SYDNEY

Louis Nowra is a playwright, novelist, essayist and screen-writer. Some of his plays are *Inner Voices*, *The Golden Age*, *Inside the Island*, *The Boyce Trilogy*, *Radiance* and *The Lewis Trilogy* (*Summer of the Aliens*, *Così*, *This Much is True*). Screen credits include *Map of the Human Heart*, *Radiance*, *Black and White*, *Heaven's Burning*, *K-19: The Widowmaker* and *Così*. His novels are *The Misery of Beauty*, *Palu*, *Red Nights*, *Abaza* and *Ice*. He was the principal writer for the 2008 television series *First Australians* and has written two memoirs, *The Twelfth of Never* and *Shooting the Moon*. With Mandy Sayer, he co-edited the influential anthology about Kings Cross, *In the Gutter ... Looking at the Stars*. His recent non-fiction includes *Kings Cross: a biography* (2013), *Woolloomooloo: a biography* (2017), fiction *Into that Forest*, *Prince of Afghanistan* and *Collected Stories*, plus the Audible audio dramas *The Divine Hammer*, *The Goodbye Party* and *Beatrice Dark*. He lives on the border between Kings Cross and Woolloomooloo and is married to the writer Mandy Sayer.

Also by Louis Nowra and published by NewSouth:

Kings Cross: a biography
Woolloomooloo: a biography

SYDNEY

Louis Nowra

a biography

NEWSOUTH

A NewSouth book

Published by
NewSouth Publishing
University of New South Wales Press Ltd
University of New South Wales
Sydney NSW 2052
AUSTRALIA
https://unsw.press/

© Louis Nowra 2022
First published 2022

10 9 8 7 6 5 4 3 2 1

A catalogue record for this
book is available from the
National Library of Australia

ISBN: 9781742235929 (paperback)
          9781742238524 (ebook)
          9781742239422 (ePDF)

Design Josephine Pajor-Markus
Cover design George Saad
Cover image Subash Maharjan, Unsplash
Printer Griffin Press

CONTENTS

To Mandy

'No one, wise Kublai, knows better than you that the city must never be confused with the words that describe it. And yet between one and the other there is a connection.'

Italo Calvino, *Invisible Cities*

*

'God made the harbour ... but Satan made Sydney.'

A Sydneysider to Mark Twain

*

'If you don't live in Sydney, you're camping out.'

Paul Keating, former Prime Minister of Australia

AUTHOR'S NOTE

This biography of Sydney is told through three strands: the first is its chronological history, the second considers some of its spaces and places, and the third consists of themes such as sandstone or water. It's through these entwining strands that I tell the story of a constantly evolving city.

Given the huge number of existing suburbs, my four chapters on certain suburbs have been arrived at through choosing, via accident or design, one from each point of the compass, in the hope that they add a special flavour to the history of Sydney as a whole. The first two volumes of this trilogy, *Kings Cross: a biography* and *Woolloomooloo: a biography* cover those two suburbs, so I don't duplicate the material here.

My Sydney is basically bounded by Chippendale, Redfern, Ultimo, Walsh Bay, the harbour, Surry Hills, Woolloomooloo and, of course, the Rocks.

PROLOGUE

EVERYONE HAS THEIR OWN SYDNEY. I can trace mine back to when I was nine years old and my father bought his first truck. My mother convinced him to take me on the inaugural trip from Melbourne to Wollongong where he could pick up a load of coke, a product of coal used for furnaces and home heating. Instead of stopping at Wollongong, Dad drove on to Sydney, telling me he was going to show me one of the most beautiful structures in the world. I had never heard him use the word beautiful before. A couple of hours later we made our way through the dense city traffic towards the harbour and then, with a flourish, he announced, 'Here we are, son, the Sydney Harbour Bridge.'

Suddenly we were on the bridge. I had seen pictures of it but they showed it from the sides. This time we were actually driving across it. I had the sensation of being inside an enormous cage. Grey steel girders with prominent rivets grew taller as we neared the middle. I gazed upwards in awe. The only thing stopping the slender girders from vanishing into the intense blue sky was an arch on either side.

'It's so huge that it takes workmen a year to paint it and once they have, they have to start all over again,' shouted my father over the roar of the engine. On reaching the North Shore, my father turned the truck around and we crossed the bridge again.

Twisting my head, I could see deep emerald green water below, stretching out to the hazy eastern horizon; ferries scuttled across the water like green beetles and yachts floated around like white cabbage moths. I was stunned and speechless. I had never seen such beauty before, one man-made, the other a product of nature.

'It's fantastic, isn't it?' exclaimed my elated father. All I could do was nod.

Back on the housing commission estate to the north of Melbourne, with only treeless paddocks and sterile cracked soil for a view, all I could think of was how mean and ugly my city was with its dirty brown Yarra River and the Princes Bridge spanning it: a squat, banal thing. It would be nearly two decades before I returned to Sydney.

My first and second full-length plays were premiered in Sydney in the late 1970s. At the time the two main theatre companies in my home town were very different. The Melbourne Theatre Company attracted older conservative audiences and specialised in English and European plays. Its opposition was the Australian Performing Group (APG) at the Pram Factory in bohemian Carlton that promoted Australian plays and themes. Its audiences were young, left-wing and aggressively heterosexual – a mixture of Marxists, feminists and anyone else of similar progressive views. Those who worked at the APG and their audiences considered Sydney theatre to be facile, politically naïve, and run by the gay mafia.

Melbourne was thought to be the epicentre of creativity and intellectual rigour, with the chauvinist certainty that it produced great art. If you left it to live and work in Sydney theatre, you were selling out. Melbourne had gravitas; Sydney was tinsel town. Because my work wasn't being performed in my home town it wasn't that hard to decide to go and live in Sydney.

My then wife Sarah and I packed our meagre possessions into a small truck and headed north to the inner-Sydney suburb of Chippendale, an industrial enclave with few residents. I had rented the cheapest house I could find. It was in Dick Street, a small terrace in a row of six that were shoddily built and seemed to cling to each other for support.

The short narrow street seldom saw sunlight and was surrounded by factories, warehouses and car repair shops. Directly behind our house was a sprawling and malodorous brewery and a grotty hotel, the haunt of the brewery workers. The pub had grubby ceramic wall tiles, fading beer advertisements from the 1940s, carpet soggy with beer and speckled with cigarette burns, and alcoholic staff so old they were less flesh and blood than spectral presences. Our house was overrun with huge brazen cockroaches, and the stink of sugar from the White Wings factory on the corner was so pungent that I thought I was suffocating from sweetness. The permanent and nauseating smell of hops from the brewery permeated our rooms and clothes and gave me a lifelong dislike of beer.

Despite living in such a dismal area and not having a car, I got to know Sydney by walking everywhere. During the first months I was constantly comparing it to Melbourne. The very topography of my new city was utterly different from my birthplace, which was flat and structured around an orderly grid of streets. Sydney's streets were a bewildering mixture of the narrow, the wide, the winding, the undulating. They were undisciplined, and the rise and fall of the terrain meant that one never knew what lay over the next rise or around the corner or where the hill or dip would lead. At times it was impossible to make sense of the city's lack of a grid. It was as if Sydney was a constantly evolving organic being.

Then there was the light and the heat. I was used to Melbourne's bleak grey skies that seem to press down on the city, causing one to mentally stoop, but in Sydney the blue sky seemed infinite and the light at times so intense it became a blinding glare. There were no harsh winters – I never wore a jumper again. For someone used to the bitter winds that blew directly from Antarctica, the temperatures in Sydney were subtropical. During the first couple of years, especially in January and February, I found the atmosphere so clammy and so humid it was as if the air was being sucked out of it, but just when I felt near fainting in the late afternoon, the curtains would start to dance, leaves began to rustle and suddenly there would be a whoosh of violent winds heralding the blessed relief of the southerly buster, bringing with it a drop in temperature and a fall in humidity that made the nights bearable. And there were the turbulent thunderstorms with torrential rain and lightning strikes so vivid they momentarily turned night into day. After the rains, the smell of rotting figs and putrescent ground litter was almost hormonal.

Nature was profuse and lush with the scents of frangipani flowers and the nocturnal flowering Queen of the Night shrub, an almond-honey fragrance so potent it would wake me as it drifted up the stairs into the bedroom of a house I ended up renting in Enmore. Walking under the giant flowers of magnolia trees the perfume was so heady that one felt giddy. Palm trees lined the streets, the purple haze of jacarandas caressed the eyes; Norfolk pines, stately and sombre, were etched against the sky. And then there were the monumental fig trees with aerial roots descending from their branches to anchor into the soil and transform into enormous buttress roots. When I played cricket in Centennial Park I'd sit under a gigantic fig that resembled one of those spooky trees from fairytales.

There were the birds, raucous and exuberant, the lorikeets with their constant shrill chatter, the ibises with their scimitar beaks, the screeching white cockatoos, the currawong with its

4

ringing double call of *curra-wong*. Then at dusk the sky was filled with bats slowly flapping their way south from the Botanic Gardens in search of fruit trees. In summer there was the piercing shrill of cicadas.

In wandering the streets at Circular Quay, my ears getting used to the growl and groan of buses, I'd feel a tingle, knowing that I was at the epicentre of Sydney's – and Australia's – colonial history. On my walk through the city, the bridge would suddenly appear at the end of a street or narrow lane, caught in the vapour of petrol fumes and water mist, its arch like the exoskeleton of some great beast. Down the bottom of George Street I was conscious I was walking on the same ground that had been trodden by Gadigal people for millennia, by Governor Phillip and those marines and convicts of the First Fleet, and in the Rocks there were old buildings that went right back to the origins of the city itself. At Circular Quay huge passenger ships lay at their moorings, ferries strained at their ropes, leaving trails of foam in their wake when finally set free. In summer the harbour was the emerald green I remembered from my childhood visit, with pockets of intense glare bouncing off a gentle swell, the horizon a moist haze. Then there were the raucous seagulls dipping and rising, eager to swiftly cadge a morsel, the slightly rocking wharves, the currents toying with the pylons. Whenever I flew back into Sydney, from the air it seemed that every backyard had a swimming pool, like bomb craters filled with water the colour of sapphires.

As if to prove that the Hume Highway from Melbourne to Sydney was the yellow brick road, within two years of settling here, I had several plays produced, two of them staged at the Opera House. How to explain my sense of elation every time I approached that magnificent structure? It was an enchanting sensory experience, especially at night, the ferries arriving and departing from their wharves, their lugubrious horns, and inside the passengers like miniature dolls in a light box. The calming sound of the waves gently slapping against the sea wall, the illuminated grinning-yet-menacing face of Luna Park in the far distance, the glowing lights of the bridge as it arched across the sky and the flurry of distant red and white lights of vehicles and trains appearing and disappearing as they crossed it. The mirrored moon on the nocturnal water, the briny smell of the sea, and right in front of me, the white shells of the Opera House like foamy tongues of waves frozen in time. They were curvaceous, feminine shapes, at odds with the straight lines of the long sweep of steps that led to the hushed interiors where, a few years after my arrival, I saw Richard Meale's opera *Voss*, based on Patrick White's novel, and thrilled at the opening scene where the chorus sings loudly and jubilantly 'Sydney! Sydney!' as if reflecting the audience's pride in the city itself and the glorious venue it was staged in.

Every city street seemed to show off handsome sandstone buildings with their Gothic, Italian and even Byzantine styles, the sandstone ranging from pale yellow to dirty orange, soaking up the sun and enticing the eye, a stone so different from the cold, brutal bluestone of buildings down south. The New South Wales Parliament was a simple Georgian structure lined with slender colonnades that was an exhilarating contrast with Melbourne's pompous Victorian Parliament building.

The harbour itself I thought I knew from its shores and the bridge, but in the first year of my migration, when I went on a cruise around it, I understood its beauty. Previously I had only noticed the occasional island, but as we sailed I took in Goat Island, Clark, Shark and Cockatoo islands and Fort Denison, with its tiny Martello tower seemingly the only remnant of a castle long drowned. For the first time I saw mysterious coves, inlets, bushland and trees that ran all the way down to the beaches, as if no humans had ever trodden on them. There were grandiose modern houses and Victorian and Edwardian mansions perched on cliff tops, but thankfully few high-rise apartment blocks like the bland phallic ones that lined the Gold Coast beaches. The previously torpid tourists around me on the deck sparked into life when the guide started talking about the huge prices paid for the houses. I laughed at how Melburnians were right: one of Sydney's favourite topics was real estate.

When I visited beaches like Bondi and Bronte, I could see just how important surfing was to the locals and how sunbakers flaunted their flesh, the men in tiny swimmers, the women topless, or both sexes sunbaking nude at special coves. It was obvious why, given the choice between going to see football or cricket, Sydneysiders preferred to embrace the sun and sand. What was also obvious in this adoration of the sun and surf was that Sydney was a city of pagans.

The locals seemed to speak more loudly, the reserved radio personalities of Melbourne were out-shouted by Sydney's raucous right-wing radio shock jocks. Even the restaurants and the food were different, as restaurant reviewer, Terry Durack, wrote:

Rosetta Melbourne is a moody, theatrical, draped and chandeliered space with a rich meaty menu, while Rosetta Sydney is all light, sunny and seafoody. Melbourne is damask cloths and crystal chandeliers, roast pork and Tuscan bistecca, while Sydney is three cantilevered levels in Seidler-designed Grosvenor Place, complete with outdoor terrace, mezzanine bar and a menu of scampi crudo with blood orange, mint and pistachio; tagliolini with spanner crab; and whole grilled baby snapper with salmoriglio.

I was struck by how people were browner, suntanned, with none of the Melbourne pallor. The women's dresses were colourful rather than the trendy funereal black of women down in Bleak City (as Sydneysiders called it), their lipstick pink rather than a shocking red. Few men wore suits, their dress was casual, many wore shorts and Hawaiian shirts, and later in the 1980s the men on floats during the Gay Mardi Gras proudly displayed as much flesh as possible and, indeed, on the streets there was more bare flesh shown by both men and women. The prostitutes in Kings Cross weren't hidden like those down in St Kilda. The strip joints beckoned with their brazen neon signs of naked gyrating women. In the tawdry Venus Room in Orwell Street I mixed with lawyers, criminals, plain-clothed detectives, actors and tourists while naked women danced on the stage or used sex toys on themselves. Sydney society seemed a potent and amoral mix of people where your origins or lifestyle choices didn't matter as long as you had money or influence. Life was there to be enjoyed and sensuality celebrated. The light and effervescence of the city seduced me.

It was easy to see why one friend had observed that Melbourne was like a nice old aunt and Sydney was like a harlot. Or as Rex Cramphorn, the theatre director, once said to me: the difference between an actress in Melbourne and Sydney was that when you said to the former that she had to play a princess she complained that she couldn't play one because she didn't know what it was to be a princess, whereas the Sydney actress asked, 'What sort of dress do I get to wear?' If Sydney looked through the Heads to the Pacific and on to America and Asia, Melbourne looked to London and Europe for inspiration.

Over the years I moved on from Chippendale to Enmore, Sydenham (directly under the flight path), to Woolloomooloo, Elizabeth Bay, Kings Cross, Darlinghurst, and to my present abode straddling the border of Kings Cross and Woolloomooloo.

Yes, Sydney can be vulgar, corrupt, facile, ugly, brash and mindlessly hedonistic, but it is also visually beautiful, sensual, playful, dynamic, with a sense of unrestrained optimism. I fell in love with it as only someone who wasn't born there could.

LOCATION, LOCATION, LOCATION

IN THE EARLY MONTHS OF LIVING IN SYDNEY I used to visit the Tank Stream bookshop, and the eponymous slightly tacky arcade near the corner of King and Pitt streets. I was puzzled by the name and it took me some time to understand its significance.

The stream is invisible now, and to see it you must go underground, where it is an anaemic version of its former self. Yet this dismal trickle that winds its way through narrow tunnels beneath the high-rise buildings of Pitt and George streets is the reason for Sydney's location.

It soon became clear to Governor Arthur Phillip after the First Fleet anchored in Botany Bay in January 1788 that this wasn't the Edenic harbour Sir Joseph Banks had painted. The bay was exposed to capricious storms and harsh winds, and there was little fresh water to be found for the 1035 men, women and children waiting to disembark in the heat of summer. Just a few miles north another harbour was marked on Captain Cook's map of the east coast, one Cook hadn't entered. Phillip decided to explore it.

The small crew rowed into Port Jackson, amazed by its beauty and its obvious shelter for ships, unlike the open water of Botany Bay. They slowly moved up the harbour, inspecting the many peninsulas, coves and inlets, examining possible anchorage sites for the fleet, hoping to find one that had a ready supply of fresh water. Eleven kilometres into the harbour, after rounding what is now called Bennelong Point, they came upon a cove that was not only deep enough to accommodate the largest ships but, more importantly, had a stream, one more like a rivulet than a river. To Phillip, there was none finer to be found in any of the coves of the harbour. It was exactly the location he needed for the settlement. As David Collins, the deputy judge advocate, put it, the site was 'at the head of the cove, near the run of fresh water which stole silently along through a very thick wood'. At the time the stream was 40 metres wide and at high tide schooners would travel up to what is now Bridge Street. This stream was so important, it would even influence Sydney's social fabric.

The water's source lay in a swampy spring a mile away on a hill in the centre of what is now Hyde Park. The stream, its banks lined with trees, dropped some 30 metres as it meandered northward over sandstone rocks and through a series of small waterfalls to King Street where, sustained by two springs, one at King Street and another at eponymous Spring Street, it flowed directly to Bridge Street, which at that time was the head of a tidal estuary. If you were to dig down around the flagstones of the present-day Customs House, you would find the sandy beach of the original Sydney Cove shoreline.

The new arrivals cared little, if at all, that this creek was also used by the Gadigal people who drank its fresh water, fished from it, and used the bark of the trees on its banks for their canoes. Proof of their occupation has been seen in recent excavations around the stream that have uncovered flaked stone artefacts made from water-worn pebbles.

*

In October 1788 a timber bridge was built to span the water at the head of the cove (the site of what is now Bridge Street). However, this proved less solid than expected when an overloaded bullock wagon broke the decking and put the bridge out of action for some time. But the bridge did provide a crucial connection between the two sections of the settlement, with the convicts and soldiers on the western side, and Governor Phillip and colonial officials on the other. This division continues today, with the wealthy congregating in the eastern suburbs, the less fortunate in the west.

It soon became apparent to Phillip that the stream was a precarious resource for the colony and in March, just two months after landing, he decreed:

> The run of water which supplies the Settlement was observed to be only a drain from the swamp. To protect it from the sun, the governor forbids the cutting down of any tree within 50 feet of the run.

When a drought came early on in the settlement, it was clear that the precious stream was drying up. In February 1791 soldier and surveyor Augustus Alt deepened the stream near Bridge Street; by November water restrictions were introduced. In his account of the early years of the settlement, David Collins wrote about these fraught times and Phillip's solution:

> By the dry weather which prevailed the water had been so much affected, besides being lessened by the water of some [ships], that a prohibition was laid by the governor, on the watering of the remainder of Sydney ... to remedy this evil, the governor had employed the stone mason's gang to cut tanks out of the rock which would be reservoirs for the water large enough to supply the settlement for some time.

These three tanks hewed from sandstone eventually held some 36 000 litres of water. To further protect the rivulet, soon nicknamed the Tank Stream, Phillip had a paling fence erected to keep out stock and protect the remaining trees lining its banks.

In 1803 the Tank Stream was further enclosed to save it from the ravages of livestock and increasing garbage. The *Sydney Gazette* was enthused by the changes where:

> ... every appearance of rubbish has been removed from its
> sides, and crystal current flows into the basin with its native
> purity. A dam secures it from the heaviest falls on the side
> that lay exposed, and a high palisade will cut off all access to
> the stream.

Despite this, the stream was used for cleaning fish and as a waterhole for pigs. The third governor, Philip Gidley King, threatened those who fouled the water with floggings, road gangs, fines or having their houses demolished.

Realising that the poorly constructed bridge had a temporal and temperamental quality to it, that same year King decided it was imperative to build a more permanent structure. This sense of urgency failed to inspire others. Work progressed agonisingly slowly, and a desperate government gathered up 'free loungers who appeared to be in want of employ' to fill in the ends of the bridge. Judges resorted to sentencing men to work on the bridge. Stone masons and labourers needed to be enticed to work harder by the payment of 'spirits'. Simeon Lord, an ex-convict who had become a wealthy merchant, was so exasperated by the leisurely pace of construction that he auctioned one of his buildings, 'A commodious stone dwelling house in the Rocks, near the new windmill ... to defray the expenses of completing the new bridge.'

The finishing touches were so frustratingly slow that the work was left to be completed by 'the labour of a few feeble women'.

Finally, in April 1804, the *Sydney Gazette* proclaimed: 'On Tuesday the New bridge was rendered passable for carriages.' This was not the optimistic opinion of most people, who cynically observed, 'The arch was not likely to stand.' But it did.

In early 1811 Sydney was afflicted with such a severe drought that the tanks were empty for several weeks, 'and those who were in want of water obliged to collect it from the small cavities in the spring course above the tanks'. Enterprising men and women collected water and sold it on for fourpence to sixpence a pail. Others, desperate for a permanent source of water, dug wells in their yards.

For a new arrival like Lachlan Macquarie, who was sworn in as governor in 1810, the colony's disrespect for its water supply was infuriating. He couldn't believe people could be so short-sighted. His exasperation was clear in the first of his decrees in 1811. The Tank Stream, he declared, 'supplied pure and good water, benefit for the inhabitants at large'. He was astonished at the casual fouling of it. He prohibited the erecting or keeping of privies near it, banned slaughterhouses (there were five along the banks at one point), tanneries, 'dying houses', breweries and distilleries. He also ordered that no one could throw dirt, rubbish, ashes, dirty water 'or filth of any kind into the tanks or stream … no linen, cloth or any article to be washed'. To give an idea of the insanitary condition of the stream, and what contributed to it, he also banned pigs, goats, sheep, horned cattle and horses from drinking from the stream. If that happened the owner would forfeit the animal.

Even dead bodies turned up in the stream. In 1816, Sylvester Scott, a young man employed at a hat business in Hunter Street, was found in a hollow of the tanks, naked and strangled, his murderer never found. The cavalier attitude to the Tank Stream continued, despite warnings, and in 1820 naked men washed themselves in water that had become downright filthy. The *Sydney Gazette*'s editor was appalled:

> With much pain we have recently observed individuals washing themselves in this stream of water, particularly in that part that runs from King Street, because that spot is secluded from every eye, that of curiosity excepted.

To alleviate this, Macquarie erected public fountains. There was one in Bent Street, and in 1820 Francis Greenway, in collaboration with Elizabeth Macquarie, designed an ornate Doric fountain in the south-western corner of Macquarie Place, between modern Bridge Street to the south and Reiby Place to the north. It was a square pavilion, with a domed roof and an arched opening on each side. A constant stream of people brought buckets to be filled, many of them servants in the houses of the colonial elites – leading merchants and those who held important posts in the nearby government offices.

But not even Macquarie could save the Tank Stream from the wilful stupidity of the populace. Its condition continued to deteriorate until the new governor, Thomas Brisbane, had no choice but to forbid anyone drinking its polluted water. Ralph Darling, the next governor, arranged for seven wells to be dug. They continued to be the main source of fresh water for the town until the completion of Busby's Bore in 1837, which funnelled water from the catchment area of Lachlan Swamps (Centennial Park) to an outlet in Hyde Park.

One can see the degradation of the Tank Stream in two artworks. In 1839 Conrad Martens painted a view of the stream from Bridge Street. On the bridge itself an Aboriginal family of four casually rest against the brick railing, shooting the breeze. Near them are the ruins of a house on the barren western bank. The low water is not fit for drinking but handy enough for two women to use it for washing clothes. Three years later John Skinner Prout, visiting Sydney, produced a watercolour titled *Old Pitt Street*. This image of the stream is almost dystopian. The water is shallow and befouled; crumbling houses on both desolate banks seem about to tumble into the water, while men and women in tattered clothes fossick in the mud.

But a purpose was found for the Tank Stream. In 1857 what was once a source supplying the colony with 'fresh and pure water' was now so debased that it became an official sewer that ran parallel to George Street. Gradually it was covered and built upon, buried under stone, bitumen and concrete. Even so, the 'purling rivulet' continued to haunt those who hoped to subjugate it. As one writer observed in the 1960s:

> What building great or small, in the line of its course, has
> not bowed to its dictates? The AMP building is built partly
> on piles driven into the muddy depths. Many an owner has
> been committed to installing pumps to deal with seepages
> in basements. The throb, throb, shows that the stream is
> still alive.

The modernist architect Harry Seidler designed the Plaza in 1963 only to find that the biggest problem was the Tank Stream, which ran underneath what used to be Hamilton Street. As he explained, 'We had to divert it under the Plaza, which seemed to float above Pitt Street on cross-hatched concrete legs.' Years later his assistant, Colin Griffiths, confessed: 'We wouldn't be allowed to do it now ... We stopped [the stream] and put in a concrete tunnel under the edge of the Plaza Building. Now we all feel a bit awkward about ruining a bit of our heritage.'

Once the beating heart of the colony, the stream now suffers the ignominy of being reduced to a smelly stormwater drain and would be forgotten except for a small group of the curious who can explore this underground system twice a year, or pedestrians who pause on the busy corner of George and Alfred streets near Circular Quay, where the Tank Stream fountain constantly gushes water. Designed in 1981 by the sculptor Stephen Walker, it is also called the 'Children's Fountain' and is dedicated to *all the children who have played around the Tank Stream*, which would explain the playful figurative and non-figurative bronze forms connected by five separate linked pools (not unlike the pools commemorating Busby's Bore in Hyde Park North). The pools display Australian flora and fauna, including a menagerie of snakes, goannas, echidnas, crabs, birds, frogs and tortoises cavorting in the water. One of its inscriptions reads, *The Tank Stream fountain recalls mankind's past dependence on this flowing stream.*

After nearly 200 years of degradation, the Tank Stream, the reason for Sydney's location, and its importance was finally acknowledged.

THE DISPOSSESSION

IN THE 1840S EORA WOMAN CORA GOOSEBERRY, known as the Queen of Sydney, told the artist George Angas of her father's reaction to the arrival of British ships in 1788: he thought them terrifying sea monsters and fled inland to hide.

'Boatswain' Maroot gave evidence to the NSW Legislative Council's Select Committee set up in 1845 'to Consider the Condition of the Aborigines and the Best Means of Promoting their Welfare'. He was born about 1793 and was the son of Maroot, an elder of the Gameygal people who occupied the north shore of Botany Bay. In his testimony he spoke frankly about his life, his family, his country (Gameygal) and the impact the British had on the Indigenous people of Sydney. He said his father had told him that when he first saw the ships of the First Fleet, he thought the sailors up in the rigging were possums.

Some Aboriginal people believed the white men were ghosts who had come from the land of the dead. Others thought that the clean-shaven soldiers were women. There were times when marines had to drop their trousers to show the Eora they were men. The sight was often greeted with laughter and recognition. Not knowing each other's languages, communication became dumb shows, dancing and singing or, in the case of the musical soldiers, playing the fife.

But what did the First Australians think of the strange actions of the invaders once they had landed, chopping down trees, clearing the land, monopolising the Tank Stream, desecrating the landscape and destroying their spiritual world of Sydney Cove, *Warrung* (Little Child)?

Radiocarbon dating suggests that Aboriginal people lived in and around Sydney for at least 30 000 years. Prior to the arrival of the British, it's estimated that there were 4000 to 8000 people in the Sydney area from as many as 29 different clans. Sydney Cove from Port Jackson to Petersham was inhabited by the Gadigal. 'Eora' is regarded the generic name for the coastal inhabitants of the Sydney district. The name Eora means 'here' or 'from this place' and was used by Aboriginal people to tell the British where they came from.

Phillip's attention was also focused on the Indigenous people he knew he would encounter. They were to be treated with kindness and friendship, and anyone killing them would be hanged. He was given strict orders on how to interact with the local population:

> You are to endeavour, by every possible means, to open up an
> intercourse with the natives, and conciliate their affections,
> enjoining all our subjects to live in amity and kindness with them.

Phillip and many marine officers were fascinated by the Eora male (for a time the women were deliberately kept at a distance by the men). Captain John Hunter described the men as:

> … bearded, naked, up to five feet nine inches tall, thin, ritually
> scarred very straight and clean made; walk very erect and are
> active. Occasionally there were kangaroo teeth in their hair and

a bone through the nasal septum, one of their front upper teeth was always missing.

The missing front tooth or teeth was a sign that the men had undergone initiation. Phillip's missing front tooth intrigued the Gadigal, who thought he had undergone an initiation.

In April 1789, 15 months after the First Fleet arrived, the Eora were devastated by an epidemic of smallpox. A horrified David Collins described what he saw:

> At that time a native was living with us; and on taking him down to the harbour to look for his former companions, those who witnessed his expression and agony can never forget either. He looked anxiously around him in the different coves we visited; not a vestige on the sand was to be found of human foot; ... not a living person was anywhere to be met with. It seemed as if, flying from the contagion, they had left the dead to bury the dead. He lifted up his hands and eyes in silent agony for some time; at last he exclaimed, 'All dead! all dead!' and then hung his head in mournful silence.

The Gadigal were reduced in number from about 60 in 1788 to just three in 1791. According to Dr Val Attenbrow in *Sydney's Aboriginal Past* (2002), two of the three were Colbee and Nanbaree. Surgeon John White fostered the young Nanbaree, who had been orphaned. Colbee's life would be further interrupted by the white men later that same year, when Phillip ordered his kidnapping, and that of Bennelong.

Phillip had become frustrated by the Eora's reluctance to enter the colony. He was desperate to learn their language and customs. Earlier he had kidnapped Arabanoo in order to learn his language. Watkin Tench reports how, when Arabanoo approached the new

Government House, he 'cast up his eyes, and seeing some people leaning out of a window on the first storey, he exclaimed aloud and testified the most extravagant surprise'. His stay was brief; he was to die of smallpox. Bennelong and Colbee were captured in November 1789. They were entertained by Phillip and the marines at Government House and saw up close the strange, cruel reality of the colonists' world. What was to repulse the Eora was the white man's cruelty towards each other: the brutal floggings, hangings, the public humiliation of the pillory, the convicts who were treated no better than beasts. There was an obvious hierarchy, something foreign to the Eora. Obviously the soldiers with their 'firesticks' and their uniforms in warpaint colours of red and white, were the warriors, and the convicts, lesser human beings. This world also had curious animals the Eora had never seen before, not only pigs and sheep, but a monkey. At first, a curious Colbee thought it was a rat, then, seeing its paws, called it a man.

He fled his prison just two and a half weeks after his capture. Bennelong did not escape for some five months. He was close to Phillip, calling him 'Father', took to the ample food and drink, and proved both intelligent and funny, mimicking marines and Phillip's French cook. For Lieutenant Watkin Tench, Bennelong was a compelling figure. He provided the lieutenant with a basic vocabulary of his language and passed on some of his people's customs. According to Tench:

Love and war seemed his favourite pursuits; in both he had suffered severely. Showed his many wounds. The wound on the back of his hand, he laughed and said it was received in carrying off a lady of another tribe. 'I was dragging her away: she cried out aloud and stuck her teeth into me ... I knocked her down and beat her till she was insensible and covered in blood.'

21

After Bennelong's escape, Phillip heard that he had joined several other Aboriginal people on a beach. When Phillip arrived, the situation was tense, and through a misunderstanding, or perhaps payback for kidnapping Bennelong, Phillip was speared by another native. Despite his savage wound, he stopped his marines taking revenge.

By late 1790 Government House was playing host to Aboriginal visitors, including Bennelong, who lived there periodically. One person who didn't like Bennelong mixing with the whites was his second wife, Barangaroo, a feisty Kamaraygal woman. She refused to be shamed into wearing clothes, and long after other Aboriginal women wore them in the settlement, she walked through the streets entirely naked. In his *A Complete Account of the Settlement at Port Jackson*, Tench describes an example of Barangaroo's mercurial behaviour:

> Not seeing Barangaroo of the party, I asked for her, and was
> informed that she had violently opposed Bennelong's departure.
> When she found persuasion vain, she had recourse to tears,
> scolding, and threats, stamping the ground, and tearing her
> hair. But Baneelon continuing determined, she snatched up in
> her rage one of his fish-gigs, and dashed it with such fury on
> the rocks, that it broke. To quiet her apprehensions on the score
> of her husband's safety, [The Reverend] Mr. Johnson, attended
> by Abaroo, agreed to remain as a hostage until [Bennelong]
> should return.

By May 1792 the Aboriginal people had become part of the settlement, but for some of the British their behaviour was hard to fathom, as George Thompson, a gunner who arrived on the *Royal Admiral* in 1792, relates:

There are three or four of the chiefs who attend the governor's House every day for their dinner and a glass of wine. Several of the officers have both boys and girls as servants, but they are so lazy that it is with difficulty you can persuade them to get themselves a drink of water. If you attempt to strike them, they will immediately set out for the woods, and stay four or five days. Indeed it is common for them to strip off what clothes they may have on, and take a trip to the woods, whether offended or not. If they were shy at the first setting in the colony, that is not the case now, for the people can scarcely keep them out of their houses in daytime.

Lieutenant William Dawes had set up an observatory at Point Maskelyne, now known as Dawes Point, where the southern pylons of the Sydney Harbour Bridge stand. Dawes, in his middle twenties, well educated, extremely proficient at languages and very religious, was the First Fleet's astronomer and meteorologist. Fascinated by the heavens, he set up the observatory with the specific aim of observing a comet that was predicted to appear in the southern sky, but the sighting never eventuated. He and his close friend Watkin Tench spent long evenings discussing Milton, the French Revolution (the news of which reached the colony a year or so after it happened), a bridge that would link the north and south shores of the harbour, and Aboriginal languages.

Many officers, like Hunter and Collins, and Governor Phillip himself, had collected a basic vocabulary of the local language, but through his friendship with a tall, 14- to 15-year-old Gamaragal girl, Patyegarang, Dawes learned the intricate grammar of nouns, adjectives, verbs and sentence construction that would allow two people to communicate with an interracial intimacy unique in the settlement.

The Aboriginal people saw the observatory and Dawes as a safe spot to share friendship and knowledge. Locals like Bennelong and his wife Barangaroo would visit, as did several teenage girls, including Patyegarang, who became close to Dawes. In the beginning she was more attracted to his gifts of bread and tea, but she quickly grew curious about this white man. Sometimes, like any teenage girl, she became exasperated by his stubborn insistence on learning her language; at other times she was intrigued by his interest in her culture. There's no doubt she was intelligent, but she was also high-spirited and mischievous. On one occasion, when Bennelong had Dawes shave him, Bennelong had to admonish Patyegarang, telling her to 'Stop making me laugh. Can't see you see he has a razor in his hand?'

Dawes' notebooks clearly show that the two spent much time together. They shared details of their daily lives that give a fascinating account of Eora traditions and knowledge. Their relationship became close, close enough for Dawes to shorten her name to Patye.

Patyegarang taught him words such as putuwa, which means 'to warm one's hand by the fire and then to gently squeeze the fingers of another person'. Other words included *tariadyaou* ('I made a mistake in speaking'); phrases like *Minyin bial naadyimi?* ('Why don't you sleep?') and *Minyin bial widadyemi?* ('Why did you not drink?'). *Matarabaun nagaba* meant 'We shall sleep separately'. There are also ambiguous phrases that have led some historians and romantic novelists to believe they had a sexual relationship. Their friendship was intimate enough for Patyegarang to take off her clothes in order to warm up by the fire (*Goredyu tagarin*). Whether this was a coquettish act or not, we'll never know. We do know Dawes teased her about not washing enough, suggesting that she could become white if she bathed

24

more. One time she threw down her towel in despair, saying, *Tyerabarrbowaryaou* ('I shall not become white').

Not only did Patyegarang share the Sydney language with Dawes, but also the Eora's view of the invasion. Eventually this led Dawes to stand up to Phillip and refuse to participate in a punitive action against the Aboriginal people when, in late 1790, Phillip, on the edge of a nervous breakdown, decided to order the capture and beheading of several natives in retaliation for the killing of convicts – especially his gamekeeper. It's obvious from Dawes' notebooks that the Eora were in despair about the occupation of their land and were afraid of the British guns.

One of the most poignant exchanges in Dawes' notebooks is Patyegarang recounting her people's horrified realisation that the invaders had come to stay.

As indeed, they had. The whites' first main thoroughfare through the colony (eventually named George Street) followed an Aboriginal path. Huts and shacks started to sprout along Eora tracks in what would become central Sydney. Aboriginal people may have become constant visitors in the settlement, but after Governor Phillip and the First Fleet marines left in December 1792, the colony lost interest in the Eora, with some treating them as pests.

Even so, the Eora were still based around the harbour and enacting their culture seven years after the arrival of the First Fleet. In 1795 David Collins attended a *Yoolong* initiation ceremony involving dozens of men and boys at *Woggan-ma-gule*, today the Royal Botanic Gardens. There the nervous young boys were initiated by having their front teeth knocked out. For some it was an excruciating affair. Collins noticed Nanbaree, a boy he knew, pressing a fish against his bloody gums to ease the pain.

*

The first pictorial depictions of the Aboriginal people by white settlers had been earnest and respectful, but as time wore on they were characterised as drunkards and pathetic fringe dwellers. Artists pictured the dispossessed Eora as: drunken women, violent husbands and neglected children. Faces became mere caricatures with no attempts at individuality. One seminal image was an etching in MacLehose's *Picture of Sydney and Strangers' Guide in New South Wales* (1839), which showed an Aboriginal family with their scruffy dogs, the drunken woman drinking straight from a rum bottle and her drunken spouse holding a bottle with one hand and attempting to hit her with the other – behind them is a malnourished child with a distended stomach.

Blanket distribution lists from the 1830s show that few people who identified as Aboriginal were living in Sydney itself. According to Dr Val Attenbrow, senior fellow at the Australian Museum, Aboriginal people:

> ... remained living in many parts of the Sydney region – in
> places such as the Mulgoa Valley, Emu Plains, Plumpton,
> Manly, La Perouse, Salt Pan Creek and Campbelltown,
> in some cases continuing to live on what had been their
> traditional campsites until at least the mid-1800s.

There were Aboriginal people on the North Shore in St Leonards as late as 1870, working as servants and stable hands. In a letter to the *Sydney Morning Herald* published on 23 September 1878, a Blues Point resident noted the presence of an Aboriginal camp at Berrys Bay, on the north side of the harbour:

Considering the vast territory which has been wrested from these poor people without any compensation I take it would be a graceful act to allow them the privilege of pointing to one of these small islands [i.e., Goat Island] in the entrance to the metropolis as still their own.

From 1879 through to July 1881 about 18 Aboriginal people, including members of the Davis and Bundle families, were camped in the government's Marine Board boatsheds on the eastern side of Circular Quay at Bennelong Point. They received weekly rations of meat, bread, tea and sugar. It was likely they were forced to live in this derelict boatshed because they were dispossessed of their land. After the camp closed, many moved south to Daniel Matthews' Maloga Mission on the banks of the Murray River. Any remaining Indigenous people were 'encouraged' to join the growing community at La Perouse, south of the city.

ALBION

BEFORE HE SET SAIL, PHILLIP SPENT MONTHS IN LONDON preparing for the long voyage to New South Wales, and in idle moments pondered what he would call the town to be established at the bottom of the world. He came up with the name Albion, a poetical term for ancient Britain. But, on landing in the cove that would become the first European settlement, he named it Sydney after the Home Secretary, Lord Sydney, a pragmatic decision that he hoped would impress him and keep him interested in the progress of the settlement.

Phillip's optimism about the future of this penal colony was rare in the embryonic colony, and soon after landing he wrote to Lord Sydney that he had no doubt 'this country will prove the most valuable acquisition Great Britain ever made'.

Phillip had grown up in difficult circumstances. His widowed mother had packed him off to a charity school, where he excelled, his astute headmaster remarking that Phillip was 'unassuming, reasonable, business-like to the smallest degree in everything he undertakes'. Characteristics that were to be noticed by anyone who worked with him.

On 12 October 1786 he was appointed the first governor of New South Wales. The choice turned out to be an inspired one. A man capable of the big picture, but knowing that God was in the details, his experience both on the water – he had made his way through the ranks of the Royal Navy and had served as a captain in the Portuguese fleet – and on land – he had a substantial farm in Hampshire – would be vital. A major problem was that, except for some general remarks about Botany Bay made by James Cook and Joseph Banks, the site chosen for the penal settlement was an unknown quantity.

Phillip had to imagine just what would be needed to establish a colony in an unfamiliar land. All the British government was interested in was a place to dump the criminals overflowing their jails now that, post independence in 1770, America would no longer take them. The result was that convicts would be punished by sending them to the furthest outpost imaginable with little hope of return. Funds were scarce, and Phillip's repeated suggestions that convicts with expertise in farming, building and crafts be included in the cohort transported were ignored. He had to constantly monitor the supplies, which were often of poor standard or not delivered at all. It was only Phillip's persistence and attention to detail that ensured the 11 ships of the First Fleet were outfitted to a standard that would both make the long voyage feasible and provide enough provisions for survival once the motley group of 1500 convicts and marines landed.

Lord Sydney and Phillip were optimistic that the colony would become more than a dumping ground; it could be the foundation of a valuable outpost of free settlers, and a bulwark against the French or Spanish. As such, Sydney stipulated that Phillip would be the governor of a civilian government, not head of a military administration of a penal settlement. Its charter of justice established a legal regime whose inhabitants enjoyed all the rights and responsibilities of English law; slavery was outlawed. However, this last did not stop Phillip contemplating whether the solution to the imbalance between male and female convicts might be addressed by kidnapping women from islands along the way.

On the evening of 25 January 1788, the *Supply* anchored in Sydney Cove after its short trip from Botany Bay. Next morning a patch of ground was cleared in the hilly, heavily wooded land, and a flagstaff erected. In the afternoon Phillip and his officers went ashore, the Union Jack was hoisted, toasts were drunk, volleys of musketry fired, and the men gave three cheers. Towards dusk the rest of the fleet began to arrive. Working parties of convicts were sent ashore and the hard work of establishing a settlement began. Trees were cut down, undergrowth cleared; sawpits, a blacksmith's forge and cooking ovens were set up. Tents and marquees were erected and livestock, provisions and stores were landed. The first few days were chaotic, but a routine was established.

When he ventured outside his large, prefabricated oiled-canvas tent ('neither wind nor weatherproof') what Phillip saw were a few miserable clusters of makeshift shelters, tents and one-room huts with walls constructed of saplings held in grooved-post frames and plastered with mud and pipeclay. Some of the roofs were clad in cabbage palm leaves, others were made of twigs and clay. A few had roofs of bark held down by saplings to stop them curling as they dried. The wooden doors and shutters had hinges of leather thongs. Fireplaces and chimneys were lined with mud to reduce the risk of fire and the floors were bare earth. To further lessen the risk of fire, most cooking was done outdoors.

The soil around the cove proved uncongenial to farming, and anything that grew was liable to be stolen by the convicts, who also pilfered from the stores and from marines' belongings. There is a romantic myth that these convicts were not hardened criminals, but the reality was that many of them were, and in the main they did not have the skills necessary to build a settlement. Few cared if it survived. Phillip had to constantly struggle against this widespread pessimism. The morose attitude of some of the marine officers, reacting to the harsh reality of their isolation

17 000 kilometres from London, eight months away by ship, infected their men.

Livestock died of disease or were killed by lightning. Unfenced cattle simply wandered off into the bush and were never seen again. Dingoes (warrigals) attacked the sheep. It wasn't long before Phillip found that few of the prisoners were used to manual labour; they worked slowly and with surly inefficiency. Only a fortnight after they came ashore, Phillip had to rigorously enforce discipline and let the convicts know that he would not tolerate thefts, insolence or assaults. One convict was sentenced to 200 lashes for hitting a marine with an adze, another sentenced to 50 lashes for stealing wood, and a third, who had stolen some bread, was put in irons and exiled for a week to 'The Rock' (soon to be known as Pinchgut Island) on a diet of bread and water. Rum was smuggled ashore and, predictably, the felons fell into drunkenness. Things became so troublesome that Phillip resorted to public hangings.

*

There was one convict who gave Phillip hope: James Bloodsworth, a master bricklayer and builder who had been sentenced to seven years transportation. Since there were no architects in the colony, he was responsible for Sydney's first buildings. More importantly, he set up brick-making kilns in an area that quickly became known as 'Brickfields' or Brickfield Hill, near the present Goulburn Street. At the time it was a considerable hill containing large deposits of clay suitable for brick-making. The bricks were good but of uneven sizes. The few horses and bullocks available meant that the convicts were yoked together like animals, dragging wagons of bricks up the rutted, stump-littered track to the settlement. Each cart was loaded with 350 bricks or 700 tiles and was hauled by a dozen men.

At least for Phillip there was hope that Government House (a 'cottage') would soon be built, as the foundations had been laid, but the first winter would prove a nightmare. Heavy rains and bitter winds turned the paths and tracks into quagmires. Outdoor work proved impossible. A kiln at Brickfield Hill collapsed and thousands of semi-dried bricks were destroyed. Huts were flooded and many disintegrated before their owners' eyes. The foundations of the governor's house collapsed and work had to begin again in the spring.

The convicts seemed beyond spiritual help, half of them not having attended a church service for at least five years before becoming prisoners. Many were from the poverty-stricken areas of cities, where churches had little influence. The colony's chaplain, Richard Johnson, held his first service in the open air to a congregation of marines and convicts on Sunday, 3 February 1788. He constantly pleaded for a church, but Phillip, who seemed to have little interest in religion, thought it could wait, and was much more impressed by the pastor's ability as a farmer (as was Lieutenant Watkin Tench, who thought him 'the best farmer in the country').

Johnson grew annoyed at having to preach either in the open air or in a boatshed that was open to the weather at both ends. As his frustrations grew, he wrote to a friend in England, complaining about his flock, observing that they would prefer the erection of a tavern or a brothel than a church: 'They prefer their Lust before their Souls, yea, most of them will sell their souls for a Glass of Grog, so blind, so foolish, so hardened are they.'

Using his own money, Johnson erected a wattle-and-daub church on the corner of what is now Hunter and Bligh streets, which held its first service in September 1789. It was a T-shaped building with a thatched roof, seats for 500 people and standing room for another 100. He rarely filled the church – many convicts saw themselves as beyond salvation in a godless world. As Johnson was to bitterly observe, 'these miserable people spend their Sabbaths like heathens'.

Phillip at least had the consolation of being able to shift into the new Government House in early 1789. It was built of bricks baked in Brickfields and from ships' ballasts, using nails and windows retrieved from stores brought from England. The lime for the mortar was made with oyster shells collected from the neighbouring coves and Aboriginal middens. Sited on a hill on the eastern side of the stream, the house 'commands the most exalted position ... and is simple without any embellishment whatever,' reported the convict painter Thomas Watling.

Further disasters tested Phillip's patience and faith in his colony. At the beginning of 1789 food stocks were dwindling. Theft of food was treated as a major crime. In January, a convict who had been stealing food at night from huts and gardens was put on trial and hanged the same day. Not long afterwards, seven marines were found to have been plundering the public stores for eight months. Six were sentenced to death and hanged the following day. Stealing food and the raiding of gardens grew more frequent and Phillip formed a night watch from among the most trusted convicts, and instituted guards for his own gardens in Farm Cove. The experiment was successful, as he proudly wrote to Lord Sydney: 'For three months not a single robbery was committed at night.'

In idle moments the governor and his two surveyors drew up a detailed plan for a town, Phillip's own Albion. It would not replicate the narrow streets, alleyways, mews and crowded tenements of London, but be something majestic. The three men imposed an imaginary grid on the settlement, with grand streets 200 feet (60 metres) wide, allotments with frontages of 60 feet (18 metres), large freestanding Georgian buildings – even a library.

This could be considered a pipe dream, a lark, an act of fantasy by three men with time on their hands, or a combination of hope and deliberate optimism to give Lord Sydney the impression that the settlement was proceeding in the manner both men hoped it would.

Phillip's plans for his Albion stood in fantastic and highly imaginative contrast to the sloppy reality of the settlement. His idealistic grid of thoroughfares was undermined by the reality of the opportunistic and practical pathways through the Rocks, tracks that took the easiest routes, and often were already established Aboriginal walking tracks.

One unimpressed female convict described the reality of the Rocks area to her family in England near the end of that first year:

> We now have two streets, if four rows of the most miserable
> huts you can possibly conceive of deserve that name. Windows
> they have none ... so that lattices of twigs are made by our
> people to supply their places.

HERE SHE COMES!

SUDDENLY THE SKY RIPS OPEN. There has been no warning. A blizzard of hailstones, some the size of golf balls, fall from the sky. Holding my hands over my head to avoid being hit, I run for cover, finding shelter under the awning of a mixed business. Soon the roads and pavements are white with hail. Above me it sounds like rocks are bouncing off the corrugated-tin awning, accompanied by the machine-gun rat-a-tat noise of hail smashing into the cars parked outside the shop, and the racket of hailstones on the roofs of nearby apartment blocks. It's so loud you have to shout to be heard.

As quickly as it arrived, the hailstorm abates. It is April 1999, and I'm living in Elizabeth Bay. When it is safe to leave my refuge, I run through the heavy rain to my apartment at the end of the road. My car, parked outside, looks as if a fiend has taken a hammer to it, smashing the windows and making hundreds of dents. The damage is no different among the battered cars alongside it.

It is thought to be the most destructive hailstorm to strike the city. Windows, skylights, solar panels and tiled roofs are ravaged. Even a year later, large parts of Sydney will still be a sea of blue tarpaulins covering devastated roofs.

Weather can determine a city's architecture, clothes, and even its social fabric. Sydney's mercurial weather is a telling example of this, and the men and women of the First Fleet quickly realised they were in a dangerously unpredictable climate quite unlike that of the Mother Country.

Governor Phillip had been astonished that, despite arriving at the height of summer, there were storms and lightning so devastating that they killed livestock and set trees on fire. On 6 February 1788 the storms reached a fearsome peak. The male convicts had disembarked at Sydney Cove the week before, and now the convict women and their children were to do so. It was a discomforting, sultry day, with frequent thundery squalls and lightning storms, the likes of which few of the new arrivals had ever seen. The women were up at five o'clock in the morning, many of them dressed in their best, excited to be on land after nearly nine months at sea, stuck in fetid and claustrophobic spaces. By six o'clock they were rowed to shore with the few possessions they brought with them or had acquired on the voyage. Their tents were not ready to house them, and there was no shelter to be found from the terrifying electrical storms, or the oppressive heat.

Surgeon Arthur Bowes Smyth, still on board his ship, wrote in his journal of 6 February 1788 in a tone of awe and fear:

> The scene wh. Presented itself at this time & during the greater
> part of the night beggars every description, some swearing,
> others quarrelling, others singing – not in the least regarding
> the Tempest, though so violent that the thunder shook the Ship
> exceeded anything I ever before had a conception of. I never
> before experienced so uncomfortable a night, expect'g every
> moment the Ship would be struck wh. The Lighten'g. the Sailors
> almost all drunk, and incapable of rendering much assistance had
> an accident happen'd & the heat was almost suffocatin.

The women had just landed and were waiting for their tents to be pitched when:

… there came upon the most violent storm of lightning and rain I ever saw. The lightning was incessant during the whole night, and I never heard it rain faster.

Near midnight a flash of lightning struck a large tree in the centre of the camp. It split the tree from top to bottom, killing five sheep and a pig tied up under it.

There were salacious rumours that during this violent storm the male and female convicts, despite the thunder and lightning and the lack of cover, engaged in an orgy of sexual abandon, as if the wicked spirits of the immoral convicts were at one with the manic ferocity of the weather.

Another surgeon, George Worgan, observed of his new surroundings:

The thunder and lightning are astonishingly awful here, and by the heavy gloom that hangs over the woods at the time these are in commotion and from the nature and violence done to many trees we have reason to apprehend that much mischief can be done by lightning here.

More 'inclement, tempestuous weather' persisted throughout the winter of 1788, making life in the nascent colony extremely onerous. Any attempt to build a hut was met with the weather's fury. For David Collins, the colony's deputy judge advocate, the volatile weather seemed to be conspiring against any progress in establishing a settlement:

During the beginning of August much heavy rain fell, and not only prevented the carrying on of labour, but rendered the work of much time fruitless by its effects; the brick-kiln fell in more than once, and bricks in a large amount were destroyed; the

roads about the settlement were rendered impassable, and some
of the huts were so far injured to require nearly as much time
to repair them as to build them anew ... Unfavourable heavy
rains, with gales of wind, prevailing nearly the whole time. The
rain came down in torrents, filling up every trench and cavity
which had been dug around the settlement, and causing much
damage to the miserable mud tenements which were occupied
by the convicts.

The marine lieutenant and historian of the first four years of
the settlement, Watkin Tench, noted another disturbing aspect
of the weather, its tendency to create permanent anxiety: 'Under
wretched covers of thatch our provisions and stores were exposed
to destruction from every flash of lightning.' But he also noted
something else: that a very sultry day would eventually bring
relief when the afternoon and early evening sea breezes arrived,
especially when the southerlies hit, causing the temperatures to
sometimes plummet as much as 15 to 20 degrees Fahrenheit in a
startlingly short time.

This longed-for wind soon earned the name the 'southerly
buster'. It became a symbol of hope and recuperation for those
who were sick. In 1820 there was an outbreak of influenza, which
probably originated from newly arrived ships. Local Aboriginal
people knew the cure and pointed to the north-west, confidently
affirming that all 'distempers' came from that quarter and that
once the southerly arrived, it would blow away the flu and health
would be restored.

The southerly could bring welcome relief from the heat, or
despair if it brought the choking dust storms that originated at
the brickworks and from sand whipped up by the winds from
the dunes of Paddington and Surry Hills. It suffocated unwary
Sydneysiders and coated everything in a thick dust, seeping into

houses through closed windows and doors. One of the most vivid memories an old woman had of her girlhood in the 1840s was 'the terrible storms of red dust which swept down Brickfield Hill, and besides almost smothering us, spoilt our nice clean clothes. All the houses in George Street had to be shut when the storms came.'

These storms brought 'destroying dust to those who ventured to expose perishable goods on the footway'. In 1826 a newspaper was amused to report that 'groups of perambulators who had sallied forth to sniff the evening gale presented a spectacle indescribably grotesque, resembling in many instances walking pyramids of sand'.

It was only with the building of houses and factories in suburbs like Surry Hills and Paddington, and on Brickfield Hill itself, that the notorious 'Brickfielder' gradually ceased to be a threat to the city and its inhabitants.

Until the southerly arrives Sydney's humidity can be exasperating, leaving you drained and exhausted, with wet patches under your armpits, sweat trickling down your neck and chest, your face flushed and shiny with a sheen of perspiration. As the novelist Elizabeth Harrower wrote, 'the humidity would get anyone down'.

The sultriness became an accepted part of Sydney life. In his *Rhymes of Sydney*, published in 1933, Colin Wills describes how the humidity brings a city to the end of its tether: people call each other names, passengers perspire profusely on the trams, people moan that they're fed up, asphalt in the suburbs 'clings like toffee to your feet', postmen are exhausted, toy dogs wheeze and pant, traffic cops' brains 'boil', golfers avoid playing, collars 'vex our clammy necks', and all anyone can do is 'stagger through the days'.

In the early years of the colony, 'the burning state of the atmosphere' could be deadly. Parrots fell dead from the sky, bats dropped from the trees, many of them plummeting to earth as they flew. Watkin Tench recorded that upwards of 20 000 dead bats were seen within 'the space of one mile'. So many bats and parrots died that the water was 'tainted for several days'.

One way to cope with the heat before air conditioners was to hang wet sheets on open windows to keep the house cool. These heat waves continued to exasperate Sydneysiders down the years. Marjorie Barnard recounts one such trying time in her 1943 novel *Dry Spell*:

> It was the third waterless summer, and the heat came down like a steel shutter over the city ... the country with its endless aching death pressed in on the city, the drought and the heat pressed on both.

Even those in the wealthy suburbs of the North Shore and Vaucluse couldn't escape it, so that:

> ... all the fine houses that had nestled so comfortably in the contours and in the greenery were forced into the light. They bulged out, exposed, and the sun tore at them. The gardens that had embowered them were perished. Tinder dry, fire had been through many of them, scorching walls and blistering any paint that remained.

Peter Corris's detective Cliff Hardy in *The Dying Trade* (1980), his suit soaking with sweat, drives his unair-conditioned car from his home in leafy Glebe to the North Shore:

> Sydney was sweltering. The roads were bubbling asphalt cauldrons and white concrete paths to hell. Most people had managed to stay inside or find some shade, but there were

several thousand of us who had to cook slowly inside mobile glass and steel ovens.

The summer temperatures caused sunstroke and fainting fits, especially for those who were not used to the climate. A *Sydney Gazette* editorial pleaded for 'some kind of shelter from the burning sun' for the laundresses working their trade at the Tank Stream: 'A woman and, we understand, it is not the only instance, while pursuing her occupation at the tanks fainted from the intensity of sun's rays, a day or two back.' There was also a theory that these hot days were conducive to madness or exacerbated mental illnesses. Frederic Norton Manning, the medical superintendent of Gladesville mental asylum, was particularly vexed about this. In his *The Causation and Prevention of Insanity* (1880), he writes of sunstroke:

> As a cause of insanity, in England, is almost unknown. It is
> far from otherwise in this colony. Five per cent of the total
> number of cases are accredited to it, and I think with good
> reason ... Many slight attacks of illness assigned to other causes
> are I believe due to the effect of heat and glare on the cerebral
> circulation ... It is in the power of physicians to prevent such
> mischief by inculcating greater care in avoiding exposure, by
> insisting on a more rational head covering for the summer
> months than a black stove-pipe hat.

So, in a practical move, weather sheds, hats and bonnets were provided for patients in the airing yards at Parramatta Hospital for the Insane and at the asylum at Callan Park.

New arrivals had to get used to the torrential rain and thunder that strikes after a heat wave. These storms would come so quickly that, if one was caught outdoors, the results could be catastrophic. In 1804 a party of picnickers comprising 14 military men and as many women rode out to South Head, a popular spot. As the *Sydney Gazette* reported they were to suffer 'one of the most general as well as violent electric shocks that perhaps ever was experienced'. The group was preparing to have their lunch under a fig tree when they heard peals of distant thunder, then suddenly there was a tremendous crash. An immense ball of fire struck a rock near them, obliterating it, and took off, crashing into the sea with a splash that rose high into the air.

The fireball caused injuries nearly fatal to everyone in the party. It was assumed that:

> ... a part of the electric fluid probably being attracted by the knives and forks on the table, took its course that way, and at the same instant ten of the company were struck down, some to all appearances dead, and others strangely affected by delirium. Mr Harris was knocked down and was supposed to have been killed but soon recovered, though part of his hair was singed, Mr Sloane was knocked down and remained in a dreadful and dangerous state for some days, Lt Laycock was lamed, Mr Blaxland had a bottle knocked out of his hand but escaped hurt. The principal sufferer was a young lady whose head was struck.

In 1820 Government House in Parramatta was hit by an 'electric fireball' that came through the dormer window in the roof, descended from the top floor to the ground floor, smashed the chamber doors off their hinges, shattering them, then made its way out through a solid wall, leaving several hundred panes of glass broken into minute particles. 'The house was almost in one instant of time left nearly a wreck, and full of a suffocating smell of sulphur.' What astonished everyone was that none of the large family occupying the house was harmed.

The approaching storms had an apocalyptic feel. The poet James McAuley, living in the inner-western suburb of Homebush in the 1920s, remembered how the sky suddenly transformed into an ominous colour, almost apocalyptic in its darkness, during late afternoon thunderstorms. One delivery man said to him as they watched a storm looming, 'You'd think the ending of the world had come.'

There are the frequent and violent hailstorms, as in 1814, thought by many to be the severest since the arrival of the First Fleet. It completely overwhelmed Sydney, extending from the tollgate, near present-day Central Station, and passing over the North Shore. According to one contemporary report, some of the hailstones:

> ... fell with incredible velocity measured nearly 3 inches
> in length and did considerable injury to the gardens,
> besides destroying almost every window facing the south.
> In Government House nearly 400 squares of glass were
> demolished, at the judge advocate's house about 200, at the
> church a further 300, [the wealthy merchant] Mr Simeon
> Lord's south windows were also entirely destroyed, as were
> those of Mr Nichols' range of storehouses.

The destructive hailstorm did its damage in only 12 minutes.

Shortly after noon one day in 1829, the sky darkened and large hailstones rained down. Sydney was said to echo loudly to the sound of broken glass. In the Scots Church nearly 200 panes of glass were smashed and in the *Sydney Gazette* offices about 70. The violence of the storm carried away the folding doors at the entrance of the Bank of Australia, then the gust rushed up the stairs to the second flight, forced open the trap door to the roof and nearly tore it off its hinges. Boats riddled with hailstones sank in Darling Harbour and the arms of the Windmill in Prince

Street, the Rocks, were shattered as if by gunfire. Roofs of pubs were blown off, shop windows shattered. It was said that scarcely a house in Sydney had not been damaged.

But it was not only the hailstorms that frightened Sydneysiders, but the thunder and lightning. In *A Bunyip Close Behind Me: Recollections of the Nineties by Eugenie McNeil, retold by her daughter Eugenie Crawford*, the family widow, Kate Delarue, was so terrified of the thunderstorms that she would rush around the house covering up the mirrors, for fear a lightning bolt would strike them and bounce off in another direction.

If the extremes of weather frightened people and made them anxious, it also affected the way Sydneysiders lived. The climate pushed women to reconsider their clothing, which too often aped inappropriate English and European fashions. Overseas visitors noted well before the 1880s that a local style had emerged. Not only were the lower class better dressed than their English equivalents, but the women and girls favoured flimsy fabrics and pale colours, especially in summer. As far back as the 1840s a British traveller commented on this distinctive Sydney style: 'On hot days the white dress, very gently worn by all classes, gives a lightness in gaiety to the streets, is very striking.' It was not only dresses that developed to accommodate the heat, but the Victorian desire for women to achieve a beautiful complexion saw colonial mothers insist their daughters did not leave the house without enormous leghorn hats complete with a strip of gossamer veil tacked round the edges.

Architecture too, has been fashioned by our weather, notably the verandah. Its introduction into Sydney came early. Because the town was seriously short of lime for making mortar, mud and clay were often used between the bricks, but these soft materials and handmade bricks were easily damaged by torrential rain. An important function of the verandah was to protect the fragile brickwork – and, of course, they became ubiquitous shelters against the hot sun.

In 1802 Governor Grose had a single-storey verandah constructed along the front of Government House. The skillion-type verandah was so common in Sydney by 1809 that a painting of the settlement by John Eyre shows many examples. It was a practical response to the climate, and with the arrival of convict architect Francis Greenway, it became a Regency stylistic device. When Greenway opened his practice in 1814, he specifically advertised his expertise with 'Plans of awnings, veranda's.'

By the 1830s, verandahs began to be built around two sides of a house. TJ Maslen, who had lived through Indian monsoons, was a vocal advocate of the verandah, noting in *The Friend of Australia* (1830) that they 'would be a great comfort during torrential rains of a winter, and in summer would soften the otherwise almost intolerable glare'. He also recommended that every street should have a verandah along each side, the same width as the footpath. This suggestion was soon taken up and photographs of Victorian Sydney show streets, houses and shops shaded by awnings.

For children, as related in *A Bunyip Close Behind Me*, the verandah became a playground: 'All around the house ran a verandah, on which we burned our feet in summer when we ran barefoot on the boards. On the hottest days the verandah kept the place reasonably cool.'

It's become increasingly obvious that present-day Sydney is divided into two by the weather. In his book *Australian Accent* (1958), journalist John Douglas Pringle asserts that Sydney is ruled by winds. The north-easterly is a sea breeze and, as it progresses inland, fades away. The winds blowing over the western suburbs bring no relief from the heat, but 'to the more favoured eastern suburbs the night breeze is a source of pride and joy; and the wealthy citizens of Bellevue Hill and Point Piper set their houses to catch it like the yachts on the harbour set their sails'.

Coastal winds fade and heat up as they flow across Sydney, causing those in the west to swelter when the coast can be eight degrees Celsius cooler. Some of this is down to Sydney's geography. There is a ridge that divides the Sydney basin, running from Camden in the south to the Hills district in the north, that traps hot westerly winds and blocks sea breezes. The current building boom in western Sydney is also creating more 'heat islands', which contribute to higher temperatures as the warmth absorbed by concrete and brick during the day is released. Traffic and air-conditioning exhausts add to the growing problem.

Temperature records show that Parramatta typically records 13 days over 35 degrees Celsius each year, while Sydney's CBD only averages four. Coastal Bondi can be 29 degrees Celsius and outer-suburban Blacktown 40 degrees on the same hot summer's day. In other words, the weather has helped to perpetuate Sydney's social divide.

SURVIVING

BY EARLY 1790 SYDNEY WAS IN DANGER OF BEING ABANDONED.
The situation was critical, with just enough food to last until the
end of May. 'Gloom and dejection overspread every countenance,'
Tench wrote, himself falling into lethargy and torpor.

Convicts were sent to Norfolk Island and others 24 kilometres
upriver to the new settlement of Rose Hill (Parramatta), which had
better soil for gardens and crops. There were less than 600 people
left in Sydney. Deputy Judge Advocate David Collins described
the dismal state of affairs in his exhaustively detailed *An Account
of the English Colony in New South Wales*:

> The military quarters had a deserted aspect and the whole
> settlement appeared as if famine had already thinned half its
> numbers. The little society that had been in place was broken
> up, and every man seemed left to brood in solitary silence over
> the dreary prospect before him.

Phillip was feeling the strain, despite his determined air of
optimism. In 1790 the sight of a dog infuriated him, appalled that
food was wasted on the dog when it should be given to humans.
'Kill your dog, sir, and I will send you a pig from the stores,' he
demanded of one owner. Not long afterwards a surgeon's mate

gloated: 'I dined most heartily the other day on a fine dog, and I hope I shall soon again have an invitation to a similar repast.'

The grim atmosphere momentarily lifted on 23 June when, with great excitement, the settlement greeted the arrival of the *Lady Juliana*. Things quickly turned sour when it was discovered that instead of food the ship had brought 222 women convicts. The news grew worse: the captain informed Phillip that the *Guardian*, a store ship sailing to Sydney, had struck an iceberg and been wrecked.

Over the summer of 1790 and 1791 drought came to the colony. Vegetables became scarce due to the lack of rain, not helped by the poor soil around the cove. The nearby farms were in a wretched condition and as the food supply dwindled, many of the pigs and poultry succumbed to heat exhaustion. The summer dragged on. 'It felt,' wrote Tench, 'like the blast of a heated oven.'

A sense of desolation and general hopelessness returned, but a fortnight later when the store ship *Justinian* arrived from London via Rio de Janeiro, the mood abruptly changed again, and a relieved governor put the colony back on full rations. But just as optimism resumed in the last days of June, something out of Dante's hell arrived in Sydney Cove in the form of three convict ships, *Surprize*, *Scarborough* and *Neptune*.

Conditions on the way out had been so appalling that about a quarter of the 1000 convicts who had embarked died on the voyage through brutality, neglect and deliberate starvation. Some who survived expired as the ships sailed up the harbour. Their naked skeletal bodies were thrown overboard, others perished when they stepped on deck and collapsed because of the bracing fresh air. Some died as they were being rowed ashore; others were too weak to stand. The Reverend Johnson went aboard the ships and found himself retching, overcome by the stink below decks. When he returned to shore he was horrified to see how 'Some creeped on their hands and knees, and some were carried on the backs of others.' Almost two-thirds of the 750 survivors were hospitalised; 90 died within a month and 220 would never fully recover. Soon the two burial sites at the Rocks were overflowing, as was the site for the marines at Dawes Point. Another burial ground was established in what is now Clarence Street, until it too filled and in September 1782 new burial grounds shifted to the area now occupied by the Town Hall.

Between July and October more transports arrived. The conditions were better on these ships but even so, of about 2000 convicts, nearly 200 died on the voyage and another 600 went down with dysentery soon after landing. The men and women were 'so thoroughly exhausted,' Captain John Hunter observed, 'that they expired without a groan and apparently without any kind of pain'.

Rose Hill's grain harvests were successful, but not enough to feed the colony. But slowly, as more ships arrived with provisions, the threat of starvation eased. Phillip began to relax and take an abiding interest in the fauna of this new world. He had two pet kangaroos that seem to have had the run of Government House, and a tame flying fox, which clung upside down from his jacket. He had been astonished to see a black swan, a bird he thought only existed in mythology. Then there were the ostrich-like emus. His gamekeeper killed one and Phillip sent the skin to Lord Sydney with the note that it was a 'very well flavoured meat'.

When not exploring the countryside, Phillip liked to spend evenings with William Dawes and Watkin Tench at the observatory. Both lieutenants spoke Latin and French and read widely, swapping quotations from Voltaire, Gibbon, Milton and Cicero, discussing issues such as slavery (all three were violently opposed to it) and speculating what lay beyond the Blue Mountains. The observatory was the intellectual hub of the tiny community.

Dawes also spent time establishing a battery near his observatory, and had long sessions with Phillip helping to lay out the streets of Parramatta and Sydney. Good humoured in company, Tench was a keen observer of men and the progress, or lack of it, of the settlement. His two books, written in an admirable and entertaining style – *A Narrative of the Expedition to Botany Bay* (1789) and *A Complete Account of the Settlement at Port Jackson, in New South Wales* (1793) – give us the best account of the sufferings during the hungry times, the difficult beginnings of agriculture, and the adventures of the first explorers, and the growing realisation that the colony would survive. An entertaining and vivacious fellow who, although always trying to find the best in someone, saw the Aboriginal way of life as confirmation of Hobbes' observation that a state of nature is a state of war. At the same time, he found the 'Indians' as intelligent and astute as any Englishman. His books convey the sheer excitement of finding himself in a strange country, with weird weather and fauna, and of being jolted upright in his hut on hearing the longed-for raucous cry of 'the flag's up', which indicated a ship was about to enter the harbour. One time he was so excited on hearing the cry that he rowed down the harbour and out the Heads to greet an approaching ship, desperate to hear news about what was happening back in England and the progress of the revolution in France.

In 1790 houses were being built of bricks. More convict ships were arriving, and the colony was settling into something permanent. It may have looked nothing like Phillip's dream city of Albion, but at least it was flourishing. And in order for it to continue to thrive it had to find a way of paying for itself. As a farmer, the governor saw the colony's future in agriculture, and as a former whaler – at the age of 15 he had joined a whaling vessel, becoming expert in stripping blubber and doing the dirty work of packing it into barrels before joining the Navy – he knew there was a fortune to be made from whaling and sealing in Australian waters.

On 11 December 1792 Phillip sailed for England in the *Atlantic* to seek medical attention for constant kidney pain (a common complaint among long-term sailors whose huge intake of salted meat was the frequent cause). He had accomplished much, and it is difficult to imagine anyone else could have succeeded as he did in establishing Sydney. It was his leadership that saved the colony. It may not have become Albion under his watch, but it had survived.

THE DISTANCE OF YOUR HEART

I'M STANDING WHERE GOVERNOR PHILLIP ONCE STOOD. I'm looking for birds, birds made out of metal. I'm outside the Museum of Sydney one warm Wednesday afternoon between Easter and Anzac Day. I had come from Kings Cross by train. In my carriage was an agitated man in his thirties, his eyes sparkling as if he had plugged into an electrical socket, singing along loudly to an obscene rap video on his phone, his voice muffled by his jumper, which he was using as an improvised face mask due to the Covid pandemic. The masked middle-aged couple opposite were, like me, trying to avoid eye contact with the madman.

Once outside Martin Place station, I walked towards Bridge Street. I found myself engaged in a sort of St Vitus dance, trying to avoid the zombies on their phones, propping suddenly, nearly walking into me or a lamppost. It's school holidays and there are whining kids and shy groups of teenagers. The crowds are dressed casually in shirts, T-shirts, shorts and slacks, so different from the huge historic photographs the City of Sydney has pasted onto the hoardings around construction sites that show men and women in the city dressed in their formal best well into the late 1950s.

I am at the museum because of an English artist. A decade or so into the twenty-first century the lord mayor of Sydney, Clover Moore, decided that the city needed some exciting street art, and her advisors came up with what they thought were cutting-edge ideas. There would be a gigantic sculpture of a blue milk crate in Prince Albert Park which visitors could enter and play, and a huge elongated piece of metal, like a monstrous white tape worm, rising up 50 metres in front of the Town Hall in George Street. The costs of these two pieces of public sculpture grew alarmingly high, the tape worm nearing $20 million alone. After public mockery and a prolonged and bruising debate, they were quietly abandoned. But there was another project kept alive.

Englishwoman Tracey Emin had become famous for her confessional art that culminated in her 1997 work, *Everyone I Have Ever Slept With 1963–1995*, which comprised an unmade bed and the names of everyone the artist had ever shared her bed with, the mattress encrusted with a detritus of cigarettes, condoms and stains of bodily fluids.

If there was one thing she shared with the artists of the shelved projects, it was that she wasn't Australian. It may have been a sign of cultural cringe or the City of Sydney (which has a dismal recent history of public sculptures) wanting to impress the international art world, but Emin's abilities in this area were unknown. Her specialities were art installations, wacky drawings and cartoony paintings.

She came up with the idea of 67 bronze birds, which she would individually handcraft. Rather than a native Australian or British species, these birds were to be hybrids inspired, she said, by her 2003 visit to Sydney for her solo exhibition at the Art Gallery of New South Wales. She had felt incredibly homesick and overwhelmed by the distance between Sydney and her loved ones in London – '17 035 kilometres to be exact'.

The birds were hybrids because, 'We're all hybrids, mixed up, mixed cultures; nobody is one culture or one thing, and Australia is a melting pot.' She also described the birds as 'angels of this Earth', and added a sentimental note about her mother: 'My mum died about a year and a half ago and every time I see a bird flying, I actually wonder is it her? Could it be her? Could she be looking down on me?'

Called *The Distance of Your Heart*, the birds were said to be the antithesis of what we typically expect from public art, which is often monumental in scale and subject. Emin explained the idea was that:

> ... when people are walking through this big city vista and by these big high buildings, they stop for a moment when they see one of these little birds; they can have a memory, a poetic thought, and just stop and think about somebody they love.

Her project cost nearly a million dollars. Each bird was to be the size of a thrush and the flock was placed in various locations along Bridge and Grosvenor streets in the CBD. They were to perch on ledges, lampposts and windowsills; peep from under benches, and sit in doorways.

Emin described her public installation as 'simple, straight-forward and accessible to everybody'. The trouble is that at times the quest to see these birds has resembled a frustrating treasure hunt. Interested seekers have braved impatient, busy crowds and either given up the arduous, neck-straining search for them, or else ended the quest exasperated at having been unable to find more than 40 or so out of the 67. Far from being accessible, many seemed to have been hidden on purpose.

I have visited the museum many times, but on this day I find it shut. The new hours are from Thursday to Sunday. I am the only person here. In front of the sandstone edifice is a herm of Governor Phillip gazing slightly towards where the gardens of Farm Cove used to be. To my right, as I face the blank windows of the museum's restaurant and front doors, there are 29 tall pillars that from a distance appear stark, almost severe. It's an installation called *Edge of the Trees*, created by artists Fiona Foley and Janet Laurence, and the elongated shadows of the pillars creep towards the entrance. These pillars are of steel, wood, clay, shell, sandstone and glass and are said to embody 'the crossroads of two cultures meeting'. Up close one can see, engraved on the pillars, the names of Aboriginal people and places, First Fleeters and plants from the area. To my left is the massive Chief Secretary's five-storey building, a late Victorian masterpiece built out of sandstone that in 1881 the *Illustrated Sydney News* boasted was 'a veritable poem in stone'.

The museum was once the site of the first Government House, built for Governor Phillip in 1789. Designed by Phillip and his brickmaker, James Bloodsworth, it was the only two-storey building in the settlement, more like a comfortable private house than a mansion. It had six main rooms, two front rooms downstairs, two sculleries and two rooms upstairs, plus upper and lower halls and a vestibule. It was not a building suitable for a hectic official life, but it was ready to receive guests to celebrate the king's birthday in June 1789. It functioned well because of a convict, the efficient, no-nonsense Jane Dundas, who quickly rose from maidservant to the position of housekeeper and was regarded by all as 'an honest, faithful and affectionate servant'.

It was the first permanent building in the colony, and quickly became the centre of the colony's administrative and social life, and a meeting place for the Gadigal and the colonisers. Both Arabanoo and Ballederry, Bennelong's friend, were even buried in its grounds.

At the back of the house were a cluster of buildings containing a kitchen, bakehouse, stables and offices and workrooms. There is an 1807 painting of Government House by John Eyre that gives the viewer a good idea of how it dominated the settlement from its position on a hill. In the foreground, two canoes with Aboriginal people indicate just how much the Gadigal and whites co-existed at the time. The military is a presence with four soldiers in a boat, and a dinghy shows a typical Sydney scene of someone enjoying the harbour. There's a steep straight path leading from the water up to Government House, with shrubs and vegetable and flower gardens on either side of it, and a huge flag, confirming the authority not only of the governor, but the British.

Government House was extended and repaired by the eight governors who succeeded Phillip. Around 1800 Governor King added a verandah and a drawing room. In 1816 Francis Greenway added extensions and a ballroom, transforming it into a faux Italianate house. But as the years went by the building leaked, some of its original structure rotted, there were constant white-ant infestations, crumbling mortar and rising damp. The rambling edifice was described as 'an incongruous mass of Buildings built at different periods', and after many complaints by a procession of occupants, it was permanently vacated in 1845 when Governor Gipps shifted into the new Government House in the Domain. The following year it was demolished without sentiment.

Not knowing what to do with the vacant site, the municipal authorities left it to become a wasteland of weeds and grasses. Terrace houses were built around its edges and in 1912 a two-storey corrugated-iron office was erected for the government architect. After that it was levelled in 1967, the unsentimental City of Sydney did what it became known for in that era – the site was paved over for use as a car park. Until 1983 it was thought that nothing remained of the first Government House. When a hasty excavation was undertaken as a prerequisite for a building development, archaeologists uncovered the original foundations, garden paths, drains, evidence of the first printing office and thousands of objects, including cutlery and crockery. It was a priceless insight into the early years of Sydney.

Because of the significance of the site, a museum was built in the middle 1990s officially known as the Museum of Sydney on the Site of the First Government House. Now simply called the Museum of Sydney, it explores the stories of this city from its origins to today, while the few remains of the original building can be glimpsed through glass openings in the floor of the museum's forecourt and foyer.

I turn around to face what would have been Phillip's uninterrupted view of Sydney Cove, whose waters were much closer than today; then it was just a quick walk down a slope to a waiting boat. Now the view is of the confronting AMP skyscraper, a curved glass building of brutal vacuity. Phillip Street on its right leads down to the Quay, and to its left, Young Street, with its view of a slice of the bridge, heads down to the harbour, which today glistens with reflected sunlight.

My task is to find the six birds that Emin says she planted around the museum. At first, I see none, then I look up at the ledge of the upper truncated walkway and see two birds staring down at me. As I take a step closer, they fly away. I head up to the walkway where half a dozen Chinese businessmen are smoking. Behind them are several large ceramic pots containing examples of native grasses and plants, but no birds.

As I set off down Bridge Street, I keep a close eye on anything that resembles one of Emin's birds. But I see none. I am surrounded by a muddle of building styles, several wonderful Victorian-era structures covered in webs of scaffolding that have workers busy renovating and refreshing their sandstone exteriors, prosaic mid-century office blocks and modern skyscrapers. The street dips as it proceeds towards what was once the bridge that spanned the Tank Stream and connected the two sections of Sydney town.

I end up in Macquarie Place, a triangular shaped oasis of trees, palms and assorted historical objects where Emin had placed a dozen of her birds and a handmade stone bird bath inscribed by the artist with the words *The Distance of Your Heart*. She chose this place because of the Obelisk of Distances designed by Greenway in 1818, from which the distance to various locations in New South Wales are measured. She saw this as 'the perfect site to measure the distance of my heart'.

Emin probably knew little about the obelisk except that it seemed a fitting visual summary of her concept. It was erected on the site where it was once thought Governor Phillip had first raised the Union Jack. The large sandstone structure functioned as the zero point for the measurement of early roads in New South Wales. It was instrumental as a surveying device for Sydney's earliest roads as part of Macquarie's civic improvements. But it was more than that. The obelisk, in the park named after himself, was Macquarie's way of confirming that the colonisation of Darug lands to the west was proceeding at pace under his governorship. It pointed out that the new town of Bathurst was 137 miles (220 kilometres) away, and gave distances to the towns of Windsor, Parramatta and Liverpool. Just seven miles away to the east was his namesake lighthouse at South Head.

Today Macquarie Place is shaded by trees with a pocket of dappled sunlight in a far corner. The plane trees face Loftus Street to the east, two imposing Moreton Bay figs are on the western side, and an oak is flanked by two clumps of Lord Howe Island kentia palms and a cluster of tree ferns on the Bridge Street side. There's also a juvenile weeping lilly pilly huddled up in the south-eastern corner. The trees are huge, especially the ficus, with its dramatic buttress roots. Because it's autumn there are dead leaves littering the paths and garden beds and there's a musky smell of decay. The two small areas of grass are temporarily fenced off and the weathered sandstone benches and ledges are a dirty grey and moss green.

The park should be a quiet oasis with any noise abated by nature, but it's not. Traffic noise competes with buzzy chatter and laughter drifting over from the nearby Customs House bar. There the customers dine and drink under huge dirty white canopies littered with rotting leaves. Only one other person is in the park, a plump homeless man with a white beard lying prone on one of the ancient sandstone benches, his snores mingling with the chirping of a few birds above him.

Hard to avoid is the enormous anchor, a relic of the flagship of the First Fleet, HMS *Sirius*, which was wrecked two years later in 1790 on Norfolk Island, much to the dismay of those back in Sydney who had relied on it as one of the few vessels capable of replenishing the starving colony's dwindling food supplies. The cannon from the *Sirius* points straight at the Customs House bar. There's the remnant of an old drinking fountain and the sealed men's lavatory with its ornate entrance built in 1907.

The location of the park itself was once closer to the harbour foreshore. It was laid out in 1810 and functioned as the town square. The south side was occupied by government buildings and the east by the Governor's Domain. Wealthy emancipist merchants such as Mary Reibey and Simeon Lord bought land on the western side; Lord's three-storey mansion was the most impressive private dwelling of his time (the heritage-listed Kyle House was built on the site in 1931). Today Macquarie Place is approximately half its original size, some of the land being resumed for the construction of Loftus Street in the late 1830s.

Once an exclusive area for the wealthy, now the shrinking park is surrounded by prosaic office buildings, cafés and bars. I pause to look across at the rear of the statue of Thomas Sutcliffe Mort. With one arm casually propped on his side, he seems to be staring at Bridge Street with its roar of cars, trucks and the piercing sounds of steel cutting into sandstone, and the passing parade of businessmen and women, joggers, cyclists and families on holiday. As for the bird bath, I can't find it. It's probably in one of the fenced-off areas.

Looking around at the park, about a third of the size of a soccer pitch, I can only see a scruffy cacophony of trees and plants and a jumble of historical objects with no connection to each other. It seems a forlorn and forgotten space that only a minuscule number of Sydneysiders know about. There's an air of visual clutter and neglect, as if it is of no importance. In any other major city of the world, this would be a precinct of historical significance and civic pride.

I pass the snoring man as I walk outside the park, around to the front of the striking statue of Mort. The imposing bronze piece was erected in 1883, five years after his death, and the inscription on the marble plinth reads: *A pioneer of Australian resources, a founder of Australian industries, one who established our wool market.* More importantly, he was one of the first in Australia to make the export of frozen meat possible by investing a fortune in refrigeration. He constructed docks big enough for any of the world's ships and became a major founder of the shipbuilding and repair industry. His statue is public recognition that a proud Sydney had evolved from a penal settlement into a wealthy, self-supporting colony and a major economic player in the British empire.

I am about to leave for Martin Place to return home without having seen one of the English artist's avian sculptures when I stop. At the foot of Mort is a tiny bird, about the size of a starling. It doesn't move. It's one of Emin's birds. The only one I have found.

THE NEW SKYLINE:
FRANCIS GREENWAY

HIDDEN AMONG SYDNEY'S SKYSCRAPERS and glass towers are remnants of the original architectural triumphs that once dominated the Sydney skyline – the creations of one man, the convict Francis Greenway.

Greenway had been in private practice as an architect in Bristol when, in March 1812, he was found guilty of forging a document and sentenced to death. This was commuted to 14 years transportation to the fledgling colony, and he arrived on the transport *General Hewitt* in February 1814, after a horrendous voyage (34 convicts died). He disembarked aged 34, height 5 feet 7 inches (170 centimetres), a good height in those days, tousled light hair, hazel eyes, with a complexion fair and ruddy that would become choleric when angry, which, over the years, was often. A few months later his wife, Mary, and their three children arrived. Greenway had obviously spent his time between sentencing and transportation wisely because he arrived with a reference from ex-governor Arthur Phillip, who praised him as 'an architect of eminence'.

In his first dispatch to England after being sworn in as governor in 1810, Macquarie had pleaded for an architect to design new public buildings. Finally, four years later, one had arrived, albeit a convict. The two finally met in July 1814, and Macquarie asked

Greenway, as a test of his abilities, to copy designs from a pattern book.

An offended Greenway responded with a letter boasting about his skills, adding that he would:

> … immediately copy the drawing Your Excellency requested me to do, notwithstanding it is rather painful to my mind as a professional man to copy a building that has no claim to classical proportion and character.

To test Greenway's architectural competence further, Macquarie asked him to critique the Rum Hospital, which was still under construction but plagued by problems. Greenway's report was scathing about its structural defects and the liberal consumption of rum by the workmen, and, as Macquarie realised, it was astute and meticulous. Much to their chagrin, the builders had to make costly alterations, and so became the first of the many enemies Greenway would make in Sydney.

He was granted a ticket of leave to begin a private practice and in 1815 Macquarie had him give advice on public works. Greenway pointed out that public and private buildings were badly constructed to such an extent that they were either decaying or would soon end up in ruins. A major problem was that contract building in the colony was a 'racket' (nothing seems to have changed in Sydney), where graft and bribes were 'practised by those whom its power has made invincible', the result being cost overruns and shoddy workmanship.

There is a sense of Macquarie weighing up the convict's ability alongside his cocky manner. What gradually tipped the scales was Greenway's relationship with the governor's wife, his 'Dearest Elizabeth'. Artistically inclined, with a special interest in architecture and landscape design, she had arrived in Sydney with a book of architectural drawings. She and Greenway pored over the illustrations and pondered how the town should look. In 1815 Greenway designed Governor Macquarie's Toll House, which was erected near where Railway Square now stands. At the time, the building marked the southern boundary of Sydney. And what a building it was. Elizabeth's input was obvious, given her liking for ornamental decoration. The Toll House was a piece of Gothic fantasy, complete with pinnacles and lancet windows.

It must have pleased the governor; in March 1816 he appointed Greenway civil architect and assistant engineer, 'directing the Planning and Execution of the Government Public Works' at a salary of three shillings a day. As an added inducement, Greenway was given a house on the corner of Argyle and George streets, rations, an assigned convict servant, coals for heating, fodder and a horse. One of Greenway's first announcements was that he would design buildings that would result in Sydney becoming a 'regular and well-built town'. His architectural philosophy never changed, often resorting to a simple domestic image to explain it: 'I consider the Government and the Public as man and wife; therefore, those who injure the one must injure the other.'

Macquarie moved quickly and ordered Greenway to design a lighthouse at South Head. A plus for the architect was that the sandstone could be quarried directly from the site. On 11 June 1816, the governor laid the foundation stones for the lighthouse and a soldiers' barracks at South Head. It was a day celebrated with speeches (as usual long and self-congratulatory) and toasts with cherry brandy.

Greenway quickly discovered that he needed more than architectural skills. His workmen were convicts and could be a sullen bunch. There was a shortage of stone masons and he had intended to use the project as a training school for masons, but the experienced men refused. It was a brittle atmosphere and created daily tensions until he provided the masons with extra money and emphasised that he would reward them with recommendations for their early emancipation. He also realised that praise rather than punishment worked better with the convicts, and he constantly encouraged good workers.

Even so, years later this quarrelsome, self-dramatising architect would complain about that time, saying, 'I exerted myself at the risk of my life.'

The lighthouse was opened on 29 April 1818. On that day Greenway was given a conditional pardon. By this stage he had ridden all over town and the outlying districts, observing that Sydney's topography needed solutions different from the flat terrain of England. There were hills, valleys, rocky escarpments and, as every good architect since has realised, these make Sydney a difficult landscape to design for. Out of these exploratory journeys he began to imagine a master plan for Sydney.

Hyde Park would become a great landscaped quadrangle surrounded by public buildings on all sides. Then there was the north–south divide of the harbour. As early as 1790 William Dawes had included a proposal for a bridge across the harbour in the notes accompanying his wildly ambitious plan for Sydney. Greenway speculated how to construct a bridge from Dawes Point to Milsons Point that would 'give an idea of strength and magnificence'. It was, of course, a pipe dream as there was no money for it and he lacked the technology to achieve it. He envisaged Circular Quay as a quay in the shape of a horseshoe, with the extremities at Fort Macquarie (Bennelong Point) and Dawes Point.

These marvellous ideas remained only dreams. Macquarie needed Greenway for more urgent tasks. Since 1788 the convicts had been allowed to either camp at night, rent lodgings, or live with free settlers for whom they worked. But by 1814 the convict population had increased to such an extent that, as far as Macquarie was concerned, leaving convicts to roam at night was 'a source of many evils'. These men needed to be housed and controlled at night, so Greenway was ordered to come up with a design.

Construction of the Hyde Park Barracks began in 1817. It was not without controversy, as some believed that the barracks was not sufficiently isolated (people later complained about the sound of the barracks scourgers 'ripping unpleasantly through the Hyde Park air'). It took two years to build. His lighthouse experience had taught Greenway how to cajole and drive his workmen, but much to his annoyance he had to spend an inordinate amount of time on tasks that should have been done by the site managers. He even found himself inspecting each of the bricks, as too many faulty ones came from the government kilns in Brickfields. He had to fire incompetent overseers and could only resign himself to the fact that the convicts working on the site would spend the extra money he gave them at the end of the working day on 'exorbitantly priced liquor' in the nearby pubs.

During construction he was also busy designing other buildings, including the police offices in George Street, plus the adjacent markets, and occasionally attending dinners at Government House. At a ball given at Government House on Anniversary Day 1818 by Elizabeth Macquarie, Greenway showed his gratitude for the first governor's recommendation by presenting 'a likeness of Governor Phillip' that was the talk of the town.

But his priority was the convicts' barracks. Gathering convict workers in the barracks overnight was intended both to separate them from the general population and to curb their criminal activities at night. Greenway's design had incorporated a high wall around a three-storey building, but there were no bars, bolts or cells inside. It was not conceived as a jail. The main building contained 12 spacious and well-aired sleeping rooms designed for up to 600 men, though there were times when it would house up to 1400 men, some forced to sleep on the floors.

It was officially opened in 1819. Facing on to Macquarie Street was the huge clock designed by convict watchmaker James Oatley, which not only symbolised how the town was becoming regulated but also orchestrated the convicts' lives more precisely, allowing the government more efficient management of their hours of work and leisure. Each morning the residents were aroused by a bell just before sunrise. They were fed a meal of hominy (porridge made from corn or grain), then they were sent outside to work. Those close enough could return to the barracks for lunch, while the rest came back in the evening for dinner, the muster and then bed.

During the next 20 years the barracks came to represent the horrors and drudgery of convict life, but for others the building was a remarkable accomplishment. *Sydney Gazette*'s appraisal of the barracks on 17 July 1819 summed up what many thought:

> The Building is beautiful at a distance, but at a near approach conveys an idea of towering grandeur. This Building is executed comfortably with the most elegant proportions of the Greek School.

While Macquarie was not as preoccupied by the potential of foreign invasion as previous governors had been, he did get Greenway to design a fort on what is now Bennelong Point, replacing the small one William Dawes constructed in 1788.

Fort Macquarie was impressive, a large square structure built of sandstone hewn from an outcrop in the Domain adjacent to the construction site. One prominent feature was the castellated walls, of which Greenway (and, one suspects, Elizabeth Macquarie) had become enamoured.

Greenway had shown Macquarie a sketch of a building for the

Government House Stables, based on the model of Thornbury Castle in Gloucester, 'only much bolder, in the size of the towers and other parts of the building'. Macquarie agreed that it seemed like a good idea and thought little more about it. But Greenway went ahead with his grandiose plan – a building up on the hill, not far from Government House in Bridge Street. It held a huge complex of stables, servants' quarters, and special offices for Elizabeth, which would fulfil a need while the new Government House, the third part of Greenway's grand plan, waited to be built.

Finished in 1821, the Stables was a building of striking appearance, impossible to ignore given its prominent position. This gothic extravagant structure quickly earned the nick-name of 'Greenway's Folly', and its cost delayed the construction of the new Government House for 25 years. Greenway's own ideas for Government house was a building complementing both the Stables and the Fort, the castellations uniting all three.

When Rose de Freycinet visited Sydney in the summer of 1819 she admired the 'lighthouse built of stone' and 'the peculiar building erected for Government House Stables. It was just like an old castle, with its towers, crenelles etc.' Intrigued, she asked if it was Macquarie's idea (and never got a firm answer). She concluded that its location was chosen because it could be seen from ships in the harbour and was all the more 'picturesque' for it. Others weren't so kind. When the Russian Akhilles Shabelsky visited in 1822, he wondered if Macquarie's Stables was a statement that 'in Sydney the horses have better lodgings than God himself'.

In 1819 Macquarie commissioned Greenway to design St James' church. The building was originally intended to be a courthouse, as both the governor and the colonial architect had plans for a large cathedral to be built on the present location of St Andrew's Cathedral, but these plans were suspended by the arrival of Commissioner John Bigge to report on the progress of the colony the same year. The capricious Bigge initially approved of the courthouse but four months after his arrival recommended its conversion to a church.

At 52 metres, it became Sydney's tallest structure for 36 years. Churchgoers appreciated its delicate Georgian simplicity and Ionic pillars, but complained bitterly of the noisy clanking of chains as convicts from the nearby Hyde Park Barracks, just across the square, stumbled upstairs to the gallery.

The church would have its critics. The *1882 Illustrated Guide to Sydney* called it 'ponderous', and a writer two years later thought it 'an ugly early Gothic building'. Once it could be seen for miles, but nowadays it seems shrunken, hemmed in as it is by skyscrapers that block out the sunlight for most of the day, so the church slumbers in gloom. Its once mighty spire, by contrast with the surrounding buildings, seems like something out of a toy town.

The arrival of Commissioner Bigge marked the turning point of Greenway's career. The architect had made many enemies with his arrogance, his criticisms of others who disagreed with him, his public allegations of bribery, his anger at political interference and his vitriolic comments about slapdash construction methods. Bigge was inclined to listen to the criticisms and cancelled many of Greenway's projects as being overly decorative, costly and unrelated to the running of a penal colony.

Exhausted from his decade overseeing an unruly colony and hounded by Bigge for 'extravagant' spending on public buildings, Macquarie had little energy for Greenway's new demands that he be paid £11 000 for his designs, calculated at 5 per cent of the buildings' costs. Greenway's stunning lack of tact and his combative letters to his former friend (caustically pointing out that he was paid a measly three shillings a day when masons received seven shillings), were a monumental mistake. Macquarie refused to pay and abused his architect in return. In one retaliatory missive he bridled at 'such language I will not stain my letter with' and called his former partner in the creation of a new Sydney, 'insulting, disrespectful and insolent'. In a feline aside in one letter, putting the former convict in his place, he mentioned that the dinners Greenway attended at Government House were a privilege that the former convict should have regarded with 'a special debt of gratitude'. What the egotistical Greenway, impulsive and intemperate, did not understand, was that in attacking Macquarie he was not only losing a patron but the one person who had supported him when he had been publicly criticised.

When the new governor, Sir Thomas Brisbane, arrived in 1821 to take over from Macquarie, he thought Greenway a 'fanatic nuisance'. Brisbane finally lost patience with the constantly complaining architect and fired him the following year.

Greenway's subsequent fortunes as a freelance architect eventually amounted to nothing. He complained about his poor treatment at the hands of the government, but he had made too many enemies, and no one wanted to deal with him. The government tried to reclaim the house he had been given, but he refused to leave it until his wife, Mary, died in 1832. Her little school at the rear of their house had provided for the family of seven children during her husband's unemployment and now there was no money coming in. By 1835 he was destitute, advertising in the *Sydney Gazette* that 'Francis Howard Greenway, arising from circumstances of a singular nature is induced again to solicit the patronage of his friends and the public'. Bankrupt and without a future in Sydney, he rode north to try and farm 324 hectares on the Hunter River, a sterile marshland he had been granted by the government. And there, in 1837, he died of typhoid, aged 59. He was buried in an unmarked grave.

He left behind some exquisite and substantial examples of Georgian architecture that are reminders of a time when both he and Macquarie tried to inspire the populace with buildings that would be the beginning of what Greenway imagined would be 'a great city, as great to equal any of beauty in Europe'.

MORTDALE,
AKA VALLEY OF THE DEAD

'YOU TWO LOOK LOST,' I HEARD A WOMAN SAY. Ali and I stop next to a bench not far from the main street. Sitting on it in the harsh sunlight is a tiny middle-aged woman dressed in a pink outfit with lips painted a bright candy colour.

'This is our first time in Mortdale,' I say. She nods, and glances up at us both, her eyes glassy. 'Are you waiting for a bus?' I ask.

She shakes her head. 'No, I'm an alcoholic and I'm just having a rest before going home.'

Ali asks if she lives in Mortdale and she says she has done so for four years but misses the neighbouring suburb of Oatley terribly.

'Oh, it is a beautiful place. So different from here. There was a sort of a wood where I used to live and now, I'm stuck in Mortdale. Anyway, I'm on my way home now.'

I have never been here before, but I am intrigued by it because of the French author, Georges Perec, whose *Life: A User's Manual* (1978) I consider one of the great novels of the twentieth century. Perec came to Australia in 1981. During the few days he spent in Sydney, he made a list of railway stations on the Sutherland line to be used for a literary thriller called *53 Days*. He died before completing it but left behind a list written in capital letters, naming all the stations from Redfern to Sutherland, with Mortdale squeezed into it. Barely legible, it seems he added it to the list as a last-minute correction after Perec originally overlooking it. Perhaps his late addition of the name was because he had been psychologically shaken and temporarily forgotten it, as its French translation is 'Death Valley' or 'Valley of the Dead'.

There are now 658 suburbs in Sydney. Architecture critic Elizabeth Farrelly expressed a typical inner-city attitude towards Sydney's suburbs in the *Sydney Morning Herald* when she wrote: 'The suburbs are about boredom, and obviously some people like being bored and plain and predictable. I'm happy for them … even if their suburbs are destroying the world.'

Mortdale is one of Sydney's middle ring suburbs in the south. My companion on this December day is Ali Nasseri. I had seen his explicit photographs of lap dancers at a Kings Cross nightclub and, impressed by them, sought him out and got to know him. He's Iranian, a couple of decades younger than me, with unruly black hair and beard. It's early December when we set out on the train; the morning promises a hot day.

We pass Sydenham with its factories and storehouses, where I used to live under the flight path. Graffiti now dominates the sides of the buildings, where before it was just discreet tags. As the train passes through Tempe and Wolli Creek what astonishes me are the high-rise apartments on either side of the tracks where I only remember grim terrace houses, cheap 1920s bungalows and parched paddocks with rusted derelict cars. These new buildings have the prosaic utility of public housing, except that they are expensive apartments for people wanting to live close to the city. In years to come they will be a dismal sight.

It takes about half an hour to reach our destination. Descending the steep station stairs into Mortdale, enter an unfamiliar part of Sydney and don't know what to expect. To my left is a wedge-shaped hotel, some hundred years old judging by the architectural style and the brickwork. We walk down Morts Road, the treeless main street and shopping centre. Outside a pharmacy is a blackboard proclaiming: *Life is better when you're laughing.* Most of the shops are cafés and restaurants with several fish and chip shops. It's a multicultural food fest: Japanese, Italian, Lebanese, Indian and Chinese. The street seems to be predominately about food. The architecture is simple and functional, with a tiny church in among the shops, its huge white banner announcing *God is Love* in red letters.

We sit under the awning outside a Gloria Jeans coffee shop watching the foot traffic. Ali sips an iced coffee and me, a latte. I notice that many of the men, mostly Anglo, are wearing shorts in the heat. There are old men using walking sticks, one even has a stick tied to his briefcase; another is so obese that I wonder if the walking stick will collapse under his weight. Two old women using Zimmer frames inch by us. Mothers push prams slowly through the shimmering heat.

Gradually the social complexion of the passing parade changes. An Indian woman wearing a sari, a red dot between her eyes, strolls past, then a plump Chinese schoolgirl, followed by a worried-looking Tamil man. Under the shade of her red umbrella a Chinese woman peers in a shop window, and a woman in a headscarf wanders up the street, as does a bald Middle Eastern fellow with a long black straggly beard a few minutes later. The different cultures grow even more diverse: a Nigerian man walks side by side with an old white man, and a young African man with braided hair saunters past; a Laotian woman wearing a traditional yellow dress with colourful accessories steps into the pharmacy next door. A four-year-old boy, hand in hand with his mother, wears a T-shirt with the message *I [heart] Roma*; two teenage boys greet one another with 'What's happening, dude?' and, perhaps, the most curious of them all given the temperature, is a taut grey-haired man in his early seventies dressed in a tidy dark blue suit and tie. There is something prim and proper about him, as if he has stepped out of another era. He seems oblivious to the heat and carries himself upright, as if, says Ali, he is a war veteran.

After finishing our drinks, we continue along the main thoroughfare noticing Christmas trees for sale outside a small greengrocer and a Lebanese restaurant displaying stencils of reindeers on its window. What strikes me as odd is that the side streets are named after those in the CBD, so we pass Macquarie, George, Martin and Oxford streets, as if they are a suburban parody of the bustling city centre. Just beyond the main shops is a plain 1950s fibro house with a sign attached to the front door, *Little House on the Prairie*. Beyond that is a nail shop filled with plump women having their fingernails manicured.

We turn left into a wide street. There are no people, but late-model cars line the kerbs. There are no houses, only three-to four-storey apartment blocks. The oldest have names like Ankara and Istanbul and are constructed from brick, with distinctive rows of bulbous white balusters lining their balconies.

The more recent apartments are made of pale brick, and have no distinguishing features, as if built quickly to provide the maximum profit for the developers. The ugliest apartment block, probably built in the 1950s, has its bland, windowless façade facing the street, with a hand-made shingle out front, announcing it is Mort's Mews.

In this street there seems to be no visual evidence of Christmas, except for one apartment where the Venetian blinds are choked with festive cards stuck between the slats. What is unnerving to someone like me who lives in the urban area of Kings Cross, which is always teeming with people, is that there is no one to be seen, except for an old Chinese woman walking through the heat under the shade of a black umbrella on the other side of the road.

Eventually Ali and I come upon a main road with fast-moving traffic. We cross it to inspect the Hurstville District Christadelphians church, an unimpressive brick structure with a large sign out the front that proclaims it's *Serving Jesus Christ while waiting for His return and His Kingdom*. A notice under it announces classes to *Learn English through the Bible*, and women-only Bible study classes every second Friday morning. Further on is the Mortdale-Oatley Baptist Church, which also has a sign: *English Taught*.

We return across the busy road to Mortdale Memorial Park, whose perimeter is lined with enormous fig trees. Prominent on the freshly mown lawn is a marble memorial dedicated to locals who have served Australia. A propeller and the tread of a tank commemorate those who fought in the armed forces, and a simple, awkwardly executed mosaic celebrates the nurses who have served since the Boer War, with the motto *Still Serving*. Beyond the memorial is a handsome bandstand with eight plain green columns holding up a simple white dome.

A few hundred metres on we come to a clear space with rolling green lawn and a stubby modern building, one of those functional council projects that from the very beginning lack a sense of permanence. This is the community centre. Inside it is blissfully cool, though empty of staff. On the walls are posters for the services in the area, including programs for the dementia group (*Outings Every Second Monday at RSL Clubs, Parks or Cafés*), the Social Knitting Group, which proudly announces it had been going for over 30 years, and a course of 'Chair Yoga with Erika'. While Ali and I explore the small building, grateful for the air conditioning, a family of three come in and chat between themselves in Chinese, waiting patiently for a staff member to come and attend to them.

Outside again, we walk across a bridge; below it the railway line winds its way around a curve between two steep inclines and vanishes from sight. The heat is enervating, I feel my face burning. Before us is an endless series of warehouses and factories on our left, and on our right is a large grey building, Punchy's Training and Nutrition. Through a window I can see an enormous room of gym equipment with only a middle-aged woman working out. Before us is a sign, *Oatley*, demarcating it from Mortdale. I peer into the shimmering distance, trying to see the paradisiacal suburb the alcoholic woman is homesick for, though Oatley seems even more industrial than Mortdale.

Oatley is a suburb obsessed by Time. Its name can be traced to James Oatley, the man who made the enormous clock on top of Hyde Park Barracks. In 1814 he was transported to Sydney for life for stealing two feather mattresses. He set up a business as a watch and clock maker in George Street, opposite the site of the present-day Town Hall. Governor Lachlan Macquarie appointed him the colony's first keeper of clocks. As well as the clock for the Hyde Park Barracks, Oatley made at least half a dozen beautiful grandfather clocks, some still in existence, and in 1831 was granted just on 71 hectares in the Hurstville district. When the local bowling club was formed in December 1959, it was inevitable that the founding members should choose a clock as the club emblem. The hands on the clock were set at 15 minutes after 10, the precise time the club was opened. The suburb was in the news in 1983 with a clock festival to celebrate James Oatley, and a square tower was constructed in the main street to commemorate his achievement with, naturally enough, a clock on each of its four sides.

From Boundary Street we turn right and soon come upon a community hall, wooden, rundown, seemingly near collapse. I can make out a faded sign, *Mortdale District Pensioners Welfare Club*. Next to it is a list of times for karate classes. Through the open door I spot a handful of middle-aged women doing yoga.

As we walk up the incline that leads to the Mortdale Hotel I say to Ali that we haven't seen a dog but maybe people keep cats. As if to confirm this, when we stop outside a vet's, there are five posters in the window announcing rewards for missing cats. But why are so many missing? Is someone killing them? Or do the cats just hate Mortdale? Have they escaped to a better place? Oatley, perhaps?

Across the street is a row of brick buildings with recessed balconies that hint at art nouveau influences – so different from the prosaic apartment blocks we saw earlier. They are shops with flats above. The date of their construction is proudly etched across the brick brow of the first storey – 1918. I was only to realise the significance of this later when I learned that Mortdale was a popular suburb for returned soldiers after the Great War.

By now it's late morning and both Ali and I are thirsty, so we make a beeline for the hotel. The only other people inside the gloomily lit bar is a trio sitting on stools at a bench, two men in their sixties and a woman in her fifties with the pale, puffy face of an alcoholic. The décor is 1970s, slightly tatty and cheaply tarted up; remnants of tinsel hang from one wall, a feeble gesture of Christmas spirit probably from last year. While I am at the bar ordering a lemon squash, I ask the barman how old the hotel is.

'Dunno, mate,' he says, 'but it's older than me and I'm thirty-six.' On display is a trophy board devoted to the winners of the hotel golfing competitions.

Ali and I take turns looking at a map of the area. I know so little that I'm amazed we are so close to the Georges River. Examining the map, I overhear one of the men, sitting not far from us, talking about Jews. I hope this isn't an anti-Semitic rant, but he's telling the other two about the time he was in Israel when the Six-Day War broke out in 1967. 'The Jews went through the Arabs like a dose of salts. Jews are really tough.' As he praises the

SYDNEY

Jews, the woman, not listening, concentrates on making up her face. With the aid of a tiny pocket mirror, she carefully applies mascara and paints her lips an even more shocking red.

On searching for the toilet, I come upon a corridor and many rooms of mirrors and glass where several of my reflections stare back at me. It takes a few moments to orientate myself. This is an enormous space devoted to pokie rooms, some designated for smokers, each cubicle separated by glass partitions. The many players seem to exist in a labyrinth of glass, making it difficult to determine just where they actually are, and who is flesh and blood and not a reflection. There are council workers in their yellow or lime vests, many Chinese, and pensioners, all mesmerised by the flashing lights, their fingers tapping endlessly at the buttons like zombies with OCD.

Just after noon Ali and I make our way back to the church with its banner of *God is Love* because I see a badly painted sign pointing to an op shop and drop-in centre just behind it. When we enter there is the familiar stale odour of mothballs common to op shops. It has rows of books, second-hand furniture, cutlery, crockery, and racks of old-fashioned clothes. At the end of the large room is a white-haired woman sitting at a table. After browsing the books, mostly popular genres like thrillers, mysteries and romance, I find a $3 copy of Cecil Beaton's *Uncensored Diaries*. Just how it got there is a mystery.

I pay the elderly lady for the book and begin to chat to her. She has lived in Mortdale for most of her life, though as she is at pains to point out, on the other side of the railway line, where there are few apartment blocks. The eastern side still has its single-storey houses, but, as she says, the Asians want new apartment buildings, which is why the western side looks so different. She remembers how the main street was once devoted to speciality shops, like wallpaper and paint, haberdashery, clothing, shoes and furniture. Now all these businesses are in nearby Hurstville and Morts Road has become a lacklustre restaurant and café strip, lacking character and community.

The way the old lady talks, it's evident she is nostalgic for the Mortdale of her youth. The influx of Asian migrants has disturbed her tight-knit Anglo community. She isn't angry, just resigned to the reality of change.

I'm curious as to the name of Mortdale. 'Oh,' she says, sparking up at the memory, 'it was named after the owner of the brickworks. It used to be near where the railway station is. It had two tall brick chimneys. I remember as a girl seeing them being demolished. The owner was a man called Mort.'

At this point oral history is undermined by facts. Thomas Sutcliffe Mort (1816–1878), whose statue in Macquarie Place commemorates his achievements in industry, shipping and refrigeration, bought a huge chunk of land in the area.

His enormous property was subdivided into farms at the same time the Hurstville Steam Brick Company was formed, known locally as Judd's Brickworks after its owner, William George Judd. The name Mortdale itself unnerved some people because *mort* was the French word for 'dead', and thus 'Mortdale' was the dale or valley of the dead. After several meetings by locals to change the name, the Department of Lands came up with a list of alternatives: Carruthers, Princemead, Wyargine and Storrieville. Local inertia meant the issue was never resolved, and the name remains.

Ali and I decide to have lunch at the local RSL, a bland, modern structure on a lacklustre street not far from the main road. It is a relief to escape the scorching heat and enter the air-conditioned building. As we pass the gaming rooms, we see a familiar figure sitting on a stool in front of a pokie, the flashing lights giving her face an unearthly glow. It is the alcoholic woman in pink who, having not gone home as she intended, is embarrassed to see us again and swiftly turns away.

The upstairs room is large, with practical tables and chairs and a lack of atmosphere that is probably due to the space being used for many different types of functions. The large windows look across at a 1960s red-brick apartment block whose windows are blank, with closed Venetian blinds and curtains so the diners can't peer in. The long tables are filled with older white women, perhaps widows, and a scattering of old men. The exceptions are two tables at the far right, where guests are celebrating a birthday, the birthday girl in a motorised wheelchair and a Chinese man with a club foot encased in a huge boot taking photographs with a professional-looking camera and expensive telephoto lens.

The lunch prices are ridiculously cheap. Ali's chicken schnitzel is so huge its edges tumble over the side of his plate. Mine is a grilled Dory, which is tasty and fresh. The staff are teenagers, four or five decades younger than the people they serve.

On our way out we peek into the pokie room. The alcoholic woman has gone. We pause at glass cabinets of photographs and memorabilia commemorating locals who had fought in the two world wars, especially the first. It makes sense that a suburb whose population increased rapidly after World War I with an influx of returned soldiers, would be proud of the servicemen, who are also commemorated in the Memorial Park.

Before returning to Sydney Ali and I walk around the lane running beside the railway station. On Morts Road we pass a plaque that denotes the site of a masonic temple. Built in 1922, it had been a meeting place for masons until 2002, then briefly used as a community hall before being demolished. The picture of it on the plaque shows a three-storey brick building (and surely the number of brick buildings in the area is a reflection of the importance of the local brickworks), with a covered entranceway supported by two simple white columns. It looks the most striking and imposing structure in the whole squat, lacklustre suburb, aside from the hotel. The local council tore it down and replaced it with a car park, the surface of which is a rough and ready amalgamation of asphalt and dirt. The improvised car park is an insult to the stern beauty of a building that seems to have been demolished out of pique.

Ali and I catch the train back to the city and, as I think over what I have experienced, I realise I was unnerved by Mortdale. The main street throbbed with people, but the side streets were empty, as if drained of life. The apartment blocks – except for the Jasmine Gardens, a recent construction which, judging by the constant flow of people in and out of it, is extremely popular with the Chinese community – were merely functional and depressively similar, as if the developers had no pride in their designs. The only building of significance left was the hotel, and even that gorgeous wedge-shaped building was undermined by its tasteless interior.

There wasn't anything memorable about the suburb. Ali was of a similar opinion and had taken only a couple of snaps. Later I was to learn that neighbouring Oatley was a haven for vulnerable species of flying fox and owls. It's surrounded by bays, with a sea pool and mangroves. The Myles Dunphy Bushland Reserve, named after a renowned conservationist, contains one of the last remaining forests of Sydney Turpentine Ironbark (the trees that originally grew around Sydney Cove), a huge park, memorial gardens and the former bowling club. Maybe the woman in pink was right – Oatley is a paradise compared to Mortdale.

SEEN THROUGH THE EYES
OF CONVICTS

IT'S A CURIOUS PAINTING. The title is *A Direct North General View of Sydney Cove, 1794*. The landscape seems alien, as if painted by someone who hasn't seen the real thing. Framed by trees that in no way resemble eucalypts, their foliage more like that of European trees, it resembles a traditional eighteenth-century classical landscape where the flora, the mean huts and haphazard buildings of the colony have been transformed into an idyllic Georgian Arcadia. The harbour is like an ornamental lake with its delicate solitary ship; squeezed between the exotic trees and bushes are some tidy cottages, neat gardens and, in pride of place, Government House. At the centre of the picture are two elegant men, one a marine in his red jacket, the other a gentleman. A languid lap dog sits at their feet as they pause for a chat, enjoying the late afternoon sunlight in a bucolic paradise.

This is the earliest known oil painting of Sydney and was once thought to have been by convict Thomas Watling, the settlement's first professional artist, but it seems that it was executed by an English artist back in London, who based his romantic vision on several of the convict's drawings. Watling's actual view of this new land was anything but romantic. One of his watercolours of Sydney Cove, done soon after his arrival in October 1792, shows a foreshore denuded of trees, basic huts, some stone and brick houses, the only two-storey building, Government House, a hill pitted with stumps and clumps of dull green trees on the horizon. The only people are an Aboriginal woman with two children in a canoe on an otherwise empty harbour. There is something forlorn about it, as if the settlement is suspended in a listless existence.

Watling was born in 1762 in Dumfries, Scotland. He had a thorough grounding in art and in 1788 he was a coach and chaise painter in Glasgow. In the same year he was sentenced to 14 years transportation for forging bank notes.

He was soon snapped up by the surgeon-general, John White, an amateur naturalist, to draw the local fauna and flora. He produced many pictures of early colonial Australia, including prolific sketches of birds, fish, mammals, plants, landscapes and Aboriginal people, including an initiation ceremony in 1795.

During his first six months in the colony Watling wrote a series of letters back home that were published in 1794 as *Letters from an Exile at Botany Bay, to his Aunt in Dumfries.* The early letters are near-hysterical with his fear of his lengthy exile and full of self-pity. Gradually he settled into clear-eyed observations and assessments about the colony: 'It will be a long time before it can support itself.' Sydney and its environs were nothing like green, fertile Scotland, 'The face of the country is deceitful, having every appearance of fertility and yet productive of no one article in itself for the support of mankind.' Yet, as he grew used to his new environment, he viewed things differently. 'To see what has been done in the space of five or six years of clearing, building and planting, is astonishing.'

*

While some convicts prospered, others dreamed of escape. Some fled into the bush heading for China, thought to be several days to the north. One man carried a paper with compass points marked on it and was eventually found lost and starving. Others stowed away in departing ships (especially American), some making up the crews. One ship was searched and found to be hiding 30 convicts. A large group of Irish convicts put their faith in a Scottish woman convict who achieved local fame as a prophet. She predicted that French warships would destroy the settlement, liberate the convicts and whisk them away from Sydney, thereby confirming the French commitment to the Irish in their centuries-long struggle against the common enemy, the English.

Some convicts became convinced that there was a colony of white people some 600 kilometres to the south-west. This wonderful place, if reached, would enable them to live a life of pleasure and idleness with all the food they could eat, a veritable fabled land, like Cockaigne, the land of plenty in medieval myth.

One emancipated convict who intrigued Phillip's successor, Governor Hunter, was Robert Sidaway. He had arrived in Sydney on the First Fleet at the age of 30. A watchcase maker by trade, he had been caught stealing and was sentenced to transportation for life. During the voyage to Australia, he was put in leg irons twice for impertinence. But in Sydney this brash-talking thief seems to have reformed. In fact, he so impressed the authorities that in November 1792 he was given a conditional pardon. Two years later, he was granted an absolute pardon and a contract as a professional baker.

Sidaway had been brought up in Horseshoe Alley in London, an ancient narrow thoroughfare that ran parallel to Southwark Bridge. It was prone to sudden flooding during high tides and had been named after the medieval pub of the same name. Although it was a bleak, damp place, Sidaway seems to have been literate, with a special fondness for the theatre. In Thomas Keneally's novel *The Playmaker*, about the first theatre performance in Australia in 1789 – a production of *The Recruiting Officer* – he makes Sidaway one of the actors. This seems a reasonable speculation, because in 1795 Sidaway approached Hunter for permission to start a theatre.

The decision to allow a theatre in what was basically a prison would have taken some time to consider. After all, the players would be convicts, and so would many in the audience. The idea of frivolous entertainment for convicts when the aim of transportation was punishment seemed a contradiction. This notion of punishment was strong in British prisons, even into the twentieth century – when the famous British philosopher Bertrand Russell was in Brixton jail and laughed loudly at something in the book he was reading, the guard had to remind him that prison was a place of punishment, not levity.

Despite the fears of the more conservative elements in the colony that the stage was a place where emotions could get out of hand, Hunter believed the settlement needed some culture, and hoped that allowing theatrical entertainment would distract convicts from more destructive pursuits, such as gambling and drinking. A 120-seat theatre was built by 'some of the more decent class of prisoner' who 'fitted up the house with more theatrical propriety than could have been expected'. It was probably a primitive slab-sided small hall or shed with a stepped floor, a pit and a gallery. It opened in January 1796 and is thought to have stood either in Bells Row (Bligh Street) or High Street (George Street) near Jamison Street.

Sidaway was the prime mover for the theatre. Given the grand name of The Victoria, it opened with performances of *The Revenge* and *The Hotel*. One of its successes was a sentimental history play, Nicholas Rowe's 1714 *The Tragedy of Jane Shore*, which was followed by other productions, including a revival of *The Recruiting Officer*.

At the time there was little cash in circulation in the colony, so the price of admission was bartered as a measure of spirits, flour, meat, or any other commodity of value. With few alternative means of diversion available, the convicts took to play-going with a passion. The unfortunate effect was that the worst among them resorted to any means to obtain the cost of admission. One convict is said to have killed an officer's dog and passed its meat off as kangaroo to get inside. Pickpocketing was rampant, as was the burglarising of the audiences' residences while they were at the theatre. In fact, such was the rise in the crime level that in 1800 the governor, believing that the theatre was exerting a 'corrupting influence' on the town, ordered it to be closed and the structure destroyed.

*

Sidaway was not the only convict to find opportunities in the colony. In 1802 George Howe printed the first book to be published in Australia: *New South Wales General Standing Orders*, comprising government and general orders issued between 1791 and 1802. Howe had been born on St Kitts in the West Indies. In his twenties he'd worked in London at various newspapers, including *The Times*. In 1799, under the curious moniker of 'George Happy, alias Happy George', he was arrested for shoplifting and in 1800 was transported to Sydney.

Not long after arrival he became the government printer, and on 5 March 1803 he inaugurated the *Sydney Gazette and New South Wales Advertiser*. The old printing press was a dismal apparatus with only 9 kilograms of type and mildewed paper, but Howe was an 'ingenious man' and despite the derisory state of the printing press, having to make his own ink, overcoming a constant paper shortage, and the persistent censorship of articles by government officers that meant having to reset type and write new pieces at the last moment, he managed to bring his paper out regularly.

In the early days he had no salary and opened up a stationery shop. He also earned money tutoring pupils in reading and 'the Grammar of the English tongue upon the principles of Drs Lowth, Johnson, Priestly and other celebrated writers ...' In 1810 his printing office was almost destroyed by a freak bolt of lightning. In the same year he found a great supporter in the new governor, Lachlan Macquarie, who granted him his first salary. In 1813 he issued the first natural history book printed in the colony, *Birds of New South Wales with their Natural History*, a collection of 18 coloured plates of Australian birds by the artist John Lewin, with short descriptions of their habits and environment. In 1819, *First Fruits of Australian Poetry*, containing two poems by Barron Field, became the first book of poetry published in Australia. He was preparing to publish Australia's first periodical magazine when he died on 11 May 1821.

Howe probably wrote most of the paper in the early years, including the poetry. One writer, decades on, criticised him for producing a newspaper that was:

> ... moral to the point of priggishness, patriotic to the point of servility, pompous in a stiff, eighteenth-century fashion; and mingles a more precious dignity with inappropriate lapses into humour that is sometimes deplorable.

This is somewhat unkind. The *Sydney Gazette* was crucial to Sydney's image of itself. It reported government edicts, crime, cultural events, shipping news, fashion, the arrival of cargo, the expansion of the whaling and sea industries, then the wool and wheat successes. There were the reports of balls, parties, cricket matches (the first in 1803, played between ships' crews), horse races and the arrival of free settlers. The *Gazette* wrote about new buildings and businesses, and the establishment of the first bank (of which Howe was a founding member). The advertisements ranged from animals to auction houses, from governesses looking for work to those who sought music students. The paper's values were on open display in its depiction of the convicts, their crimes, foul language and especially the obstreperous behaviour of lazy and drunken female convicts. These stories were reported in a sardonic condescending tone, often verging on the insulting. It was sometimes smug, moralistic, and containing blatant and servile praise of the government and its officials, but it had a sense of humour, a macabre appreciation of the foibles of a penal settlement growing into a town sure of itself, even, at times, refreshingly cocky.

*

In 1798 John Lancashire arrived in Sydney to serve seven years transportation for forgery. He became a strange and familiar figure in town; short, emaciated, with a slightly pitted face, the result of smallpox. He was a draftsman and house and ship painter and soon found employment in Robert Sidaway's theatre as a scene painter. In 1800, the same year the theatre was shut down as a corrupting influence, he was again in trouble for forgery. He wriggled free of the charge and others, as he was to do for the rest of his life (for example, he was arrested for selling illegal spirits, but never convicted), his glib tongue and mendacious nature a help rather than a hindrance in his dealings with the law. Governor King was so irked by him he described Lancashire as 'possessed of every art of cunning that human nature could turn to the worst of purposes'.

Lancashire's only known painting is *View of Sydney, Port Jackson, New South Wales, taken from the Rocks on the Western Side of the Cove, 1803*. It reveals his limitations as a painter. In true primitive style he gives every detail equal value with scant regard for the laws of perspective. Yet there is an attempted fidelity to what he sees, and the cheerful colours and sharp focus give Sydney a mesmerising intensity that hovers on the edge of the surreal. He shows us the Rocks in the foreground from where he views the town. On the western side is the shipbuilding yard. Merchant ships preen in the harbour, and, still on the western side, a few sturdy single-storey houses and their gardens dot the cove. The bridge crossing the Tank Stream gives an illusion of stability. On the eastern horizon are windmills, and Government House with its extensive kitchen gardens, whitewashed houses and government warehouses.

What comes across is a settlement that is firmly established around the cove, its air of permanence hinting at a bright future.

THE CULT OF THE BODY

IN THE FIRST DECADES OF WHITE SETTLEMENT one thing that intrigued visitors to Sydney was how the convicts, soldiers, free settlers and, in particular, young women, seemed to have developed a selective blindness towards the nudity of the Aboriginal people, a feature of early colonial life foreign visitors often commented on. There were attempts to put petticoats on the women and shirts and trousers on the men to instil modesty, but there was a stubborn resistance to this by some of the Eora and on the street the Europeans would discreetly look away or pretend they didn't notice the lack of clothing.

Soon, nakedness was adopted by the Europeans when swimming, whether in the harbour or the Parramatta River. Governors, especially Macquarie and Darling, became frustrated at the brazenness of male nude swimming and, unable to ban it outright but deeming it an offence to women especially, insisted that nude bathing was illegal during daylight hours and banned it in public places like the harbour foreshores where women and children were likely to see the swimmers.

In 1833 the Fig Tree Baths were built in the harbour at Woolloomooloo, yet there were still reports of nude bathing in Manly and parts of the Bondi foreshore. Slowly, over decades, swimwear in the twentieth century became skimpier for both sexes, until in the 1970s there were discreet nude beaches, and even on Bondi and Bronte beaches women went topless. With the growing popularity of the Gay Mardi Gras the city became used to a parade of semi-naked male flesh as gym-buffed men proudly flaunted their oiled, muscular bodies on floats or marching proudly behind them.

It's impossible to ignore the intoxicating forces of the Sydney climate and its superb beaches; they combine to create an inimitable sensuality, a cultivation of the body beautiful, where the body itself is both performance art and a celebration of it. This is perhaps more obvious to a visitor or someone like me when I first came to live in Sydney and was astonished by the casual attire even on the streets, with men in shorts and open-necked shirts and women in flimsy dresses with revealing cleavage.

What also became obvious to me was that this adoration of the human body and the worship of sun and sea verged on the pagan. For Sydney artists the siren call of paganism distinguished them from Melbourne artists.

In the late nineteenth century Sydney Long, an elfin-sized man with an outrageous ego, defensive and thin-skinned, went against the popular realism of bush paintings to imbue nature with a sensuality missing from the work of Australian impressionists. His moody 1894 painting *By Tranquil Waters* created controversy. It showed naked boys bathing in the Cooks River, one of them playing a reed pipe. Its absence of shame was appealing to many, and the way he had transformed the bush into a poetic idyll was unique. He followed this with one of his finest paintings, *Pan*, a key example of a symbolist-inspired painting. It is set in the twilight of a gum tree Arcadia, where the pagan god of nature plays his reed pipe to a gathering of elongated nymphs and satyrs whose sensual dance is harmonious with the bush, as if nature is responding to the piper's music.

It was a painting that the bohemian artist Norman Lindsay would have enthusiastically endorsed. Lindsay saw Australia 'as the last country on earth where paganism can flourish naturally'.

Norman Alfred William Lindsay had been born in country Victoria but shifted to Sydney at the turn of the twentieth century to pursue a career as an illustrator, painter, etcher, political cartoonist, novelist and polemicist. He became a household name considered, by people he called 'wowsers', a pervert and pornographer. As one critic wrote, echoing the thoughts of others, 'His subjects suggest an artist with an imagination in an advanced stage of decomposition.' Though as Robert Hughes says in *The Art of Australia* (1970), 'I doubt whether his works have promoted anything beyond a little masturbation.'

One of his most controversial works was *The Crucified Venus*. A naked, voluptuous woman is being nailed to a cross by a demented monk; below her are screaming misogynist men, leering bystanders, and a mob of ranting ecclesiastics. It was a deliberate act of blasphemy and it enraged people, as Lindsay knew it would. As far as he was concerned the ancient Greek and Roman civilisations were destroyed by Christianity, with its hatred of hedonism and the flesh.

In *The Witches' Sabbath* he painted a swirling cloud of naked women having a riotous party. In another work, *Port of Heaven*, pirates find paradise not in treasure but a swarm of nude sirens. In several works portraying his erotic visions of bacchanals, horny satyrs cavort with luscious naked femme fatales, their bodies intermingling to such a degree that the eye cannot rest as it tries to disentangle the riot of limbs, naked breasts and hairy chests.

Lindsay was rake thin, an almost cadaverous, bird-like man. His wife Rose described him as 'looking like a half-starved jockey', but his female subjects were stout Amazonians who could have crushed the painter between their ample breasts. He was not physically robust enough to do his own etching and printing so

Rose, who also modelled for him, undertook those onerous tasks for decades. Despite using many different models, the women all appeared disturbingly similar, or as Hughes writes: 'melon-breasted, ham-thighed playmates ... elephantine buttocks ... the very embodiment of adolescent sexual fantasy'.

In 1930 *Art and Australia* published an issue devoted to his work. Newspapers called it a 'filthy and obscene' magazine and police raided the publisher. It became a *cause célèbre*, and despite calls for Lindsay's arrest, he avoided going to court. The publicity only increased his fame and infamy. If anything, it confirmed his drawing power. Fellow artist Arthur Streeton, worried he might not get enough people into his solo exhibition in Sydney, erected a booth in the corner of the gallery with a placard reading *For Men Only*. Inside was one of Lindsay's pen drawings. The image may have been innocuous (two lovers with doves hovering over them) but the word spread that one of Norman Lindsay's spicy pictures was at the showing.

As his biographer, John Hetherington, notes, Lindsay's work made an extraordinary impact on the public:

> No other artist had ever stirred Australians in general as he
> did, some marvelled, some fulminated, but they took notice.
> His riggish fauns and frolicking satyrs, bacchanals, bewigged
> gallants, wanton nude women, captured the attention of people
> who had never heard of Velasquez or been in an art gallery.

His exuberance appealed but it was more than that, it was his brazen treatment of sex and desire that cast the spotlight on him for most of his life. Sex was a wonderful and joyous thing: 'Sex is not only the basis of life, it is the *reason* for life,' he said.

Lindsay had a tireless nervous energy. Passionately honest, he read widely but not deeply, and was a mesmeric speaker. Not a good conversationalist, but a brilliant monologist, Lindsay expounded his philosophy of life in a loquacious cascade of words, leaving no room for doubt, attacking bourgeois notions of art, Christian morality, and proclaiming that the artist is the most important member of the community. ('The earth exists only as a mudflat for the generation of a few geniuses.')

He viewed much modern art with disgust. Artists like 'the obscene Gauguin' and 'mental savages like Matisse and Picasso' produced work that was 'a disease of the mind'. Jazz made him nearly 'homicidal'. Freud was evil and wallowed in the unclean depths of the subconscious, whereas Lindsay's own demons were healthy. He was drawn to the past, a pantomime world of cavaliers, troubadours, Greek gods, courtiers, imps, ribald satyrs and sexually free women. His art was a costume party, propelled by an Antipodean reworking of Nietzschean vitalism. It was a world where the great artist was typically spurned by society, as he believed himself to be. His dislike of modern life was epitomised by Sydney's cars, smoke, and jostling crowds, their faces filled with anxiety. He was not alone in his belief that modernity was a disaster. Overseas, people like Matthew Arnold and John Ruskin in England and Henry Adams in America were also what T Jackson Lears called 'antimodernist vitalists', men who shuddered at the devitalising shallowness of the urban souls they saw around them. As Adams put it, 'all the steam in the world could not, like the Virgin, build Chartres'.

Lindsay died in 1969. His adoration of the body, especially the female body, had a powerful impact on women who wanted to flout the puritan morality of the time. In 1943 24-year-old Constable Lees wandered into an art gallery where an exhibition influenced by Lindsay was being held, and was shocked by 'the nude paintings … the female figures unadorned are obscene'. Four of the artist's models were called to testify in court. They were a tetchy bunch, and one of them, Dawn Anderson, told the court, 'There is a greater dignity of line in the nude than in the clothed female form.' Another one, who had modelled for Norman Lindsay, declared, 'Apparently Constable Lees can't tell the difference between art and French postcards.' Holly Faram, who had modelled for William Dobell and Norman Lindsay, was not only unembarrassed on the stand but played the role of the offended one: 'I was brought up to believe that anything natural was pure and good. Constable Lees' remarks shock me more than I can say.' Charges were dismissed.

One of Lindsay's deepest friendships was with an English sculptor, Rayner Hoff, who had come to Sydney in 1923 to teach at the art school housed in the former Darlinghurst Gaol. Hoff revelled in the sunny, warm climate and became a keen surfer and swimmer.

Hoff, according to Rose Lindsay, was 'short, stocky, dark and very brisk'. He lived for his art, had a keen sense of humour, and was 'always ready to have a hearty laugh at life in general'. She got to know him well because, even though he was married, when not teaching he would spend as much time as possible with her husband. Hoff and Lindsay were 'more than friends', and they would spend all night talking on 'that most inexhaustible of all subjects, art'. His friendship extended to sculpting a delicate bust of his hero.

The majority of Hoff's students were female (including Rosaleen Norton, the Witch of Kings Cross, who always said Hoff was the man 'who freed me up'). This was unusual in the 1920s. Most women chose painting or commercial art rather than sculpture. It was a daring pursuit for these young women, who had to sculpt from naked models. Hoff himself liked to sculpt naked women and in 1924 produced one of his best works, *Gael*, a female with large breasts and hips, one hand over her breasts, a highly erotic and self-absorbed figure.

The men and women of Sydney's beaches fascinated Hoff, as did beach sports and the popular practice of eurhythmics. Hoff and his students often portrayed beach scenes in their work, as in Hoff's bas relief *Pacific Beach* (1932). In interviews he frequently advocated for much scantier beachwear:

> The whole attitude is different in Europe. Here we are isolated and overrun with wowserism. There are really only two schools of thought at many bathing places on the Continent. One says that as little as possible should be worn, and that should be of a thin, silkish material, which will admit the sun's rays. The other school sees nothing wrong with nudity, complete and unashamed.

His enthusiasm even rubbed off on JS MacDonald, director of the notoriously conservative Art Gallery of New South Wales, who encouraged artists to visit the beach where, 'On golden and milky sands, bodily excellence is displayed the year round, clearly defined by the sun in an atmosphere as viewless and benign as the air of Hellas as described by Euripides.'

One of Hoff's best students was Barbara Tribe, a keen swimmer, who personified the perfect sun-bronzed body that epitomised the work of the Hoff school. She rhapsodised over the cult of the body:

> I doubt if even the Ancient Greeks produced better examples of beauty and grace. We don't allow our bodies to become flaccid ... the call of the sun, surf, great open roads ... is all too strong for any to resist. Hence, we are active, virile, and few nations show such an average body of perfection.

Tribe's enormous plasterwork, *Bacchanalia* (1934), was an unabashed depiction of sexually charged nymphs and fauns, naked women and men, writhing in an ecstasy of sexual abandon. Her fellow student Victoria Cowdry was also a great admirer of Lindsay, and it shows in her graduate work, a nude self-portrait that glows with a brazen sensuality.

Still, Hoff's adventurous spirit could upset people. The trendy Ambassador's Café bought a huge painting of mythological subjects painted by Hoff and his students in 1927, but there were complaints about the nudity. One student recalled, 'It was quite shocking in those days to see half demons/half humans on the wall. One of the boys had to go into the nightclub to trim off the penis of Pan.' Barbara Tribe remembered Hoff having to 'alter certain male features which were protruding amidst topless women, fauns, nymphs, children and angels surging forward and disappearing out of the edge of the right-hand side of the frame'.

As Hoff became engrossed in the demands of designing sculptures for the Anzac War Memorial in Hyde Park, his sensual, curvaceous female nudes were transformed into stylised art deco figures, becoming almost ethereal presences rather than flesh and blood. This created a rift with Lindsay. As far as the prophet of 12 Bridge Street (where Lindsay kept a studio and salon of like-minded acolytes) was concerned, Hoff's figures seemed puritan and had lost their sexual vitality. To Lindsay it seemed that these ghostly figures were symptomatic of Hoff's decaying marriage. When the sculptor died in his early forties after injuring his kidneys while surfing, Lindsay considered his death to be self-inflicted: 'It's absurd to suppose that chance has anything to do with such an ignominious death as being dumped in the surf. That only happens to a man who is already morally dead.'

But for Hoff the body was always a metaphor for a modern Australian identity, as exemplified in his *Australian Venus* (1927), a work alive with sexual tension – the Australian woman as the ultimate sensual being. As art critic Lorraine Kypiotis said of Hoff's artistic practice, 'The body became the primary metaphor for a modern Australian identity, based on the classical perfections of the ancient Greek model, and imaged as a virile product of the nation's outdoor environment to create an optimistic celebration of life.'

Photographers also discovered the sensuality of Sydney's beaches. Perhaps the most influential were a husband and wife, Max Dupain and Olive Cotton. Dupain's 1938 photograph, *On the beach. Man, Woman, Boy*, shows the three naked bodies fused with soft and hard patterns of sand and sunlight. There's an aura of robust health, fertility, virility, innocence, on display. Dupain's national beauty type was a woman intimately bonded with nature, as in his *Souvenir of Cronulla* (1937) where a naked female is superimposed over the sea and sand. His archetypical men are extremely physical, each muscle straining with concentrated effort, as in his *Discus Thrower*, featuring the taut body of a naked man caught in the swirling action of hurling a discus, as if embodying the spirit of the ancient Greeks.

One of Olive Cotton's portraits of her husband is startling in its unblinking female gaze. He has just emerged from the sea, his torso bare, and is caught lost in thought. Titled *Max after Surfing* (1939), it is an erotic ode to the masculine physique. Max is an Apollo, his handsome body sculpted by the invigorating play of light and shadows. Perhaps one of her best photographs is one taken in 1939, *Only to taste the warmth, the light, the wind*. It's a black and white image of a beautiful swimwear model shot from the side, only her shoulders and head showing. She's facing a gentle sea breeze, which wafts over her youthful skin, her eyes closed as in a state of bliss. It's a beguiling and sensual image of a contented woman at one with nature, the sun, sea and sand.

It's hard to think of another photograph that so aptly sums up paganism as a state of spiritual bliss.

The previous year, young Sydney-born photographer Laurence Le Guay, 21, produced a montage photograph, *The Progenitors*, that took the idea of the body into the realm of the mystical. There is no doubt he was fascinated with the German concept of body culture that thrived between the two wars. In the image the nude man and woman are massive figures within an industrial landscape of factories and chimneys. The naked woman looks skyward with one hand pressed to her temple, while the man is seated at her feet, gazing up at her, the quintessence of female strength and beauty, in barely concealed awe. They are a modern Adam and Eve who will create a new race that will be part of a modern industrial empire. Le Guay had freed the body from the beach and placed it in a world not of sun and sand, but a place where bodies are part flesh, part technological marvel.

Both Le Guay's and Dupain's pictures of nude models became known to the rest of Australia in *Man* magazine, which started in Sydney in 1936. But even the tame nude photos in *Man* occasionally caused problems. The company was warned of approaching crackdowns and on these occasions, as one staff member recalled, '*Man* magazine was temporarily sanitised to resemble the *Catholic Weekly*. As soon as the all-clear sounded, naughty bits went back into print and everything reverted to normal.'

If anything showed the difference between attitudes to sex in Sydney and Melbourne it was World War II. William Dobell was amused by the American servicemen who populated Kings Cross, and Donald Friend painted and drew the sexual anticipation of men and women hooking up and partying. It was all very different from the gloomy moralising of much painting down south, where Albert Tucker painted a grim nocturnal Melbourne populated by grotesque whores and leering soldiers. After the war Melbourne painters, many of them socialists, portrayed their city as a bleak place filled with the downtrodden working class, and filled with a sense of hopelessness. Even the middle class, as in John Brack's *Collins Street 5 p.m.*, were brow-beaten clones, their business suits armour to hide their shameful bodies.

Two Sydney painters in the 1960s and 1970s celebrated the sensual body. Brett Whiteley painted numerous nude women, but mainly his wife, Wendy. He thought the nudes were sensuous, but these languid women are painted a pallid white, which seems to drain all the sexual energy out of them, their typically elongated bodies as unappetising as a white mollusc removed from its shell.

Then there was the underrated Richard Larter, whose work had a pop art exuberance that poured out of him once he arrived in Sydney from England. Many of his works are brightly coloured and draw on popular culture, reproducing news photographs, film stills, and images from pornography. His frequent model was his wife, Pat, who poses in suspenders, generally naked, with unashamedly open legs. All of these works celebrate the erotic energy of his wife.

Larter approached his paintings determined not to produce the slick eroticism of *Playboy* magazine but to duplicate the sensibility of what he called 'the less salubrious type of magazine … where girls who are actually doing intercourse know what they're doing and the expressions and posing is far more honest'. In order to achieve this, he had no hesitation in showing the pudenda of his wife. Pat's poses range from parodies of porno magazine photographs to the luscious *Seated Nude* (1964), to rear views of a naked Pat on all fours. Some critics would like to believe that these paintings parody cheesecake sexism, but there is a strong strand of Larter's lust for his wife that gives many of them a hardcore sexiness.

Pat was essential to Larter's vision of sexuality. She was an artist who had been adopting some of the poses in her work before he appropriated them. She was not only his muse but also a performer, and as such could be considered his collaborator, in that she created the many sexual positions and personae her husband utilised for his work. It is instructive to see works where Larter used professional models, as in *Blonde Nude* (1991). Without the input of Pat, some of the photographs resemble pin-ups from *Playboy* and lack the sexual vitality and interplay between artist and subject.

Pat brought a vitality, a sense of unashamed exhibitionism to her husband's art, and the dynamic bond between them meant he was unafraid to embrace the extremes of eroticism. Because of this the works reveal a wonderful sense of mutual pleasure and sexual happiness, a theme that could be called Sydney paganism.

Whiteley's and Larter's sexual images were a long way from Norman Lindsay's nudes, but they were evidence that the puritans and wowsers who had hounded him and many others had been finally defeated.

PLOTTING SYDNEY'S DESTRUCTION

IN THE EARLY YEARS OF SYDNEY the settlers were blissfully unaware that in their eagerness to alleviate their isolation from the rest of the world, their hospitality twice brought them to the edge of destruction.

In March 1793, Spanish vessels sailed into Port Jackson, the first foreign delegation to visit the new colony. The British were excited and wined and dined their visitors over a month. Like the Eora, the visitors were horrified by the cruel way the convicts were treated, and they were disgusted that, as they made their way back to their ships at night, they were often accosted by brazen prostitutes and 'easy women'.

Their artists made two sets of illustrations, flattering ones that they presented to their naïve hosts, and secret drawings that they took back to Spain showing the class divisions in the settlement. One illustration they gave the British was of happy, well-dressed locals in a bucolic setting; one they kept to themselves was of convicts being used like beasts to haul a cart carrying upper-class women along a muddy, rocky track.

On returning to Spain, one of the captains, Jose Bustamante y Guerra, analysed the chances of a military invasion of Sydney: 'The entirely helpless state in which I observed that settlement in 1793, and the general discontent of its inhabitants, would so facilitate its conquest that I believe it would be achieved with the surprise that the convincing presence of our fleet would cause.'

The plan would be to disguise a fleet of gunships to resemble British supply vessels until, upon entering Sydney Cove, they'd open fire with 'red hot' cannon balls that would set alight the frail buildings and raze the settlement. Anything of value would be taken, the rest destroyed. After the destruction the next step would be to make prisoners of the entire population of around 4000 and transport them all to South America, where they would help build Spanish colonies. The devastation would make the British abandon the colony forever. But the plans were never followed through. The Spanish had to turn their attention to wars against the French and soon found themselves a declining imperial power.

In late April 1802 the French ship *Le Naturaliste*, captained by Jacques Hamelin, sailed through the Heads. Despite the frequent animosity between France and Britain, this embryonic outpost of the British empire was excited by *Le Naturaliste*'s arrival.

The vessel was one of two ships commanded by Nicolas Baudin that had set out from France in 1800 on a voyage to map New Holland, collect specimens of flora and fauna, and conduct other scientific investigations. On board were artists, naturalists, zoologists and cartographers. Baudin captained the sister ship *Le Géographe*. An affable man and competent commander, he was often sick and not suited to leading such an arduous expedition and dealing with a scientific team that was sometimes unmanageable and contemptuous of navy discipline. One of Baudin's enemies aboard *Le Géographe* was François Péron, a naturalist and explorer who developed an intense loathing of the captain. It was no wonder that an exasperated and weary Baudin would complain: 'I must say ... that those captains who have scientists ... aboard their ships, must take with them a good supply of patience. I admit that although I have no lack of it, the scientists have frequently driven me to the end of my tether and forced me to retire testily to my room. However, since they are not familiar with our practices, their conduct must be excusable.'

Hamelin had taken *Le Naturaliste* and parted company with Baudin's ship when he ran low on food and water, and made a dash to Port Jackson. Over the three weeks they were there, the French captain and his officers were feted by Captain Philip Gidley King, the third governor of the colony, with balls and dinner parties. Once refitted, *Le Naturaliste* set out for France, only to be driven back by bad weather. On his return to Sydney, Hamelin found that *Le Géographe* had arrived in June, with low supplies and only four men fit for service. Baudin and his crew were to remain in Port Jackson for five months, exploring Sydney and the outlying districts, making maps and sketches.

Péron was impressed by the Sydney he encountered: 'How much reason had we for astonishment on beholding the flourishing state of this singular and distant colony. The beauty of the post was the admiration of everyone.' He was amazed at how quickly the colony had expanded in just 14 years, and painted a picture of a thriving colony with successful whaling and sealing industries, productive farms producing large quantities of wool, hemp and wine, and a burgeoning trade with China and the Pacific Islands, supported by convict transportation and investment in its military administration. Even the cemetery impressed him, noting its striking monuments, 'the execution of which is much better than could reasonably have been expected from the state of arts in so young a colony'.

Like the Hamelin crew, Baudin and his officers were feted by the colonists, though Governor King was irritated by Péron's garrulous French patriotism and his Gallic condescension. His incessant quests for information led some, like the explorer Matthew Flinders, to believe that Péron's intense interest in the colony was more than suspicious.

One of the artists on the French expedition, the naturalist Charles Lesueur, drew maps of Sydney and also made many drawings and watercolours. His *Sydney in 1803* is a realistic depiction of the town, showing three Aboriginal men in the foreground, two making a fire, while one blows on it to help ignite it. The Frenchman detailed the fences, the gardens, tracks and streets, the windmills on the treeless horizon, the whitewashed houses, the military barracks, the clock tower and the harbour, a busy hive of sailing boats and merchant ships. On the foreshore men are unloading cargo while another trio of Aboriginal men go about their business.

Lesueur made several maps of Sydney, one so detailed it even included the site of the old gallows (near the corner of Elizabeth and Market streets) and the new gallows (somewhere around Liverpool and Pitt streets). Seen in another light, the map takes on a more ominous aspect, carefully depicting the locations of the government commissariat stores, the military barracks, gun batteries, the prison, the house of the military commander and Government House.

In fact, the French, like the Spanish, were a duplicitous bunch. Péron was collecting information about a potential invasion of the colony, which was located strategically on the edge of the Pacific Ocean. The drawings and maps were to be used as the basis for a French assault. Troops would land at Botany Bay, then attack the settlement and easily overwhelm the poorly trained British garrison. Such a plan, reasoned Péron, would be supported by a spontaneous uprising of the Irish convicts.

Baudin bought needed supplies, including casks of flour and salt meat, and the 20-ton schooner *Casuarina* to help continue his exploration of the Australian coast. When *Le Géographe* sailed out of the Heads in November, Sydney was saddened to see it depart, little realising it carried with it Péron's firm recommendation that the colony 'should be destroyed as soon as possible and that ... we could do it easily now'. Péron knew that time was of the essence because he saw that Sydney was growing rapidly and warned, 'We will not be able to do it in 25 years' time.'

OLD SYDNEY TOWN

OLD SYDNEY TOWN IS DECAYING, its pioneer huts rotting, the fences tumbling down and the narrow dirt streets overgrown with dandelions and weeds. It's a forlorn spectacle, like a long-abandoned movie set. It had opened in 1975, a replica of Sydney Town in the first decade of the nineteenth century, with one-storey and occasional two-storey whitewashed houses, a tavern, and many visitors' favourite re-enactment, floggings.

The open-air museum and theme park was built near Gosford, about an hour's drive north of Sydney. This living tribute to early Sydney was extremely popular for a couple of decades, eventually clocking up six million visitors, including countless students, as it was part of the school curriculum. It was also a pilgrimage for many to imagine the world of their forebears. As the rollicking song in the television commercial had it: 'I want to go back to Old Sydney Town, to find out why I'm me.'

The construction was overseen by heritage architect Robert Irving, who convinced his students to carry out historical research and help construct the buildings, learning to make bricks, wattle-and-daub, shingles, tiles, thatch and other materials the convicts used in the pre-Macquarie period. They even recreated Bennelong's hut; the original having been the first privately occupied brick building erected in Sydney. The students and workmen also researched the decorations, furnishings, clothes, food and activities of the era. Some of the buildings included the large reception complex (Heritage Hall), the first pub (the King's Head Tavern) as well as modern restaurants and cafés. A significant handful were never finished, including the jail and the church. The enormous windmill was almost completed but never operated.

Actors played soldiers, convicts, blacksmiths, government officials and floggers, the strands of their whips containing red dye. All told there were over 30 authentically reconstructed buildings, the large pool of a nearby creek a stand-in for Sydney Cove. There were soldiers on parade, loud artillery cannons, pistol and sword duels, a convict rebellion, a magistrate's court (*'Be part of a typical trial of the day as colonial justice takes its course … See convicts tried, convicted and punished'*), bullock rides, horse-drawn wagons, and function halls, including one called the Cat-O-Nine Theatre. Tourists could have a 'chat with townspeople as they go about their business', and be part of 'an adventure back into history as we wander the streets and discover the lifestyle of Old Sydney Town'. What was missing were Aboriginal people, but the visitors didn't seem to mind or even notice.

Three years after the complex opened, it was used for the television series *Against the Wind*, which was set in the period between 1798 and 1812 and followed the life of Mary Mulvane, the daughter of an Irish schoolmaster, who is transported to New South Wales. The 13 episodes were based on a real family, the Garretts, and despite what would now be considered cheap production values, and the liberties taken with history and actual people, it's a solid introduction to the lives of convicts at the time.

The simulacrum of Old Sydney Town served the series well, as it did for other films, television productions and advertisements. However, the town's immense popularity began to wane and at its closure in 2003 the owners blamed what they called the 'instant gratification' of a young generation that paid more attention to computer games and thrill-rides 'than a leisurely stroll through history'. In 2012 a committee was formed to re-open the park but the plans came to nothing. Two years later the Heritage Hall went up in flames and a large cache of important artefacts and documentation was lost. Now the remaining structures are decaying as nature reclaims the site.

The replica of old Sydney was based on an exquisite and richly detailed map of Sydney in 1807 drawn by the former Irish convict James Meehan. He was a schoolteacher and surveyor back in County Offaly and had arrived in Sydney in 1800 after being transported for his active involvement in the outlawed Society of United Irishmen. In Sydney he was immediately snapped up by the Survey Department where, as Governor King soon noticed, he was 'a Man of Abilities'.

He proved himself an indefatigable surveyor and explorer. He traversed mountains, rivers and barren plains in the hinterland of New South Wales, Port Phillip and Tasmania, sometimes, as when exploring the area from Camden to Jervis Bay, using Aboriginal guides, Bundle and Broughton. He nearly drowned a couple of times, broke his arm falling from a horse, was on the cusp of starvation during one expedition, and was said to have spent more time under the stars than under his own roof.

He had a house near the corner of Argyle and George streets, where it was rumoured the first Catholic Mass was celebrated in secret in 1803 by Father Dixon, who had come out to the colony on the same ship as Meehan. Priests were only allowed into the colony and permitted to hold services in 1820, so in 1803 this was a more courageous act than it might seem now. The surveyor received an absolute pardon in 1806 but did not return to Ireland and it seems the reason was his de facto wife, Ruth Goedaire, who had recently arrived from England, though by this stage he was obviously enthralled with this new land. In spite of his successes and hard work, his Irishness held him back. Later in his career Governor Macquarie supported Meehan in his bid for the post of surveyor-general, however the British government was appalled at the idea of a former Irish political prisoner occupying such a high office, and instead gave the position to John Oxley, a naval officer with no experience in land surveying. Meehan remained deputy surveyor, responsible for all the field work in town and in the countryside.

His religion was important to him, though as one friend said, 'it did not lie like a misplaced millstone'. In 1820 he chose the site of what would become St Mary's Cathedral near Hyde Park. As he pegged it out, he attracted a small crowd, some of whom were Catholics who urged him to extend the area to enlarge the block the church was to be built on. He retired in 1822 to his 800-hectare property in Macquarie Fields where he built what was called 'Meehan's Castle'. The area around his huge farm, and neighbouring Bankstown, attracted so many of his countrymen that it became known as Irishtown.

Meehan became a favourite of Macquarie, who invited him to dinners at Government House and paid a handsome tribute to his talent and fulfilment of his arduous duties, saying, 'I believe that no man has suffered so much privation and fatigue in the service of this Colony as Mr Meehan has done.'

Prior to Macquarie's arrival, Governor Bligh thought the same thing, and had ordered Meehan to conduct a complete survey of Sydney Town. In Bligh's mind a map would enable him to accurately envisage how to control the town's growth and stop illegal land grabs and shonky developments by the bully boys of town, the military officers.

Meehan's 1807 map has all the main streets of Sydney Town,

with every house and its occupant marked, as well as government buildings and installations. It is a remarkable record of where the elite resided: the officers, doctors, merchants, the newspaper publisher, officials and Governor Bligh. It also showed the location of the Female Orphans' Asylum near the corner of Bridge and George streets, created to train abandoned and unwanted girls or those who were taken away 'from the destructive connections and examples of their dissolute parents'. The Orphans' Asylum held about a hundred girls and had been founded in 1801 by Anna King, the sympathetic, persistent and efficient wife of Governor King. Its success was gradually mitigated by the school's proximity to the military barracks, and the increasing frequency of the orphans hightailing it over the walls and falling pregnant to the soldiers and visiting sailors. Eventually in 1829 it was shifted to Parramatta, away from the temptations of Sydney, and became part of the Female Factory.

What becomes apparent in studying the map is the huge amount of land devoted to the military barracks. The space it takes up – the site bounded by present-day George, Barrack, Clarence and Margaret streets – emphasises that Sydney was basically a garrison town. It also illustrated how the town was expanding along King and Market streets, west towards Cockle Bay and a mile or so south to Brickfields. There was one main thoroughfare to the east and that was South Head Road, which led to the coast and was sparsely populated, but held a splendid villa, the house of a wealthy Irish convict, Sir Henry Browne Hayes, a Protestant from Cork and a zealous Freemason. He was not a political prisoner like Meehan but an impulsive and haughty creature, who regarded himself as the main player in the theatre of his life and those all around him as his extras.

In 1803 Hayes picked out a section of the harbour foreshore to buy. The 42 hectares of land was 11 kilometres outside of town towards South Head, then considered countryside. His house had two pyramid-capped turrets, symbolising the twin pillars of Freemasonry. Twenty acres were cleared for farming, and over a thousand fruit trees were planted. At the rear of the secluded estate were steep hills with virginal bush. Because he imagined the land resembled the poet Petrarch's estate in Southern France, 'Vaucluse', he named his new house after it. In 1805 a friend described Hayes and Vaucluse House to his mother:

> As we sail down the Port of Sydney the beautiful house of
> stone, built by Sir Henry Hayes on his land at the end of
> the harbour and his animals grazing peacefully there ...
> [I] momentarily regret at the loss I would feel without his
> society, this idea cost me some tears.

For several years Hayes avoided town and spent most of his time at Vaucluse House entertaining guests, sailing, indulging in Freemason rituals and attempting to establish the first Masonic Lodge. Macquarie pardoned him and he returned to Ireland in 1812. The house passed to the party boy John Piper and then the politician William Charles Wentworth, who considerably extended it. It would eventually be owned by the state, where it remains a much-visited museum, a remnant of upper-class living in the nineteenth century.

*

On Meehan's map, a street lurches south, down to the sordid area of the brickfields where *hoi polloi* lived and, as Meehan notes, 'These houses are irregularly built, very few good.' The other aspect that jumps out at the modern viewer is how different Sydney Cove (Meehan also called it 'Warrang') looked. It is untouched and stretches inland in an irregular fashion, waiting to be tamed into Circular Quay during the 1840s.

In 1804, three years before Meehan made his map, a survey had been taken of the number of houses in the town. There were 420, exclusive of the military: in the military district there were 160, Brickfields had 72, Cockle Bay 18 and Farm Cove eight. The total number was 678, with the non-military population of the town hovering around 2100 people.

Some houses were basically hovels, collapsing in strong winds, their thatched roofs a constant fire hazard. One time fire took hold as a result of a spark from a chimney in Pitt Street and devastated a row of houses. The town's tallest structure, an elegant clock tower 50 metres high built with local bricks, tumbled down after heavy rains in 1806 due to a lack of enough lime in the mortar. As one Sydneysider wrote, some of the main streets were not only dangerous but, 'impassable after dark, save with the risk of breaking an arm or a leg, by numerous pits and hollows … Having myself lately plunged into one of those occasional recesses in Pitt's Row.' Only a few Sydneysiders seemed to care about the state of the streets and, as the writer discovered, one man was even stealing earth from the street 'to level his yard'. The government, and even private citizens, made futile attempts to fix the roads by filling the potholes and ruts with broken bricks. An exasperated Bligh published a government decree: 'The Inhabitants of the Town of Sydney are expected to keep the Streets opposite their respective Dwellings in Good Repair and the Footpath clean.' But people seldom took any notice of it.

Residents had their own gardens and many grew peach trees, both for the fruit and to make a strong cider. This type of alcohol was promoted by the government and every person who produced two hogsheads (around 240 litres) of peach cider 'which the governor judges to be the best shall receive a cow from the government as a reward'. People also dug their own wells, but at night many were left uncovered, and these provided a watery grave for drunks and unwary children, one boy even drowning in the hospital well.

The Rocks was a lawless place with its honeycomb of huts, hovels and narrow streets and alleyways, a refuge for convicts, emancipists, seamen, whalers, deserters, ruffians and criminals. The range of races and nationalities was astonishing, a cosmopolitan mix of English, Irish, Scots, Māori, Americans, both black and white, Tahitians and even 'Hindoos'. Thefts, muggings, brawls, illicit stills, prostitution and drunken revelry were a disturbing concoction to the more law-abiding inhabitants. Drunks brawled in the streets and lanes, taking on the police who had come to arrest them. House robberies were epidemic. Gardens were raided, trees and even fences stolen.

Stolen items included casks of rum, the railing enclosing the tomb of a child from the burial ground, the front gate of a house in George Street, a fat black sow weighing 60 kilos, a silver watch and an emu. Servants were robbed of their clothes, a silver dessert spoon filched from the officers' mess, and a 'Derwent' magpie stolen from its cage ('easily recognisable by its inimitable mimicking of a puppy in distress'). One brazen robber stole some watermelons from a garden and returned a few days later to steal some more. He was shot at, and in fleeing left his bags and bludgeons behind.

Other thieves were not so lucky. A man who tried to steal some chickens was shot in the face, 'his eyes blown out of his head'. The man who fired the shot had been placed as a guard due to the frequent thefts of poultry. When James Harris, a labourer, was shot and killed in the act of robbing a garden in Chippendale, the coroner's verdict was 'justifiable homicide'.

The wealthy merchant Simeon Lord had armed watchmen to keep thieves from his warehouse. Other shopkeepers and householders didn't have the money to buy protection. Naked thieves squeezed down chimneys, some were caught stuck halfway down, others ran from the scene of the crime covered in soot. One robber was caught red-handed with a desk containing £24 and three pieces of gold, having broken a door frame to get in. More common was smashing a window late at night and a hasty snatch of anything that could be quickly sold on. Wine was a frequent target, as were chests of tea, frocks and even silk handkerchiefs. One woman caught a thief in the very act of stealing her bed. Even those few settlers who were living on the outskirts of the town (now the inner suburbs) were not immune. In 1806 William Page would emerge from his hideaway in the brickfields and rob isolated farmhouses in Redfern, Chippendale and Surry Hills. He even broke into Dr Harris's warehouse in Ultimo and then had the audacity to return the next day, claiming he was sent to repair the damage. He was captured in a stake-out in the vicinity of Central Station and quickly hanged.

Those convicted of minor crimes were sentenced to the public pillories, sometimes with their ears nailed to the headboard. In 1812 Michael Simpson, Thomas Brown and William Bailey were put in the stocks in the marketplace for 'unnatural acts'. On occasions such as this the police would allow verbal abuse, jeers, spitting, and even the throwing of vegetables and fruit at the victims, but would step in if rocks or stones were hurled.

Hangings were public and both spectators and the *Sydney Gazette* expected a show of remorse from the criminals and were appalled when someone like Thomas Welch 'gave no signs of contrition for his offence, but unhappily appeared to be little affected at his melancholic situation'. Some criminals were petulant, others showed no remorse or even emotion. Some made speeches to the many spectators, confessing their sins, others exhorted prisoners who were forced to witness the executions to 'shun those vile practices which prevailed among them: gambling, drunkenness, theft, and the total neglect of religion'.

One woman, Mary Grady, 20 years old, was convicted of robbing a house and sentenced to death. She was driven to the scaffold in a cart while the men who were to die with her walked alongside. On approaching the gallows, she fainted several times and 'the nearer she approached, appeared more and more affected by the horrors of her condition, of which she did not appear sensible until her death warrant was read to her'.

Convicts working for the government began early in the morning and finished mid-afternoon, their days regulated by the ringing of bells and drum tattoos. They worked from Monday to Friday, starting at sunrise. There was an hour's respite between eight and nine, and then they worked without a break until 3.30. The weekend was spare time when they could hire themselves out to settlers, earning money to pay for their lodgings or to buy goods. Those who misbehaved were forced to sleep in irons in the jail. Floggings and the screams of pain that accompanied them were so common that few of the public took any notice.

For those who enjoyed the pretend floggings at Old Sydney Town, the reality would have been an appalling sight. One eyewitness recalled a particular incident:

This was an old offender and had been flogged repeatedly; this was the first time he was punished with the regulation cat; he bellowed at every lash and writhed in agony; his back was very much lacerated, and more blood appeared than I have observed on any other criminal; when taken down he seemed much exhausted and cried like a child.

And then there was a young man who:

> ... had been punished before; at the first lash he cried out, which he did during the whole of the punishment, and struggled most violently, calling out that he could not stand it, and praying to be taken down ... he begged for some water, which was given him; his back was much lacerated, and he appeared a good deal exhausted when taken down.

The punishment could be stopped when a surgeon announced the offender was close to death, then the victim would be taken to hospital to recover. This may take weeks, during which time the victim was haunted by the knowledge that when he was reasonably recovered the punishment would be continued.

HOWLING AT THE MOON

MEEHAN'S MAP WAS A BEAUTIFUL WORK that gave the impression of a tidy and efficient town, but it was at odds with the reality of a Sydney whose buildings seemed exhausted, not unlike the present condition of Old Sydney Town. The year that Meehan drew the map, Governor Bligh walked all over Sydney, taking notes he sent on to London. What he observed and his recommendations give some idea of the condition of Sydney's major buildings. The Master Builders House needed plastering, whitewashing, windows repaired, and the foundations shored up. The dockyard needed sheds for boats, the blacksmith's shop and watchman's hut needed plastering, whitewashing, new doors, shutters and a staircase ... And so the list went on and on, including Government House, which needed replacements for doors, windows, shutters and floors, 'all in so rotten a state'. No building seemed immune from neglect and shoddy workmanship: the windmills, the bridge across the Tank Stream, the government stables; the new church had a collapsed wall. Even the executioner's hut required new doors, window shutters, a fence and, like so many buildings, required immediate plastering and whitewashing. As for the wooden hospital, it was so decayed it was not worth repairing. 'The Other Hospital' needed new doors, windows, shutters, floors, the repairing of broken windows – all in all, it was 'in a ruinous state'.

Sometimes it must have seemed as if the town was a menagerie. Packs of stray dogs roamed the streets, attacking livestock, chasing after horses, biting children, 'the wretched animals prowling around for food to the annoyance of the public'. There were constant calls for 'the curs and useless dogs to be destroyed'. You could tell the dogs that people had attempted to kill or capture – canines with ears and tails cut off were a common sight.

The dogs roamed far and wide, making their way to surgeon John Harris's 94-hectare property. His two-storey house, 'Ultimo', had been built by convicts in 1804 and he had transformed the bush into an English-style parkland where imported Indian deer grazed. The feral dogs ran down the deer and killed many of them, causing Harris to issue a public warning that any dog venturing onto his property would be shot on sight.

Another animal causing problems was the pig. By 1808 there were nearly 20 000 pigs in the colony. Responsible owners tethered their swine, but others let them roam free to scavenge in the streets and devastate gardens. The government ordered people to erect fences to protect their gardens and if they didn't, then the householder wouldn't be awarded damages for the animals' destruction. Pigs were constantly polluting the Tank Stream, the town's only water source. A game for drunks was to cut off a pig's ears and eat them raw. The wild swine, as if in payback for this treatment, attempted to eat children and, in some cases, took huge bites out of them.

There seemed to be as many feral goats as pigs and the two often came into conflict. In one instance, several goats went missing down at the lawless brickfields. One was found mangled and half-eaten by a couple of enormous swine; other goats were suspected of being eaten by pigs 'supporting themselves almost entirely upon a fare of chance'. Pigs also dug up corpses in the cemetery (now under the Town Hall).

Parrots and cockatoos were household favourites, and they were everywhere, in cages or on perches with wings clipped, squawking and swearing. There were constant queries in the *Sydney Gazette* about lost or stolen parrots and advertisements for native animals for sale. Some people even kept black swans. Kangaroos were popular pets, and visiting sailors sold monkeys to the public. A sergeant in Pitt's Row owned a koala and two cubs, and a judge advocate had a native owl. One poor family, consisting of a husband, wife and two children, had four dogs, three cats, five parrots and a kangaroo.

In 1806 there were 1808 children in the settlement, of whom 908 were illegitimate. Of the 1216 women living with men, only 360 were married. Like the stray pigs and goats, children ran free, many unschooled. For the boys and girls, the pigs were dangerous fun. Boys bludgeoned them, threw rocks at them, assaulted them with sticks and buried axes in their heads. Children themselves were also victims of the colony's dangers. They were accidentally scalded, drowned, attacked by dogs, fell into wells, were stamped on by horses and run over by carriages. They also wounded and killed one another. Some children were cut with glass and disfigured for life, others were accidentally speared by their friends; one boy accidentally cut off his playmate's fingers. On Guy Fawkes Night children drank rum, let off fireworks and ran wild.

By 1813 a quarter of the white population of Sydney was aged under 12. Some children attended school, some worked at home, and others wandered the streets looking for trouble. One 15-year-old boy attempted to murder another boy the same age by shooting him.

In an all-too-common incident at that time, a pack of boys in the Rocks chased a small group of Aborigines through the streets, hurling insults and throwing rocks and stones at them. Near the jail in George Street, one of the boys went to throw a large stone at an Aboriginal woman and in retaliation one of the Aboriginal men threw a larger stone at the boy that hit him so hard the boy thought his thigh was broken. This single act made the young mob even more hostile and they went to attack 'the meek, well-known Bungaree' who happened to be passing by. One of the thugs ran at Bungaree, threatening to dash out his brains and was only stopped when a bystander intervened.

Most male convicts were visible, digging roads, chopping down trees, acting as builders' labourers, making bricks, tramping through the unmade streets in chain gangs and loading and unloading ships. Female convicts, however, pressed into working as servants, were less visible. Many lived in the stables of houses, in lean-tos or huts where their behaviour would occasionally disturb the tranquillity of their employers.

It was easy to stigmatise these female servants as lazy, uncouth and dishonest. The stereotype was common, yet a different picture emerges when, in the early 1830s, the *Sydney Gazette* and *Sydney Herald* began reporting on female servants tried in the courts. Their crimes cover a wide spectrum: smiling too much, howling at the moon, being drunk, violent, backchatting the master or mistress, being caught with a lover. Once convicted, the women were transported to the Female Factory in Parramatta in a huge windowless black carriage. Occasionally they were escorted up the Parramatta River on a steamer.

Designed by Francis Greenway, the Factory, which opened in 1821, served several purposes. It was a residence for newly arrived female transportees, a place of punishment for those who had committed crimes in the colony, an asylum for the elderly or mad, a labour exchange, a marriage bureau where men would come to choose a wife, a hospital for the sick, a maternity ward, and a real factory that manufactured cloth (linen, wool and linsey-woolsey).

The women spun, knitted, plaited, washed, cleaned, or, if in the dire Third Class, broke rocks and picked oakum, untwisting old rope to obtain loose fibres to be used in caulking ships, a tedious job and tough on the fingers.

The building had all the appearance of a penitentiary. Three storeys high and with a forbidding sandstone solidity, its occupants were divided into three classes. The First Class were recently arrived convicts and the destitute, who were allowed to earn money for themselves and receive visitors. Women in the Second Class were generally pregnant or nursing a child. Not allowed visitors, these women could advance to the First Class section after three months of good behaviour or, if badly behaved, be demoted to the Third Class, the category for women who had been convicted of crimes committed while in service. Their hair was closely cropped, and they were forced to do hard labour. Food and clothing ranged from reasonable in the top class to grim in the lowest one.

The notoriety of the Female Factory even spread overseas. In 1937 the German Douglas Sirk directed *Zu Neuen Ufern* ('To New Shores') starring the legendary musical star Zarah Leander. Its protagonist is Gloria Vane, an English music-hall singer who, in the 1840s, takes the rap for her aristocratic lover Sir Albert Finsbury when he forges a cheque. She is sentenced to seven years in the Female Factory. Sir Albert, unaware of all this, has gone off to New South Wales himself, where he woos the governor's daughter. There is a delirious section where Leander as Gloria and her fellow prisoners sing and make baskets like 'slightly dishevelled chorines in a *Gold Diggers* movie' as one cynical film reviewer put it. Gloria, like many a real woman of the times, can only escape the dreadful Female Factory if someone agrees to marry her. A local farmer, Henry Hoyer, takes pity on her and she marries him, happily becoming a farmer's wife. Sirk's portrayal of the conditions in this bleak Sydney prison was his oblique criticism of what was happening in 1937 Nazi Germany.

For convict women assigned as servants, domestic work was tedious, endless, hard and long. She served dinners, cleared tables, did the laundry, organised for the bath water to be heated and delivered, made beds, mopped and swept the floor, cooked, cared for the mistress's clothes, helped her dress and undress, washed and dressed her hair, carried away her stinking chamber pot, and was on call at all hours. She was at the mercy of the temper of her employers, and often had to avoid the lecherous attentions of her master and ignore the insults of her mistress if she was perceived to be lazy, slow or suspected of thievery – or even eating more than she was allotted. It was no wonder that many of them rebelled.

Women judged to have committed petty crimes were fined five shillings. If they couldn't pay, they were sentenced to the stocks near the police station in Druitt Street. In 1825 the *Sydney Gazette* reported one normal day in court where 11 people were to be sentenced, 'of whom two were of the softer sex'. The nine men were sent to work the treadmill for ten days while 'one of the nymphs, despite the upper part of her face about the eyes was disguised and discoloured, was destined to a seat in the stocks for three hours'.

But it was the women sent to the Third Class of the Female Factory who intrigued the reporters. They wrote up the women's court appearances in a light-hearted, condescending manner that no doubt amused their readers and confirmed their views of the immorality and unruliness of the women.

Servants who stole from their masters and mistresses – favourite targets were jewellery, money, tobacco and clothing – only proved their innate criminality. One woman was found with stolen property in the lining of her bed and knives and forks under the floorboards. Ann Craig was arrested for stealing from her mistress, but on the way to the watch house the incorrigible woman filched a snuff box from the waistcoat pocket of the constable who arrested her. Other popular stolen goods were ribbons, gowns, stockings, frocks, crockery, watches and combs. One servant was discovered hiding a stolen ring in her mouth. Even desperate acts of stealing food resulted in being sent to Parramatta, whether it be chickens, mutton or, one of the most sought-after substances, green tea. If anything irritated the women more, it was how miserly mistresses would water down their cups of tea.

Their personal lives were not their own. Lovers were discovered under beds and in stables. In order to get some privacy, many a woman made for the Domain, where shrubbery and trees offered some sort of sanctuary from patrolling policemen. One servant, Elizabeth Gardener, was caught snogging an actor; another Elizabeth was found laughing and giggling with several men, all of them drunk and jolly. A Selina Harding was found with 'a young blade', tying a handkerchief around his neck. She tried, in vain, to avoid arrest by sweet talking the policeman. Another woman caught smoking with 'a regular flash cove' pathetically lied that she was in the Domain to buy a pint of oysters. One brazen woman was found making love 'in a romantic nook overhanging the cove'.

Few days in court passed without women being punished for drunkenness. It was a common pastime. Drinking and alcohol developed a long list of slang terms, including muzzy, maizy, groggy, lushey, slewing, getting nappy, blue ruin, lamb's wool and a ball, which had to be explained to perplexed judges and magistrates who sometimes didn't understand what the women were saying, so thick were their Irish and Scottish brogues and so incomprehensible their slang.

Some women were found in the streets so drunk they needed a wheelbarrow to cart them to the watch house. If not caught in a sly grog shack, they might be discovered by their master in the act. One was found 'snoring like a pig' on the sofa in the parlour, surrounded by fag ends of her lover's cigars. Many stole from their mistress's liquor cabinets or master's wine cellars. Once they had the bottle of spirits or wine they drank it quickly and not far from the scene of their crime, only to be found 'speechless drunk' or 'walking on her head instead of her heels'. Some with the Dutch courage of drink abused their employers. Typical was a drunken Catherine Barrett, singing 'My Pretty Page' and simultaneously banging a pan with one of her shoes, the clamour keeping the whole household awake, 'little dogs and all'.

If alcohol liberated the behaviour of some, others needed no such stimulant to run wild. Ann Taylor, 'of a pugnacious disposition', waved her fist in her mistress's face, threatening her with, 'There's muscle for ye – hit me with a sledgehammer.' Another servant struck her master with a box of dominoes. Mary Carr pointed a knife at her mistress, saying, 'Here's your fucking breadbasket.' A furious Julia Birmingham grabbed her mistress by the hair and banged her head against a wall; another servant seized her master by the collar of his coat, held him aloft and shook him 'until his knees chattered together', then ripped up his shirt, declaring she wished she could 'lay his heart bare in the same manner'.

Many a woman reached breaking point and smashed up everything in the house she could lay her hands on, including furniture and crockery. In some cathartic outbursts women danced around the house singing at the top of their lungs, laughing loudly or, what was weirdly popular, performing a Native American war dance. Other servants refused to work, or ran away; many hid in the Domain. One enterprising woman hid for days in one of the crannies in Cockle Bay, a hideaway she stockpiled with food; for company she had a cat and a parrot who whistled 'A bumper of burgundy fill for me'. After a four-day search one servant was found hiding in the oven of the military barracks in George Street. Some disguised themselves as men (a sailor's outfit was common), others were found drunk, dancing and singing in the streets.

In court many of these women answered back to the judges, attacked the policemen who arrested them or shouted obscenities, but it was their defiant words after being sentenced to the Female Factory that indicated just how much they hated their masters and mistresses and the work they had to do. 'If you take me back I'll never do you an hour's good,' one woman shouted at her mistress. Matilda Wildboy wagged her finger in her master's face and sneered, 'I'd rather be a dog, and bay [at] the moon, than work for you!'

One servant, Jane MacDonald, sentenced to two weeks, shouted at the judge, 'Send me for six months, if you like – I'll never go back!' The judge, saying he'd 'tame this shrew', added 38 days to her sentence for contempt of court, which only riled her more, 'You may send me for years, if you like, for I'll never go back!'

One woman up on a charge of insolence was so angry that she hit her hands together 'with', said the reporter, 'the fury of a maniac', and screamed, 'So help me God, I'll never go back to my master's service – I won't, I won't, I won't!'

There were women who simply sneered on hearing the length of their punishment and affected a blasé attitude. When Catherine Ryan was sentenced to six weeks, she shrugged, 'Oh, I can stand six months for that matter.' Others refused to leave the courtroom and lashed out at the constables. 'I'll run away when I come back!' yelled one, and with that, turned around and floored a policeman with a punch. The other policemen struggled to put a pair of handcuffs on her and then, as she screamed and fought, it took three constables to remove her from the courtroom. One woman was so ferocious it took six constables to carry her out.

There's a sense that by the time these women got to court they knew they had nothing left to lose and revelled in their insubordination, determined to insist on their status as human beings and not go quietly. It was as if, having been stripped of their dignity, they found strength in their white-hot fury. Their dramatic explosions were fuelled by a larrikin energy. Many felt they were less like servants than slaves, entirely at the mercy of their masters and mistresses, and even the miserable circumstances of Third Class at the Female Factory were preferable.

The tone of the newspaper reports of these women in Sydney in the early 1830s was one of mockery, especially of the Irish, but at least these women were no longer invisible. Their protests, whether it be insolence, drinking, stealing, violence, dancing, howling at the moon or doing 'the Cherokee war dance', were acts of defiance in the face of exploitation and demeaning treatment.

A NEW BEGINNING

AFTER TWO YEARS OF UPHEAVAL, Sydney welcomed its fifth governor, Major-General Lachlan Macquarie, with celebrations throughout the town. Windows were covered with beautiful illuminated transparencies, one proudly featuring the image of the first ship built in the colony; pieces of coloured glass lit from behind dazzled the eye, verandahs blazed with countless lamps, archways were garlanded with flowers, portraits of George III adorned front doors – all this to an endless soundtrack of a military band playing 'God Save the King' and 'Rule Britannia'. At half past eight in the evening a huge bonfire was lit. Fireworks lasted until ten, followed by banquets, many drunken speeches, garrulous tributes to the new governor, and dancing until dawn.

With the departure of Arthur Phillip, the colony had been captured by the New South Wales Corps – the notorious Rum Corps, who controlled the lucrative rum trade to the point where rum had become the colony's de facto currency. The Corps took the law into their own hands, not afraid to bully anyone or smash up the house of someone they disliked. Hunter, Phillip's successor, on the cusp of 60, was perhaps too old for a task better suited to a younger man with more energy and conviction. By 1806, when William Bligh was sworn in as governor, things had gone from bad to worse. His attempts to bring the Corps to heel, combined with an abrasive personality, led to his ignominious overthrow by the very body he had been charged to control.

With the arrival of Macquarie, the dark ages of the illegitimate regime ended.

Macquarie was 48 and the first army man to govern the colony – his four predecessors had all been naval men. He had been born on the Scottish island of Ulva to poor parents. Realising he could only look forward to eking out a living as a tenant farmer like his father, he joined the army at the age of 14 and, ambitious and cunning, rose through the ranks to lieutenant colonel. In the process, he earned a considerable amount of money, much of it dubiously acquired – like many British officers, he joined in the sacking and plundering wherever he went, adding to his loot. He had been a soldier and little else, fighting in far-flung places such as India, America, Jamaica and Ceylon. The 20 years he spent in India had given his complexion a swarthy hue. Tall, broad shouldered, active and energetic, he had a micromanaging style and an autocratic manner that would end up irritating many. Sydneysiders got used to seeing him riding or walking around town, often wearing his heavily braided, bright scarlet uniform. His second wife, Elizabeth, 16 years younger, was also Scottish; a daughter had been born in Scotland but died in infancy. A son, Lachlan, would be born in Sydney in 1814.

The couple arrived from England on 28 December 1809 accompanied by Macquarie's 73rd Regiment, which was to relieve the crooked New South Wales Corps. Intending to stay five or six years, Macquarie was sworn in on New Year's Day, 1810. In fact, he would stay for 11 years and become New South Wales' longest-serving governor, making more of an impact on Sydney than any other governor. His first aim was to restore order in a colony where the military had established a kleptocracy, and to send those who had been leaders in the rebellion against Bligh back to England for trial.

The Sydney he inherited had been allowed to stagnate in the interval between governors. The finest residence belonged to the wealthy ex-convict Simeon Lord. The main structures were the stone bridge over the Tank Stream, the King's Wharf, the timber yard (a large enclosed area where the convicts worked), the Female Orphans' Asylum fronting George Street, and the granary and stores (also on George Street). Along the ridge of York Street stretched the barracks.

Small rickety huts and houses dotted the Rocks. Described as 'a fortress of iniquity', neither the Rocks' topography nor its inhabitants could be tamed. It was a place of steep hills, winding tracks and narrow lanes that followed the line of least resistance. To Macquarie this was chaos where there should be grids of straight lines.

A third of the population of around 10 000 were fed and clothed at the expense of the crown. Convicts scavenged for anything that might be of use. Oil lamps and homemade tallow candles supplied light to houses that had floors of brick or trodden clay, causing the inhabitants to suffer from 'rheumatiz' and 'brownchitis'. Cups, mugs, spoons, platters, bowls and saucers were of iron, tin or wood. Soups were made of wallaby or possum bones. Wooden troughs and empty barrels were used for holding water. Wholemeal bread baked in dripping was a luxury food. Maize, ground by windmills and watermills, was made into hominy (boiled dried maize), corn cakes and bread. The quality of the bread was a frequent issue. In the year Macquarie arrived there was a rash of bad quality bread at several bakehouses from grain that had been imperfectly ground, which meant it was riddled with grass seeds. Many people who ate the bread were affected with debilitating symptoms such as violent headaches, 'dimness of sight', trembling of joints, extreme drowsiness, and vomiting. As the *Sydney Gazette* remarked, 'Its narcotic or stupefying qualities are well known.' Convicts and the poor seldom ate meat, and when they did it was more likely to be salt pork, some of which had been in casks for a year.

A few industries were booming. The tanning of leather made from the skins of cattle, kangaroos and seals 'cannot be surpassed'. Several potteries turned out plates, basins, cups, saucers and teapots. Clay tobacco pipes, once expensive at sixpence each, were now manufactured in the town and only a penny each, something that was much appreciated as smoking was endemic. There were four breweries, and many people brewed their own beer in addition. In his *The Present Picture of New South Wales*, published in England in 1811, former convict DD Mann was most taken with the 'respectable' and tastefully decorated shops that appealed to women, noting that 'Articles of female apparel and ornament are greedily purchased.' Mann tried to put a positive spin on the colony, but he could not avoid the glaring truth of the damage alcohol caused:

> Most of the people in the colony, male and female, give
> way to excessive drinking … The evils consequent upon
> the unrestrained use of [spirits] have proved from their
> first introduction into the colony, and still continue to be,
> the fertile sources of social disorder, of domestic misery, of
> disorders, and of death.

It seemed to Mann that there was nothing a governor could do, whether by threats, entreaties or punishments, to stop it.

For entertainment there was cricket, sailing, cockfighting, shooting, fishing and kangaroo hunting (good kangaroo dogs were rare and costly). Convicts drank prodigiously and gambled wildly, some even staking the clothes they wore, so when they lost, wrote Mann, they 'stood amongst their companions in a state of nudity, thus reducing themselves to a level with the natives of the woods'.

Years later Macquarie was to look back at his first impressions of Sydney with no sense of nostalgia:

> I found the colony barely emerging from infantile imbecility,
> and suffering from various privations and disabilities ...
> agriculture in a yet languishing state; commerce in its early
> dawn; revenue unknown; threatened with famine; distracted
> by faction; the public buildings in a state of dilapidation and
> mouldering to decay; the few roads and bridges formerly
> constructed almost impassable; no public credit nor private
> confidence; the morals of the great mass of the population in
> the lowest state of debasement, and religious worship almost
> wholly neglected ... public works had been neglected ... and the
> general moral state of the mass of the people was one in which
> the evils attendant upon promiscuous cohabitation between men
> and women were exaggerated or alleviated by a copious flow of
> very inferior alcohol.

Free settlers, most of whom were convicts who had long since completed their sentences, far outnumbered the convicts, but they continued to be treated as prisoners and second-class citizens. There seemed to be a pervasive sense of hopelessness in the colony, a lack of civic pride and a listless drift towards an unknown future.

Macquarie was horrified by the huge number of 'concubines' attached to the officers and 'immorality and vice so prevalent amongst the lower classes [and] the custom so generally and shamelessly adopted of Persons of different Sexes COHABITING and living together unsanctioned by the legal ties of MATRIMONY'. Some of his earliest orders were to stop couples cohabiting without marriage. Further, constables were told to enforce the laws against Sabbath-breaking, and a regular church parade was introduced for convicts in government employ.

By October of his first year, he began to see a distinct improvement in public morality. Attendances at church rose and the marriage rate increased. Schools were established, the number of pubs reduced from 75 to 20 and clandestine stills seized. A delighted Macquarie claimed that there had been 'a very apparent' change for the better in the 'Religious Tendency and Morals' of the colony. In the same month he opened a new marketplace, and proclaimed Hyde Park.

The pace of Macquarie's restructuring increased. His priorities were to build a new army barracks, a new general hospital and a turnpike road to Parramatta. The George Street barracks were completed by the end of 1810. Macquarie's newly arrived regiment, the 73rd, was the first occupant. By 1815 a giant wall, 10 feet (3 metres) high and two feet (61 centimetres) thick, with four gates, one on each side of the rectangle, enclosed the whole area of 16.5 acres (6.7 hectares), between George and Clarence streets. The idea was to restrict the interaction between the military and inhabitants of the town. The result was that the barracks sat like an enormous citadel in the heart of the settlement, dominating the town and reinforcing the authority of the military.

Despite Macquarie's attempt to segregate the army from civilians, drunken brawls continued between the redcoats and the populace, often in the lawless Rocks. One deadly weapon a soldier had was his belt with its heavy metal buckle. When swung at full speed it could cause severe damage to a face or head. Eventually the commander of the garrison banned the wearing of belts on leave. The large number of soldiers presented a continuing problem for Macquarie with their easy access to spirits, their strutting arrogance, and their predilection for women 'of loose morals'. If any one case showed the problem of the garrison troops mixing with the locals it was an incident in 1813 when two officers slipped into civilian clothes and, drunk, banged on the door of an old man in Pitt Street, wanting to be let in. When he refused to admit them, they beat him to death with heavy sticks. Instead of being charged with murder, they were convicted of manslaughter and sentenced to just six months hard labour. No wonder many Sydneysiders despised these haughty redcoats.

It was obvious that Sydney was in desperate need of a new hospital, so in November 1810 Macquarie contracted the principal surgeon, D'Arcy Wentworth, and two other important colonists, Garnham Blaxcell and Alexander Riley, to build one. By this stage Macquarie realised it was almost impossible to curb 'the use of spiritous liquors' as Castlereagh, the secretary of state for the colonies, had demanded, and instead used it to his advantage. The government would supply the trio with convict labour, food and 20 oxen to help with the building, but the partners were to construct the hospital at their own expense in exchange for the right to import 202 500 litres of Bengal rum over a period of three years.

It seemed a cheap way of gaining an urgently needed medical facility. Macquarie was counting on the tyranny of distance working in his favour. By the time the London office heard about his actions (which they strongly criticised), the building was well underway. The Georgian-style hospital opened in 1816 and remains a functioning example of early colonial architecture, the oldest public building in Australia. After serving as a hospital, in 1853 it became the Mint, established to deal with the influx of gold from the goldfields, which continued to operate in the south wing until the 1920s. The north wing has been Sydney's Parliament House since 1829, when Governor Darling appropriated it.

It was not only the morality of Sydneysiders that had appalled the new governor, but the unruly nature of the town itself. Typical of Macquarie's attempts to bring order was regularising street names – what had been known as Sgt Majors Row and High Street became George Street; Stream Row was widened and became Pitt Street, and so on. Further, any stock found wandering in Hyde Park would be confiscated. Even the traffic attracted his attention. Children were maimed and adults nearly trampled to death by horses; gigs overturned or crashed into each other; road rage was a frequent problem; and drunks were run over by carriages or trampled by cattle being driven into town. Macquarie decreed that the driving of cattle and carts, riding and walking should be on the left of roads. Enforcing this English practice, he declared, would avoid unnecessary injuries.

Determined to control every aspect of Sydney life, Macquarie introduced the first building code into the colony, requiring that all buildings were to be constructed of timber or brick, covered with a shingle roof, and include a chimney. If one needed a further example of Macquarie's attention to detail it was his order that all buildings, public and private, be numbered, the cost of painting the numbers to be paid by the occupiers. John Eyre was appointed to paint the numbers on the eastern side of the Tank Stream, while James Richardson was to do the same on the western side. The painters were to be paid an excellent fee of sixpence for every house, which, as the governor said without a hint of irony, 'every inhabitant will cheerfully pay'.

Eyre was an interesting choice. He had been transported for housebreaking and arrived in 1801, aged 30. A prolific artist, he lived a precarious existence trying to hawk his works to the few patrons available, whose stinginess rankled him. He produced drawings and watercolours of Sydney and small towns. Before returning to England in 1812 he struck up a friendship with

DD Mann and provided four engraved views of Sydney for Mann's *The Present Picture of New South Wales* (1811). Perhaps his most curious painting was *East View of Sydney*, produced the year before Macquarie arrived. The huge rocks of the western side of town block most of our view. Framed by the rocks are nine Aboriginal men. Eight are sitting watching one demonstrating how to throw a spear. Beyond them, in the background, is the busy harbour. Although the scene of the Aboriginal people dominates the eye, it's as if they are living in a cocoon of their own culture, unaware that the world of Europeans in the background will come to dominate their lives.

In his struggle to eradicate the use of rum as the unofficial currency of the colony, in 1813 Macquarie purchased 40 000 Spanish dollars and set up a small mint in Bridge Street. These coins, their centres punched out to create the holey dollar and the dump, became Australia's first official currency, which would continue in use until 1829.

It's obvious that the governor relied on his wife. Elizabeth's personality seems obscured by time but her journal of the seven-month journey to the bottom of the world shows a vivacious woman fascinated by the world around her. Back in Scotland she was known for her ability as a landscape gardener and her interest in architecture. She was more tactful than her husband, a much-needed attribute, a perfect hostess with a highly developed sense of style and refined artistic taste that tended towards the rococo. She undertook arduous travels in Tasmania and across the Blue Mountains. Her husband acted like Adam, naming lighthouses, rivers and towns after himself, but he also indicated how much he valued his wife, naming, among other places, Elizabeth Street and Elizabeth Bay after her and, of course, there is Mrs Macquarie's Chair, a rock cut into a bench shape on Yurong Point, where it is said she sat rapt in the spectacle of the changing light on the harbour.

When they arrived in Sydney, both Macquarie and Elizabeth had been dismayed by how toxic the relationship between blacks and whites had become. Those Aboriginal people who lived in Sydney were outcasts, shunned by most Europeans, mocked and insulted. Many were left to beg or take refuge in drink.

Just as he was determined to lift the colonists out of spiritual squalor, so Macquarie set about forging a way for the original inhabitants to live alongside the British and helping them avoid beggary and drunkenness. He outlined his plan, proclaiming that he would 'always be willing and ready to grant small Portions of Land, in suitable and convenient Parts of the Colony, to such of them as are inclined to become regular Settlers and such occasional Assistance from Government as may enable them to cultivate their Farms'.

He established Australia's first Aboriginal reserve at Woolloo-mooloo. It was to be managed by Aboriginal people themselves and whites could only enter if invited. The plan was for the recipients to earn money through their vegetable gardens and fishing. It was not a success. Neither was another of Macquarie's ideas. He gave a generous amount of land at George's Head on the North Shore to 15 Aboriginal people to farm. They were provided with implements, stock and convict instructors in farming. A feast was held to celebrate, and Macquarie decorated his friend, the Sydney identity Bungaree, with a brass plate inscribed *Bungaree: Chief of the Broken Bay Tribe*. The venture failed but Bungaree kept the brass plate, wearing it everywhere, even though he had no tribal authority. He was a gregarious and intelligent man with several wives – one of them was Cora Gooseberry, 'the queen'.

These efforts existed alongside reprisal missions. In 1816, when Macquarie heard that nine settlers had been killed by blacks in three separate incidents, he responded as the military man he was, ordering a retaliatory expedition. Force would be met with force. He ordered his soldiers to 'apprehend all the Natives you fall in with and make Prisoners of them'. He had a list of those he believed were guilty of the killings and went on to explicitly order that 'You are to spare all Women and Children.'

On a moonlit night, his troops raided an Aboriginal camp in Appin, firing their guns, killing some, panicking the women and children, causing them to blindly leap to their deaths in a gorge. In all 14 bodies were found.

*

Although he prided himself on his self-discipline, Macquarie had an autocratic nature he struggled to control. He was frustrated that the wall around the Domain was frequently being smashed or scaled, allowing criminals to hide their stolen goods in the wild and rocky shrubbery and women to frequent there for 'the most indecent improper purposes'. What annoyed him most was that these lawbreakers were only given a slight reprimand when caught. Exasperated, he had three men arrested for trespassing on the Governor's Domain and, greatly exceeding his authority, denied them a trial and had them flogged by the hangman. He was criticised but didn't care, as 'it certainly had the desired effect and put a complete stop to those Trespasses and breaking down the Government Wall, as well as the gross indecencies'.

It is said that Macquarie had a sense of humour, but it's nigh on impossible to find examples of it. Because he prized his honour so highly, he hated being mocked. One way people ridiculed their enemies was to write nasty things about them, roll up the unsigned paper and drop it where it could easily be found. These anonymous satirical verses were called pipes. When a pipe was written lampooning Macquarie's vanity and his propensity to name everything after himself, the culprit, former convict

Dr William Bland, was charged with libel and received a sentence of 12 months imprisonment and a fine of £50. At the completion of his sentence, Bland returned to his practice and proved to be a significant medical and political presence in the colony long after Macquarie had departed. His eminence is now forgotten, even to those who live in the narrow street in Woolloomooloo named after him.

If Macquarie thought he could jail or gag his opponents then he didn't count on his nemesis, John Thomas Bigge, who arrived in Sydney late in 1819. He had been sent to set up a royal commission to examine Macquarie's rule, including his expensive building program and his 'ill-considered compassion for convicts'. It was not only the governor's seemingly lenient treatment of convicts that went against London's demand for a harsher penal settlement, but his promotion of emancipists like Francis Greenway, the colony's architect, and Dr William Redfern, a magistrate, as well as his encouragement of ex-convict merchants like Simeon Lord and Mary Reibey. Macquarie had even had the audacity to invite these men and women to Government House for dinners and balls.

To some people it seemed strange that Macquarie favoured emancipists, but he had quickly realised in his first years as governor that he needed their expertise and, as a man of humble origins who had risen through the ranks, he knew that men of promise need not be of noble birth. These sort of men and women worked hard once given their freedom, knowing full well that the possibilities available in the colony were more than they could achieve back in the Mother Country.

What mortified Macquarie was that he had to comply with this pompous royal commissioner's directions and give precedence to him. Bigge was an affront and challenge to his authority, and although a stickler for the law, the commissioner sometimes seemed to operate outside it by taking evidence informally, often in private, and making no distinction between sworn and unsworn testimony. He entertained gossip and hearsay, adding them to his increasingly long list of damning criticisms of Macquarie as a person and as governor. Bigge had no idea about the running of a convict colony like New South Wales and was more experienced in the slave colonies of the Caribbean and Mauritius.

Macquarie's fears were realised when Bigge delivered three long reports criticising many aspects of his policies, including his extravagant spending on public works, alleged mismanagement of convicts, and his preference for emancipists, even though he had brought 'peace if not harmony' to the colony. Bigge recommended that the 'wasteful and expensive' building program be curtailed, and that money be spent creating harsher conditions for the convicts. There were many more criticisms, most of them minor.

Macquarie was relieved to see the back of Bigge when he sailed off to London in 1821, and, worn out, was also keen to return to Scotland. Three months after the new governor, Thomas Brisbane, arrived, Macquarie, accompanied by his family, his Indian manservant (a former slave), and many Australian animals and birds, sailed out of Sydney in February 1822, cheered by a 'harbour full of people'.

But the damage Bigge had done to his reputation in London was immense. Macquarie fought for a pension and official recognition of his achievements as governor, but it was a gruelling and frustrating struggle. When he died in 1824, he had still not received his pension.

However, in the colony he was not forgotten. How could he be, given that streets, squares, rivers and buildings were named after him and his wife? But there was something more. Residents knew that although he had viewed the colony as a giant jail, he had seen its potential to be, as he wrote back to his superiors in London, 'one of the greatest and most flourishing Colonies belonging to the British Empire'. Some of the elites had intensely disliked him, especially his favouring of emancipists, but he had shaken Sydney out of its torpor, ridded it of military corruption, and transformed it from a penal settlement into a town.

THE WATERY HEART OF SYDNEY

Mag draws back the curtains from the glass wall. The lights
are on above the Harbour. She speaks triumphantly.
MAG: There! Sydney!

— Patrick White, *Big Toys*

AS THE CRUISE BOAT PULLED OUT OF CIRCULAR QUAY we swayed
slightly in the wash created by a ferry churning to a stop in its
bay. We were setting out on the harbour, accompanied by seagulls
wheeling and squawking overhead. I had been living in Sydney
for months and it was my first time on the harbour. I had been
prodded to go on a sightseeing cruise by an incident earlier in
the year. A Russian cruise ship had docked in the harbour in
January 1979 and a beautiful 18-year-old girl in a red bikini,
Liliana Gasinskaya, squeezed through a porthole, dived into the
water and, after a 40-minute swim, climbed up onto a wharf in
Pyrmont, rushed up to the first person she saw, a man walking his
dog, and in broken English asked for clothes and assistance. She
later asked surprised officials for political asylum. The incident
was on the front page of newspapers across the globe. Later
in the year she was on the cover of the first issue of the men's

magazine, *Australian Penthouse*. Her journey from communism to capitalism had been meteoric. The amusing and outrageous incident (something I thought could only happen in my adopted city) reminded me that if I were to become a Sydneysider, I had to experience the harbour, the very reason for the city's location.

I knew none of the beaches or inlets and only one bay, and that was because of a short story I had read a few years before, called 'The Jumping Jeweller of Lavender Bay'. I asked the guide if we would be going there. He shook his head and shook his head again when I asked if he knew the story by Hugh Atkinson. It was about James Pratt, a middle-aged jeweller living in a stale marriage who takes the ferry from the eponymous bay into the city every workday. One morning he's running slightly late and has to jump onto the ferry instead of using the gangplank. In his simple jump he sees, while in flight, a different plane of existence. There, below him, is a world of golden sand and sitting on a mat, is a beautiful yellow-haired young woman. Each morning after that he waits for the ferry to depart so that he has to jump further, and the longer the jump, the higher he rises to get a better view of that beautiful world. His business starts to decline, his drab marriage collapses. Every morning as he prepares to jump the ferry passengers and bystanders urge him on. Even newspapers report on his strange behaviour. One morning he rushes through a throng of reporters and photographers, leaps towards the departing ferry and, in the arc of his jump, he rises high enough to see further into the enchanting world – where the young woman is beckoning to him – and believes he is finally going to enter it. But he doesn't make the ferry and his body is never found.

For a Melburnian who had never been on a ferry, the story gave these harbour workhorses a magical aura, and as the cruise boat moved out into the deep water, every time I saw a ferry I thought of the story.

We passed the Opera House, whose curvaceous white sails dazzled in the sunlight, then Fort Denison, which looked like a partly submerged castle, and then Clark Island. What I had never seen from shore were all the marinas, pontoons and jetties. Yachts sailed past, as did speedboats and green wooden ferries; a couple of container ships laboriously headed west. On board my boat were Japanese tourists, people from interstate and those who, like me, lived in Sydney but were venturing out onto the harbour for the first time. The sun bounced off the water, whose colour changed from a greenish emerald to an inky blue. I hadn't realised just how many bays and inlets there were and how much of the native bush remained. There were tiny sandy bays between peninsulas, like webbed feet, where men, women and children played or sunbaked as if, on this workday, they didn't have a care in the world. Some peninsulas seemed to elbow their way into the water, others dipped their toes into it, and piers and wharves were like fingers testing the temperature of the harbour while many of the inlets and small bays were coyly elusive, as if you had to go out of your way to find them.

The guide's commentary was broadcast all over the boat and was sometimes accompanied by the Japanese guide. Most of us half-listened until suddenly there was a rush to the starboard side. The guide was pointing out mansions on the slopes of Point Piper and reciting the names of the famous people who lived in them. But what intrigued the tourists most of all was the cost of the houses. The prices awed the sightseers as they gazed, gobsmacked, at the huge houses with their gorgeous gardens, Olympic-size swimming pools and huge bay windows reflecting the sun like golden eyes.

We sailed past Shark Island, Camp Cove and moved towards the Heads. The water became agitated as a strong sea breeze rocked the boat, then we turned and sailed back, hugging the North

Shore. Standing at the bow I looked at the distant city hazy in the sea spray and imagined Governor Phillip and his three rowboats passing through the Heads, where wild seas were pounding the imposing cliffs, and then suddenly finding themselves in this calm, uterine space dotted with islands, and finally discovering the sheltered cove that became the beginning of Sydney.

Those sailors had no idea of the age and formation of what Phillip called 'one of the finest harbours in the world'. The harbour is a drowned ancient river valley carved out of sandstone. The Parramatta River and its tributaries were repeatedly flooded by the ocean during interglacial periods. Up to the end of the last ice age, the sea levels were 100 metres below those of today, and the shoreline was some 30 kilometres further out to sea. Rising temperatures and the thawing of glacial ice raised the ocean to the present-day levels around 6000 years ago. A 2-kilometre wide entrance, framed by North and South Heads, leads to the vast waters of the harbour. Depths vary greatly. The Heads entrance is quite deep, at 35 metres, and just west of the Harbour Bridge is one of the deepest chasms, which is more than 50 metres deep. The North and South Heads guard this beautiful natural harbour, protecting its 245 kilometres of foreshore, its gently sloping ridges, tranquil bays and sandy beaches from gales and ocean swells. There are 50 beaches scattered around the foreshores. Below are underwater canyons, forests of seaweed, sponge gardens and seagrass meadows.

What is little known, even to Sydneysiders, is that there are over 600 species of fish in the harbour. The reeds and kelp forests are home to old wives (their name derives from the grinding noises these distressed fish make with their teeth when they are caught), snapper, mulloway, tarwhine and lower order fishes, leatherjackets and luderick. There is the tasty red morwong, a good substitute for snapper with its red upper body and two horns above the eyes.

Trevally, yellow fin bream, eastern pomfrets and silver batfish are common, as are pufferfish and wrasse.

Wobbegong sharks drift among the rocks or along the seafloor, their fleshy whiskers projecting from the upper lip, waiting patiently to pounce on large fish, even other sharks, and sometimes resorting to cannibalism of smaller wobbegong. There are bull sharks that can turn nasty, Port Jackson sharks that come in to breed, and even the aggressive grey nurse sharks. The colonists of the First Fleet were shaken out of their complacency about the benign nature of the harbour when they saw an Aboriginal woman torn in two by a shark. Over the years sharks have fatally attacked people from Darling Harbour to Middle Harbour. The last fatal attack in the harbour was in 1963. Marcia Hathaway, a 32-year-old actress, was wading in Middle Harbour while on a boating trip with friends when she was savaged by a bronze whaler.

Occasionally a lost or dying whale will come through the Heads. Governor Phillip once interrupted an Aboriginal feast on a dead whale at Manly. In 1811 a black whale was killed near Bennelong Point and, in 1819, boats belonging to Captain Piper, the wealthy party king of Sydney, pursued a whale in the harbour for five hours without success.

Invertebrates outnumber fish, both in varieties and numbers. There are over a thousand species of molluscs. Octopuses and cuttlefish are common. Then there are the snails, sea slugs and chitons clinging to rocky reefs. Crustaceans, like the eastern rock lobsters and prawns, thrive. Mussel and oyster beds once covered the rocky foreshore. Oyster beds were prolific and provided nutritious food for Aboriginal people, who left countless middens of the shells as testament to their fondness for them over hundreds, even thousands of years. Two centuries of city growth almost wiped out the once common Sydney rock oyster

(*Saccostrea glomerata*). The much larger mud oyster (*Ostrea angasi*) had disappeared forever from Sydney Harbour by the 1870s.

What was obvious to the colonists was how important fish were to the clans dotted around the foreshore. There's a painting by Governor Philip Gidley King that shows Indigenous people cooking and eating fish around a campfire soon after the arrival of the First Fleet. The colonists were intrigued that it was the Aboriginal women who fished on the harbour, while the menfolk fished from rocks or the beach. The women paddled their bark canoes (*nawi*) with their hands or using bark scoops, and would sometimes spend long hours dangling shell hooks on lines made of acacia fibre, chewing and spitting out mussels as burley, chanting songs of invitation to the fish. Women did the fishing in canoes while seated next to a fire that smouldered on a hearth of sand or stones. Men used three- or four-pronged fishing spears made of grass tree stems, throwing them from the shoreline or occasionally balancing upright on frail canoes.

Thomas Watling, the convict painter, wrote home to his aunt in Scotland explaining why the women had fragile bark canoes rather than something sturdier:

> Their huts and canoes are extremely rude, but when we consider their non-acquaintance with iron tools, and the hardness of their wood, it is more surprising that they can use it at all – it being so ponderous as to sink immediately in water, renders it entirely useless that way, consequently no succedaneum [substitute] here could be so easily moulded, or so fit for the purposes of forming their little vessels as the bark – and this, both as builders and sailors they manage with a singular dexterity.

The first Australians had lived on the south-eastern edge of Australia for thousands of years before the sea started rising around 11 000 years ago. They were witnesses to the remorseless flooding over generations, having to adapt and gradually move inland, eventually retreating to the foreshores where the waters finally stopped rising. By then, what had been a river valley was a deep, sheltered harbour of coves, headlands and promontories, with three estuarine appendages leading north, north-west and west.

The Eora established territories around the harbour based upon family groups. By the time of the arrival of the First Fleet there were at least eight clans occupying specific parts of its foreshores. These 'saltwater people' gathered much of their food from the harbour and its waterways. The land and harbour itself had great social and spiritual significance.

The sandstone may have been useless for axes or clubs, but it was ideal for engraving, and there were carvings on rock platforms all along the waterways. Many were images of the animals they saw and hunted and which probably served a totemic purpose. Given their reliance on food from the harbour, there were many petroglyphs of fish. Prime examples are an engraving on a headland in Cammeraygal country on the north of the harbour, which illustrates a whale or large fish with a human figure inside and other engravings showing fish, sharks, and what might be a fairy penguin.

For the people of the First Fleet the harbour seemed to have an abundance of food, and one day in 1790 sailors and convicts hauled in 4000 fish. But, as the Eora knew, during the winter months fish could be scarce, as the starving colonists soon discovered, and fish were sought further afield in bays and rivers up and down the coast.

As the colony grew, the harbour became a working port for convict and migrant ships, battle ships, exploration vessels, American whalers and merchant ships. The people who worked around the foreshores were intrinsic to the culture and commerce of Sydney. Boatbuilders were designing and constructing vessels in Sydney Cove within 20 years of the settlement. In 1831 the first steam-powered vessel was seen on the harbour, and soon local shipwrights competed successfully with competition from abroad.

After Circular Quay was completed in 1844, it became the main docking place for shipping, and shipwrights moved further west. Wharves and jetties crowded the shore from the Quay to Pyrmont. For Sydneysiders the ships were links to home, the carriers of news, cargo from across the world, and new settlers. When Joseph Conrad visited in 1880, he declared, 'Circular Quay is the integral part of one of the finest, most beautiful, vast and safe bays the sun ever shone on.'

The traffic on the harbour – incoming, outgoing, and connecting the northern and southern shores – was so active that in the early 1920s the author DH Lawrence wrote of 'huge restless, modern Sydney whose million inhabitants seem to slip like fishes from one side of the harbour to the other'. The poet Kenneth Slessor saw the harbour's many coves and the ferries and skiffs that serviced them as 'a dispersed and vaguer kind of Venice'.

Venice may have its gondolas, but Sydney harbour has its ferries and they have long been one of the city's most distinctive attractions. The ferries were central to a number of novels and stories of the interwar period, including Eleanor Dark's 1938 novel *Waterway*. One of Dark's characters, Lady Hegarty, boards a ferry with a feeling of relief, because,

> For the next three quarters of an hour she had nothing to do but sit still and watch the harbour where, the tall Norfolk pines still stood in the garden of Admiralty house, and the little steps which had intrigued her as a child still lead down to its wharf and the deep water, gold and green over the yellow rocks ...

The bays swung into the land down the long northern shore, Neutral Bay, Shell Cove, Mosman, Clifton Gardens; the red rooms of the houses and the mingled greens of gardens and bushland came down to meet the grey of the rocks at the water's edge.

Ferries from Circular Quay to Manly had started in 1854 and most other ferry services also date from the latter half of the nineteenth century. The ferries didn't distinguish between the residents of harbourside mansions and the tenants of workers' cottages in Watsons Bay and Lavender Bay. For one of Dark's characters:

> Ferries were the friendliest things on the harbour, even in the daytime, but especially at night when everything was so inky dark, so unfamiliar. There they were still, busy and confident, transformed now by the lights which made long pathways of shivering, yellow reflection across the black water; and down the centre of each path blazed one long, magnificent streak of colour – green on the starboard side, red on the port …

In 1904 the ferries carried 9 million passengers, compared to the 30 million carried by rail and 131 million by tram. Sydney's ferries reached their peak annual patronage of 47 million in 1927. It was the bridge that helped reduce harbour congestion. Following its opening in 1932, the number of passengers abruptly fell from 43 million in 1931 to 20 million in 1933.

On 3 November 1927 Sydney witnessed the greatest disaster in the history of its harbour when forty people, including children, were killed in a collision between the Watsons Bay ferry *Greycliffe* and the liner *Tahiti*. The tragedy featured in Dark's *Waterway*, and it preyed on the minds of other writers, too. Christina Stead was living at Watsons Bay at the time and one of her stories in *The Salzburg Tales* (1934) features the ferry disaster. Sumner Locke Elliott's *Careful, He Might Hear You* (1963) ends with a similar event. In Shirley Hazzard's *The Transit of Venus* (1980) the two sisters at the heart of the story are orphaned by a ferry tragedy.

There have been other ferry and boat accidents that resulted in deaths, too numerous to mention. Some were caused by momentary distractions, or naïvety about the waters and the winds, which may not be as savage as those outside the harbour itself, but can still be dangerous. I quickly appreciated the vagaries of the harbour when I learned sailing. Nearing the Heads, the water could be dangerously choppy, the afternoon winds would spring up without warning, so if the yacht's sails were not attuned to the new direction of the winds, it could be difficult to control the boat. One also needed to be constantly aware of other vessels and the ferries, and how a ferry's or speedboat's wake could jostle a small craft so violently there was a danger of falling overboard. At night, one had to be even more aware when navigating the dark waters. It was all too easy for a late-night lark to turn into a disaster.

On a cold night in May 2008, just before 2.30 a.m., a half-cabin work boat collided with a trawler. Six of the 14 mostly young passengers, who had previously been at a party in Balmain, were killed. The man at the helm had been drinking, snorting cocaine and smoking marijuana. It was one of the worst peacetime tragedies on Sydney Harbour.

*

As the city developed, the harbour and the nature of its traffic changed. Tankers and cargo ships became rarer, diverted instead to the huge container terminals at Botany Bay; from the 1960s the numbers of yachts and party boats increased. Industrial parts of the foreshore were turned over to parks and apartments.

When Darling Harbour was transformed as part of the Bicentenary celebrations, its extensive working structures were obliterated. Other rapid transformations of the working waterfront occurred around the harbour.

The finger wharves at Woolloomooloo, Walsh Bay and along the foreshore of Circular Quay, once vital parts of a working harbour, are now home to cultural hubs, posh apartments and restaurants. The development of Barangaroo into exclusive apartments, towering office blocks and a casino has hastened the dramatic renovation of this once enormous section of the working harbour.

The harbour itself has always been a watery garbage tip. In 1910 it was reported that the commissioners of the Sydney Harbour Trust were attempting to minimise the further pollution of the port. In the space of six months 1114 dogs, 375 cats, 946 rats, 63 fowls, three goats, 125 bags of ash, 239 bags of meat, 18 pigs, 8 sheep, 20 rabbits and hares and a sunfish were recovered and removed from the waters. For decades harbour cleaners were towed by a boat on a wooden scow, pulling out rubbish with a gaff. Today dog-boat men in small wooden launches search the sheltered coves and inlets, towing steel scows into which they dump the floating rubbish. They collect tree branches, metal drums, plastic milk crates, clothes, dead animals, plastic bags and hypodermics by the hundreds. Twenty-one men are employed to clear Port Jackson's foreshore and to keep shipping lanes free from navigation hazards including floating fridges, large engines, logs, boats rescued after they have sunk at moorings, as well as hundreds of tyres and cars (fished out by floating cranes), dead pigs and dogs, and tonnes of rubbish and household junk.

The harbour was contaminated by more than 200 years of industry, exposing it to metals, organic waste and microplastics. The *Clean Water Act* of 1970 led to the closure of Sydney's most polluting industries. Now that commercial fishing has been banned, fish stocks have never been higher, especially salmon, kingfish, yakka and tailor. Peer down into the water from any wharf and you'll see big bream cruising around. Slowly the harbour is returning to a pristine cleanliness, though it's still advisable not to eat any fish caught west of the bridge.

*

Two major contaminated sites were Goat Island, once a shipyard and arsenal – originally called Me-Mel and said by Bennelong to have been passed on to him by his father (and recently handed back to the Aboriginal people) – and Snapper Island, an abandoned outcrop in the inner harbour that is being recolonised by sea birds. It was once a naval training base with a distinctive huge ship's mast, now lost. In a 1900 article in the *Sydney Morning Herald* the islands in the harbour were described as 'The amethystine archipelago of happy islands floating peacefully on a turquoise tide.'

All the islands at one time or another were put to use. In the first months of settlement Garden Island served as a kitchen garden for the crew of HMS *Sirius*. Another, further along the harbour, and nearly a hectare in size, was picked as a site for a garden by Lieutenant Ralph Clark, a marine of the First Fleet. At a time of acute rationing and hunger, naval officers were allowed to have their own vegetable gardens, which were worked by convicts. Clark established a garden, but he was frustrated to the point of anger when produce was stolen. As he noted in his diary: 'Some boat had landed since I had been there last and taken away the greatest part … it is impossible for anybody to attempt to raise Garden stuff here, before it comes to perfection they will steal it.'

During the nineteenth century the harbour islands would be used as fortifications, for shipbuilding, laboratories, and as prisons; they would be denuded of trees, and carved up for sandstone to help construct Circular Quay. Garden Island would be connected to the foreshore and Snapper Island radically reshaped.

Governor Phillip eyed a small island (then called Rock Island), named Mat-te-wan-ye by the Gadigal, one kilometre to the east of where the Opera House now stands, as a place of punishment which became known as Pinchgut (now Fort Denison). A few years later Governor Hunter erected a gibbet on it. One convict hanged and then gibbeted there was Francis Morgan. He had been transported to the colony in 1793 for life as punishment for a murder. A man with an uncontrollable temper and brutal impulses, he was executed for bashing Simon Raven to death in Sydney. Morgan's body was hung in chains on Pinchgut. His rotting corpse was not only a warning to those convicts in the settlement but also to those arriving by ship. His skeleton was still hanging there four years after his execution, rattling in the breeze. With the cockiness of the unrepentant criminal, Morgan said to the hangman that the only thing worth mentioning about Pinchgut was the superb view of the harbour from his high elevation, and he was sure there were no more beautiful waters in the world.

Later the island was used for a time gun, for navigational aids and for tide gauge facilities. During the Crimean War in the 1850s, the British colony feared a Russian naval attack. Given Pinchgut's key position just outside Sydney Cove, fortifications were built (urged on by the impatient governor, Sir William Denison) and completed in 1857. One distinctive feature was a Martello tower, the last one built in the British empire.

Like Fort Denison, Garden Island was fortified against a Russian invasion, but its most dramatic transformation occurred during World War II with the construction of a large graving dock and the reclamation of 12 hectares of land connecting the island to the tip of Potts Point. An elaborate tunnel system was built under the island and within it was a power station, offices and air-raid shelters. The wharves of this naval base now stretch the length of the eastern side of Woolloomooloo to the end of the original island, and when the warships are at anchor, this part of the city and the western side of Potts Point reverberate night and day with the vessels' throbbing engines.

Just off Birkenhead Point is Rodd Island, a hunk of rock once known as Snake Island, for obvious reasons. It was named after the Rodd family who lived on the western shore of Iron Cove and used the island for recreation. Less well known is that between 1888 and 1894 it was the headquarters for a scientific research program led by Doctor Adrien Loir, Louis Pasteur's nephew, to find a microbe to control Australia's rabbit plague. The rabbits had become so numerous and so destructive that Henry Parkes, the premier, offered a £25 000 reward to anyone who could solve the problem. Loir's name might well be forgotten except for his relationship with the French actress Sarah Bernhardt.

The most famous actress in the world during the nineteenth century, 46-year-old Bernhardt had arrived in Sydney in 1891 and brought with her more than 100 pieces of luggage and a menagerie of pet animals, including a bear. Loir and the actress met when her dogs, a St Bernard and a pug, were quarantined on the island where Loir was living and working. They quickly became friends and visited each other, either at her rooms at the Hotel Australia or at his house on the island. The romance blossomed but only one thing stood in its way. Bernhardt hated facial hair on men and Loir had a flourishing handlebar moustache. One Sunday the actress told Loir, 'When I come back to the island, if you have shaved off your moustache, I will kiss you.' The young Frenchman, 20 years younger than Bernhardt, didn't need a second invitation and when she returned to Rodd Island, he was clean shaven. Their affair was so passionate that the actress pretended she was ill and cancelled her Brisbane tour. Despite this, Bernhardt, well known for her appetite for young men, women, and even the Prince of Wales, returned to Paris alone – except for her huge retinue of servants and her many animals, which now included a possum and cages of parrots.

After Loir departed and his laboratory was dismantled, a dance floor was installed on the island in the early twentieth century and the place became a Sydney party spot. Throughout the 1920s, 30s and 40s people travelled there for the regular Gypsy Tea Dances.

The largest island in the harbour is one the Gadigal called Wa-rea-mah, now known as Cockatoo Island. When the First Fleet came it was a heavily timbered sandstone knoll. The vegetation is now gone. Once rising 18 metres above sea level, like Fort Denison it provided stone for construction sites around Sydney, including the Circular Quay seawall, and as its height gradually dropped, the island's area was extended by 12 hectares.

In 1839 it was chosen as the site of a new penal institution by Governor George Gipps. Between 1839 and 1869 the island was used as a convict prison, visible from the mainland, its prisoners invisible. Convicts were transferred from grim Norfolk Island to hellish Cockatoo Island. After a few years, prisoners went there from Sydney itself. Some of them were trained to become boxers for the amusement of the guards and the superintendent, others who misbehaved were locked in underground solitary cells no bigger than coffins. One prisoner on Cockatoo Island was the bushranger Captain Thunderbolt, who escaped in 1863 to begin the crime spree that made him famous in the colony. There's a popular legend that his wife swam across to the island with tools to aid his escape, and once he was free, they both swam back to the mainland.

The convicts constructed their barracks and rock-cut silos for storing the colony's grain supply. Between 1847 and 1857, they were used to dig the Fitzroy Dock, Australia's first dry dock, on the island, a back-breaking task not helped by constant hunger and vicious whip-wielding guards. The dock, named in honour of the charismatic Governor Fitzroy, would be modified extensively over the decades and the island would also make room for a second dry dock and shipbuilding facilities. In 1869, the convicts were relocated to Darlinghurst Gaol and the prison complex became an industrial school for girls and a reformatory. In 1913, it became the dockyard of the Royal Australian Navy and during World War I many ships were built, repaired and refitted there. At its peak during the war, some 4000 men were employed on the island.

Many of the islands in the harbour are now idyllic sites for recreation; picnics, cultural events, concerts, camping and parties, their pasts reduced to plaques and historic walking tours.

*

In contrast to all the pleasure-seeking, the harbour is also a death site. People drown in it, accidentally or on purpose; some bodies are plucked from the water, others vanish into a watery grave. Almost from the beginning of white settlement, an abnormally high number of people drowned – they fell off boats, went for a drunken dip, tumbled off jetties unable to swim. In the nineteenth century most people couldn't even tread water, and drownings were frequent.

Suicide by drowning started with convicts who, despairing of their situation, threw themselves in the water seeking oblivion. When the bridge was opened people jumped off it into the waters below, which would invariably kill them. Some jumped off other bridges. In December 1965 a tabloid published a photograph of a naked young woman floating on her back, her body discreetly covered by rippling waves, her face in a state of bliss. She had just unsuccessfully attempted suicide in Middle Harbour.

Not long after I shifted into my present apartment near the top of William Street, on the border of Kings Cross and Woolloomooloo, I frequently ran into Star Delaney, a transgender woman who rented upstairs and seemed to be increasingly troubled. Another tenant who lived across the landing from her began to worry when he hadn't seen her for ten days. After knocking on her door and getting no answer, he had the police break in. There was a suicide note, but no body. She had neatly stacked up everything in her apartment as if ready for the removalists. A policewoman asked if Star had any identifying marks. Her friend said she had a tattoo of the symbol for infinity on her wrist. It didn't take long for the symbol to be matched to a body that had been plucked out of the harbour ten days before. If it hadn't been for the curious neighbour, no one would have claimed her body.

Other bodies, eaten by fish or crabs, or unrecognisable after being in the water too long, are not claimed. Others, like the cartoonist Joe Lynch in 1927, just vanish.

There are two different versions of Joe's death. For his friend, the modernist poet Kenneth Slessor, the cartoonist was on a ferry heading to Milsons Point, his overcoat filled with bottles of beer. When tired of the slow progress of the ferry – 'or even life itself' – he stood up and announced that he could swim to shore faster and dived overboard. A deckhand leaped after him, life belts were thrown. The passengers saw Joe wave cheerfully to them and strike out for the shore, only to vanish. His body was never recovered. Another version has Joe, his overcoat filled with beer bottles, on a ferry to the North Shore. A larger ferry passed his near Bennelong Point, its wake rocking the smaller vessel and, too drunk to steady himself, Joe fell overboard into oblivion.

Joe's death and the fact his body was never found obsessed Slessor, and in the 1930s he began writing a poem about him that would finally be published as 'Five Bells' in 1939. This magnificent long poem is more than just a eulogy for Joe; it's a profound meditation on time and memory, all concentrated in the imagery of the harbour.

*

Painters have long been attracted to the harbour. It was said by the *Bulletin* that it was Arthur Streeton, rather than Governor Phillip, who was 'the discoverer of Sydney Harbour'. Streeton would describe Sydney in lyrical letters as 'a land of passionfruit and poetry', with balmy air under 'a warm palpitating sky'. He was one of the first painters able to capture the cerulean hue of the Sydney sky and sea in paint that would take his name: Streeton Blue. It was a saturated blue colour with gold tones, able to depict both the radiant blue of midday and the soft 'love in a mist' blue of late evening.

During his first visit to Sydney, Streeton had painted Coogee Beach and the Heads, but he returned to Sydney in 1891 and stayed at Curlew Camp on the eastern shores of Mosman Bay, where he joined similar-minded artists living in tents at Little Sirius Bay, painting *en plein air*. Streeton wrote of the gorgeous landscape:

Around the tent climbed the begonia and Clematis and Sarsaparilla the rough winds broken for us by an exquisite fusion of tender gum leaf. Honeysuckle (like the trees of the old asters). Cotton plants heath and a wild cherry (bright green at our tent door) and a beautiful flood beneath. All is splendid.

The other artists included his friend Tom Roberts, Charles Conder, Elioth Gruner and Sydney Long, 'promoting an alternative to the bourgeois lifestyle and escape from suburban conservatism'. An artist would land at the Musgrave Street wharf and follow the track across Curraghbeena Point to the shore opposite the camp, then cry out 'Coo-ee'. On hearing the coo-ee, a boat would set out across the bay from the camp to pick up the visitor.

Many artists down the years have been entranced by the harbour. Brett Whiteley had a house in Lavender Bay and his studio overlooked the harbour. A busy social scene revolved around the Whiteley house with a constant stream of international visitors, including artists and film stars. Parties were loud with lots of drinks and recreational drugs, and his Lavender Bay paintings evoke a Dionysiac vision of life. His numerous harbour paintings show the water as electric blue, almost like something out of a technicolour movie. Nearly all of them are framed by the interior of the house, looking out, as if the artist is afraid to venture into the world, not so much showing us the real harbour, but his solipsistic vision of it.

His friend Peter Kingston gives us something closer to the truth in his paintings. He grew up in Watsons Bay and lived opposite Luna Park. His most important influence was Whiteley, whom he thought, 'Full of energy, quick, like mercury.' But Whiteley's narcissistic self-infatuation collapsed into a brittle mannerism that tilted towards the grotesque. This was far from

Kingston's vision. He looked closely at the environment of the harbour, its bays, work boats, wharves, boathouses, the night ferries lit up like Christmas trees (sometimes uncannily empty, as in reality). His harbour waters are alive, fluid, mobile, not like Whiteley's dead water. At times there is pathos and mystery in the small white wakes left by vessels beyond the frame, but there is a curiosity and a generosity in his work, as if the harbour itself has determined his character and life.

Like these painters, everyone has their Sydney Harbour. For Herman Kant, writing in *Walkabout* magazine in 1973, Sydney is 'a city pierced by the sea ... and shaped by water – it has hewn the character of the city's buildings – and its people ... man and nature each leave their mark on the other'.

There's no doubt that the harbour has shaped the city and its people. Its beauty is obvious, and its many bays, inlets and peninsulas give the foreshores a fluid shape, where one can never be sure what will be around the next turn. The two great structures, the bridge and the Opera House, mimic the curvaceous shapes of the hills and slopes of the harbour that seem to rise up out of the sea mist.

The harbour is an essential part of the city, its watery heart. At times just to stare at it is to be mesmerised by its shifting colours and wave patterns. It's a playground of hedonist activities, like sailing and swimming, and recreational events like Sydney's New Year's Eve celebrations and the start of the Sydney Hobart Yacht Race. One scoop of land like Walsh Bay can contain a hub of high art, theatre, music and dance while looking across the harbour at the huge grinning face of Luna Park, a tribute to popular culture. To sail on this magnificent cathedral of water is to breathe in the briny essence of Sydney.

DISTRACTIONS

OBED WEST WAS BORN IN 1807 TO CONVICT PARENTS who worked hard and eventually owned a huge property, 'Barcom Glen', surrounded by Darlinghurst, Paddington and Rushcutters Bay. He became an unforgettable presence in Sydney at 193 centimetres tall and weighing just over 100 kilograms. A successful farmer and land speculator, in old age he was to prove he was also possessed of an astonishing memory. In 1882 he recalled in detail the George Street of the first decades of the nineteenth century.

He structured his memories around a walk along George Street from the Rocks to its southern end in Haymarket, and the result gives a vivid picture of Sydney slowly finding its identity separate from the Mother Country. Sydney Cove had one public wharf, King's Wharf, which was sufficient for unloading the ships that arrived at irregular intervals. For the young Obed, the boat-building around the cove was a desultory affair that seemed to lack any sense of urgency. Every week convicts would congregate outside the Government Storehouse to get their rations.

What attracted the young Obed was the post office, run by Isaac Nichols, once the superintendent of convicts, now postmaster. The whole town would pick up letters from his house and, as there was no postage, everyone had to pay cash for the letters they received and those they sent. A little further on was the Government Printer, George Howe, and just beyond his building on the corner of Essex Street was a large paddock. This was only one of many paddocks that pockmarked the long main thoroughfare. Most, if not all, of the houses and shops were set back from the street; many had gardens with fruit trees, cedar or oak trees, even Norfolk pines. Mrs Edwards kept her cows in one large paddock in Barrack Lane, and this was one of the first dairies in the colony. There were a couple of butchers, several solicitors and bakeries along the way. But as Obed observed, 'the business done at this time was not great, and a spectator could almost at any time during the day count the number of people engaged in and about the business centre'.

The centre of business activity was the market on the corner of George and Market streets. It was enclosed by a four-railed fence, with the entrance gates between George and York streets. Along York Street were sheds in which 'all manner of wares were exhibited and sold'. The carts bringing goods from outside the town were arranged along George Street.

At the southern end of the market were the Central Police Offices, which had originally been built by Macquarie for a butter market, but had been converted into a police station. It was close to the pillories, a source of entertainment for shoppers and gawkers. The wooden pillory could accommodate two people at a time, and in Market Street there were four stocks. These were placed on a frame raised about 2.4 metres high, to give the spectators a better view of the tormented victims.

Where the Town Hall is now was the burial ground, and Thomas Dick lived next to it in a wattle-and-daub cottage with a thatched roof. His job was to herd the cattle belonging to the townspeople to the outskirts to graze. A solitary man, his murdered body was found in the harbour at the foot of Bathurst Street. Having no relatives in the colony, his land reverted to the

Crown and Macquarie set it aside for an Anglican cathedral, St Andrew's, which took decades to build.

South of Bathurst Street was considered the manufacturing part of Sydney, with a brewery, a tannery, clay for making pipes, a bakehouse and granary (which doubled as a theatre, according to Obed, where 'many terrible blood and thunder tragedies were enacted with the price of admission being a dump cut out of a holey dollar'). Further on were blacksmiths, a wheelwright, a cabinet-maker, a small steel mill, and many impoverished Sydneysiders living in humble wattle-and-daub houses with thatched roofs. A bridge had been erected over a creek flowing from Elizabeth Street that crossed George Street.

In the journey south Obed remembered the impressive number of public houses: The Cat and Fiddle, Hen and Chickens, The Bull's Head, Manchester Arms, White Swan, Royal Oak, Spotted Dog, The Black Swan, The Dog and Duck Inn, and The Harp.

Down at Haymarket Square was the government brickworks and near it the tollgate to Parramatta. Beyond this there were no more houses, but there was a large pond that spread over Dr Harris's 'Ultimo' estate. It was noted for its ducks and teal and, according to Obed, provided 'many a good day's shooting'.

One sport he did not mention that became one of Sydney's favourites was boat racing. In 1818, for a sizeable prize, four boats raced from Bradley's Head (Booraghee) into the cove (a distance of three and a half miles or 5.6 kilometres), taking 15 minutes to do so. Three of the competitors were captains of ships anchored in the harbour. Captain Piper, a military officer and the colony's collector of customs duties, was the winner.

Under Macquarie, racing, cricket and athletic tournaments were fostered, but he brought in laws against bare-knuckle fighting, which nevertheless continued in bushland near the brickfields or across the harbour. Cockfighting remained popular, and there were secret bouts of bull baiting where, as one report put it, spectators 'were amused by the diversion, in the course of which a number of dogs were killed or crippled'.

For the elite of the town there were balls and parties. Isaac Nichols and his wife, Rosanna, were very popular, and their home was a centre of social activities. A typical ball was held in late summer 1813 for 50 men and women. 'One of the most pleasing private entertainments that we have for some time witnessed,' reported the *Sydney Gazette*. Not long after seven in the evening there was spirited country dancing and after that, 'a cold collation, elegant and sumptuous – the wines were exquisite'. There were innumerable enthusiastic royal toasts, then more dancing and drinking until four in the morning.

Then, of course, there were the popular Sunday promenades in Hyde Park, which would begin at 5.30 in the evening, except during heat waves, when they would start at 6.30. Men and women walked and talked and listened to the military bands. Fashionable women wore silks and panjums and palempores – dresses which showed Sydney's reliance on the trade from India. The less wealthy wore prints and turkey-coloured or black-checked ginghams and straw bonnets. Topaz was fashionable for brooches and pins.

Foreign visitors were a welcome distraction. When *L'Uranie* sailed into Sydney Cove in late 1819 it was greeted with gun salutes. The captain, Louis de Freycinet, had been in Sydney way back in 1802 as a member of Baudin's expedition. The Sydney he encountered this time had been transformed.

He was leading a scientific expedition that would circum-navigate the world. The voyage had already received some notoriety back in France because Louis' wife, Rose, was on board. It was illegal to have a woman on a navy vessel, so she had disguised herself as a man, but disembarking from *L'Uranie* in Sydney, she wore a dress. Also on board was the only civilian, Jacques Arago, a botanical artist. He wrote in his *Voyage autour de monde* that he was 'astonished' at how quickly Sydney had become 'a flourishing city'. He couldn't contain his admiration for the 'Magnificent hotels, majestic mansions, houses of extraordinary taste and elegance, fountains ornamented with sculptures worthy of our best artists ... rich furniture, horses, carriages ... immense storehouses ... the streets wide and straight,' and mused how amazing it was to find such a beautiful city so distant from Europe.

What also stunned Arago was how nonchalant Sydneysiders seemed to be when passing or talking to Aboriginal people in the streets who paraded 'their disgusting ... hideous nakedness'. If that wasn't enough, he was invited to a rich merchant's house to witness naked Aboriginal men, armed with spears and clubs and fortified by liquor, fighting one another. What disturbed him was that the spectacle was eagerly witnessed by girls aged 15 to 18 'encouraging' the fighters. On another night he witnessed a brutal fight between Aboriginal men in the backyard of a pub.

These spectacles were a popular feature of Sydney life. Back in 1814 Alexi Rossiisky, a Russian who came to Sydney on the *Suvorov*, attended a fight in Sydney between 50 Aboriginal men, all naked, each carrying three spears, a shield and a club. The furious and bloody battle was witnessed by local Aboriginal people and whites. The Russian was dumbfounded by the brutality of it all:

> It is impossible to imagine the fury and abandon with which
> they attacked and beat one another and fought back ... some
> were beaten to death by blows to the temples, [there was the]
> clash of shields, wild cries of the victors, the piteous howls of
> the wounded, the bloodied faces and broken limbs.

The contest lasted for two hours and what appalled him was how the whites egged on the fighters. 'It is frightening to think how unsparing the British are of humanity. It has become an enjoyable form of entertainment to watch the torments of their fellow mortals'.

Arago was of the same mind, repulsed by the way Sydneysiders embraced these base entertainments, and how they would give the Aboriginal men alcohol in order that they would lose control during clashes that often became fights to the death. He wondered how 'culpable are the English for not checking these disorders'.

Rose Freycinet's experience of Sydney did not take in such violent spectacles. She and her husband were overwhelmed with invitations to balls and dinners. In her letters she mentions how she mingled with the elite, including Elizabeth Macquarie (Macquarie himself was said to be unwell). There was a party at Captain Piper's 'country seat'. Because his mansion was unfinished, the dancing was held in the garden, overlooking the harbour. There was a reception at a prominent lawyer's, dinner parties, balls, one 'a brilliant affair'. She visited the Government Houses in Sydney and Parramatta, the Botanic Gardens, and the 'peculiar' Government Stables, the 'very fine' Convict Barracks, and she thought the new hospital was 'magnificent'. There were suppers with their tedious long-winded speeches and much dancing even when 'it seemed too hot to dance'.

She and Louis were taken special care of by the Fields. They were a cultivated couple. The husband, Barron Field, was a judge and fancied himself as a poet, with two poems included in George Howe's *First Fruits of Australian Poetry*, published that year. Field had once met Wordsworth, but nothing of the romantic poet's talent rubbed off on him and his creaky verses were quickly lampooned as 'Barren'. Both he and his wife, Jane, spoke French, and Rose was particularly impressed by Jane's extensive knowledge of French literature. Her husband was much more impressed by Jane's 'ravishing ankle'.

The Freycinets' praise of Sydney was only tempered by two incidents. One was when their collection of silver plates was stolen. As Rose remarked ruefully, 'It would be astonishing not to find thieves here as it would be not to meet Parisians in Paris and an Englishman in England.' The other was when *L'Uranie* set sail for Europe and Louis discovered ten Irish convicts had stowed away on board. Not willing to waste time returning them, he set them to work as crew.

Like Arago, Rose was 'very sorry' to leave Sydney after her month-long stay. She and her husband, like the Russians of the *Suvorov* five years before, would always remember the rapturous reception given to them by the locals (the Russian crew had been carried off their ship and taken to hotels to get riotously drunk) and the impressive progress of Sydney.

*

Another woman impressed by young Sydney was Lady Amelia Forbes. When she first saw the harbour in 1824, she was entranced by the scene that met her:

> How can I describe my sensations upon that eventful morning? There being very little wind, it took us nearly two hours to sail up the harbour to our anchorage at Sydney Cove, during the whole of which time fresh beauties in scenery arrested our attention. The numerous bays, the white sandy beaches, and the green-capped islets made a picture more like a glimpse of fairyland than actual reality. And this paradise was to be our home!

In her memoir *Sydney Society in the Days of the Crown Colony*, Amelia writes about Sydney with a mixture of bemusement and excitement. What she wasn't prepared for were the duels. With a sense of irony, she describes two, saying, 'duels at this time were not infrequent, though I never heard of anyone being damaged'. But there was one 'that much disturbed our social circle'. That duel was between the attorney-general, Saxe Bannister, and Dr Wardell, who insinuated that Bannister took his legal instructions from the governor. The parties met at daybreak and shots were exchanged with bullets perforating the clothes of both men. Then there was the duel between her 'very intimate friend', the explorer and surveyor-general, Thomas Mitchell, and Stuart Donaldson, who later became the first premier of New South Wales. Three shots were fired, one of which just missed Mitchell's ear, and one went through Donaldson's hat. By then the seconds had had enough and stopped the duel.

Lady Forbes and her husband, a judge, were invited to government levees, balls and dinner parties. Many 'brilliant receptions and balls' were held at Government House, where guests spilled out onto the lawns that extended all the way to Sydney Cove. One especially memorable occasion was a ball and supper given by Ralph Darling, who followed Brisbane as governor in 1825, and his wife, Eliza. At around eight o'clock coaches 'conveying beauty and fashion', came up the driveway. The ballroom was 'brilliant with chandeliers'. Trellis arches of Gothic design were intertwined with laurel leaves and roses that made the room 'resemble a bower of flowers'. There was a sumptuous dinner, after which 40 ladies and gentlemen danced French quadrilles in the ballroom 'until the close approach of the Sabbath morn made the elated group disperse for more solemn duties'.

If anyone represented the elegance and high spirits of an optimistic Sydney it was Captain Piper. Born in 1773, he came to the colony with the New South Wales Corps in 1792. He was an immediate social hit, gregarious and generous, with a penchant for pleasure and the eager pursuit of happiness. In 1801 he acted as Macarthur's second in a duel with Colonel Paterson and was sent to Norfolk Island for six years for his trouble. There he was acting commandant and became the lover of 15-year-old Mary Ann Shears, the daughter of a convict. He returned with her to Sydney and later in 1813 resigned from the Corps and was appointed a naval officer. His responsibilities included the collection of customs duties, excise on spirits and harbour dues, and control of lighthouses. All this proved very lucrative, with Piper taking a sizeable, if sometimes illegal, percentage of all monies collected.

Three years later he was granted 77 hectares of land on Eliza Point, now Point Piper, and there he built his stately pleasure dome overlooking the harbour. 'Henrietta Villa' was notable for its large ballroom adorned with a cupola. The interior was fitted out in luxurious fashion and the constant stream of guests either took a boat to the property, sometimes accompanied by Piper's personal band of musicians, or rode in a carriage along the South Head Road to the isolated villa. There were glittering balls, elaborate dinner parties and musical evenings. Piper and his seemingly permanently pregnant Mary Ann (she had 13 children) were the perfect host and hostess, the cynosure of Sydney society.

In a period of a few years Piper, in what seemed a frantic state of elation, bought up land in what were to become the western suburbs, in the North Shore, Rose Bay, Botany Bay, and even Bathurst. But by 1827 he was financially stretched and in the following year he was found to have gravely mismanaged the finances of his office and was suspended. Now he had no money coming in and creditors were after him. He was in despair, but

continued to entertain lavishly. One evening he invited guests for
dinner and, after excusing himself, gathered his musicians and
ordered them onto a large barge. He directed it towards the Heads,
ordering the band to play some of his favourite tunes and then,
near the windy Heads, he jumped overboard into the churning
waves. The musicians, at risk to their own lives, retrieved him
with difficulty.

They sailed back to Eliza Point where Piper marched off the
barge and returned to the dining room, his wet and dishevelled
appearance causing 'a sensation' among the shocked guests.
Further humiliation followed when he had to sell 'Henrietta Villa'
and most of his other properties before shifting out to Bathurst.

Piper's rise and fall became a template for many spendthrifts
and risk-taking Sydney developers right down to today, those
whose fortunes fluctuate wildly but, while on top, provide Sydney
with glamour, glitz and the dizzy promise of material happiness.
Their optimism and revelling in pleasure rub off on others. As one
society woman lamented of Piper, 'the want of animation created
by the absence of a well-known public favourite' was felt by many
and specially 'his ladies [who] regretted the absence of that star'.

Lady Amelia Forbes was to survive her husband, who died
in Newtown after a long illness in 1841. He had been a highly
respected chief justice, and a street in Woolloomooloo was named
after him.

THE SHAME OF CLONTARF

FEW PEOPLE LIVING ON THE OTHER SIDE OF THE HARBOUR have heard of Clontarf. Nestled between the Spit Bridge and Manly on the North Shore, it has to be sought out. On the shoreline there is a narrow strip of sand and 300 metres of level land that rises suddenly in a cliff face so vertiginous that recently a man fell to his death from a rock ledge while gardening. From the beach you look up to what resembles an amphitheatre of green haze, trees and tamed bush and shrubs that successfully hide its many mansions, some costing $10 million or more. This 'hidden gem', as the real estate agents call it, seems so peaceful, yet it was once considered the most shameful suburb in Sydney.

The secluded stretch of flat land is sprinkled with Moreton Bay and Port Jackson fig trees, their sprawling canopies giving much needed shade. Norfolk pines, their razor-sharp outlines etched against an intense blue sky, line a beach of white sand facing the tranquil waters of Middle Harbour. Although Manly, and the Pacific Ocean, are ten minutes away by car, this cove has none of Manly's tacky apartment blocks, tourists, volleyball courts appropriating the beach, or unremarkable restaurants with bored staff touting for diners.

I am visiting Clontarf with the painter Craig Handley. He's a friend who lives in Woolloomooloo and drinks with me at the

Old Fitzroy Hotel. He knows Clontarf and intends to sketch it, perhaps for a painting. I wanted to write about a suburb on the North Shore and decided I liked the name of Clontarf. No one at the pub had any idea where Clontarf was, and when I asked around, only Craig knew. It's difficult to get to by public transport and Craig drives, which is handy for me. His present interest is Australian beach scenes, so we have come to the right place.

It's a hot and humid weekday and there is a noticeable lack of men. Women are either in the shallow water of the shark netted enclosure playing with their children or lying on the sand sunbaking under a brilliant blue sky like suburban sybarites, maybe the perfect subjects for one of Craig's paintings. Nearby, on the northern corner, is a clutter of imposing yachts and speedboats. Across the waters to the west is the Spit Bridge and beyond it, the suburb of Seaforth. To the south, through the heat haze, is the wide entrance to Middle Harbour between Grotto Point and Middle Head (Gubbuh Gubbuh).

In his exploration of Middle Harbour in April 1788, deputy Judge Advocate David Collins saw 'the forests of unsettled country' and noted, with something akin to horror, 'the bare idea of being lost in them; as from the great similarity of one cove to another'. As far as he was concerned the area 'did not promise to be of any benefit to the settlement'.

But by the late nineteenth century Middle Harbour had become a hugely popular place to visit. For the *Illustrated Sydney News* of 15 December 1866, 'The delights of Middle Harbour include making up a party and chartering a small steamer to visit the spot ... a good day's trip to skirt its shores and explore all the numerous bays and inlets which form a part of it.' On Sundays and holidays steamers ran from Circular Quay to the Spit, where boats could be hired to continue further up Middle Harbour, where nature was untouched and beautiful. 'Here,' one writer observed, 'we have the true primeval solitude ... we might be hundreds of miles from any civilised habitation.'

It was remote enough from central Sydney that Cockfighter's Point was a place where the sport could be indulged without interference from the authorities, as was bare-knuckle boxing. In the late 1840s hundreds, if not thousands, of men would sail up Middle Harbour to watch illegal fights. In 1847 an indignant *Sydney Morning Herald* called the bouts 'scandalous outrages', with both the spectators and boxers 'deserving the name of neither Christians nor gentlemen'.

The most popular destination in Middle Harbour was Clontarf. Its flat sandy shore made it an ideal picnic spot. By the early 1860s it was, said the *Sydney Morning Herald*, 'the oldest and also the largest most sheltered pleasure grounds in the harbour'.

The growth of the middle classes in late nineteenth-century Sydney meant more people had more time for leisure, and pleasure grounds sprang up around the harbour. One of the earliest examples was Cremorne Gardens, established in 1856 and named after similar gardens in London. Perhaps the most popular were the pleasure gardens at Clontarf run by the Moore family for over three and a half decades. At first the Moores supplied only hot water and basic shelters from the sun, but as the years went by, and competition from other pleasure grounds increased, Clontarf offered bars, dining rooms and dance halls. Quoits, skittles and cricket bats were available for hire. Bands played all day and people danced. Food and drink, including alcohol and 'temperance' beverages, were available. There were tightrope walkers, jugglers, and such bizarre stunts as attempting to cross the harbour in a tub drawn by six geese. The temperance drinks were especially popular with church organisations, which would sometimes entertain up to 3000 people.

On Boxing Day 1870, over 6000 people visited the opening of the dancing pavilion. By this stage there were cricket pitches, running tracks, shooting galleries, swings, razzle dazzles and donkey rides.

So it was no wonder that Clontarf was chosen for a picnic in honour of the first British royal to tour Australia, Prince Alfred, Duke of Edinburgh, the second son of Queen Victoria. The occasion would make Clontarf's name infamous throughout Australia, Britain and Ireland.

My own visit to Clontarf is 150 years to the day, almost to the hour, since 12 March 1868, when 35-year-old Henry O'Farrell, born in Ireland but raised in Australia from the age of eight, waited impatiently for the prince to arrive. He was wearing a new suit, and in his pockets were two revolvers. The day before he had practised target shooting in Waverley and had surprised himself with his perfect aim.

His life in Melbourne had been one of melancholia and failure. He had wanted to become a priest but failed. He fell into debt after losing several jobs and took to drink. A year before Alfred's Australian tour, O'Farrell suffered a severe mental breakdown with bouts of delirium tremens and fell into prolonged periods of paranoia, during which he threatened to shoot people. He left Melbourne and travelled to Sydney with money his sister had given him. At first he stayed at the Clarendon Hotel on the corner of Hunter and George streets, but because of his strange behaviour, muttering loudly to himself, talking endlessly about the Fenian movement and how the British had wronged Ireland, he was forced to shift further along Hunter Street to the corner of Pitt, where he booked into the Currency Lass Hotel. He spent hours jotting down a stream of consciousness of unconnected thoughts, concluding that 'Vengeance for Ireland is sweet.' The Fenians had staged an unsuccessful revolt in Ireland the year before, but

O'Farrell took it on himself to avenge this failure by assassinating the Duke of Edinburgh. He wrote letters to newspapers and relatives in Dublin telling them what he intended to do, believing that by the time the letters arrived he would be dead.

He was tempted to shoot Prince Alfred at Circular Quay, but the time wasn't opportune, just as it proved difficult to gain entry to a ball held in Hyde Park. But Clontarf was easy to get to, it only took a ferry ride. Now all he had to do was be patient. The picnic had been organised as a fundraiser for the Sydney Sailors' Home by barrister and politician William Manning, and it attracted a crowd of over 3000 Sydneysiders eager to get a glimpse of the royal.

Alfred was 23 years old, conceited, wilful, and with a grandiose sense of entitlement. He had been living such a debauched life with dubious friends that a worried Queen Victoria decided to send him to the bottom of the world in the hope of removing him from temptation and teaching him how to behave like a royal. It was the longest and most dangerous royal tour ever undertaken.

The prince's retinue included a Scottish piper and a pet monkey. Australians greeted him everywhere he went with parades, banquets, the laying of foundation stones, fireworks, tours, and shooting parties where he could bag possums and rabbits to his heart's content. Despite shooting hundreds of our local fauna, he made it clear that he missed the thrill of killing elephants as he had done in South Africa on his way out from England. One consolation was that in Australia he could indulge in his favourite recreation of bedding attractive women, married or not. Sydney greeted him with massive and adoring crowds of 50 000 in the Domain and another 50 000 at a fireworks display in his honour.

His intention was to spend as little time as possible at Clontarf because he wanted to explore the rest of Middle

Harbour. His ferry arrived just after two and the prince stepped ashore to a rapturous reception. He walked along the beach to where 300 Aboriginal people were ready to perform a corroboree and present an exhibition of boomerang throwing. O'Farrell squeezed through the crowd and caught up with the prince just ahead of him. When he was some two metres away, he pulled out his Smith and Wesson and fired a shot into the prince's back. The royal fell, screaming out, 'Good God, my back is broken!' At first the spectators thought it was fireworks, but Manning, who was accompanying the prince, immediately realised what had happened. He tackled O'Farrell to the ground, unable to stop him firing off two more shots. One bullet hit the ankle of George Thornton, the former Sydney mayor.

Close by was Thornton's daughter, who later reported in her diary:

> It's impossible to imagine what a shock it was to us unless you had been there. It was an awful moment. What I see most vividly in my mind is our noble prince falling [on to] his hands and knees and then over on his back, look up and muttering two dreadful 'Ohs'. I only have a dim recollection of a revolver being held close to the prince's back but I did not see the man at all. [When she saw her father limping] I almost screamed out 'ah Papa what is the matter' and he said, 'I'm shot. I'm shot.'

A woman cried out 'The Prince is shot!' Others joined in: 'He is shot and has fallen down dead.' 'The Duke is killed!' Men and women cried, some fainted. Amid the confusion and distress Alfred was carried to a tent where doctors examined him as he groaned in pain and pleaded for air. Outside the cry went up, 'Kill the wretch!'

The crowd attacked O'Farrell wanting, as one newspaper reported, 'to tear him limb from limb'. People shouted and screamed, 'Lynch him!', 'Hang him!', 'String him up!' He fought wildly as men punched and kicked him and women threatened to kill him with their scissors.

By the time he was carried to the wharf most of his clothing had been torn off, his eyes were blackened, his face and body badly bruised and he was bleeding from several wounds. When he was placed on the deck of the steamer *Paterson* he was unconscious. But no sooner was he on board than a number of sailors prepared a rope to lynch him, and were only stopped when Chief Justice Lord Newry intervened. The prince was rushed to Sydney in another steamer and taken to Government House to be examined and operated on by surgeons, who discovered that the bullet had just missed his spine and major organs after being deflected by the cross-over of his Indian rubber braces.

His luck held. Five days before, the first professional nurses had arrived in Sydney after being trained by Florence Nightingale, and they tended the prince night and day. During the two weeks he remained in his makeshift ward, he was entertained by the band from his ship and people took turns to use large fans to ward off the mosquitoes which were 'positively maddening'.

The day after the attempted assassination nearly 20 000 people attended what was called 'an indignation meeting' in the Domain. The anger was fuelled by a sense of wounded national pride, fear and horror. 'The Shame of Clontarf' devastated Sydney and the rest of the country. As *Empire* put it:

This can at least be understood – that the deplorable disgrace
to this colony – that it should have harboured such a wretch as
this murderer to violate its hospitality, must rest upon this part
of the country for a long time to come.

Fenians were regarded as terrorists are viewed today, and even though O'Farrell claimed he belonged to the organisation, his membership was entirely imaginary. The shooting resulted in vitriolic abuse towards Catholics and the Irish. There had always been a fear of Irish insurrection since the days of the First Fleet, and Catholic convicts had been forced to attend Church of England services. O'Farrell's actions would entrench decades of sectarian distrust and abuse.

The Irishman seemed remarkably calm in Darlinghurst Gaol and during his trial. When he was questioned about why he had shot the prince, he replied, 'Come, come, it is not fair to ask me such a question as the prince is all right – the prince will live, you need not fear about him – it's only a side wound. I shall be hanged but the prince shall live.'

He was proved right. Despite attempts for him to be spared on the grounds of insanity, as well as Alfred's plea for a stay of execution until he received advice from his mother, O'Farrell was found guilty of attempted murder and hanged.

In his book *Cruise Around the World 1869–70*, James Bruce, a Royal Navy lieutenant, described how Clontarf had become a place of:

> ... world-wide reputation ... the chosen ground of the would-be assassin ... and how close the picnic spot has come to being as famous as the Washington Theatre, with him succumbing to the same fate as Abraham Lincoln and Henry O'Farrell as notorious as John Wilkes Booth.

In *An Illustrated Guide to Sydney, 1882*, Clontarf could not escape its infamy and is described as a 'favourite place of recreation ... possessing a melancholy interest in being the scene of the attempt on the life of the Duke of Edinburgh'.

Today there are two aluminium panels attached to a cottage on the beach at Clontarf and inscribed with the events of that day. Few people read them as most are intent on picnicking, swimming or sunbaking. It was eerie to stand where the attempted assassination took place, but the sun had drenched all mystery from the deed, and the women in their bikinis were at odds with the image of formal Victorian suits, top hats and heavy frocks of that day 150 years ago.

Just when the stigma attached to Clontarf was fading, on Boxing Day 1880 a bored journalist decided to visit the famous pleasure grounds. William Traill, a leader writer for the young *Bulletin* magazine, hadn't been there before and was shocked by what he witnessed, '[I had] dropped into the middle of a saturnalia of vice ... such open, reckless and flagrant immorality as I had never before had any notion of.'

A few days later he wrote an editorial headed 'The Larrikin Residuum' and was unrestrained in his outrage:

> [The] intemperance and ravages of excesses ... [and] worse
> still, amidst the flushed, panting, bevy of young girls, clinging
> in romping abandon to promiscuous partners, were some
> unworn childish faces with the devil's mark not yet stamped
> on their foreheads – but obviously preparing to have the
> seal set on them before another day ... The males barely
> restrained themselves to a semblance of decency – the females
> resented no familiarity. The devil had broken loose.

The brothers Thomas and William Moore, who ran the grounds, sued the *Bulletin* for £1000 in damages. Many witnesses were called during the trial and nearly half agreed with Traill's assessment. It was said that earlier in the year a Sunday school group, caught up in a crowd of 2500, had been frightened by the unruly behaviour of a mob of larrikins. Witnesses for the *Bulletin* had seen rowdiness and people swimming in the nude and heard obscene language. One man, John Joseph Horan, said that at Clontarf there were 'greater facilities for vice and immorality down the harbour in consequence of there being much more bush and scrub, than in any other picnic grounds'. In contrast witnesses for the Moores said they had never noticed any bad or rowdy behaviour at the pleasure grounds.

The jury returned a verdict for the Moore brothers with damages of one farthing. The problem for the owners of the *Bulletin*, JF Archibald and John Haynes, was that the judge ordered them to pay the fees of the solicitors and counsel on both sides, a total of £1500. It was a prohibitive amount of money and supporters of the *Bulletin* could only raise £800. Haynes and Archibald were arrested in March 1882 and the two men walked from George Street up to Darlinghurst Gaol, followed by a huge crowd of supporters and journalists. It took them two hours because they frequently stopped at hotels along the way for drinks. The pair spent two months in the debtors' prison until the extra money was raised. On release, newsmen greeted the two men at the jail gates and accompanied them in a triumphal walk into town, which became a bar crawl, stopping at hotels until they ended up at the Royal George Hotel thoroughly drunk.

Even though they didn't publicly admit it, the Moore brothers realised that some of the evidence against them had an element of truth, and so they organised that one of the brothers, or an employee, would stand guard at the ferry terminal at Circular Quay, making sure larrikins and unsavoury types didn't embark for Clontarf. The next year Manly pleasure gardens had to deal with 400 larrikins causing a riot, some of them the same offenders at the Clontarf disturbances

The trouble was that the court case had damaged Clontarf's reputation and it was now in competition with Correy's Gardens, the pleasure grounds at Cabarita on the Parramatta River. It promoted family fun with merry-go-rounds, swings and every luncheon table decorated with flowers grown on site. Its dance hall had a special timber floor and the bands that played there were some of the best in Sydney. You could wade into the calm water, swim, fish, catch prawns, go rowing, listen to a ten-piece string orchestra or an opera company, buy fresh fruit, vegetables and flowers grown on the grounds and in the summer months dance under the stars. As commentators approvingly remarked, at Correy's Gardens 'the best order prevailed' and there was no 'rowdyism'.

In the early years of the twentieth century Clontarf's added attractions included an 'aeronaut' who, on his first attempt, rose into the sky, gave a trapeze display and then parachuted from the balloon into Middle Harbour, only to find himself surrounded by sharks. Terrified, he escaped by swimming frantically to the closest beach, far from the pleasure grounds. By the turn of the twentieth century the crowds were dwindling, aside from a brief revival in 1909, when a group of Māori built a traditional village, performed hakas and dances, sold souvenirs and showed their curious audiences their methods of cooking.

But pleasure grounds were becoming a thing of the past. At Tamarama Beach Wonderland City was launched in 1906, promoting itself as the largest open-air amusement park in the southern hemisphere. People could ride in a balloon, take a trip in an enormous miniature train on a two-mile (3.2 kilometre) switchback railroad around the cliff top, stroll across a bridge built over an artificial lake, rollerskate, or enjoy themselves at a shooting gallery. The whole area had so many gaily coloured electric lamps that it was dubbed 'Fairy City'. It only lasted five years, and by the end of World War I, pleasure gardens were no longer popular.

After the war there were calls for the state government to buy Clontarf for public recreation. As one nostalgic supporter said, 'Clontarf is the most ideal picnic ground around Sydney and with a few improvements could be made a harbour paradise.' The government wasn't interested and subdivided the land.

It didn't sell and during the Great Depression of the 1930s the area between the present-day marina and Clontarf Point became a tent city of the unemployed. Tents were created out of the surrounding bush, covered with hessian coated with a mixture of whitewash, lime and fat to make it weatherproof. Later in the 1940s it was said you couldn't give the land away. But by the late 1950s it began to flourish as a safe, conservative, family-orientated suburb attracting the middle to upper middle classes, but if it thought it could escape notoriety, history was to toy with Clontarf one last time.

In June 1960 the first prize in the Opera House lottery was £100000 (about $3 million today), and it was won by Bazil Thorne. Bazil lived in Bondi with his wife, two young daughters and his son, eight-year-old Graeme. The details of the lottery win were published on the front pages of newspapers and reported on the radio.

On the morning of 7 July Graeme was kidnapped on his way to school, and a ransom demand swiftly followed. The case became a national sensation. Eventually Graeme's body was found in Seaforth, the suburb next-door to Clontarf, and it transpired that the little boy had been taken first to the kidnapper's house in Clontarf – though whether he was killed there or was already dead when he arrived will never be known.

The case was to prove a watershed for the development of forensic science in police work. Pine needles from two species of cypresses (*Chamaecyparis pisifera* and *Cupressus glabra*), not present where the body was found, were identified on the blanket the body had been wrapped in, along with Pekingese and blonde human hair. Scientists established the time of the boy's death from the contents of his stomach, fungi on his shoes and fly larvae.

But how to identify the two trees which, according to experts, were a rare combination in North Shore gardens? In a piece of serendipity, the Clontarf postman was an amateur botanist and, having read about the exotic trees, recognised them in the front yard of a house at 28 Moore Street, less than two kilometres from where the body was found. At the time of Graeme's kidnapping, it was the home of Stephen Bradley and his family. Bradley faced court in early 1961 and was sentenced to life, the maximum penalty for murder.

For most of the nation the horrific crime 'marked the end of innocence in Australian life'. Kidnapping for ransom was thought of as an American phenomenon and was unknown in Australia. Besides the obvious change in the media no longer reporting the names of Opera House lottery winners, the case was a watershed moment for forensic science in the solving of crimes.

After this final shaming, Clontarf developed into a somnolent, verdant enclave that, like much of the North Shore, radiates a self-satisfied Anglo gentility and is now one of the most salubrious areas in Australia. It's as if it has cocooned itself from the riff-raff and rowdies of its pleasure garden days, and no one now mentions Henry O'Farrell or Stephen Bradley.

PICTURES OF SYDNEY

IN 1848 THE ARTIST JOSEPH FOWLES PRODUCED a hugely influential book, *Sydney in 1848*, and the *Sydney Morning Herald* wrote that anyone who wanted to give friends back in England an idea of what Sydney actually looked like should send them a copy of it. Fowles had always felt himself to be an important painter, but his reputation rests solely on the strength of this book.

On the five-month voyage out to New South Wales Fowles kept busy illustrating a journal and playing the flute. When he arrived with his wife and daughter in 1838, he intended to earn a living as an artist, but quickly realised this would not be possible, so instead leased a farm, 'Figtree', along the river at Hunters Hill from wealthy Mary Reibey. For three years he and his wife worked hard growing fruit and vegetables, which they shipped to Sydney with timber Fowles had felled himself.

Always fascinated by sailing, he bought a yacht and in 1843 discovered, as had many before him, just how treacherous the harbour could be. He and three friends sailed down the harbour to watch a regatta. As they returned in the late afternoon, the wind suddenly picked up, and Fowles decided to head for nearby Bradley's Head, but before they could reach shelter, a westerly squall overturned the yacht and it sank immediately. The four men were thrown into the water and only Fowles and a second man survived.

The money from his small farm enabled him to open a studio on Harrington Street in the Rocks. It was the perfect location for someone setting out to establish himself as a marine painter, as it was just a short walk from the docks. If he wanted to amuse himself, he could join the spectators at the Quay and the crews of the moored ships to watch the butcher clerk races. When there was a signal from Flagstaff Hill that a ship was approaching Sydney, the excited butchers' clerks would sprint down to the water and hire a boat from the watermen. The clerks would then row furiously down the harbour, aiming to be first aboard the ship, some even racing out through the Heads in a rollicking wide-eyed ride. The winner secured the order for supplying the ship with fresh meat and vegetables during its stay in port. If Fowles needed esoteric information for his ship paintings he could easily mingle with sailors and whalers at the nearby Ship and Mermaid in Gloucester Street, a popular pub for officers and crews.

Then there were the sounds he would have heard. Up the hill was St Philip's church and the frequent tolling of the death bell. One toll was for a child, two for a woman, three for a man. Of a Sunday it would be hard not to hear Mr R Pigeon and his followers preaching about the end of the world in the streets of the Rocks. At night he'd hear the drumbeat coming from the military barracks and hear the running footsteps of soldiers hightailing it from the many hotels in the area to get back to their barracks in time. Then there was the nightwatchman who lived nearby: a stout fellow, with a big coat down to his ankles, carrying a rattle, a lantern and a short staff, he slowly made his rounds, calling out the hour and making sure all was right in the area. As he came to each store, he'd shine his lantern on the front door lock to make sure it hadn't been tampered with, and if it had, he'd shake his rattle as violently as possible to attract the police.

By July 1847 Fowles decided it was time to exhibit eight

paintings. Only one was not of ships or maritime scenes. The paintings are a stolid likeness of ships out at sea, but they lack vividness and animation. The reviews were scathing, one saying the 38 year old was attempting too much for a young man, and another pointing out that he couldn't even paint a storm.

Perhaps the reviews set him on his new artistic path, or he had so fallen in love with Sydney over his decade in the developing colony that he set out to change English misconceptions about it. In 1848 he produced the first of his etchings illustrating central Sydney and announced his reason for the project:

> The principal object of this Work is to remove the erroneous
> and discreditable notions current in England concerning this
> City ... We shall endeavour to represent Sydney as it really is –
> to exhibit its spacious Gas-lit Streets ... its Public Edifices, and
> its sumptuous shops, which boldly claim a comparison with
> those of London itself.

A book intending to attract English migrants entitled *Emigrant's Guide to New South Wales* was published around the same time. In it the author, JC Byrne, set out to portray the best picture of Sydney he could:

> Hundreds of ships lie still, as if sleeping on the calm waters of
> the port, beneath; busy thousands congregate at the wharfs and
> the chief thoroughfares; whilst numerous rocky promontories
> clothed with verdure are dotted with the villas and country
> mansions of Sydney merchants ... [the] chief streets lined with
> continuous ranges of stone or brick edifices, some being shops
> and stores of noble dimensions, where every article for common
> use or luxury is to be met with. There are not a few handsome
> and spacious private houses.

But Byrne was unable to ignore Sydney's drinking culture: 'the number of licensed places for the sale of spirits is perfectly astonishing'.

Fowles felt what was missing from Byrne's work was the sense of Sydney as a city. Although smaller than some cities in England, it was just as architecturally impressive. Byrne's guide lacked a sense of wonder at just how far Sydney had advanced in 60 years. People back in England only had a vague idea of Sydney and still thought of it as a vulgar colonial outpost rather than the refined Georgian city it had become. Fowles was not interested in representing the people of the city, but in showing how far Sydney had progressed by illustrating its buildings.

The work was initially serialised over 20 issues, one every fortnight between 1848 and 1850. They were completely unexpected from someone considered a journeyman artist. As the architectural historian Morton Herman has written, 'Only a draftsman and an architect can really appreciate the prodigies of labour that went into ... this wonderful record of early Sydney.'

His work contained accurate and precise drawings with accompanying descriptions of the streetscape, whether commercial, religious, administrative or residential; each building and house rendered exactly. The work does not cover the whole of Sydney; many of the streets of the Rocks are not included, and the southern end of York, George and parallel streets are not represented because Fowles didn't consider them architecturally significant. Those streets he etched are filled with harmonious buildings, few of them over three storeys high, in an orderly procession of charming drawings. Few of the noteworthy buildings now remain, such as the Obelisk in Macquarie Place, and sections of Horbury Terrace in Macquarie Street. Of the nine churches illustrated by Fowles, only three are still with us: St Patrick's, St James', and the Congregational.

The details are extraordinary. Take, for example, the eastern side of George Street between numbers 432 and 376: 'City Toy Bazaar', ironmonger, wine merchant, importers and dealers, warehouse, steam coffee warehouse, tailor and draper, White Horse Tavern, harness makers and saddlers, solicitors, Robinson's warm vapour shower and medicated baths, and the Australian Drapers' Association. At 404 was a passage to the rear of the Theatre Royal, which had frontage on 400–402 Pitt Street. Directly behind it, on George Street, was the Royal Hotel, built in 1840 after the old hotel was destroyed by fire. The Royal was the most famous hotel in Sydney (where the Dymocks building stands now). A little further on are wholesale and retail hardware shops, a foundry, a family grocer, a whip maker and tobacconist, auctioneers, a boot and shoe warehouse, a stationer and bookseller, a draper, a chemist, more ironmongers, a tea mart, and the popular Crown and Anchor Tavern. In another street he even stops to draw 'a small cottage occupied by Hart, a philosopher, who produced the first daguerreotype on copper'.

The Sydney he records is a gorgeous colonial city of clean-lined, delicate architecture that seemed, to some later readers, a fanciful representation of the city. But architectural drawings still exist of the vanished buildings Fowles recorded, and comparisons of the two prove Fowles' veracity.

His work gathered acclaim as each issue unveiled a city in all its Georgian magnificence. He captured the imagination of its inhabitants, revealing an environment they had taken for granted as something to be proud of. His career never looked back. His reputation enhanced, he became an art teacher, acknowledged on his death as 'The Father of Drawing in Sydney'.

Fowles' precise and clear-eyed views of Sydney couldn't be more different from those of Conrad Martens, the colony's first professional painter. Martens' works are romantic and emphasise the natural features in and around Sydney. His watercolours and oils of Sydney Harbour and the Heads are full of theatrical interplays of light, the drama of nature, and bucolic calmness. When he paints a view from Macquarie Street, he turns his back on the homes and public buildings in order to face the Domain, which, with its sheep and herder, seems as far removed from the city as possible. He earned money undertaking commissions for the wealthy, rendering their mansions and villas in an enchanting picturesque style. Invariably framed by a foreground of virgin forests, the houses of the rich – whether it be Alexander Spark's 'Tempe' on the Cooks River, or Alexander Macleay's 'Elizabeth Bay House' – seem cocooned in an Arcadian paradise and could be in England, except for the Australian vegetation, which is conveyed in a blur of green beauty. The mansions in their solitary splendour are stately bastions of civilisation, carved out of nature, imperious and serene. But it's more than that; these depictions of colonial wealth and personal prestige are a deliberate attempt to erase the colony's foundation as a penal settlement. Transportation to Sydney had ended in 1840, but it was still a very present memory.

For the writer Louisa Meredith, who arrived in Sydney with her new husband in 1839, Sydney was a 'truly wonderful ... large and busy town' reminding her of Bristol or Liverpool. She made sketches of parts of it, but one day in 1840 she sat down at Mrs Macquarie's Chair and sketched the North Shore, a subject that had seldom attracted other artists. To Meredith the low hills of the north side of the harbour were monotonous, the shoreline busy with boats and yachts. Her drawing only shows two houses, both two-storey Georgian villas.

The North Shore was still basically bush. In James Backhouse's *A Narrative of a Visit to the Australian Colonies*, his first impression of Sydney in the late 1830s to early 1840s, was that it resembled a large English town. What is intriguing is that he mentions something no one else seems to have written about: the air of Sydney after sunset was impregnated with an eerie and beautiful perfume. This was the scent of the *Brugmansia suaveolens*, a large Brazilian shrub that was 'cultivated in almost every garden'. It produced striking flowers like white trumpets, and every part of this alluring plant was alarmingly toxic to humans and animals.

Backhouse visited the North Shore, and found trekking the thick bush hard going. He was surprised to come upon a large Indigenous family sitting around a small fire, with several dogs and a cat. Though they spoke 'tolerable' English, he thought their whole appearance was 'degraded and forlorn'. They sought out the washings of rum-casks, and got drunk on it. One of the men had gone to town to buy bread, but the rest were afraid he would spend the money on drink.

One amateur artist who tried to convey the reality of the young city was John Rae, whose drawings and watercolours are the opposite of Fowles' austere perfection of Georgian Sydney. Rae had studied law back in Scotland before emigrating to Australia in 1839 at the age of 26 to become an accountant. In 1842 Sydney Town was incorporated into a city and a year later Rae became the city's first full-time clerk and legal officer. He developed a reputation as a diligent, incorruptible public servant, but he also fancied himself as a poet and artist. He gave lectures on art and Robert Burns, and one can see the Scottish poet's sense of humour in his own verse and artworks.

In 1844 Rae published a prose account in the *Sydney Morning Herald* of the Mayor's Fancy Dress Ball, held at the Victoria Theatre in Pitt Street. It is an affectionate if satirical portrait of Sydneysiders partying hard. He had heard criticisms that such an event shouldn't be held in a time of economic difficulties, but Rae knew most Sydneysiders wanted 'an invitation to dance and be merry'. The 99th Regiment was the band and tables heavy with food were at both ends of the stage, which was lit by a huge chandelier and dozens of gas lamps. The dress and upper circles were for the invited guests and those who weren't were in the gallery, 'spectators of the carnival'. Rae marvelled at the diversity of the costumes:

> ... a never-ending series of living pictures of different ages and
> countries that could not be surpassed ... among the gaudy array
> of Eastern garbs, glittering with Barbaric pearl and gold, there
> were many complete and handsome Highland costumes.

One settler, dressed up as an Aboriginal man and wearing 'an old, tattered blanket' burst into a circle of waltzing couples and gave 'a facsimile of an Aboriginal dance'.

Rae also wrote a long series of satirical verses about the night where 'the news soon spread like wildfire through the city/and naught was talked of but the Fancy Ball'. What becomes clear is how equalitarian Rae thought the occasion was, with its mixture of Governor Gipps and 'the blooming damsel with the rosy lips/ the matron sage, the veteran frail and bald/the merchant and the soldier and the sailor/the shoemaker, the draper and the tailor/ and numbers more I need not mention'. As he was to write, 'One leading and most agreeable feature of the evening's entertainment was the total absence of all class feeling.'

And you can see this in his watercolours – Sydney as an egalitarian society (unless, of course, you were Aboriginal). His pictures of Millers Point, Hyde Park and the main streets of the city are depicted with an amused and sharp eye, with some parts merely rutted roads and wonky old houses. A main thoroughfare like York Street is lined with houses, hotels and shops, few of them over two storeys high. It has Rae's familiar patient horses and their carts, but what comes across is the languid pace of the city. No one seems in a hurry as they gossip, shop and stroll down the centre of the street oblivious to the horse traffic. Another watercolour shows the military barracks in Wynyard Square, and it's only in Rae's picture that we realise just how much space the barracks took up and how it dominated the city. The Domain is gated with only a carriage, pulled by two horses, making its way through the basic entrance gates, while two horsemen rest and talk in the distance, giving it the appearance of a country estate. New Government House, shown from a roughly graded Macquarie Street, stands alone in a state of ersatz grandeur. Despite its reputation as a bustling thoroughfare, George Street's traffic is sparse, the only activity being two men hauling casks as one of Rae's unflappable horses waits for its cart to be loaded. A bystander leans against a lamppost in the foreground as if he has all the time in the world.

Rae drew several pictures of Hyde Park and the feature that intrigues a modern viewer is the large spaces between the isolated buildings in the background, whether it be St Mary's, Lyons Terrace, Hyde Park Barracks, or the distant windmills on the ridges. Each stands alone, almost like civic trophies. One picture shows a few couples wandering arm in arm across Hyde Park while plump sheep graze nearby. In other pictures there is a cricket game in progress watched by curious spectators as children play and couples promenade. The road running alongside the park is rutted deeply by carriage wheels.

One can see Rae's humour and interest in people in a Hyde Park watercolour featuring 'The Flying Pieman' at the extreme right selling his pies. He was one of Sydney's eccentrics and when hawking his pies, shouted incoherent proclamations. He had become famous in Sydney for his endurance walks. It was rumoured that the cause of these bizarre undertakings was an unhappy love affair. One 'pedestrian feat' was to walk from the Obelisk in Macquarie

Place to Parramatta and back again in six hours; another was beating the coach from Windsor to Sydney by seven minutes. During one feat he had himself horsewhipped to spur him on. On another occasion he walked from Campbelltown to Sydney carrying a 32-kilo dog. To top that triumph, he undertook another walk, this time carrying a goat weighing 42 kilos, with an added dead weight of 5 kilos, from Brickfield Hill to Parramatta in seven hours, winning, as he did on many occasions, a large wager. As he walked with his characteristic single-minded intensity, onlookers mocked him, but he didn't care, even though, as one reporter wrote: 'his peculiar and vivacious manner made him the butt of almost all'. Contemporary sketches show him as an athletic figure with a 'distracted expression'. One depicts him in a blue jacket, reddish breeches, white stockings and shoes, wearing a top hat with coloured streamers and carrying a long staff decorated with ribbons. Eventually he went insane and died in Liverpool Asylum.

Perhaps one of Rae's best works is a watercolour of the turning of the first sod for the first railway in Australia in 1850. It's a delightful evocation of a city thrilled by the prospect of modern transport. In the foreground are prancing horses and their riders, unaware that the train will eventually supersede them. Dogs run around barking excitedly. At the right-hand side is a handful of Aboriginal people, some bored, others intrigued by the air of excitement. Men, women and children mingle and chatter, all exuberant with the significance of this moment. The actual day was dreary and wet, but Rae pushes the symbolism further by painting it as a sunny, radiant day for Sydney.

Rae later became the commissioner for railways, so it's no wonder his own enthusiasm at the beginning of the railway age is apparent. He went on to photograph Sydney, residing in the grand three-storey mansion 'Hilton' in Liverpool Street, which had a camera obscura at the top to take in the views.

His Sydney is confident, a hybrid of English mores and Australian optimism, with a pulsating sense of unlimited opportunities for everyone. This confidence tipped over into overconfidence in the late 1830s and early 1840s, when Sydneysiders borrowed huge sums of money to mortgage their houses, and buy investment properties, pastoral estates and sheep stations. The German explorer Ludwig Leichhardt, who arrived in Sydney in the beginning of 1842, quickly sized up the situation, noting that Sydneysiders had been 'Intoxicated with previous success – (a success so unprecedented as to be in itself a warning to the wise) – the highest as well as the lowest of the colonists had launched forth into every species of extravagance and wild speculation.'

The depression hit hard. Overborrowing, a severe drought, a financial crisis in Britain, a slump in land sales and incomes, meant a run on the banks, six of which had to close. From February to the end of December 1842 there were more than 600 insolvencies, a rate of nearly two a day. The *Sydney Morning Herald* described it in almost apocalyptic terms:

> 1842 will long be remembered as one of the darkest eras in the
> history of New South Wales. Its commercial aspect was fearfully
> dismal ... black clouds hung over it and thick fogs covered it ...
> a storm and tempest did set. Commerce, agriculture and even
> the great staple our 'golden fleece' were alike laid prostrate by
> the blasts of pitiless adversity.

Costly homes were sold for trifling sums and some of the rich found themselves living in poverty. It got so bad that on New Year's Day an angry mob gathered in Hyde Park and hurled abuse at Governor Gipps for not doing enough for the unemployed.

Louisa Meredith and her husband lost properties and their homes, as did Martens, who, without commissions or a public to buy his paintings, had to sell up and find cheaper lodgings for his family and beg for financial help from his brother Henry in London. Martens had painted 'Tempe' for Alexander Spark, one of the wealthiest men in Sydney. At the time of Martens' romantic depiction of the estate, Spark had 35 servants and 'Tempe' was a palatial mecca for balls and dinner parties with important guests such as bankers, merchants and large landowners. He had a library of 500 books and European paintings, as well as owning many properties, including a gorgeous villa, 'Tusculum', in Potts Point. He was an agent for two dozen ships, and owned many stores in town as well as prized stallions. When the depression came, many of the friends for whom he had guaranteed loans were suddenly bankrupt. In a frenzy, Spark sold off properties, shares and ships, but to no avail. In 1844 he was declared insolvent. His diary entries show him falling into a deep melancholy, believing his financial ruin was divine punishment for his sins.

But by 1844 a slow economic recovery had begun. That year, in a heartening sign for the city, after seven years a huge engineering project, the construction of the Semi-Circular Quay, was completed. It had involved reconstructing Sydney Cove with an artificial shoreline. The mouth of the Tank Stream, which flowed into Sydney Cove at the western end of Circular Quay, was filled in. Because of its shape, the Quay was originally known as 'Semi-Circular Quay', but the public soon shortened it. Wharves were constructed on the southern shore and in 1845 the imposing Customs House was opened, facing onto what would become an increasingly busy port.

RIDDING SYDNEY
OF THE BIRTHSTAIN

TRANSPORTATION ENDED IN NEW SOUTH WALES IN MAY 1840.
Since the 1830s a growing number of free settlers had arrived,
many of whom were annoyed about sharing their city with the
criminal detritus of Britain. The mere sight of their convict
uniforms and the sound of their clanking leg irons as they trooped
around town was a reminder of why the First Fleet landed in
Botany Bay.

In August 1848 the shift away from Sydney's identity as a
penal colony was underlined when the 11th Regiment marched
out of the barracks and up the hill to Paddington where the
Victoria Barracks had been built amid the sand dunes (its long,
sober two-storey Georgian buildings feature in Fowles' book).

For nearly 40 years the barracks had dominated the centre of
the city, a constant reminder that it was a garrison town. Locals
and visitors had flocked there to hear concerts and watch the
drilling of the 600 or more soldiers in their brilliant red uniforms.
On Sundays spectators lined the streets to see the fife-and-drum
bands. Playing 'Hark the Merry Christ Church Bells' and 'I'm
Ninety-Five', the bands would march up to St Philip's church.
After the service the musicians would lead the troops back to the
barracks, playing more tunes. For four decades the soldiers had

strutted around town, as if above the law, and had made the Rocks their hedonist sanctuary for drinking, whoring and brawling.

After the barracks was vacated, a quietness settled on that part of town and the government divided the immense space into allotments to be sold off. The square on which the demolished barracks had been built was named after Major-General GB Wynyard, who commanded the garrison at the time the land was divvied up. If the removal of the soldiers to Paddington was a sign that the penal colony had become a proper and respectable city (six years earlier, in 1842, it had been incorporated as a city), the following year brought a stark reminder of its foundation as a prison for convicts.

In June 1849 the *Hashemy* sailed into the harbour with 212 convicts. The day after the ship's arrival thousands of enraged Sydneysiders protested the landing of what they called Britain's birthstain. As one newspaper reported:

> The merchants closed their stores, the shopkeepers put up
> their shutters, the mechanic laid down his tools of trade, and
> the great body of the citizens headed down to Bridge Street,
> near Circular Quay, and gathered under the shade of the fir
> trees. The speakers' platform was one of the Sydney omnibuses,
> named 'Defiance', which was painted in large golden letters on
> each side.

When the charismatic politician and barrister Robert Lowe clambered upon the knifehead (a seat on the roof of an old-fashioned omnibus), the thousands of people cheered wildly. Lowe was 38, tall, spare, with a quiet contemplative air about him, belied by his ferocious debating style. He was remarkably boyish looking with a very pale face crowned with wavy white hair, bushy white eyebrows and white eyelashes and eyes constantly squinting in the glare. As was his habit outdoors, his eyes were hidden behind dark-coloured spectacles. He had albinism, and it was the albinism that caused him to migrate to Sydney.

He had graduated from Oxford and practised as a lawyer, but developed severe headaches and a painful nervous twitch of the eyes. Doctors warned him he would go blind within seven years and, determined to make the most of his allotted time and reasoning that the Australian light would be beneficial for his sight, he arrived in 1842 with his wife, Georgiana.

Lowe oscillated between the law and his role as a New South Wales parliamentarian. His speeches in parliament were feared by the opposition, as was his cutting wit. He was equally at home in the courts and in 1844 undertook the defence of a man reviled by everyone, John Knatchbull had been a ship's captain back in England, but after being found guilty of stealing with force, he was transported to New South Wales in 1824.

Seven years later he was charged with forging Judge Dowling's signature on a cheque. He was sentenced to Norfolk Island and, seemingly unrepentant, took part in two mutinies en route. He returned to Sydney in 1839 to serve out his sentence. After gaining a ticket of leave he was set to marry in early 1844, but he was broke. His solution was to visit the shop of Ellen Jamieson, a poor widow, and as she was serving him, he repeatedly smashed her head with a tomahawk. She lingered for a few days, then died, leaving behind two orphaned children. The 'abominable wretch' was soon caught.

Lowe's defence was unique for the time. He argued that his client yielded to an irresistible impulse and could not be held responsible for his crime. Lowe brought up the idea that insanity of the will could exist apart from insanity of the intellect. The novel argument failed and Knatchbull was sentenced to death.

The murder horrified and enthralled Sydney. The execution

was held outside the gates of the three-year-old Darlinghurst Gaol. It was scheduled for nine o'clock in the morning, and just after dawn scores of excited men, women and children began making their way across Hyde Park towards Darlinghurst Hill. By the time Knatchbull mounted the scaffold, the crowd was estimated at 10 000, nearly a third of Sydney's population. As the *Australian* reported, 'Captain Knatchbull ascended the fatal scaffold without trepidation or fear and was launched into another world with a noble and fervent prayer trembling on his lips.' Once he was hanged the bell of distant St Philip's tolled three times.

In a generous gesture, Lowe and Georgiana adopted the murdered woman's two young children, Bobby and Polly Jamieson, who went to live with the Lowes in the newly completed 'Bronte House' in Nelson Bay, the name given to the bay at Bronte Beach once occupied by the Bidjigal and Gadigal people. 'Bronte House' was six and a half kilometres from the city but so isolated at the time that Lowe considered it his 'country residence'. The mansion was approached by a long gravel carriageway, now Bronte Road, which curved down a hill. The beautiful sandstone villa has a slate roof, two entrances, one on the western side, the other on the eastern, and includes romantic circular and hexagonal corner turrets, and deep bay windows. (A second storey was added in the 1880s.) The view over the ocean is breathtaking. The estate was enormous at 17 hectares and included the beachfront itself, a cliff south of the house where the stables were located, and a waterfall of 18 metres that ran through Bronte Gully and Bronte Park.

We have a fair idea of how the house, the estate, the gardens and the wild shores of the bay looked thanks to Georgiana Lowe's sketches. She was a skilful artist and enthusiastic landscape gardener. With the help of the head gardener, Hugh Beattie, the garden was so successful that she sold the surplus produce at the Sydney market. She grew annuals and vegetables but also an exotic collection of plants grown from seeds that Leichhardt's assistant gathered from each new flower and tree discovered on the German's exploration of far north Australia. Her drawings are in the Martens style, with 'Bronte' estate as a romantic, Arcadian enclave.

By the time Lowe was hammering home his message from the top of the bus that transportation should cease and the *Hashemy*'s convicts not be allowed to sully the city, he was wealthy and famous. Even the caricatures of him with albinism viewing the world through a telescope-like magnifying glass were light satire. He was known as a man of great intellect, one of the most eloquent in Sydney, but to some arrogant and inflexible.

Because of his wife's homesickness and illness, Lowe and Georgiana returned to London with the Jamieson children. He became an important politician, a leader writer for *The Times*, an author of dull poetry (some of it set in Sydney and the bush), and was elevated to the House of Lords, where he became Viscount Sherbrooke.

His oratory that day in 1849 resulted in the dispersal of the convicts from Sydney. Of the 212 convicts on board, 45 were sent to distant Moreton Bay and the rest were only allowed ashore once those employing them had given assurances they would be sent to the countryside – no convicts were to remain in Sydney. It was the end of transportation in New South Wales. Just as the removal of the military from the centre of the city helped the emancipists and free settlers to forget the reasons for the first settlement, so the gradual elimination of the sight of convicts in the streets removed all evidence of the 'birthstain' from Sydney.

THE TRAGEDY OF THE *DUNBAR*

IT WAS NEAR MIDNIGHT ON 20 AUGUST 1857 and the merchant and passenger ship *Dunbar* was approaching the entrance of Port Jackson. It was difficult to navigate the vessel in the heavy rains and strong gale-force wind. Twenty-year-old Able Seaman James Johnson was on deck with Captain Green and the crew. The night was so dark a seaman could not see the crew member alongside him. The captain shouted above the howling gale, 'Does anyone see anything of the North Head?' The mate yelled back, 'No, I see nothing of it.' Then the second mate suddenly shouted a warning, 'Breakers ahead.'

Before the men could react, mountainous waves pushed the ship side-on until it struck the cliffs of South Head. Then the screaming began. The passengers rushed up on deck, imploring God to help them. Captain Green, on the poop deck, remained calm and self-possessed as the passengers shrieked and cried. Women ran about the deck wearing only their chemises, crying out to be saved. Five minutes after the crash the vessel began to break up, and within an hour it had been smashed to smithereens. A huge wave lifted Johnson and threw him up onto the rocks among the shattered timber and rubbish. He could see nothing in the darkness and could only hear the roar of the surf. He sat on a rock ledge, shivering, constantly soaked by the crashing waves. As dawn broke, he saw dead bodies carried in by the sea, then dragged out again by the undertow. The only thing that remained of the three-masted, full-rigged ship was the foreyard.

The bodies, and parts of bodies, the cargo and remains of the ship were funnelled into the harbour, littering the beaches, bays and inlets. It seemed there were no survivors, until Johnson was found two days after the disaster with not so much as a scratch, still clinging to a high ledge on the cliff face, unable to climb to safety. Of the 122 on board (63 passengers, 59 crew), only the able seaman had survived.

It was one of Australia's worst maritime disasters and traumatised Sydney as no other shipwreck had done. Few of the population of 55 000 did not know of someone who was a relative or friend of the dead. The impact was profound. As one newspaper said, 'Nothing else but this calamity has been talked about or thought of.' What horrified Sydney was seeing the mutilated bodies floating in the water or unexpectedly finding them in an inlet or on a beach. Men sailed out on the harbour collecting corpses or limbs. One of the most assiduous was Philip Cohen, who owned a hotel on Manly Beach. Every day he went out by himself recovering bodies. One morning he saw a drowned man and as he was dragging him into his boat an enormous shark grabbed the body and, after a desperate struggle, Cohen had to give up the fight and helplessly watch the shark disappear beneath the waves with it.

Five weeks after the disaster a funeral was held for the victims. A day of public mourning was declared. Shops and most of the pubs were closed. Flags on the ships in the harbour were at half-mast and 'the city wore a most dismal aspect'. The procession of seven hearses and a hundred private carriages began at the morgue in Circular Quay and, accompanied by a military band playing the 'Dead March' from Handel's oratorio *Saul*, slowly made their way to Camperdown cemetery, the streets lined with thousands of weeping mourners.

The hearses contained the remains of 22 victims; some were whole bodies, others were unidentified trunks or limbs of men, women and children. In a candlelit ceremony, they were interred in a single large tomb. As a journalist observed, 'scarcely greater grief and sympathy could have been manifested around the graves of the nameless strangers'.

The calamity haunted Sydney. Alfred Dampier, an actor-manager who made his name with stage adaptations of *For the Term of his Natural Life* and *Robbery Under Arms*, was not one to miss an opportunity to exploit misfortune and realised he could make money out of the city's grief. In 1887, he produced an epic four-act drama, *The Wreck of the Dunbar*. The hero is a young pilot on the lookout at South Head. It was a melodrama filled with action, young lovers, the hero saving the life of James Johnson, and the requisite dramatic storm scenes. It starred Dampier and his daughter, 'Miss Dampier', whose important scene in the churchyard was drowned out by the orchestra on opening night. One reviewer called it 'a free admixture of pathetic and ridiculous situations'. If the show was a critical failure, there were some irreverent members of the audience who made the opening night memorable. During the intervals, and even during the performance itself, 'there were disturbances on the floor in one locality, where a particular riotous spirit seemed to be in possession ... these incidents appeared to afford almost as much entertainment as the performance itself'.

Despite the bad reviews the play proved so popular that it was adapted into a film in 1912 starring the celebrated actress Louise Lovely. *The Wreck of the Dunbar or The Yeoman's Wedding* promoted scenes of 'the intense lovers, two thrilling scenes, the terrible Gap, the doomed ship, the wreck of the *Dunbar* in all its awful realism, the rescue of the sole survivor – the daring feat performed in the actual spot.' The film, now lost, enthralled Sydney and it ran for three weeks.

Three years later James Johnson died. He had worked for the maritime board in Newcastle and, as fate would have it, in 1868 the steamer *Cawarra* was wrecked just outside the entrance to Newcastle during a gale. He rowed his boat to the wreck and rescued the solitary survivor. Johnson died in Sydney after making a pilgrimage every year to the site of the *Dunbar* wreck and the place where providence saved him.

SYDNEY CREATES ITSELF

IT'S ALMOST AS IF THE SANDSTONE IS ALIVE. It can change colour, from grey to snotty green to a golden hue. It can take on a brooding drab air when damp, and then, after it dries, assume an affable yellow. It can be stained by weather to an inky dark green or be a pristine bright mustard. At times it seems as if it is a living creature as water seeps from its pores, and the stone itself hosts lichens, mosses, creepers, ferns and orchids, and can live in a symbiotic relationship with the exposed roots of fig trees. Left to the elements it can be sculptured into weird shapes, creating honeycombed caves and dramatic overhanging ledges. Beneath the thin cover of the soil the sandstone is soft and grey, but when harvested, it transforms itself in a matter of weeks, hardening as it oxidises and, in an act of sublime metamorphosis, becomes a rich honey colour.

Wherever one looks in Sydney it is impossible to avoid the sandstone buildings that rose from the very bedrock of the city itself. It was carved and shaped for glorious buildings, warehouses, hospitals, churches, bridges, barracks, walls, graveyard headstones, schools, stables, steps, pavements, gutters, gatehouses, toll houses, mansions with baroque decorations adorning their façades, beautiful sculptures, Parliament House and Government House. Even in the suburbs it's hard to avoid the sandstone lying just below a thin crust of soil as knobs of it push through lawns 'like hide through a bad taxidermist's work'. For over 100 years the stone gave Sydney an inimitable appearance and helped to define its urban character. As one recent writer, Robert Irving, says of it, 'It's a kind of bass note, an ever-present reminder of its Georgian beginnings and more ancient past.'

Yet for the men and women of the First Fleet the sandstone was a bitter reminder of the problem of feeding the colony. Lying beneath a thin coating of earth, it was the basis of the nutrient-poor soils that made it so difficult to grow crops. Even if Governor Phillip had wanted to use the stone as building material, there were no suitable tools to exploit it.

The Eora had no crops to farm so the poor soil meant nothing to them. Their farm was the harbour with its fish and oysters. The sandstone was used for art. The Sydney area contains the largest collection of rock art in the world. Its durable quality means that many rock carvings and drawings still exist, though many are hidden under houses and office blocks. Sandstone caves and overhanging ledges provided the clans with shelter and a medium for artwork. The Eora used coloured clays to paint and draw their stories on sandstone walls, and on the harder stone carved designs and figures, including Dreamtime creatures, human beings, animals and, of course, fish. Rock drawings and carvings can still be found around the harbour from the foreshore of North Head to Manly, Bradley's Head, Wollstonecraft and Vaucluse, to mention only a few sites.

Perhaps the most poignant sandstone carvings are those at the North Head Quarantine Station, which was established in the 1830s. They are the creations of passengers and sailors from arriving ships and those quarantined during local outbreaks of smallpox and typhoid. The majority of inscriptions are carved into the cliff that runs down to the wharf where the inmates disembarked and, they hoped, where they would eventually embark for the city, which was achingly close across the harbour. The inscriptions are in all languages: Chinese, Italian, English, Arabic, Russian, Greek, Japanese. Some are elaborate, as if carved by a stone mason. From teenagers to old men and women, there are messages, pleas, dates, commingling with the names of vessels, medical staff, passengers, or just a single name. Many are memorials. In the graveyard, elaborate sandstone headstones are roll calls of the dead, decorated with flags, crowns, anchors, shipping insignias and crests.

Sydney rests on a sandstone shelf. Called Sydney Yellow, it's found in layers from a centimetre to many metres thick, often extending at the same thickness for many kilometres. The rock outcrops within a 260-kilometre radius of Sydney sustain a unique flora and fauna of remarkable diversity – for example, the sandstone supports more tree species than exist in all of Europe. Experts believe that the sandstone started to form about 220 to 195 million years ago in the Triassic era, when most of the region was under water. Sandstone itself is made up of sand grains worn from rocks by weathering and transported by water or wind. It accumulates particle by particle in parallel layers and is welded together by a form of natural cement. The size of the sand grains determines the texture of the stone. The colour originates in both the sand grains and the nature of the cement.

For those who came into Port Jackson by ship, the sandstone greeted them as sheer coastal bluffs, two ancient and separated monuments, North Head and South Head, seeming to guard the harbour. These craggy surfaces are weathered by the Pacific storms and turbulent waves, salt spray and ferocious winds. The stone itself seems as if sculpted in a frenzy; the result is enormous piles of rubble at the bottom of the cliffs. For some these imposing sea cliffs can seem sombre and forbidding, but the rugged and ragged texture of the surface also provides vivid examples of geological patterns and infinite variations in shading, light, colour and mood, all determined by the mercurial weather originating in the Pacific. For a long time these cliffs were to Sydneysiders, especially to those approaching by boat, what the welcoming white cliffs of Dover are to the English.

But what to do with the sandstone and how to utilise it? From the beginning of his governorship Macquarie set about exploiting the stone. It helped that gradually better tradesmen, some with expertise as stone masons, began to arrive, either as convicts or specialist free settlers. By 1803 there was only one private residence built of sandstone. The stone was expensive because of the tremendous amount of work involved, first with quarrying and shaping the stone, then dressing it. Early use was restricted to windowsills, hearths and pavements, but most of it became ships' ballast.

Macquarie was the first to recognise the attractiveness of sandstone as a building material, and a quarry was opened up on the north-west side of Observatory Hill, initially to provide stone for the new hospital – the biggest project of the early years of his governorship.

The quarrying was done by convicts and was an excruciating physical task. In his watercolour panorama of Sydney in 1821, Major James Taylor portrays a gang of convicts working in a quarry around Millers Point. The convicts seem in no hurry as they laboriously dig out the sandstone and then cut it into narrow oblong stones about a metre long.

It became clear that sandstone was under everyone's feet. One just had to dig down, sometimes only a metre, to uncover it. People with money used it to build their palatial homes without going to the effort of transporting it from the major quarries. Many a mansion was constructed from stone dug up on the property itself, germinating into a building before one's eyes. Most of the gorgeous sandstone houses in upmarket Hunters Hill rose up out of small quarries on site, and yet, unlike the brutal scars in the landscape of Pyrmont and Ultimo, there is little evidence of them now.

Macquarie's architect Francis Greenway became a strong advocate of quarrying on site. The Sydney stone was generally of exceptional quality and there were no transportation costs. He recommended the location of Darlinghurst Gaol because it contained a vast amount of sandstone, and there was more than enough to build the gaol and its thick walls seven metres tall. Although construction was started in 1822, the jail did not open until 1842. One of its beautiful features, a sublime example of architecture and workmanship, is the elegant roundhouse. Although built for the incarceration of criminals, it seems a self-contained artwork, and is entirely at home in what is now the National Art School.

The 1840s and 1850s saw an escalating number of sandstone buildings. Perhaps one of the finest was the University of Sydney, which became a part of the Victorian tourists' itinerary. In 1874 the English author Anthony Trollope enthused over it, calling the Great Hall 'the finest chamber in the colonies', and that no college in Cambridge or Oxford possessed a hall 'of which the proportions are so good'.

The original designer was Edmund Blacket, at the time the colonial architect. He was drawn to the project from the beginning. In 1853 the government offered the university just on 52 hectares about three and a half kilometres west of the city, an area known as Grose Farm used for grazing dairy cattle. It gives the modern Sydneysider pause to realise that the selection of this site was greeted with uproar because it was considered so remote, 'it being built out in the wilds of the bush ... so far away as to make it difficult of access'.

After sullen agreement from the parties concerned, the site was confirmed. Blacket knew this was going to be one of the most important commissions of his career. He resigned as colonial architect and set about trying to convince the committee to accept his design, which was based on the Gothic Revival style and had undeniable associations with the grandeur of Oxford and Cambridge. What he needed was someone to help him visualise it, as he knew the committee would struggle to make sense of his plans. In a brilliant stroke he paid for his friend, the artist Conrad Martens, to paint a watercolour of the finished buildings. Martens' romantic, misty confection helped sell the architect's vision.

Using Pyrmont sandstone, construction started in 1854, and in 1857 the professors and their students, some 44 of them, moved into their new premises. This first building, now known as the eastern range, was completed in 1861. This impressive structure, perched on a hill overlooking the city, seems an unbroken link to the architecture of those medieval universities back in England. As the first university in Australia, it meant that young people didn't have to travel to the Mother Country to finish their education. Blacket's noble and imposing structure became a source of great civic pride in a colony trying to define its own identity.

What also intrigues about the buildings are details that are seldom noticed. At each corner of Blacket's high tower, surmounting the main building, is an octagonal minaret, and between each of these minarets is a handsome clock. The original Fisher Library has two lions, fine examples of sandstone carving, each flanking the entrance doorway, like stern guardians of knowledge. All around the magnificent quadrangle are carvings haunting the heights, some are angels and kangaroos, others are griffins, gargoyles, and nightmarish demonic creatures who gaze down on dreamy unsuspecting students.

One can argue that these buildings are Blacket's greatest achievement, but he also demonstrated his skill designing sandstone villas, commercial offices, hospitals, schools, warehouses and especially churches. For 40 years he was the pre-eminent architect in Sydney. His awed contemporaries called him 'the Wren of Australian architecture'. Modern critics are more severe, noting that despite his important contribution to Australian architecture and his positive influence on others, his work 'lacks invention and imaginative insight' and that 'he put tradition before innovation'. But that was precisely the point and why he also dominated ecclesiastical architecture until his death.

He was a decent, honest, devout Christian who disliked controversy and shied away from social acclaim. He had been born in Surrey in 1817 and trained as a skilled draftsman, but he had ambitions to become an architect. His father gave him a stipend that Blacket used to spend a year sketching and recording details of English medieval architecture. If anything determined his architectural vision, this appropriation of the past was to become an enduring influence, and one that would exasperate his twentieth-century critics.

After disembarking in Sydney in 1842 he set up a business as an architect and in 1849 reached the prestigious rank of colonial architect. Although he was the designer of many buildings, large and small, his heart lay with the dozens of sandstone Anglican churches he designed. Critics complain that they seem exact replicas of the English churches so many Sydney clerics remembered from back home (for example, St Andrew's, next to the Town Hall; St Mark's, Darling Point; St Paul's, Redfern) but that was the point: they were a cure for homesickness in this new country.

His churches were for the glory of God, and he took his duties as a churchwarden and alderman seriously. It's sometimes challenging to comprehend in our increasingly secular age how important churches were to Victorian Sydneysiders, not only as houses of worship, but as centres of social life and community. For example, the wealthy, dignitaries and important government officials attended small St Mark's church in Darling Point of a Sunday, creating a buzzing epicentre for social and political networking.

Blacket's decision to use Pyrmont sandstone was to have far-reaching consequences for a newly arrived Scotsman, Charles Saunders. He had come out to Australia at the age of 28 from Devon, where he had trained as a stone mason. It didn't take him long after he arrived in 1852 to see the potential of the sandstone in north-west Pyrmont, and he leased the land from the Harris family the following year.

Saunders was in luck, there were dozens of Scottish stone masons in Sydney. Their existence was due to a self-righteous prig, Dr John Dunmore Lang, for decades a shrill presence in Sydney as a Presbyterian minister, religious demagogue, politician, historian, journalist and jailbird (debt, criminal libel). He had arrived in 1823, and quickly became celebrated by some and detested by others for haranguing his congregations about the sinfulness of convicts and emancipists, all this driven by his conviction that the end of the world was approaching. His wild-eyed sermons condemned what he considered to be the immorality and licentiousness of contemporary Sydney. The minister's outrage extended to fancy dress balls, picnics on a Sunday, and the pervasive drunkenness. Lang's solution was to flood Australia with free migrants who would bring sobriety and piety to the unruly town. He sailed back to Britain in 1830 and personally selected 140 men and women to emigrate, including Scottish tradesmen, especially stone masons from Clyde.

The immigrants arrived in 1831 and Lang installed the

masons at the quarry in Millers Point. Over the next decades they were to help transform the landscape of Sydney. They were a skilled, tight bunch who knew their financial worth, so much so that their trade union was the first in the world to win the eight-hour working day, in 1855. They deserved their wages, which were high for the time, as stonecutters were subject to a range of lung diseases such as bronchitis, pneumonia, and a disease known as 'stone masons' phthisis', now known as a form of silicosis or industrial dust disease.

By the middle 1850s there was a huge demand for sandstone and Pyrmont stone was found to be a harder rock that did not erode and crumble as easily as stone from sites in Kent Street and Bennelong Point. It was Blacket's demand for Pyrmont sandstone that put it on the map. Over half of the 44 quarrymen working in Pyrmont were kept busy for nearly a decade supplying stone for the first buildings and later the magnificent Great Hall and colleges of the university.

Although the sandstone was praised as a building material, it was the Scottish quarrymen who had the arduous job of digging out the stone and shaping it. It wasn't long before the stone masons resorted to vivid Dantean names to distinguish the differences between the hardness of the stone and the level of difficulty in quarrying it. The best stone was 'Paradise', a soft rock that was easy to carve, its quarry near present-day Quarry Master Drive and Saunders Street. The Purgatory quarry was near present-day Pyrmont Bridge Road, and Hellhole was where Jones Street is now. In a nice irony the stone louvres in the main tower of St Mary's Cathedral came from Purgatory and the flagstones from the Hellhole. The excavation of stone from the Hellhole created a deep pit, and after rain it would become a lake, which delighted the local Pyrmont children who would have 'canoe races' on planks, and boys would show off with diving competitions.

The gruelling yet precise work of the quarrymen was recalled by one of the Saunders family:

> The stones were cut out by drilling along the backs and sides of the stone with guttering made and then wedges were inserted in the base of the block and hammered in one at a time. The block was then lifted with steam cranes, broken into smaller blocks and then taken to dressing sheds for working in their ultimate shapes and sizes. In the dressing sheds the machines for planing, sawing, turning the stone blocks into only the finished shapes, then the masons would take over and complete the final dimensioning and finishing.

Saunders was a commanding figure, eloquent, hardworking (a notable example of the Protestant work ethic), and quick to defend himself and his precious sandstone. Locals and workmen always remembered him on his grey horse as he oversaw his quarry empire, day after day. He was not only a skilled horseman, but he adored his hardworking Clydesdale draughthorses, of which there were generally about 60, with special stables built in a former art gallery. The horses were essential for carting the sandstone blocks. The streets and tracks of the Pyrmont peninsula became rutted as the Clydesdale teams transported the blocks to building sites at Sydney University, the Colonial Secretary's Office, the Australian Mutual Provident Society, the Australian Joint Stock Bank, the Great Synagogue and the Queen Victoria Building. Crowds lined the streets as the keystone of the main arch of the General Post Office, weighing nearly 24 tonnes, was delivered on a specially constructed wagon pulled by 26 Clydesdales.

Saunders was intensely proud of his quarries and would invite mayors, society mavens and journalists to watch the controlled blasting of stubborn pockets of sandstone. He frequently wrote letters to the newspapers extolling his product and describing how it was highly sought after in countries like New Zealand and Canada, and bragging about the first prizes the stone had won in Chicago, India, Melbourne and Amsterdam.

As his empire grew, he built around 50 workmen's cottages and shops in Pyrmont. They perched on top of an escarpment looking down at the workplace below with its machines, cranes and upwards of 300 workers toiling in the heat and wet: quarrymen, stonecutters, farriers, engineers, blacksmiths and carpenters.

He and his son, Robert, introduced the latest quarrying and stone-working equipment and techniques to Australia, including steam cranes, large steam-powered multi-blade stone saws, and heavy planing and profiling machinery. By the 1880s, 130 to 140 loads of stone were being carted from the quarries each day for buildings, ships' ballast, the construction of road and railway bridges, and roadside kerbing, much of which still lines Sydney's streets. The firm was the dominant supplier of sandstone for over 50 years. By 1855 the popularity of the stone meant that Saunders needed more land to quarry, and in that year the government gave him quarrying rights to nearby Darling Island. His firm removed all the stone, levelling the island, and filled up the narrow channel that separated the island from the mainland. There is now no physical sign that there was once a Darling Island, though the name persists for this area of Pyrmont.

Charles and his family were making a fortune when, in 1893, the 69-year-old patriarch made a sudden change in his life. He handed over the reins of the company to his very competent son, Robert, and became licensee of the Quarryman's Arms Hotel in Harris Street, still operating today as the Quarryman's and one of the last vestiges of Pyrmont's quarrying history.

Saunders was responsible for reshaping the landscape of

Pyrmont. The damaging effects of quarrying are evident in the suburb's vertiginous cliffs and discoloured escarpments.

Yet the stone was sculpted into Sydney's most beautiful buildings, and if there is one architect responsible for this city of sandstone, it's Blacket's protégé, James Barnet. Born in Scotland in 1827, Barnet came to Australia in 1854 and 11 years later became colonial architect, a post he held for 25 years. His appointment as colonial architect heralded the start of a boom in public building in which Pyrmont sandstone was to feature prominently.

A brilliant yet controversial architect, Barnet favoured an increasingly florid beard that hid a complex character. His enthusiasms were balanced by private bouts of melancholia, just as his meticulous attention to detail could be undermined by his inattention to expensive practicalities (something that would cause him persistent trouble with tight-fisted bureaucrats). He was constantly dogged by an enfilade of severe criticisms from art critics, royal commissions, parliamentary committees, miserly government officials, jealous rivals and the usual naysayers who are a feature of our cultural life.

Strongly influenced by the Italian Renaissance, Barnet despised the clutter of what he considered useless ornamentation and decoration, 'surmounted with blazing red tiles from France'. His works are spread throughout the city, many of them beautifully designed, their sombre sturdiness alleviated by the honey-coloured stone. They are reminders of the optimism and splendour of Victorian Sydney.

His work ethic resulted in an amazing range of constructions that encompassed defence works, courthouses, police stations (a delightful example is the Water Police Headquarters in Phillip Street), post offices and the Macquarie Lighthouse on South Head that replaced Greenway's original lighthouse. In the city itself there are many fine examples of his work: the General Post Office, the Colonial Secretary's Office, the Public Works and Land buildings, Customs House, the Gothic mortuary station in Regent Street, a wing of the Australian Museum, and the charming Callan Park Asylum, which provided inmates with a series of linked sandstone buildings that gave the grounds an air of serenity.

His masterpiece was regarded as 'one of the finest specimens of architecture in the colony', and one whose impact 'on the mindset of the colony was profound', yet it almost destroyed his health and his career. In 1864 Barnet was asked to design the General Post Office, which would stretch between Pitt and George streets and feature a new major road, opening up Martin's Lane to become Martin Street. The immense project would take 23 years and employ dozens of stone masons imported from Italy. The building is composed primarily of Pyrmont sandstone. The northern façade has been described as 'the finest example of the Victorian Italian Renaissance Style in New South Wales', and measures 114 metres along what is now Martin Place, making it the longest sandstone building in Sydney. The George Street arcade is supported by sandstone piers on granite bases, with three-quarter columns of polished granite and Corinthian capitals also of sandstone. In fact, the use of sandstone was described as being 'without parallel in the city'.

The enormous project faced many obstacles and progress was slow from the beginning as engineers had to find a way to enclose the Tank Stream that ran below the foundations. The project was also blighted by two controversies that drove the colonial architect to distraction. One was the clock tower (Barnet referred to it as a campanile). There was a four-year argument between the original designer, Angelo Tornaghi, and Barnet over the choice of bells. The Italian believed that light tubular bells should be used because conventional bells would be too heavy and cause the tower to collapse. Barnet won this tedious and very public battle. But the second controversy was to hound him for years.

Praise was universal for the white marble statutory group featuring Queen Victoria flanked by allegorical figures on the Martin Place façade, but it was the carved sandstone figures in spandrels over the Pitt Street doorway arches that caused uproar. Barnet commissioned an immigrant mason Tomaso Sani to sculpt 'realistic' depictions of real people in high relief (one was of Barnet), 'illustrating aspects of contemporary colonial society ... to signify the integral place of the General Post Office in colonial life'. The vitriol was immediate and long-lasting. The sculptures were lambasted as caricatures and 'comical', contrary to the time-honoured practice of sculptures featuring classical allegorical figures. According to architectural historian Philip Drew, 'The Sani Reliefs Affair was largely responsible for ending the career of Australia's most important nineteenth-century architect.'

The criticism was relentless and questions were raised in parliament. There were scathing reviews in the press, anonymous threatening letters, public abuse by fellow architects. The government appointed a board of experts to report on the carvings and unanimously recommended the sculptures be cut out and blocks of stone inserted in their place. As a telling example of our cultural cringe, the opinions of English critics were sought. The president of the Royal Academy called the figures disgusting and 'degrading to the sense of sight'. Barnet fought back with lectures, letters to the editor, and with praise from his supporters. In a dramatic volte-face, the Legislative Assembly, realising the controversy had got out of hand, voted in favour of retaining the sculptures, a ruling the newspapers, who wanted to keep the controversy going, ignored, calling the decision 'astonishing' and 'extraordinary'.

He may have won but the cost to his reputation was considerable and enduring. Although the carvings are now acknowledged as 'the beginning of art in Australia', and the building itself hugely significant in the shaping of Sydney's urban grid and the Martin Place precinct, Barnet was thought to have tarnished the reputation of the Colonial Architect's Office. He resigned from his position and the government, as philistine governments are wont to do, replaced his office with a considerably reduced entity, the NSW Government Architect's Office, a bureaucratic black hole that would swallow up any maverick creative impulses architects may have.

It wasn't long before Barnet's vision was vindicated, and the General Post Office became a focus of colonial pride and, like Sydney University, a symbol of Victorian Sydney's confidence and wealth.

At the turn of the century steel and concrete became the preferred building materials. Of the Pyrmont rock extracted in the early 1900s, much was fashioned into kerbstones for Sydney's streets and trimmings like windowsills and doorsteps.

It seemed the sandstone that so dominated the architecture and economy of the nineteenth century was a thing of the past. But the stone returned as a visible and exciting presence when the Barangaroo Reserve opened in 2015. The Barangaroo complex, with its often-controversial jigsaw of office towers, swanky restaurants, exclusive shops, lanes, alleys, galleries and public spaces, is one of the world's largest urban renewal projects, covering an area of nearly 22 hectares. About six hectares of it became the Barangaroo Reserve. The park has a subterranean arts space, a series of flourishing gardens and lawns, and an urban forest. For the naturalist and writer Tim Flannery, the grounds are 'best understood as an act of restitution as expressed in Sydney's unique sandstone'.

The late eighteenth-century shoreline has been restored and cleansed of its industrial past. More than 10 000 sandstone blocks form the park and were sourced from the site itself. Many of the blocks remain encrusted with oyster shells from their long immersion in the harbour. Some sparkle with pebbles of quartzite, others reveal a delicate fossilised leaf or fragment of wood. Footpaths are lined with enormous sandstone blocks, which, if you look closely enough, show sloping lines formed by ripples in the sand that moved with the current. As Flannery writes:

> If you know how to read these ancient ripple marks you will never get lost in Sydney ... [because] the ripple lines invariably point north, following the downstream direction of the ancient river.

The sandstone is a beautiful monument that fuses the complex history of our city with its prehistoric and industrial pasts. Visitors and flaneurs can now see just how crucial sandstone was to the history and transformation of Sydney.

HOW A DYNASTY ENDS:
THE FAIRFAXES

THIS IS HOW A NEWSPAPER DYNASTY ENDS AFTER 178 YEARS, in a room crowded with gawkers, buyers, reporters, all with thick auction catalogues in hand, as 1000 objects are paraded and bid for over a weekend. And what objects they are: antique sideboards, a seventeenth-century highchair, a croquet set, credenzas, a 25-piece dinner service, Persian rugs, gilt clocks, cherub name placeholders, paintings by Hans Heysen, Ray Crooke, William Dobell's controversial Archibald-winning portrait of Joshua Smith, and an unexpected curio, a life-sized stuffed bear on wheels for adults and children to ride. It was a display of wealth and privilege and revealed to the snooping public just a sliver of the opulent world of several generations of Fairfaxes.

John Fairfax, born in 1804 in Warwick, England, was a newspaper owner, printer and bookseller. He came out to Australia in 1838 with his wife, mother and three children and only £5 in his pocket. He worked as a journalist and librarian until he and his partner, Charles Kemp, finally scrimped up enough funds to buy the daily *Sydney Herald* in 1841, changing its name to the *Sydney Morning Herald* the following year.

Both men worked long hours, seven days a week (Sunday morning church a respite), doing almost everything themselves:

reporting, editing, writing the leaders, as well as helping with the printing. In 1853, while briefly in England, John purchased the first steam press to be used for printing a newspaper in Australia and, in the same year, bought out Kemp and installed his son Charles as a partner.

The *Herald* became one of the most influential and esteemed newspapers in the British empire. This wasn't enough for the hardworking proprietor, who soon branched out into insurance and banking. A deeply religious man, he helped establish the Pitt Street Congregational Church, where he was senior deacon. In the volatile, sectarian Sydney of the time, he was known for his tolerance. It was a trait that would run through generations of the family.

One of his prized possessions was 'Ginahgulla' in Bellevue Hill, a mansion built on the street of the same name in 1858. It would remain in the family until the end of World War II.

It was Warwick Fairfax, born at the turn of the twentieth century, who of all the Fairfaxes seemed to personify the famous name with his sense of civic duty, sumptuous homes, lavish parties, passionate love of art and music, metaphysical obsessions and shrewd business sense.

He was born at the new family home, 'Fairwater', designed by the great architect John Horbury Hunt, in Point Piper, an only child. There was something emotionally awkward about him. At 188 centimetres tall, softly spoken with a long face that took on a lugubrious mien when concentrating, sad blue eyes and wavy hair, his shyness was often interpreted as condescension. One of his editors said of him that he was 'rather like a sensitive, intelligent, slightly neurotic don'. Fluent in Greek and Latin, he went to Oxford where he studied philosophy, politics and economics. If anything preoccupied him until his final days, it was the eternal mystery of life. He believed that the only way to endure existence was to find a purpose and, as he wrote, 'I prefer an incomprehensible God to a meaningless world.'

Warwick became managing director of John Fairfax and Sons at the age of 28. By this time the firm owned several other newspapers, but, captivated by the arts and modernity, he bought *The Home*, which was to become a hugely influential magazine of modern culture, and *Art in Australia* (launched by Sydney Ure Smith in 1916), which promoted new Australian artists. He derided our cultural parochialism and was a prominent defender of the controversial award of the Archibald prize to William Dobell for his portrait of Joshua Smith, a decision that was a turning point in the slow acceptance of modernism in Australian art. Unlike other members of the Fairfax family, he was beguiled by ballet and even wrote a damning critique in his own newspaper of Sydney's Borovansky Ballet, comparing it to the visiting Kirsova Company and ridiculing it as 'a row of sheep'.

During World War II he faced a resurgent *Daily Telegraph*, driven by its new owner (and Fairfax's future enemy) Frank Packer. In response he modernised the *Sydney Morning Herald* by banishing public notices and advertisements from the front page. His politics were pragmatic and at times his newspaper, although basically conservative in the Victorian era, urged voters to abandon their usual loyalties and vote for the best candidates whether they be conservative or progressive. He often used his paper to comment on politics, convinced that when politics matter, 'it matters desperately and tremendously'.

The rivalry between him and Packer (mostly on Packer's side) spilled over into vitriol in January 1945 when the *Daily Telegraph* went after him with a ferocity seldom seen in the battle between the two main newspapers. Written by Sydney Deamer, a former editor of the *Sydney Morning Herald*, and no doubt 'enhanced' by the *Daily Telegraph*'s venomous editor, Brian Penton at the instigation of Frank Packer, it was a derisive, sarcastic portrait of over 5000 words, sneering at Warwick's wealth, making snide remarks about his failing marriage, his ancestors, his privileged education and aloofness from 'the man on the street':

> No man wielding so much power in New South Wales is known
> to so few people in Sydney. He is never to be seen chasing a
> tram or strap-hanging in a bus. He doesn't attend race meetings
> or prize fights, doesn't bet – on the dogs – and is never seen
> breasting the bar. It is not that he is a snob. He was brought up
> in a very genteel manner, cushioned from the rough edges of
> life, and would feel intrusive if he tried to mix with the mob.

The relentless assault mocked the eyeshade he wore in the *Herald* offices, commenting that it was the only thing that made him seem like a newspaperman, and that when the *Herald*, nicknamed 'Granny', did undergo changes in its format, few of them were Warwick's ideas. As Deamer sneered, 'He is not necessarily the innovator of the innovations of that journal. Very likely only a few, diffidently projected, came from him.'

It was a brutal portrait, much of it unwarranted, but it did point out just how insulated Warwick was from the ordinary Australian. But he didn't care. The ridicule only added to his contempt for the vulgar and envious Frank Packer.

After divorcing his first wife in 1945, he married Hanne Anderson, a Danish divorcee 12 years younger than him. The marriage seemed to set in motion a determination not only to try to puzzle out the meaning of life, but how to present his thoughts to the select few who had the intellectual capacity to understand them. He self-published *Metaphysics of the Mystic* in 1947, followed a couple of decades later by *The Triple Abyss: Towards a modern synthesis*. The latter, at 465 pages, was Warwick's synthesis of

Western and Eastern religions, where 'Man is not only a spiritual being, he is part of God's creation where our lives are infused with three types of cosmic energy: physical, mental and spiritual.'

For Warwick it was illogical 'to believe in a drop of water because its actions are reasonably predictable and not in God because his are not'. As he surveyed the modern world, he came to the bleak insight that:

> The Communists have now come to the same conclusion
> as the Czars and the mediaeval Popes and Emperors and the
> eighteenth-century despots – we are not ready for freedom,
> whether it be freedom of action, political freedom or freedom
> of thought.

The book (which I struggled to finish) and its confused ideas, subjective rantings and pompous certainty, meant everything to Warwick, but no one listened. He likened himself to Cassandra, crying out in the wilderness of the modern world. No wonder the public thought him, as one newspaperman put it, 'an odd fish'.

He also had a craving for a creative outlet for his talents and he took up playwriting in the 1950s. His first effort, *A Victorian Marriage*, was performed in Sydney by the John Alden Company in 1951. The play had the unfortunate fate of following a highly successful season of *King Lear*. The plot concerns a celebrated actress, Carlotta, who is pursued by three suitors, including a father and son. One distinctly unimpressed reviewer conveyed the audience's bafflement as to why they should be interested in a play set in Australia in 1875 concerned with 'a gentry class' that had 'nothing characteristically Australian about it, apart from its New South Wales setting'.

The criticisms didn't faze Warwick and in his 1952 play *Vintage for Heroes*, at the Independent Theatre, he ventured into a world even further removed from the average Australian, setting it in ancient times. Its theme was the contrast between two national types and two ways of life, the Greek and the Roman. The two worlds are contrasted, as are two branches of Platonic philosophy – the philosophy of love and beauty in sexual relations, and the continuity, if not immortality, of the soul.

For 'HSN', the theatre reviewer of the *Sydney Morning Herald*, this must have been a delicate task given his proprietor was the playwright. The reviewer hints that there were too many explanatory speeches, and the reincarnations in the final scene verged on the risible. Other scenes involving a daughter cutting open her veins, after being deserted by her lover, and a Greek colony where residents recite verses by Sappho, popped up without any justifiable narrative reason and were just plain daft.

At the end of his review 'HSN' praised the beautiful costumes and concluded that the play 'involves handicaps and difficulties beyond the normal experience of an author or producer; yet at its first performance last night … reached a very considerable success'. One hopes he kept his job.

No doubt an audience filled with friends and relatives of the Fairfaxes helped make opening night a triumph, but the plays and his metaphysical works revealed Warwick as living at one remove from Australian society, inured to most people's daily struggle for food and rent. It was obvious he lacked the common touch and was unaware of it.

Then, much to the surprise of everyone, he divorced his wife. Hanne retaliated by bringing a lawsuit against Warwick for 'restitution' of conjugal rights and naming her replacement as the Polish dress shop owner Mary Symonds. If that weren't embarrassing enough, Mary's husband Cedric issued a supreme court writ against Warwick alleging that he had induced Mary to leave him. For such a private man, these accusations drove Warwick further into himself. He divorced Hanne and, in a midnight ceremony, married Mary in 1959, a decision that in Sydney social circles 'raised eyebrows all the way'. They were an odd mix – Warwick, reserved, watchful and self-contained; Mary, vivacious and gregarious, a party girl. They had a son, Warwick, and adopted two more children, Charles and Anna, but James, Warwick's son from his first marriage, always considered Mary a parvenu with plebeian taste in art, and made it quite clear to his stepmother that she didn't belong in the Fairfaxes' rarefied world. On one occasion when she tried to curry favour with him, she gave her sophisticated stepson a pair of gold champagne flutes. He sniffed that they were 'vulgar'.

Strong willed, Mary ignored the spiteful gossip and steeled herself to become Sydney's great hostess, at various times alienating her children, but devoting herself to her husband. Her constant mantra to staff was that 'Everything should be done to please him.' In 1967 the couple shifted into 'Fairwater', where he had been born. Its gardens sloped down to the harbour and witnessed some of the most glamorous bashes ever held in Sydney. As newspapers and magazines breathlessly reported, there were dinners that seated scores of guests, dog shows, fashion parades, charity balls and cocktail parties, with visitors ranging from mining magnates and politicians to artists, opera singers, socialites, celebrities and film stars from here and overseas. At one memorable party there was an ice sculpture of a kangaroo, its pouch filled with caviar.

Mary was in her element, gushing, gossiping, dancing and being the perfect hostess while the host, a spectral presence in a bespoke conservative suit and expensive silk tie, drifted through these events, nodding, smiling, saying the right thing, dazzled by his wife's charisma. At one point Mary even hosted her own

TV chat show, where she interviewed famous people, including a personal favourite, Liberace. Perhaps the high point of the couple's social life at 'Fairwater' was in 1973 when they held a ball for 800 people to celebrate the opening of the Opera House with a guest list that included Imelda Marcos, film stars like Rex Harrison, the Duke and Duchess of Bedford, Rudolf Nureyev and, of course, Liberace. Columnists belonging to the Fairfax media cooed with wonder, while the opposition papers ridiculed the pompous extravagance of it all.

When Warwick died in 1987, he left behind a considerable portfolio of newspapers, including *The Sun*, the *Sun-Herald*, the *Canberra Times*, *The Age*, the *Australian Financial Review*, a range of magazines in Sydney, plus radio and television stations. But he had lived at one remove from the world around him, viewing Sydney through the windows of his Rolls-Royces, cocooned in his opulent world of balls, parties and live-in servants at 'Fairwater', slumming it on huge country properties where he could pretend to be a man of the land by spending a fortune breeding cattle. He remained an enigma to the general public and perhaps even to himself as he struggled to find the meaning of life.

Now that her husband was gone there was no retreating from the world for Mary. Well into her eighties, she embraced her role as the grand dame of Sydney society, with 'Fairwater' the epicentre. When guests arrived, they filed past a huge bronze statue of a muscular Adonis by Rodin that stood in front of stained-glass windows in the foyer. As the guests continued deeper into the bowels of the mansion, they passed dozens of framed photographs of Fairwater's mistress posing with Kirk Douglas, Imelda Marcos, Pope John Paul II and Ronald Reagan, so that by the time they met their gracious, tiny hostess, they were suitably awed as she hoped they would be.

It was Mary and her son Warwick who were to destroy the

Fairfax empire. Almost as soon as her husband was placed in the family vault in 1987, Mary commanded her son to return to Australia from America and, together, they conspired to take total control of the company. Warwick was an unworldly, weedy and needy 26 year old who had been educated at Oxford and Harvard. A devout Christian, he would resort to fervent prayer when things went wrong, kneeling and weeping, demanding to know why fate was toying with him. Mary and her son, in the throes of a *folie a deux*, set about taking control of what they had always considered his birthright.

The bizarre aspect of this venture was that, under the terms of a family agreement, his half-brother James would have eventually passed on his shares to Warwick, making him the largest shareholder and, almost certainly, chairman of the company. But he and his mother could not wait, and Warwick borrowed $2.5 billion at his mother's request. One of his first steps in his audacious bid to take over John Fairfax Ltd was to buy out other Fairfax family members. James, realising that his half-brother was out of his depth and liable to fail disastrously, quickly sold his shares to him. With over $300 million to play with, James – gay, urbane, and with an exquisite taste in all things artistic – spent his remaining years collecting art and donating money to conservation and medical programs, deliberately cutting himself off from the Fairfax empire in his light-hearted and occasionally waspish memoir, *My Regards to Broadway* (a reference to the street where the Fairfax newspapers once had its headquarters).

Young Warwick and Mary's quixotic undertaking soured quickly, as their takeover coincided with the stock market crash. By 1990 the company had collapsed and was placed in receivership with debts of $1.7 billion. Mary personally lost a staggering $190 million. A humiliated and teary Warwick, praying for guidance from an indifferent God, fled back to America, and his mother followed soon after to escape the ignominy and ridicule. She spent her time and energy on an enormous penthouse, complete with ballroom, across three floors of the Pierre Hotel in New York. For five years she entertained lavishly. On one occasion her doctor forbade her from flying due to ill health, so she ordered her chauffeur to buy a Rolls-Royce and drive her to Los Angeles.

Warwick stayed in America and gradually put together a new life as a guru teaching people how to recover from their failures. Mary eventually returned to 'Fairwater'. It bustled again with gardeners, a butler, cooks and maids who made their careful and silent way through the labyrinth of stairways and rooms in what was called 'a real-life version of Downton Abbey'. In this hermetic world, amid the fading curtains and old-fashioned furniture that had seen better days, Mary lived out her remaining years, surrounded by loyal staff and nurses.

Her happiest times were the months she spent every year, assisted by a personal secretary, compiling eight-page Christmas cards filled with sentimental verses, inspirational quotes and pictures of her grandchildren, who had little idea that their parents were often estranged from their grandmother. She died quietly at home in 2017 at the age of 95. The Fairfax media empire was no more, sold off to a television station, Channel Nine, ironically once owned by the Fairfaxes' rival, Kerry Packer. She was not to know that even her beloved 'Fairwater' was to lose its association with the illustrious Fairfax name when it was sold for $100 million in 2018 (making it the most expensive house in Australia). The buyer was a brash young man with an unruly beard, Mike Cannon-Brookes, who had become a billionaire with a tech start-up.

HYDE PARK NORTH

HEMMED IN BY MAMMON, RELIGION AND HISTORY, its surface hiding a labyrinth of subterranean tunnels and a moving footway, Hyde Park north is a diverse, even cluttered space of unconnected enclaves, thoroughfares and disparate entrances and exits, dominated by nearly 600 trees – many of them imposing fig trees along the main avenue, as well as strategically placed clusters of palms. The park itself has spacious lawns, manicured garden beds, pompous statues and a gorgeous fountain as its centrepiece.

In the morning the twin pointed shadows of St Mary's spires creep over the gardens, and near sunset the ominous shadows from the skyscrapers on the western side loom over the park as office workers head home, scurrying down into the two underground railway stations or hurrying across the park to walk up William Street to their apartments on the ridge in the east. At night the park becomes an enchanting space where hundreds of fairy lights glitter in the fig trees like fireflies and spotlights transform the sculptures of the Archibald Fountain, creating a theatrical chiaroscuro. Floodlights shine on the cathedral's western façade, burnishing the sandstone with a soft orange glow, and thousands of lights in offices and hotel rooms reveal a modern city that never sleeps.

During the day the park is constantly in use, a place of light and shade, both a thoroughfare and a refuge for office workers who sit on benches eating their lunches; some read books, others stare at their smart phones. The weary lie on the grass, basking in the sun. From Park Street, the central pathway northwards is a long shadowy archway of fig trees. At the end of it, you emerge into the glare of sunlight and before you is the shimmering haze of water from the Archibald Fountain.

Near the entrance to St James station is a giant chessboard where pensive men slowly pace the edges of the black and white squares, contemplating where next to place their half-metre tall pieces, watched by a handful of chess aficionados and the homeless. Close by, deep in the gloom of massive fig trees, depressives with closed eyes lie on their backs like the living dead, ignoring the strutting ibises, panting joggers, shoppers with their bags of purchases, the tourists grinning for selfies, the troops of noisy schoolchildren, and mothers pushing their prams along the many paths slicing through the park.

At the northern end, facing Macquarie Street, is a statue of the eponymous governor. Erected in 2013 to commemorate Lachlan Macquarie, it must be the worst public sculpture in Sydney. Dressed in a military uniform, Macquarie clutches a rolled-up proclamation in one hand while the other, like a claw, points north towards his architectural achievements. The figure stands awkwardly, as if poised to fall. He has a confident smirk and vacuous eyes comically at odds with the inscription describing how *The chisel of gratitude shall portray the beloved and majestic features of General Macquarie*. In fact, in keeping with his class and the era, the governor seldom laughed, let alone smiled. Where is the autocratic hauteur, the sharp intelligence that initiated the building of St James' church and Hyde Park Barracks, both almost within touching distance?

It's a pity the statue is so clumsy because without Macquarie there would be no park. Back in 1792, before he returned to

England, Governor Phillip had reserved the land for use as a common where animals could graze and the locals gathered firewood (so successfully that it was soon denuded of trees). Successive governors didn't know what to do with it until, shortly after landing in Sydney, Macquarie declared it a park, naming it after the one in London. On 6 October 1810 he announced its dimensions:

> The whole of the open ground yet unoccupied in the vicinity of the town of Sydney, hitherto known and alternately called by the names of 'The Common', 'Exercising Ground', 'Cricket Ground' and 'Racecourse', bounded by the Governor's Domain on the north, the town of Sydney on the west, the Brickfields on the south and Mr Palmer's premises on the east, being intended in future for the recreation and amusement of the inhabitants of the town, and as a field of exercise for troops, the governor has thought proper to name the ground thus described 'Hyde Park'.

All told it would be 16.2 hectares in size and basically rectangular in shape.

He then had what is now northern Hyde Park converted into a 10-furlong racecourse. (The circular shape of the park at its northern end is a reminder of this former activity.) The 73rd Regiment, which had arrived in Sydney with Macquarie in late 1809, cleared the ground and on 15 October 1810 Macquarie opened the first race meeting in Sydney. The three-day event excited the whole town. A grandstand was erected near Market Street, and signs warned that any dog wandering on the track would be shot. Horses galloped on a circular course clockwise towards Macquarie Street, then along College Street, around Liverpool, then across Elizabeth Street to the winning post at the grandstand in Market Street, a distance of two kilometres. Macquarie attended every day of the three-day meet, which concluded with a grand ball.

There were balls and dinners for the upper classes in tents on Hyde Park and in the houses of the elite. The lower classes found their fun in drinking and, as the *Sydney Gazette* reported, betting huge amounts on cockfighting:

> The amateurs of cocking were on the bye days amused with
> their favourite sport, at a house in the vicinity of the park.
> A number of battles were fought, and the pit was crowded
> each day.

Hyde Park almost didn't survive Governor Darling's proposal in the early 1830s to sell it off for housing development. The decision was delayed, and the new governor, Richard Bourke, appalled by the idea, vetoed the plan and re-affirmed the area's status as a park.

Cricket matches were played in the north-west corner where, said one witness, 'It was not unusual to see a ball hit over into Castlereagh Street, for in those days nearly all the houses were cottages with low roofs.' After the game thirsty cricketers would walk to Tanks' Hotel on the corner of Park and Elizabeth streets. Although cricket was to be played in Hyde Park until 1856, there were constant arguments with quoits players, whose activities dug up the wickets. Far from being the staid amusement played on the decks of passenger ships, quoits was keenly contested with huge wagers laid on the games. Rugby, hurling and boxing also became familiar sights in the park, as did military exercises and drills. With so much activity it's no wonder that nothing grew. A sketch made in 1842 shows a bare, slightly uneven surface surrounded by a simple wooden fence.

The area remained without grass or trees until 1854, when paths were made, lawns sown, gardens dug and trees planted. There was a central avenue of Moreton Bay fig trees and a huge bandstand. In a few years the park had 'clover always in abundance, and in a good season had all the appearance of an English field covered with white daisies'. On summer evenings people listened to bands and the fashionable promenaded in the cool southerly breeze. The central avenue, known as 'Lovers Walk', was always crowded, particularly of a Sunday night. On the Queen's Birthday there were extravagant displays of fireworks. It became a popular spot on Sunday afternoons devoted to oratory where men lectured rowdy crowds on 'Religious, political, socialistic and atheistic subjects'.

Civic monuments were installed, a statue of Prince Albert, husband of Queen Victoria, in 1866 (his baleful presence now stands outside Hyde Park Barracks) and a bronze statue of lawyer and politician William Bede Dalley erected in 1897. This is an odd work. Far from it being an idealistic portrait, its realism is refreshing. It shows him as he was: short, stout, wearing his familiar buttoned-up frock coat. Few people take any notice of it and know little about the man, and that's a shame because his is the story of a local boy made good, one whose life was shaped by Sydney. Born in nearby George Street in 1831 to convict parents, he studied diligently at St Mary's seminary just across the road, became a lawyer and politician, and frequently gave rousing speeches in the park where his statue now stands.

A jovial and genial man, he cut a dashing figure in colonial Sydney, with colourful cravats, flowers in his buttonholes and ornate frock coats. An epicurean (his body shape confirms this), he greeted everyone as 'Old Boy', gave generously to struggling artists and writers like Henry Kendall, and was one of the most imposing and eloquent men at the bar. His success in the court was legendary except for two celebrated cases: one was his failed defence of the bushranger Frank Gardiner, whom he had known as a boy; and in 1867 he tried to save Henry O'Farrell from the hangman after he shot the Duke of Edinburgh at Clontarf. He was a member of important social committees, hated animal cruelty, opposed the death penalty and was a defender of the Chinese at a time of White Australia hysteria. A strong nationalist, he was also a fervent supporter of our ties to Britain. He was loved by many and a public subscription after he died in 1888 quickly raised the money for his statue, which, appropriately enough, faces down Macquarie Street to the buildings of the Law Courts and Parliament House that played such a significant role in his life.

By the time the Dalley statue was erected, Hyde Park had become 'This noble, well grassed, well-kept reserve ... a great public resort with many seats for visitors, while the beds of flowers would cause a western floriculturist to turn green with envy.' By 1890 it was also becoming notorious for prostitutes, whose pick-up spots were around the drinking fountains. Because it was a depression, the park was a refuge, remarked the *Sun*, for 'the large number of houseless of both sexes, who have nowhere to lay their heads but among the clover-scented grass'.

If there is a constant, it's that the park offers refuge for those who have no other place to go. As one *Sydney Sun* reporter noted in 1920, in 'Dreamers in Hyde Park', many of the unemployed returned soldiers filled:

... seat after seat with its crew of dreamers, staring with lack-lustre eyes at the cropped turf and visioning who knows what in the air before them? Most of them wore overcoats, in fact, it would seem that most of them sleep in their overcoats; and their clothes are weird and faded … The older men stoop over their sticks in solitary seats and commune with nothing but their memories.

But the park was to be totally gutted a few months after this article was published with the coming of the City Circle rail line. The whole area was dug up and six years later the reconstruction of the park commenced and imported soil was laid down to improve the fertility. By 1930 photographs show the central path lined with only lampposts. There was grass but noticeably few trees, only scrawny saplings.

By the 1950s, the trees had matured, the bandstand had been demolished and replaced by Sandringham Garden in the south-east. It's a memorial to kings George V and VI and was opened by Queen Elizabeth in 1954.

This peaceful, seductive spot was designed by the Lithuanian immigrant Ilmar Berzins, the first qualified landscape architect in Australia who went on to design the exquisite Arthur McElhone Reserve in Elizabeth Bay and Fitzroy Gardens in Potts Point. One of his influences was the Canadian landscape designer Christopher Tunnard, author of the seminal *Gardens in the Modern Landscape* (1938). The book promoted the idea that parks were outdoor 'rooms', comprising contemplative elements, diverse plant species, flowerbeds and intricate walling or paving. All these concepts are on display in Hyde Park. For one supporter, Berzins' work was 'small scale interventions in the public domain … he held a passionate belief that all people need to enjoy nature and that nature, in turn, can ameliorate the human temperament'.

In the far north-west corner, where cricket was once played, is a special water feature. Not many people notice this unobtrusive and tranquil water sculpture, and even fewer know its name and what it means. Off the main paths and partly hidden behind clumps of ferns and the glossy green leaves of *Monstera deliciosa* is a fountain, its presence announced by the gurgling murmur of falling water (on my visit, mixed with the loud grunts of two sweaty men working out). It is a series of four shallow irregularly shaped basins made of concrete with inlaid pebbles, growing progressively larger as they descend, the water trickling downwards from the top basin. Constructed in the early 1960s, it was designed as a homage to Busby's Bore, for several decades the city's main water source. Without the bore, the city would have been in severe trouble. However, like the Opera House and the recent light rail construction, it became infamous for spiralling costs, delays and conflict between an impatient government and the contractors.

It became apparent in the early 1820s that Sydney was in the midst of a water crisis. The Tank Stream was so polluted that it was a health hazard, private wells dotted the city, so many of them that an area like the Rocks was dangerous at nights, with exasperated authorities pleading with householders to cover the wells because so many people, especially drunks, were falling into them and drowning. Other sources of water were costly exercises, with barrels of water being transported from the Blackwattle Swamps in the west or as far afield as the swamps of Botany.

John Busby, a surveyor and engineer in England, Scotland and Ireland, migrated to New South Wales with his family in 1824. One of his duties was to supply the town with water, a task that was to become hugely controversial. He was nearing 60 when Governor Brisbane asked him to construct Sydney's first water supply. After months of experimentation, Busby found the finest water to come from Lachlan Swamps (Centennial Park). It was, he said, 'perfectly transparent and colourless, free from every taste and smell, and so soft as to be fit for washing and every other domestic purpose'. He suggested that the main pump be driven by a steam engine or a huge treadmill propelled by convicts. Naturally the government favoured the latter plan because, after all, it reasoned, there was an unlimited supply of convicts given that transportation was likely to continue for a long time.

But in 1825 Busby came up with a new plan. Although more expensive, it would prove cheaper over the long term. The idea was to drive a tunnel a little over four kilometres from the swamps to Hyde Park. He estimated it would take three years to construct. In order to cut costs, it was decided to use convicts because they were cheaper than hiring labour. The unforeseen consequence of this was that the tunnel would take ten years to complete.

Work finally started in 1827, but what the government hadn't reckoned on was Busby's reluctance to go underground to oversee the project. He was afraid of the convicts, believing them to be 'vicious, drunken and idle'. Up to 140 unsupervised men, using hand tools, had to cut through sandstone, avoid quicksand and pipe clay, and shore up the sides and roof of the tunnel with slabs of sandstone as it inched its way into Hyde Park.

Needless to say, the tunnel didn't progress in a straight line but ran the course of least resistance in a series of detours and side-steps. If confronted by a difficult section, the convicts would make their way through an easier path. The result was blind alleys, half-hearted attempts, and inconsistent heights and widths. The egregious tunnel can vary from one metre square in places to large caverns over three metres high and three and a half metres across.

The languid pace of the tunnelling bemused the citizens, who took to calling Busby 'The Great Bore'. An exasperated Governor Bourke, believing that part of the problem was that the engineer was too old to closely supervise the work, ordered that Busby's son, William, take on the job as overseer, the salary to be divided between father and son.

Finally in June 1837 the bore was completed. The water

emerged from an elevated pipeline resting on a sturdy trestle in Hyde Park near Market Street. A painting of 1843 shows the contraption, with horses waiting to cart huge barrels of water into town to sell. At its peak the bore delivered up to 1 820 000 litres daily, but during times of drought much less, and during those trying times carts had to wait three or four hours for their turn and locals were forced to pay up to sixpence for a bucket of water. The bore was Sydney's sole source of water until 1859. Few, if any of the people now passing through Hyde Park know just how crucial the bore had been to Sydney's survival.

Busby's Bore may have been the first tunnel under Hyde Park, but since then a honeycomb of tunnels and passageways has sprouted beneath the park. Besides the two railway stations, St James and Museum, there is also a ghost railway platform at St James station. Built in 1926 as one of the first underground stations in the nation, St James was to be part of a rail network extending to Bondi and the northern beaches. Devised by John Bradfield, whose next project was the Sydney Harbour Bridge, the railway line was never finished due to the Great Depression.

Time has stood still on the dirty ghost platform, still with its old heritage signs, archways, frames waiting for posters and railway beds empty of tracks. This is an eerie place, only open to the public once a year. Armed with torches that barely penetrate the echoing darkness, the intrepid explorer has to navigate a flight of stairs where the only sounds in the oppressive silence are your own footsteps and heavy breathing as your lungs get used to the limited oxygen and stale air. Reaching the bottom, the visitor is confronted by tunnels which can only be reached by wading through corridors of knee-high water where you are greeted by the first of several huge flooded chambers, one with a dome roof and a huge bell in the centre of it, which was used to replicate the sound of Big Ben for a film.

Lying some 30 metres below Hyde Park, the labyrinth of abandoned tunnels continues for a kilometre in each direction from St James station, finishing to the north just past the entrance to the Cahill expressway on Macquarie Street. One of the pools, known as Lake St James, runs for a kilometre between the State Library and the Conservatorium of Music. Apparently the water is fresh enough to drink. It's said that during high tide eels slip into the water between the sandstone cracks in the sea wall at Farm Cove.

On the other side of the chamber is a maze of narrow passageways that zigzag from one tunnel to the next. What people above ground don't know as they walk through the shade of the many huge fig trees is that their roots descend deep under the surface, in a slow and determined effort to penetrate through the soil and concrete tunnels seeking moisture from the freshwater lakes below. Their roots dangle helplessly from the ceiling like Gothic cobwebs; on the walls white crystallised fungi sparkle when brushed by the torchlight.

Once considered useless, these tunnels were transformed into bomb shelters for 20 000 people during World War II. The soldiers who were stationed in this spooky world filled in their time by writing messages on the walls to their loved ones above ground (*I love you my dearest wife Robyn Foreman*) or merely recording dates, names and ranks.

After the war this spot became a mushroom farm and then movie makers discovered it. Scenes from *The Matrix* were filmed here, and later an Australian film, called *The Tunnel* naturally enough, used the location for the story of a film crew that investigates the disappearance of homeless people. One by one a monster in the lake kills off members of the crew.

It's as easy to imagine a horror story being made down there, as it is to believe the many urban myths associated with it, including that a gigantic albino eel lives in one of the subterranean lakes. What does seem to be true is that in the 1970s witches practised secret black magic rituals there, leaving behind wall paintings of pentagrams, a skeleton cross and, representing hell, a heart on fire.

Back on the surface, another tunnel shoots off from the north-east corner of Hyde Park, and is just as disconcerting in its own way. It is a moving walkway, its walls illustrated not with images of black magic but two long rows of murals. Except for those who park in the Domain car park, few people are aware of it. Its entrance is meekly signed before one descends an abrupt set of stairs that lead towards an increasingly ominous rumbling sound. At the base of the stairs two 200-metre walkways lie side by side, one in each direction.

The journey through the shadowy tunnel takes five minutes as it slowly slips into the depths of Woolloomooloo. The rubber conveyer belt feels unsteady under the feet as if surfing a viscid wave. The murals are painted in a weird variety of styles, from the professional to the naïve. Images of Sydney pass in a blur of feverish colours: scenes of Aboriginal life, a ship towing the Sydney Harbour Bridge, a girl holding a fiery globe, starry skies, beaches, blue and red trees, schools of deliriously bright fishes, marine animals, harbourside apartment blocks, seagulls, seascapes and sunbakers – all in all, a hallucinogenic portrait of Sydney. The belt suddenly shudders to a stop and, if pedestrians are not careful, they can tumble off it, as many have done.

When it was built in 1961, it was the longest moving walkway in the world and considered a symbol of the future of modern transportation, but now it has morphed into what Vanessa Berry, in her book *Mirror Sydney*, calls a quaint example of 'retro-futuristic novelty'.

Hyde Park has another hidden history, when it becomes a site of danger and cruelty. During the late nineteenth century gangs of violent larrikins lurked in the shadows at night and attacked passers-by. In 1885 a mob savaged a woman while one attempted to rape her. In 1894 two 'enraged women' attacked a man and left him impaled on a spiked fence. The year before, an act of violence originated in a kiosk near Market Street. The 30-year-old owner, incensed that three men refused to pay for their pies, followed them down William Street shouting out to them that he wanted his money. When they mocked him and told him to fuck off, he took a revolver from under his apron and shot one of them dead. Satisfied at having taken his revenge, he returned to his stall to calmly serve other customers.

For women it could be a perilous place at night. In 1928 a young woman sat on a bench with a man she had arranged to meet. They appeared to be getting on well, then he took out a razor and slashed her face several times. She broke away from him, blood streaming from her wounds, while the man took off down to Woolloomooloo Bay and jumped in, drowning himself. He left behind his clothes and a diary; the last entry said he would 'do' the girl and then commit suicide.

Not long afterwards a homeless woman was found raped and dead, her corpse hidden under newspapers. If these incidents seem things of the past, they're not. In 2013 an 18 year old left a nightclub and, drunk and disorientated, entered the park, not realising a 52-year-old man was following her. When he grabbed her, she tried to flee, but he held her tightly, threatening her, 'I'm not going to kill you if you go with it.' He then orally and anally raped her. A jury found him guilty, and he was sentenced to 11 years.

Hyde Park has been a place of high emotions. Unions have demonstrated there, and people have created carnage. The day after the Sydney Harbour Bridge was opened on 19 March 1932, hundreds of drunken revellers descended on Hyde Park, trampling on flowerbeds, vandalising park furniture, digging up lawns and strewing rubbish. One of the more violent demonstrations occurred in 2012 during a Muslim protest against an American anti-Islam film *The Innocence of Muslims*. The protesters chanted peacefully outside the United States Consulate General in the city and then the 300-strong crowd moved on to Hyde Park, where things became ugly. The mob clashed with police, throwing sticks, stones and bottles at them and chanting 'Down, down USA'. Some of them carried placards and flags that said *Behead all those who insult our prophet, Our dead are in paradise, your dead are in hell, Shariah will dominate the world*. Six policemen were injured and two hospitalised.

These incidents are the exception, of course. Like the park of the same name in London, and Central Park in New York, Hyde Park is a verdant oasis, a place where stressed city workers, the sad, the homeless and visitors come to connect with nature, albeit in its stylised and tamed form. It's not only a sanctuary from petrol fumes and workplaces, but traffic noise is muted to a background hum by the trees and vegetation. What one notices is that the park itself nowadays verges on the inchoate. There are disparate enclaves, separate from each other, scattered across the park, containing visual surprises for the visitor who comes upon them.

All these eclectic fountains and enclaves and bisecting paths gravitate, like planets around the sun, towards one stunning piece of art deco sculpture, perhaps the most beautiful public statuary in Sydney. This is the cynosure of the park – the Archibald Fountain. Situated at the intersection of the main avenues, it is encircled by open space and a rim of flowerbeds. The hexagonal fountain is 18 metres in diameter and features bronze statues of dolphins, gods and goddesses, and turtles. A towering Apollo, six metres high, dominates the mythical figures of Diana, Pan, and

Theseus and the Minotaur. Behind Apollo is a delicate spray of water representing the rising sun and at his feet water spouts from his chariot horses. Around the large basin six tortoises expel jets of water.

The fountain was financed by JF Archibald, the founding editor of the *Bulletin*. Archibald was of Irish descent, but he adopted a French persona and the first names Jules François. A mercurial character, he was the victim of sometimes crippling melancholia, one time ending up in the Callan Park Asylum. His fortunes having recovered after the ignominy of being jailed for debt after the Clontarf defamation case in 1882, he bequeathed his fountain to Sydney as a commemoration of the close association of France and Australia in the Great War. He insisted a French sculptor be chosen, and this commission was taken up by François Sicard. The Frenchman's original design of Hercules slaying the lion caused some consternation, as it was thought this was a snide reference to the conquering of the British lion. Sicard changed it to the more tactful theme of Theseus slaying the Minotaur.

Installed in 1932, Sydney took to the fountain immediately and it became a favourite spot to meet and relax. By the following year the artist Herbert Badham portrayed it and the surrounding area as a place of quiet contemplation. Three figures sit on a bench in front of the fountain; a man and a woman who are reading, while a middle-aged man in an overcoat stares directly at the painter as if to say, *This is the life*. All three are indifferent to a gardener heading out of the frame as he patiently mows the lawn. The central location of the fountain and its naked, straining Theseus also attracted men seeking men, and by the 1950s it was a gay 'beat', slyly featured in Kylie Tennant's 1967 novel *Tell Morning This*.

Now it attracts hundreds if not thousands of people daily, from the curious to visitors, tourists and school groups and is thought to be one of the most photographed sites in Sydney. Everyone gravitates towards it, milling around its red granite border, larking, and gazing at one of the most prized examples of art deco art in Australia. Though one cannot help but notice that its playful, muscular gods and goddesses, with their air of erotic tension and violent paganism, seem a deliberate challenge to the Catholic fortress of St Mary's just a short distance away.

THE WORLD COMES TO SYDNEY

BARNETT LEVEY'S THEATRE ROYAL, Sydney's 'first permanent theatre', opened in 1833 with the nautical melodrama *Black-Eyed Susan*. The evening finished with 'the famed highly comic farce', *Monsieur Tonson*. Music was provided by the 17th Regiment. It wasn't long before the theatre gained a reputation for 'rowdiness in the pit and gallery', with prostitutes mingling with the audiences and brazenly scanning the foyers for clients.

Levey was not a good businessman. His quick temper, litigious ways and furious arguments over his underpayment of actors meant he was forced to lease the theatre to others. It's hard to gauge the standard of the theatre productions of the era except through reviews, which could be caustic. In 1838 the romantic drama *Gil Blas* was, in one critic's opinion, 'an indifferent success ... where several of the actors were palpably ignorant of their parts'. In the same year there was the first performance in Australia of *Maurice the Woodcutter*. Set in Germany, the play was a delirious melodrama involving tyrannical princes, wilful barons and, of course, the innocent woodcutter, who is jailed for killing a hare. The theatre reviewer of the *Commercial Journal and Advertiser* wrote that Mrs Taylor, who played Maurice's wife 'very ably sustaining the character of Marie', was to swoon at one point. A fellow actor, Mr Lee, was supposed to catch her in his arms, but either through 'gross negligence ... or from a worse motive', didn't attempt to catch her. She hit her head on the stage and was knocked unconscious. An announcement was made and 'the curtain fell'. Mrs Taylor's husband, who had a role as a supernumerary, was said by one reviewer to be, 'intolerable. His braying ... becomes truly disgusting.'

The Theatre Royal was to burn down in 1840, but two years earlier Joseph Wyatt had built the Royal Victoria in Pitt Street. It opened with *Othello*, with a Miss Arabin playing both Desdemona and Emelia, while her husband blacked-up for the title role. The new theatre seemed to symbolise, as one journalist summed it up:

> Sydney's phenomenal progress of fifty years as a colony.
> Look at her churches and schools, and theatre, her ships and
> commerce, and it must be allowed that she has made prodigious
> advances from a wild and uninhabited forest to a community
> of influential men, where skills in arts and sciences and useful
> literature flourish as much as they do in England, in proportion
> to the paucity of our population.

The Royal Victoria became notable for providing 'worthy' entertainment, with well-behaved audiences. It may have staged Shakespeare, European playwrights, and famous melodramas, but the pantomimes directed by Andrew Torning made the money. He also thrilled Sydney audiences with plays especially written for 'his highly trained dogs Lion and Neptune' and 'his wonderful dog Dragon'. Torning was also a decorator and painter. His work was on permanent display at the Shakespeare Tavern on Pitt Street between King and Market, the 'rendezvous of the man about town'. Inside was the Shakespeare saloon, 'a well-proportioned room, lighted from the roof, richly and artistically decorated with wall murals depicting scenes from the works of Shakespeare'. The multi-talented Torning was also celebrated in Sydney for starting the city's first organised fire brigade in 1855, perhaps influenced by the regularity with which theatres burned down.

If you didn't want to watch plays, there was Ashton's Amphitheatre in York Street, which specialised in equestrian events. One of the best performers was a 15-year-old Aboriginal boy, the trick rider Mungo Mungo. His most memorable feat was to stand on the back of a horse as it ran around the circular space, then two men would hold a huge tablecloth out over the track. As the horse ran below the cloth, Mungo Mungo jumped over it and as the horse re-emerged on the other side, he landed feet-first on its back.

Sydney began to attract international actors and singers. New theatres such as the opulent Prince of Wales on Castlereagh Street (it would burn down in 1860 and then again in 1872 during a performance of the panto *The House that Jack Built*), faster steamship travel, and an Australia made rich by the gold rush and wool exports, made it a viable destination for international theatre companies and actors, who realised they could make a fortune from middle-class audiences hungry for quality overseas acts.

In 1854 Torning, manager of the Royal Victoria, engaged American actors, including a teenage Edwin Booth of the famous Booth family (his brother John Wilkes Booth would assassinate President Lincoln in 1865). Edwin used the tour to make a name for himself in plays such as *Hamlet*. The *Sydney Morning Herald* thought his performances were 'quite an event'. The same year, the famous soprano Catherine Hayes arrived in Sydney to perform at the Royal Victoria, causing 'an excitement wholly unparalleled in the theatrical annals of this colony'. She sang arias from operas and entranced audiences with her version of 'Home Sweet Home' and brought the Irish in the theatre to tears with 'Oh, Steer My Bark to Erin's Isle'.

The following year, 1855, was memorable for the number of touring international theatrical stars, 'who dodged each other from city to city, town to town'. For one enthralled journalist, 'It is pleasing, therefore, to see the impulse which, for the last twelve months, has been given to the Australian stage by the successive arrival amongst us of actors and actresses of talent never before witnessed in these colonies.'

The most celebrated actor was Gustavus Brooke, who had been born in Dublin and became famous in London and the United States before touring Australia with his company. An excited Torning, who had picked up some publicity tricks while in America, stuck up posters everywhere, a novelty that didn't please some people, including one critic who sniffed, 'The good people of Sydney did not take kindly to the flaring, puffing posters with which Mr Torning covered the hoardings of the city announcing the advent of the great tragedian.'

Brooke performed the title role of *Hamlet*, played Shylock, Romeo and Lear. One awestruck reviewer summed up his talent and appearance:

His mental talents for the profession were of the highest order ... a classical face of the Roman type and a well-formed majestic figure with a voice of exceptional volume and roundness ... he was well educated and had the manners of a polished gentleman ... all fitted him for the highest position in the realms of dramatic art.

His Othello was thought remarkable, as was that of his Desdemona, played by the brilliant Fanny Cathcart in a performance that was 'almost too painfully portrayed, and we suggest ... that its fearful consummation should take place ... out of sight'. Sydney's excited hospitality was sometimes overwhelming; years later both Booth and Brooke would blame their alcoholism on their Antipodean tours.

The success of these stars saw more actors arrive from England, including the great tragedian Barry Sullivan, who played Macbeth at the new Theatre Royal. By now Sydneysiders, having seen many international stars, could compare them. Sullivan was thought to be 'one of the best Macbeths of our time', but as one exacting reviewer observed, 'in the colloquy commencing *I have done the deed; didst thou not hear a noise?* we missed the hoarse whisper and impressive monotone employed with such thrilling effect by Mr Brooke'. Sullivan also had a talent for electrifying audiences with special effects. When he staged *Faust,* he arranged for bellringers at nearby St James' church to ring a peal of bells at the right dramatic moment in the play, spooking the audience.

International visitors began to arrive to satiate their curiosity about the colony, and in 1858 *The Stranger's Guide to Sydney* was published. The cheap, slim book was written for 'those who have but a short time' and it described four basic walks which would help the visitor take in much of Sydney, together with Hackney Coach, Omnibus and Steam Ferry timetables.

A more thorough and boastful guide, *Handbook to Sydney and its Suburbs, a First Traveller's Guide* was published in 1868. It began, of course, with a description of the beauty of Port Jackson, and then went on to extol vistas and buildings that it thought would appeal to visitors. There was the attractive drive to South Head, 'the old road hugging the seacoast, whilst the new one, studded with villas and gardens, skirts along the bays and inlets of the inner shore of the harbour'. If you wanted invigorating air, then Manly was the fashionable bathing place to visit. George Street, between Watermen's Stairs and Barrack Street, was, compared to the rest of George Street, 'of a very old-fashioned and decayed appearance, reminding one of some of the old seaport towns of England'. If you wanted some intellectual stimulus, then there was the Sydney Mechanics' School of Arts in Pitt Street.

Established in 1833, its library had 13 000 volumes, all Australian newspapers, plus many leading English ones.

Petty's Hotel, on the corner of York, Clarence and Jamison streets, was 'the first hotel for international visitors'. The two-storey building had a gorgeous ornate verandah, 40 bedrooms, and 'a tastefully laid out garden … that gave all the appearance of a gentleman's mansion'. The *Handbook* called it 'one of the best in the colonies. The building is a credit to Sydney … The resort of the most distinguished visitors to Sydney, including English and French noblemen.'

For those who walked the streets of Sydney, there was the Botanic Gardens, where the visitors from the Mother Country could relax to the sound of English birds that had been imported into the colony. A new residential area was Wynyard Square, the site of the old barracks vacated by the army in 1848, with many of its splendid houses owned by Jewish merchants.

At the Currency Lass Hotel, on the corner of Pitt and Hunter streets, you could eat wallaby soup, roast goose, boiled turkey with oyster sauce, roast fowl, roast lamb in mint, roast wallaby with jelly, 'with the usual bill of fare'. In George Street 'the bucks and Brummels of the Colony' visited the Café Française, where there was, noted Frank Fowler in his *Southern Lights and Shadows,* good food, chess sets, billiard tables, marble-topped tables, papers like *The Times* available, as were the popular sherry cobblers and ices; presiding over it all were 'an entertaining hostess and a big, bloused, lubberly, inoffensive host'.

The finest town houses were in Macquarie Street, some up to four storeys high. John Askew, in his *A Voyage to Australia and New Zealand,* was entranced:

The best time to see this neighbourhood in all its glory is on
a summer's evening … when the drawing rooms are a blaze of

light. There is the rich tones of the piano ... accompanied by
the sweet melody of female voices ... Beautiful ladies, dressed
in white, may be seen sitting on the verandahs, or lounging
on magnificent couches, partially concealed by the folds of
rich crimson curtains in drawing rooms which display all the
luxurious comforts and magnificence of the East.

Tourists and curious writers and journalists began to arrive in
Sydney. The English novelist Anthony Trollope visited in 1871
and was immediately struck by the city's irregular street grid:
'One may walk about it and lose the direction in which one is
going. Streets running side by side occasionally converge – and
they bend and go in and out, and wind themselves about, and
are intricate.' What surprised him was the city's deceptive age,
observing that 'the antiquity of Sydney ... strikes an Englishman
as being almost absurd'.

H Mortimer Franklyn, who wrote *A Glance at Australia in
1880*, thought the lack of building regulations, as well as the
topography of the town, resulted in haphazard street plans that:

> ... gave the impression produced upon the visitor fresh from
> the rectangular formality of a younger capital in a neighbouring
> colony, that [the city] is unicolonial and free of the dreadful
> newness and the garish rawness which characterise most
> Australian centres of population.

Richard Twopeny noted in his *Town Life in Australia* that Sydney's
wealth was most apparent in its 'impressive buildings, both public
and private, created from Pyrmont's golden sandstone'. Like
Trollope and Franklyn, he remarked on the city's eccentric layout,
but conceded:

... it must not be imagined that it is poorly built ... the handsomest are the Treasury, the Colonial Secretary's Office, and the Lands Office ... The Colonial Secretary's Office is ... lofty, massive and dignified outwardly, elegant and spacious inside ...

The wealth even extended to newspapers such as the *Sydney Morning Herald*, which could afford to have 'correspondents in almost every capital in Europe, including St Petersburg'.

You can see this middle-class wealth and growing economic prosperity in a painting by Montagu Scott titled *A Day's Picnic on Clark Island* that was shown at the 1870 Intercolonial Exhibition held at Prince Alfred Park. The picture is a marvellous example of Sydney pleased with itself and its material progress. It depicts a picnic party on a bright sunny day with women in the latest overseas fashions – long wide skirts with bustles. The men are in frock coats and top hats. Bourgeois activities reign. In the colourful crowd there are young women waiting for oysters a man is knocking free from a rock, while a solitary woman is spearing something in the water with her parasol. Young men and women flirt under the gimlet eye of a mother, people drink French champagne, others use a rock as a picnic table, waiting for a slice of ham being carved by a man. On the narrow beach a man is playing fetch with his dog, more people are disembarking from a boat and, in the corner of the painting, a man and woman are conducting, as the reviewer in *Sydney Illustrated* noted, 'an umbrella courtship, bespeaking that passion which is old as the hills, and which will endure as long'. This is a middle-class paradise, Sydney's Island of Cythera.

For sailor and future novelist Joseph Conrad, it was Sydney as a port city that captivated him on his first visit in 1878:

From the heart of the fair city down the vista of important streets could be seen the wool-clippers lying at Circular Quay – no walled prison-house of the dock that, but the integral part of one of the finest most beautiful vast and safe bays the sun ever shone upon. Now great steamliners lie at these berths, always reserved for the sea aristocracy – grand and imposing enough ships, but here today and gone next week; whereas the general cargo, emigrant, and passenger clippers of my time, rigged with heavy spars, and built on fine lines, used to remain for months together waiting for their load of wool. Their names attained the dignity of household words … The night closed rapidly upon the silent ships with their crews on shore. Up a short steep ascent by the King's Head pub patronised by the cooks and stewards of the fleet, the voice of a man crying 'Hot Saveloys' at the end of George Street, where cheap eating houses (sixpence a meal) were kept by Chinamen (Sun-kum-on's was not bad) is heard at regular intervals.

In 1879 Pfahlert's Hotel, on the corner of Carrington and Margaret streets, published a visitor's guide subtitled *How to Spend a Week in Sydney* that recommended the Domain for walks and to watch cricket, the palms and cycads at the Botanic Gardens and the Head Quarter's Band that played in its rotunda when 'the weather is fine – which is the rule'. Steam launches were available to hire to carry one to the pleasure gardens at Manly, Clontarf, Chowder Bay and Athol Gardens. Visitors could take a ferry up the Parramatta River to inspect 'the very famed Asylum for the Insane'. The adventurous tourist could search the rocks at low tide for oysters, 'for which Sydney Harbour is so remarkable'.

A more thorough visitors' guide was published three years later, *An Illustrated Guide to Sydney 1882*. Like Pfahlert's Hotel visitor's guide, there is an obvious pride and confidence about the city as a national and international destination. One of its first entries was to calm the visitor about the 'evil reputation' of the Rocks. The notorious Brown Bear Lane and Maori Lane were once 'scenes of riot', where policemen were beaten nightly and robbers did not hesitate to murder, 'but nothing of this kind now occurs'. Much of the Argyle Street area of the Rocks was occupied by the Chinese:

> … who pursue their different avocations with considerable profit in commercial circles as shopkeepers, carpenters, and furniture makers, druggists, fancy goods sellers and vendors of curios and nick-knackery. With the exception of sixteen Christians, they all follow the religion of Confucius and have temples in little back rooms. Opium smoking is common but not carried out to excess.

The *Illustrated Guide* went out of its way to acknowledge Sydney's earlier crime-ridden and poverty-stricken areas, but emphasised they were gone. For example, in Rowe Street, off Pitt Street, the poorer classes had once occupied the crumbling houses, but now the area was 'a foreigners' quarter, where hurdy-gurdy artists, street musicians, and others congregate making an uncertain living by such means'. York Street near Barrack Street was transformed after hundreds of shanties were demolished to make way for warehouses, auction rooms and machine shops.

However, at times the guide seemed almost nostalgic about Sydney's raffish past:

> At the corner of Market and York was one of the queerest as well as the most notorious taverns of olden days … kept open for receiving the dregs of society. It was no infrequent thing for a couple of hundred of the aged, blind, lame and other

unfortunates of both sexes to be congregated in and around the
building at one time.

Macquarie Street remained, as the *Handbook* had stated, 'the
aristocratic quarter', but the Royal Hotel was now the favourite
headquarters of rich graziers and intercolonial visitors. It boasted
nearly 100 rooms, spacious corridors and a grand saloon. The
saloon for ladies was entered by a separate street doorway 'and
supplies a want long felt in Sydney'.

A flaneur could take in the many magnificent sandstone
edifices, including the Public Lands and Mines offices at Bridge,
Bent and Gresham streets, 'perhaps the largest public building
in the city', the Chief Secretary's and Public Works offices at
Bridge and Macquarie streets, the gorgeous General Post Office,
the pseudo-Gothic Government House, and the Town Hall,
where a visit to the top provided 'a bird's eye view of city and
the suburbs'. It was acknowledged that the old parliamentary
buildings were 'not at all prepossessing, and the accommodation
within very unsuitable for either legislators, reporters or strangers'.
But there were newer buildings like the Treasury, the Museum,
and Customs House at Circular Quay to explore.

A place to relax and enjoy yourself was down south in Botany.
During the holiday season:

> ... people often use a steamer, or may take a tram car, hire a
> cab to the richest wildflower region around Sydney. [There you
> will find the] Sir Joseph Banks Hotel, with well-kept gardens,
> quoit grounds, skittle alley, dancing pavilion ... in fact all the
> surroundings necessary to brush away the cobwebs of the city
> from the brain of excursionists.

In a walk through the glorious Botanic Gardens (Trollope called it one of the best of its kind in the world), one couldn't avoid James Barnet's Garden Palace, the Sydney International Exhibition Building completed in 1879. Pressured by the government to design and finish work on the project in nine months, the frequently sick Barnet had to oversee the work that continued day and night, and also account for the spending. As usual he went over budget and, although the splendid result was applauded by the public, he was censured by the parliament. As the *Illustrated Guide* said of the building, 'it is not too much to say that a new era was marked in the advancement of the colony'.

The palace housed Australia's first International Exhibition. This was a period when cities like London, Paris and Philadelphia held international exhibitions showing off their countries' industrial and manufacturing advances, as well as their art and agriculture. For Sydney, as many critics pointed out, such a large undertaking would cost a fortune, and there were incessant squabbles about the cost and design. There were also concerns that the city would be embarrassed on the world stage by the decrepit houses in the Rocks and around Darling Harbour. Animals roamed loose on the streets and there were always large numbers of dead animals that had to be removed. A look at the Inspector of Nuisances report from 1875 reveals some startling figures: 10 419 fowls alone had to be removed (most people had chickens in their yards), dead rats came in second with 4016 removed, followed by 2667 dead cats and 1337 dogs. Despite the increasing urbanisation, among the dead animals that had to be collected were possums, kangaroos, wallabies and koalas.

After a year of quarrels and vacillations, the government gave the go-ahead in January 1879 for the construction of the Garden Palace.

Eventually it covered 20 hectares of the Botanic Gardens. The ostentatious structure stretched from what is now the Conservatorium to the front of the State Library. Four towers and a magnificent central dome dominated the city skyline. The north tower incorporated Sydney's first hydraulic lift, which enabled visitors to take in elevated views of the harbour. Inside were machinery halls, a huge art gallery, display halls and band-stands. Outside were temporary buildings for livestock.

Despite the predictions of doomsayers, the Garden Palace opened on 17 September 1879 with a spectacular parade of mounted police, steam fire engines, even bearded druids in flowing robes. There were 724 classes of goods and produce from Australia and overseas. Locals could not compete with inter-national machines and inventions, but from all over Australia came examples of agricultural wealth, plus examples of kerosene shale, a large petrified tree from Lismore, stalactites, fossils and an enormous variety of timbers. Aboriginal people were represented by an ethnological display, as if they had already died out. There were cultural and artistic events, and visitors came from overseas and interstate.

Sydney was on the world stage for the first time. As the London *Times* observed, 'the eyes of the world are centred for once on Australia, and at seeing a lively competition between American, European and British manufacturers'.

Once the exhibition was over, the Garden Palace was used as a dumping ground for the paperwork of various government departments. At dawn on 22 September 1882 it burned down in a spectacular inferno. The windows of houses in Macquarie Street were blown out by the heat, and blackened pieces of iron landed as far away as Rushcutters Bay. Records, including land titles, railway surveys, the grand organ, paintings, objects from the new Technological and Mining Museum and the details of the 1881 census were all consumed by the flames. Arson was suspected but never proved.

Despite the fire, the exhibition had made the rest of the world take notice of Sydney and, in turn, it gave the city a sense of confidence and pride that verged on cockiness, something that has remained in the Sydney psyche.

THE DIVIDED CITY

IN 1870 THE COLONIAL ARCHITECT JAMES BARNET WAS looking for someone take photographs of Sydney, especially its architecture, for the London International Exhibition. In January 1871, on Barnet's recommendation, the New South Wales government commissioned Charles Percy Pickering to 'prepare a number of photographic views of Sydney and its suburbs'.

Pickering was born in England and came to Sydney in 1855, where he worked as one of the city's few professional photographers. By 1860 he had opened larger premises in the southern end of George Street, where he excelled at taking portraits. His studio became so popular that his address was reduced to 'Pickering. Brickfield Hill'.

He became famous as 'The Family Photographer', and besides specialising in the middle classes, he also photographed the infamous, including bushranger Frank Gardiner. His business also cornered the market in *cartes-de-visite* ('in a rich brown tint'). He continued to experiment with photographs and in 1870 he was commissioned by the *Illustrated Sydney News* to produce a huge panorama of Sydney. It was this photograph that secured him the government commission.

In 1872 a large folio, *Photographs of Public and Other Buildings, &c. Taken by Authority of the Government of New South Wales, at the Request of the Secretary of State for the Colonies*, reproduced 166 of his Sydney photographs. Considering that the photographs were of Sydney in 1871, the frontispiece of the book seems strange. It's a reproduction of Frenchman Charles Lesueur's engraving *Sydney in 1803*, which depicted Sydney as a primitive and impermanent settlement. It was chosen for the frontispiece as a deliberate and dramatic contrast with the Pickering photographs of Sydney 70 years later, showing just how far the city had progressed.

The book's images were of Sydney's buildings: libraries, churches, banks, the Treasury, the Australian Museum, post offices, the Australia Club, the stately *Sydney Morning Herald* building in Hunter Street, schools, the Glebe Island abattoirs, the Redfern mortuary station, the Royal Hotel, Sydney University, Government House, Darlinghurst Gaol, the Exhibition Building, Fort Macquarie, and many others, including, of course, photographs of the harbour and Botanic Gardens.

The *Sydney Mail* considered that most of the buildings Pickering had photographed 'would be an ornament to any city'. Some considered the images austere but 'beautiful specimens of photographic art'. The unsettling aspect of them for the modern viewer is that Sydney looks like a ghost town. The buildings stand alone in their sandstone glory, but Pickering went out of his way not to show any people, except for occasional children who have snuck into a shot and stare back at us as if they are the only humans left alive. Even the abattoirs are empty of workers. It's an unnerving, eerie Sydney.

It was left to the amateur photographer Arthur Syer in the 1880s and 1890s to show Sydney as a vibrant, bustling city. Syer's images are some of the world's earliest street photographs. They were secretly taken with one of the first hand-held cameras, nicknamed the 'Detective Camera'. With it the pictures could be shot quickly and the camera unnoticed. According to the *Sydney*

Mail, it resembled 'a square case ... disguised as a ... shoeblack's box, or even a book. The operator places it upon the ground, or under his arm, the pressure of the pneumatic ball opening or closing the hidden lens at the required moment.'

Syer was the brother of the artist Walter Syer (aka the illustrator 'Cue'), a friend of the brilliant English cartoonist Phil May, who for three years worked for the *Bulletin*. Arthur supplied May with surreptitiously taken snapshots of ordinary people in daily attire, and the Englishman used the photographs to provide an authentic atmosphere for his cartoons. It's obvious looking at the 170 photographs that Arthur became obsessed by this new camera and how it could catch people unawares.

Judging by Walter's painting of his brother, Arthur was handsome and urbane. During much of this time the two brothers lived together in North Sydney, a place that didn't much interest Arthur. For him the action was on the other side of the harbour, from Circular Quay to the Randwick racetrack.

In his photographs Sydney life teems around Circular Quay, with wharf labourers going about their back-breaking business, barrow boys hawking their wares, and men and women rushing to catch a ferry to Manly or a steam ferry to Watsons Bay. Hundreds of men load and unload ships. Syer's pictures show why Sydney was Australia's maritime metropolis: even in the heart of the city of a quarter of a million people, the sea was never far away. Looking down Pitt Street, the ships seemed, as people often remarked, to 'lie in the street'.

Descending the steep streets to the daily throng at the Quay was a visual cacophony of the grand warehouses of the wool exporters and international cargo importers, the offices of steamship companies, brokers and insurance agents, and the dense traffic of horses and carts making their noisy way to and from the wharves. Wool comprised more than half of Sydney's exports, and the months when it arrived from the countryside to be shipped to the world were the city's busiest each year.

Along the western shore of the Quay were merchant ships, and to the east, along Bennelong Point, were the largest and fastest European steamers. After the passengers disembarked, the dock would be a swarm of huge sea trunks, porters, boarding house runners and wide-eyed immigrants waiting for transport, the poorer ones carrying their meagre belongings as they set out to search for cheap lodgings in the Rocks.

In other Syer snapshots women sell fruit, a gentleman in a top hat buys a banana from a street vendor, someone with his back to us pushes a man in a wooden wheelchair, and a Chinese man carries newly purchased supplies of food. There's a diverse range of different faces and ethnic groups around the Quay and nearby streets. The port city was becoming home to a cosmopolitan mix of different cultures and languages.

The photographs are so evocative that one can almost hear the noise of the clomping horses, smell their dung and hear the cries of hawkers and street vendors.

At the busy Pyrmont Bridge, ships' masts like needles point into the smoky sky. Horses are everywhere, carting bales of wool stacked so high they can barely fit under the Argyle Cut tunnel, or with their noses in their feed bags. In an 1881 survey, it was estimated that nearly 20000 horses passed along George Street every day, and over 10000 along Pitt Street.

There are people crowding George and Pitt streets and the Rocks. Women in heavy dresses ward off the harsh sun with parasols, all men wear hats of various styles, including bowlers, top hats and derbies. Hawkers haggle with customers, shoe shiners are busy, a double-decker steam tram waits to pick up passengers, mounted police patrol the city and cleaners rid the streets of horse dung.

Up on Observatory Hill goats graze untethered, and at Randwick racecourse, an all-male crowd, many with bristling moustaches, hurry to place their bets. But there is also a Dickensian atmosphere in the narrow treeless streets of the Rocks, where dirty children in rags race their billycarts or, bored, loiter outside their exhausted terrace houses. There are only a few photographs where silence seems to reign. One is of a thoughtful young woman sitting in a huge aviary gazing at the birds, and another of a young girl taking her pet duck for a walk on a leash.

What we can't hear are the street musicians. By the early 1890s there were some 100 boys trying to earn a living busking in the city's streets. Genteel women, down on their luck, advertised their skill as teachers of English, French, music and dancing. Others resorted to prostitution, working in brothels, soliciting on the streets, in bars or theatre foyers. For the poor and homeless there were the dismal City Night Refuge and Soup Kitchens.

For the wealthy mistress of the house there was the constant problem of finding staff. Fewer women wanted to be domestic servants. The wages were inadequate, the living conditions generally dire, the mistresses too stern and the hours too long. Young women wanted more personal freedom and leisure time and preferred to work in factories or shops. Magazines and newspapers didn't tire of satirising uppity maids. In a *Bulletin* cartoon in 1883, titled 'What Will It Come To', a mistress, having heard the bell ring, goes to the front door. As she opens it, the housemaid, standing on the stairs behind her, says, 'Oh, please, m'm, if that's anybody for me, I'm not at home.'

By the early 1890s there were obvious marked differences between the Sydney suburbs. An 1895 guidebook identified Alexandria, Annandale, Arncliffe and Auburn as working-class suburbs ('the houses being small').

Sydney's upper class clustered on widely separated promontories overlooking the harbour at Hunters Hill, North Sydney, Vaucluse, Point Piper and Darling Point, where old money and the nouveau riche congregated, built villas and imposing homes, networked and went to St Mark's church together. The villas were famous. There was 'Fiona', the estate of banker and sugar refiner Edward Knox; 'Quambi', the Italianate pile of the chief justice, Sir Frederick Darley; and 'Greenoaks', home of Mrs Thomas Mort, widow of the famous wool broker, shipyard proprietor and art collector. From her windows she could see the spire of St Mark's church, which her husband had endowed. Closer to the waterfront were 'Lindesay', home of the ironmonger and parliamentarian John Macintosh; 'Swifts', the 42-room Gothic-style mansion owned by the brewer Robert Tooth; and 'Carthona', a villa built by the explorer and surveyor Sir Thomas Mitchell. Other posh suburbs were Elizabeth Bay, Potts Point, Gladesville on the Parramatta River, Rose Bay and Strathfield – in all these places 'the houses are mostly large and are surrounded by beautifully laid out grounds'.

But there was another Sydney in the late nineteenth century, the old Sydney of the poor and working class who could not afford to move to the new suburbs. Darling Harbour had become a ramshackle, fetid slum where men, women and children eked out lives hemmed in by gasometers, coal yards, smokestacks, derelict wharves and dilapidated sheds. Beyond Pyrmont Bridge was the nauseous stench of factories and their chemically harmful outflows, boiling-down works, stinky drains and leaking privies, wharves piled high with raw materials for iron foundries, timber mills and railway workshops. In a small enclave in the malodorous alleys off Sussex Street there were more than 100 people living in 21 two-roomed houses with only three privies, one of them out of order, so most had to use the communal cesspits.

In 1884 Bruce Smith wrote in the *Melbourne Review* that, 'street after street of this class of houses have far less land than is allotted to similar sized houses in the closely packed suburbs of London'. Smith blamed the absence of a rectangular grid, which created the city's many dead-ends and cul-de-sacs, which in turn created slum enclaves. As for the Rocks, most of the area was a hive of wretched hovels. In his 1885 book, *Botany Bay Past and Present*, F Myers was horrified by what he saw:

Who can conceive of a community of civilised folk … with deliberation, wilfully, constantly pouring all their filth into the beautiful blue basin which nature has provided at their doors, making of Circular Quay a pestilent stink, of Darling Harbour a feculent swamp, fouling, polluting, slowly destroying everything.

The main thoroughfare of Sydney seemed different, but only because the shanties and decrepit buildings were hidden from passers-by. In the article 'Rookeries of George Street, 1886', a reporter from the *Globe* accompanied the lord mayor, a city health officer, an architect and the inspector of nuisances on a tour of the street and its cross streets. What they saw appalled them. A store front may 'have pleased the eye … but in the back decrepit human beings were working away for a pittance'. In Bathurst Street the back wall of one shop was about to collapse, the sheds of a gun shop needed to be demolished, part of the Liver Hotel in Liverpool Street was falling down.

Houses in further cross streets were marked for demolition. The unsanitary conditions, disgusting odours and dire appearances of these rickety homes, 'were in every way repulsive'. As he strode further down the street, the lord mayor marched into shops and houses, instantly condemning them. He even condemned hotels like the celebrated Dog and Duck on lower George Street.

Of course it was in these purlieus that diseases like yellow fever and consumption were rife. In 1881 there was an outbreak of smallpox. The first case reported was a Chinese child, the son of On Chong, one of Sydney's leading merchants. As the epidemic spread through the Rocks, Darling Harbour and Woolloomooloo over the next few months, the press stoked anti-Chinese feeling. Hundreds of letters were published calling for the expulsion of the Chinese and an end to their migration, and individual Chinese people became targets for violence. Two decades later, the new federal parliament would pass the *Immigration Restriction Act*, which became known as the White Australia Policy, restricting the immigration of non-British citizens.

These grim areas were even more disturbing as the breeding grounds of violent and territorial larrikin gangs. Joseph Conrad wrote of the Rocks Push around the Quay:

> The night humours of the town descended from the street to the waterside in the still watches of the night; larrikins rushing down in bands to settle some quarrel by a stand-up fight, away from the police in an indistinct ring half hidden by piles of cargo, with the sounds of blows, a groan now and then, the stamping of feet, and the cry of 'Time!' rising suddenly above the sinister, and excited murmurs.

Three years later there was another outrage, this time on the other side of town at Mount Rennie (now Moore Park). On 9 September 1886, 16-year-old Mary Jane Hicks took a cab ride through Waterloo, where the driver Charles Sweetman sexually molested her. Hearing her screams, a group of larrikins from the Waterloo Push chased Sweetman off. Instead of helping Hicks to the hospital, they took her to a clearing in the bush and gang raped her for two hours before police showed up. Nine of the gang, all under 20, were sentenced to death. Sweetman was given a jail sentence and the lash.

There was an outcry about the savage sentences. Leading the protest was barrister William Bede Dalley – the one-time defender of would-be royal assassin Henry O'Farrell – who noted that Mary Jane had not been a virgin at the time and argued that the prosecution of rape cases was for 'the protection of absolutely pure women'. The death penalty as a deterrent was designed as protection 'for this class of persons and this class alone ... Indeed, where some women were concerned, their conduct was such as to encourage the crime.' After many protests for clemency five of the sentences were reduced to a decade in prison.

It was as if the people of the slums lacked any social conscience or morality. To the alarmed and outraged middle class, it seemed as if the larrikins were synonymous with barbarism.

A YOUNG WOMAN'S WORLD
IN THE 1890s

FOR YOUNG ETHEL TURNER, SYDNEY IN THE EARLY 1890S WAS
vibrant, exciting, and full of the finer things in life. She had been
born in Yorkshire in 1870, and her mother, after being widowed
twice, migrated to Australia with her three daughters. They lived
in genteel poverty for two years until Ethel's mother married
Charles Cope in 1880. Cope may have been despotic, with an
unhealthy adoration of his stepdaughters, but he was financially
well off.

Ethel and her sister Lilian ('Lil') were educated at the
prestigious Sydney Girls' High School. After leaving school the
two sisters founded and edited a sixpenny monthly, *The Parthenon*,
which lasted for three years. At various times the mercurial Ethel
wanted to be a millionairess, a famous actress, a famous author
and a famous painter. She kept diaries from 1889 until 1952.
Some of the most vivid entries are in the early years, when as a
young woman she partied, danced, picnicked and flirted her away
across Sydney before finding fame with her first children's book,
Seven Little Australians.

She and her family lived in Paddington and later Newtown
with servants, washerwomen, cooks and gardeners. The house at
Newtown was on the posh 'Avenue'. It was enormous and newly
built on a large block of land with 'a good carriage drive', tennis

courts (Ethel liked playing the game) and a 'lovely ballroom'. The house had a drawing room, an enormous dining room, a conservatory and six bedrooms, tiled hearths and a modern system of electric bells. Attractive and vivacious, Ethel was wooed by several men and took delight in being either 'a beast' to them or coquettish. It was a life that could only be envied by her servants.

At the age of 19 she attended many dances and proudly detailed how many men she danced with and how many times. One of her favourite experiences in 1889 was going to the Lord Mayor's Ball in a brougham. For the occasion she wore a white silk dress with pink roses and maiden hair. 'I did my hair very high and wore an aigrette [a headdress consisting of a white egret's feather] in it'. She shopped at the upmarket David Jones, attended Sunday church services, which passed in a bored blur, went to theatricals at the Victoria Army Barracks in Paddington, where she flirted with a Colonel Spalding, and had picnics at Bondi and Watsons Bay, among other places.

Ethel's social world became one of university boat races, tennis, ferry rides in the moonlight and once, having arrived too late to catch a tram from Circular Quay, walked all the way home to Newtown with her sister. She continued to string along a suitor, Herbert Curlewis, who was studying law at Sydney University, frequently admonishing herself in her diary entries for her capricious behaviour towards him, saying 'unkind things' or 'being in such a temper with him'.

Suddenly, on 2 September 1890 there is a more serious entry: 'There was a riot today in Sydney and 2 men killed. It is a fortnight since the strike started.' She was referring to the Australian maritime dispute. It had begun in August after negotiations broke down over longstanding pay and conditions claims. Industrial action quickly spread to seamen, wharfies, and then gas stokers. Coal miners as far away as New Zealand were locked out after refusing to dig coal for non-union-operated vessels. A few weeks later 28 500 workers were on strike. The dispute was over more than just pay and conditions, it was a conspiracy by the employers to destroy trade unions.

Police were used to break up marches and the army was called in to support the police. Violence broke out in ports around Australia between the military and the strikers, union and non-union workers. For 20-year-old Ethel, 'the strike was awful'. The unionists failed to sustain their dispute, basically due to a shortage of money. The jubilant employers cut wages by up to 30 per cent.

Later in the same month the strike was forgotten when she went to the eagerly awaited Government House Ball, where she ticked off on her dance card the number and names of men she danced with, including several German officers from the ship *Leipzig*. The badly treated Curlewis decided to woo this unpredictable girl with the poems of Swinburne. He copied out half of the Englishman's book of poems, 'a sort of expurgated edition because Mother won't let me have the book'. Ethel found the poems 'glorious' and wished she was allowed to read them all.

In November she patched up her friendship with Louise ('Louie') Mack. It had been nearly two years since the schoolfriends had argued and ruptured their close bond. Mack came from a family of 13 children and lived in Redfern, close to Newtown but a world away from Ethel's bourgeois existence. Mack was lively, intelligent and wild, feckless with any money she earned. Like Ethel, she wanted to be a famous writer but, despite writing some promising early novels and poems, she would never achieve the fame she dreamed of.

The two women were competitive but needed each other for moral support and stimulating conversations about literature, love and life. Resuming the friendship, Mack would visit Ethel and they would stay up until dawn talking. Ethel's stepfather was so jealous of his stepdaughters' boyfriends that Ethel had to continue her rollercoaster relationship with Curlewis (a brilliant student at ease with Greek, Latin and Italian), by meeting him at Mack's home. Over the five years of their courtship the patient Curlewis was undaunted by Ethel's frequent and unpredictable rejections of him.

Ethel took Mack with her on picnics and trips on the harbour, where she liked to sit at the bow, excited at being drenched by the waves. She wrote essays on Goethe and attended the Women's Literary Society classes, where, on one occasion, the discussion papers debated the topic 'Is Realism in Literature Desirable?'. Her stamina was extraordinary: debates, chess, tennis, singing lessons, visiting clairvoyants, and many picnics (Mosman, on the harbour in a steam launch, Double Bay, Kogarah, and the pleasure grounds of Clontarf). There were shopping excursions, visits to dressmakers, and calls on friends with her mother, when both wore hats and gloves and left their cards with the servants if the woman of the house was not at home.

Most middle-class households employed at least one servant. The servants' misdemeanours took up much of the women's conversations. 'Many society ladies managed to get through an entire session without raising another topic.'

Ethel seemed to dance her way across Sydney; at Government House (where she was appalled to see two girls, 14 and 16, wilfully dancing as if they had already made their debuts), and Victoria Barracks ('Captain Taylor is conceited because he was so good looking'). There was a dance at Elizabeth Bay, another one where she danced 'Swedish', and one at Dulwich Hill, where she did the barn dance, noting in her diary the next day to 'never, never be married. It gives me a choking kind of feeling.'

In July of that year she saw *Cleopatra*, starring 'the divine Sarah Bernhardt', at the new Her Majesty's Theatre on Pitt Street.

At the time it was the largest and best equipped venue in the city. The fear of fire was strong, and the theatre had extensive fire precautions, including a brick firewall and an asbestos drop curtain. (Even so, 15 years after the theatre's completion, on Sunday, 23 March 1902, a fire broke out during a performance of *Ben Hur* 'with real horses and chariots'. The asbestos safety curtain failed to operate, and the interior of Her Majesty's was destroyed.)

Sydney saw 'the woman of genius' perform the role of the consumptive courtesan in *La Dame aux Camélias*, and critics said she held the audiences spellbound. Over the season she also performed in *Tosca* and *Cleopatra*. As one theatre reviewer reported:

> Her name has been on every tongue for days past. She has been the general and absorbing topic of conversation. In the newspapers, in the clubs, in the hotels, in the streets, her visit has been discussed almost to the verge of weariness.

Ethel thought the night she saw Bernhardt was 'divine', though she 'fell in love with the actor playing Marc Anthony', and, as a slight on her love-struck suitor, wrote in her diary, 'I wish Curlewis was like him.' Though she was thrilled a few days later when she and her sister Lil went to Sydney University without a chaperone ('terribly wicked but no one saw us') to meet Curlewis, who took her out on the river in a skiff.

She and Mack shared books, with Mack giving her the popular and slightly risqué *Love-Letters of a Worldly Woman*, and she read Ada Cambridge's recently published *Not All in Vain*, judging it as 'better than any book I have read'. She didn't know that the Melbourne author was at the time in Sydney, visiting Arthur Streeton's camp at Little Sirius Bay, where she was researching her next novel, *A Marked Man*, in which her hero, Richard Delavel, escapes the social restrictions of his unfortunate early marriage by staying at the bohemian artists' retreat. While in Sydney, Cambridge became fascinated by the city, especially the colonial heritage of the Rocks and Dawes Point, the mansions dotting the harbour, and the port itself.

Ethel was entranced by the harbour and liked nothing more than picnicking on ferries and boats, but near the end of 1893 she became horribly aware of just how dangerous the waterway could be when she noted in her diary, 'a terrible boating accident'. The yacht *Ripple* had sunk, drowning five people. The water police raised the yacht with grappling irons and inside it they found a gold stopwatch, two men's macintoshes, two women's mantles and ladies' umbrellas. Of the three women and two men who died, only one of the women could swim.

The Turner family shifted to Lindfield on the upper North Shore, an outer suburb then considered country. It was to be the inspiration for Ethel's *Seven Little Australians*, written in 1893 and published the following year. Set in the suburban bushland of Sydney, it follows the adventures of the seven naughty Woolcot children, their serious army father Captain Woolcot, and faithful young stepmother, Esther.

It was an immediate success and has remained in print ever since. Ethel deigned to marry the future Judge Herbert Curlewis in 1896. Her friendship with Mack was severed by the tyranny of distance when Mack went off to live in London and Europe, eventually becoming a celebrated World War I journalist. Unlike Ethel, Mack remained true to her bohemian sensibility, tossing off novels for quick money, scandalising wowsers with erotic verses, marrying or living with the 'wrong' men, and dying in poverty. By contrast her friend ended up a wealthy widow in suburban Mosman.

*

Ethel's social world and her experiences of Sydney couldn't have been more different from those of Rose Soady. Born in 1885, she was the third of nine children of English-born parents. Finances were tight, her father was a labourer. Rose was raised in bushland near the Lane Cove River, and would go on to become an artist's model, printmaker and wife of Norman Lindsay, whose legend she burnished despite their tempestuous relationship.

Later in life she wrote *Ma and Pa, My Childhood Memories*, recalling her youth in the 1890s. On special occasions the family would venture into the city:

> As there were no motor cars the people surged all over the roadway, only getting out of the way of hansom cabs, or trams ringing their way through the mob. The popular mashing [flirting] ground was up in King Street, along Pitt to Market Street.

Unlike Ethel, who frequented David Jones and expensive boutiques, Rose would mingle with the shoppers looking for bargains in the less salubrious end of George Street, between Bathurst and Goulburn streets, where 'Housewives [were] bent on buying trousers for their husbands, or cotton frock prints at fourpence or sixpence a yard.'

Favoured spots for window shopping were the arcades, especially the Strand Arcade, which, when it opened in 1892, was described by the *Daily Telegraph* as 'The finest public thoroughfare in the Australian colonies.' It went on to report that many unsightly old buildings had been demolished 'and given in their place a palatial building that will be a credit to any city in the world'.

Running between Pitt and George streets, the arcade was three storeys high and featured protruding galleries, cedar staircases, tiled floors, cast iron balusters, timber-framed shopfronts and a gorgeously tinted glass roof to reduce glare. The goods may have been out of the price range of Rose and her family, but that didn't matter. This arcade, and several others built in the late 1880s, gave Sydney women the illusion that they were as sophisticated as the women shopping in the exclusive arcades of Paris and London.

Her mother liked to go out on a Saturday night, and Rose vividly recalled one time when the two of them came upon an amazing sight in a tea shop in King Street:

> The whole of its window [was] made into a Chinese room,
> with the figure of a Chinese gentleman wearing a long pigtail
> and all dressed up in a Mandarin robe seated at a table slowly
> raising a cup to his mouth and taking a sip of tea, then bowing
> his head to the onlookers as he lowered the cup; a musical box
> just inside the door played a tune.

This was the Loong Shan Tea Shop at 137 King Street. It was owned by Quong Tart and featured marble fountains and ponds with golden carp. Upstairs was a reading room frequented by some of Sydney's most important men and women. Louisa Lawson, Henry's mother, drank tea and wrote pieces there for her feminist paper *Dawn*. In 1898 Tart opened his luxurious tea rooms, the Elite Hall, in the brand-new Queen Victoria Building, an enormous, imperious and magnificent Romanesque-style building of several floors with shops, warehouses, and market stalls in the basement, the whole building serviced by four hydraulic lifts. Quong Tart's tea rooms were on the ground floor near the centre of the markets, fronting George Street. A swish carpeted staircase led to a function hall on the first floor. It had a capacity for 500 people and included a stage with an exotic carved proscenium.

Quong Tart had arrived in Australia in 1859 aged nine with his uncle, who deserted him. In Braidwood he lived with a Scottish storeowner, learning English with a decidedly Scottish accent. Later he was taken in by a wealthy family where he became, as he said, 'an English gentleman' and a Christian. He eventually owned silk shops and a network of tea rooms in the Sydney Arcade, the Royal Arcade and King Street and, of course, his most successful venture, the Queen Victoria tea rooms. He married an English woman, Margaret Scarlett, and had six children.

His acceptance by Sydney was at odds with the strong anti-Chinese sentiment at the time. He was a spokesman for the Chinese community (one that was gradually drifting from the Rocks down to Haymarket) and an interpreter. He founded one of the first Chinese merchant associations in the city, helped set up a Chinese consulate, and cajoled the Chinese government to raise the issue of the maltreatment of the Chinese in Australia.

His philanthropic activities were prodigious, providing dinners, gifts and entertainment at his own expense for Benevolent Society homes, newsboys, the Aboriginal poor and inmates of asylums for the destitute. He campaigned against the opium trade when the drug was a widespread addiction in both Sydney and Melbourne.

His Queen Victoria rooms was popular with high society, and members of the 1891 Federation Convention spent many an hour dining and debating there, but most importantly it was a place for the women of Sydney, who saw it as a tranquil sanctuary from the vulgar and cacophonous world outside and were grateful for its non-smoking rooms. Women writers met there, women's bicycle clubs were formed there, and suffragettes devised their political campaigns. One famous visitor who was to address the Women's Missionary Association at an afternoon tea was Robert Louis Stevenson, but because he was ill his mother read a paper he had written, 'Missions in the South Seas'.

Quong Tart was one of Sydney's most famous and well-loved personalities, mingling with the social and political elites. He wore bespoke European suits, and at social functions would dress either in Mandarin robes or in a kilt and sporran, and on occasions recited Robbie Burns' poetry, played the bagpipes, or sang Scottish ballads with his distinctive Scottish burr.

In August 1902 he was brutally bashed with an iron bar and robbed of a few pounds in the Queen Victoria Building. The burglar, Frederick Duggan, a 'dim-witted thug', was jailed for 12 years for what police thought was a robbery gone wrong. Quong Tart never fully recovered and died a year later, aged 53. The crime shocked Sydney, and at Rookwood cemetery thousands of people came to mourn him. He was buried in the ceremonial robes of a Mandarin of the Rose Button (which had been conferred on him by the Chinese government), which were only partly covered by his masonic apron.

Visiting Tart's tea rooms was one thing, but as far as Rose's father was concerned, the streets were no place for his young daughter. The brazen flirting unsettled him. One time Rose saw two young men in a city street, one of them whistling at two giggling girls in floral frocks and large feathered hats who were passing by. The cocky whistler pushed his straw boater to the back of his head and nudged his mate, saying, 'Come on.' Rose's appalled father looked at the men racing after the girls and warned his daughter, 'These streets are no place for young gals.'

But to Rose, nothing compared to the drama of Paddy's Market in Haymarket, a rowdy, uncouth place where Ethel would never have ventured. To Rose this was an extraordinary spot, a cacophony of:

> ... noises made up from everyone doing something in their
> own way. Pushing cases about, rolling barrels, screaming orders

to assistants, the clank of irons, buckets and tins ... The stall holders had hands at mouths shouting their wares under the naked lights that streamed ribbons of flame in the breeze ... All the banging and shouting could not drown the laughter and chatter of the crowds, or the crowing of roosters, the only discordant note in this rumbling din was the crack of rifles from the nearby shooting gallery.

Like many of the kids and young couples, Rose would always make for the ice-cream stall with its rows of coloured jellies in tumblers, 'like a stain glass window'.

*

Rose's pleasures were simple, but Eugenie McNeil, the same age as Rose, lived in a world of affluence in Hunters Hill. In her memoir of the 1890s, *A Bunyip Close Behind Me: Recollections of the Nineties*, she describes how every morning her father, top-hatted and frock-coated, would walk down to Fig Tree Wharf to take the ferry into the city. Men like him carried sticks with elaborate silver tops 'and raised them in salute when they met other gentlemen of their class, but when they encountered ladies they doffed their toppers and bowed deeply'.

Eugenie was born in 1886 into a house where all the rooms were papered and even the ceilings with their ornamental cornices and elaborate centrepieces were covered in damask paper. 'We used to crane our necks upwards to pick out the shields, wreaths, fiddles and suits of armour that made up the pattern.' Inside the cluttered Victorian home were marble clocks, ormolu ornaments and silver-mounted emu eggs, and vases of pink Venetian glass with frilly edges. Most rooms had floor-length French windows.

The kitchen and servants' quarters were a nightmare by modern standards. All around the house ran a verandah, on which we burned our feet in summer when we ran barefoot on the boards. On the hottest days the verandah kept the place reasonably cool.

The last Thursday of every month her mother was 'at home':

The ladies who came were mainly local and they wore their best mantles, sat gingerly on the edges of the drawing-room suite and made genteel conversation. They all left a piece of seed cake or half a chicken sandwich on the side of their plate to show their good breeding. On the wall of every room in Auburn Park was a bell push, which communicated with a jangling board in the kitchen ... These afternoons were the only occasions when a servant was summoned so formally. Mary or Honour or Lily appeared with fresh hot water and scones. She wore a white starched apron and an embroidered cap with black velvet ribbons and long streamers.

Tinkers were always pestering the kitchen staff for jobs to patch pots and pans and kettles at a time when such things were repaired and not just replaced. There were strange remedies for illnesses. A teacher, worried about Eugenie's anaemic sister Lydia, confidently recommended that she drink a glass of blood every day.

A visit to the city meant a trip on a bus after the ferry ride from Hunters Hill. Until the end of her life Eugenie remembered the smell of damp straw on the floor of the bus in winter. The driver would whip the horses and soon the family would be galloping down George Street, the wooden blocks making a loud clatter under the horses' hooves. The uneven streets around Haymarket and Brickhill were regarded as 'the downfall of many a horse'.

For the teenager the city only seemed to begin once she reached St Andrew's Cathedral and the Town Hall. It was next to 'the palatial new Queen Victoria Markets, which we all thought the last word in architectural magnificence'.

Once at Town Hall, Eugenie would demand to go to the fortune teller on the corner of Market Street. On top of his small table a green budgerigar would walk over to a row of strategically placed envelopes, look up and down the row and then select one, holding it in his beak until young Eugenie had paid threepence. She would tear open the envelope and eagerly read her fortune.

She need not have worried. Her fortune, like those of Ethel Turner and Rose Soady, would be a bright and fulfilling one.

THE PLAGUE

RATS CAUSED ONE OF THE GREAT HEALTH CRISES IN AUSTRALIA
when the bubonic plague emerged in early 1900. The outbreak
spread from the waterfront through the city. Millers Point resident
Arthur Payne (or Paine) was diagnosed on 19 January with the
first reported case. He and his family were shipped to the North
Head Quarantine Station on 24 January, and their house in Ferry
Lane was fumigated. Over eight months in 1900, 303 cases were
reported.

The plague was introduced by infected rats arriving in ships
at Darling Harbour (Tumbalong). The unsanitary and filthy
wharf areas and nearby houses provided a perfect environment
for the disease-ridden rats to breed. Fear of catching it, and
fear of the rats that spread it, tore through the city. Areas were
quarantined, cleared of rubbish, disinfected and lime-washed.
Sydney City Council established a Plague Department and
employed 450 labourers to carry out house-to-house inspections,
cleansing and disinfecting drains, sinks and WCs to prevent the
spread of the disease. Rats were targeted, and over 9000 rodents
were destroyed in one week in March 1900.

Peter Curson, in his *A Time of Terror: The Black Death in
Sydney*, says that 'Although the plague outbreak produced only
a handful of cases and deaths, it produced scenes of mass panic,
fear and hysteria never before encountered in Australia's history.'

Thousands fled Sydney. The Victorian railways cancelled a monthly excursion train between Sydney and Melbourne, fearing that its cheap fares would attract the plague-prone working class. A pamphlet, *Prevention of Plague: Instructions to Householders*, opened with the dramatic, and necessary, statement: 'Plague is present in Sydney. It has been introduced by diseased rats and there is a great danger of it spreading further.'

The City of Sydney and other municipal councils quickly realised they were unprepared and, overwhelmed by the outbreak, urged Sydneysiders to do their part:

> Very great and special pains must therefore be taken by householders to thoroughly cleanse their houses internally, their eaves, their gutters, and their drains ... Municipal authorities are seldom provided with large staffs, and nuisances [hygiene issues in public spaces] sometimes exist for long before they are detected and dealt with. Every ratepayer should make a point, therefore, of reporting every nuisance which he observes in his district to the Council Clerk ... All rats, therefore, must be exterminated as far as possible, and the attack upon them should be simultaneous in the healthy and infected neighbourhoods.

Bounties were offered on the number of rats caught before they were incinerated. This was a boon for the many unemployed and there were brawls between men to become part of the limited number of paid rat catchers. Eventually 108 000 rats were exterminated by officials, with untold more killed by householders.

Realising that the slum conditions in the Rocks area were a perfect breeding ground for the rodents, authorities removed people from their unsanitary and overcrowded dwellings. Local residents were employed to undertake the cleansing, disinfecting, burning and demolition of the infected areas, including their own homes. All makeshift buildings and sheds in bad repair had to be pulled down and removed. Policemen wore special leggings to prevent fleas jumping on their legs. Large parts of the docks were sealed off. Religious fanatics appeared on soapboxes in the Domain, raving that the plague was the wrath of God for the wickedness and lust prevailing in Sydney.

As with the earlier smallpox outbreak in 1881, at first the Chinese were blamed, and there were several incidents where members of the local Chinese community were verbally and physically abused. One woman remembered, 'Everyone was urged to kill rats and a bounty of a shilling for every rat tail. The Chinese proved the best rat catchers. It was at first thought it was because their premises were dirtier than others, but a thriving factory was discovered in Lower George Street where Chinese workers were making tails out of the rest of the skins.'

In September 1900, after 103 deaths, the city was declared free of the plague and the yellow flag that had flown at the Quarantine Station was taken down.

The demolition of the slums during and after the outbreak was a pivotal moment for Sydney. It became apparent that there were too many dwellings, mostly built between the 1840s and the 1880s, that had fallen into irretrievable disrepair. Many were on tiny plots of land with few rooms, and sometimes there were seven to eight adults and children to a room. A basement in Sussex Street was found to have a dozen people living, eating and sleeping in one room, with a cesspit in the corner of the room, which had not been emptied or cleaned for years. There were instances of one dwelling being built in the backyard of another, or just tacked on to an existing dwelling.

By November 1901 a large area of land to the west of George Street, near Circular Quay, became the Rocks resumption.

According to one newspaper report, 'the curious and uncanny nests of old houses, many dating nearly a century back ... are squat, rat-ridden, and unwholesome; rooms so low that one can touch the ceilings are rapidly being pulled down'.

Most of the narrow lanes and grim thoroughfares of the Rocks that peeled off from Cumberland, Sussex and Kent streets were quickly demolished and, in the process, the government turfed out some 800 families.

Not content with removing slums from the area that was the epicentre of the plague, the state government finally granted the city council the power to resume slums in other areas, with more than 700 houses resumed in Ultimo, around the Belmore markets near Central Station, and in the Haymarket area to make way for new market buildings and warehouses. As the Sydney City Council's Town Clerk said of the plague, 'it was the greatest blessing that ever came to Sydney, viewed from the standpoint of the future welfare of our city'. One could say that in some respects, the rats transformed Sydney for the better.

THE DOMAIN,
THE FIRST WORLD WAR
AND DRINK

IN 1888 THE *SYDNEY MORNING HERALD* PUBLISHED AN ARTICLE about the Domain, noting:

> The outer Domain is occupied on a Sunday afternoon by a dozen assemblies of the most diverse schools of religious thought, from the narrowest Calvinism to the most comprehensive latitudinarianism. They preach, argue, and wrangle a little noisily, perhaps, but with the greatest good humour, until teatime, and then go decorously home satisfied with having begun the week well.

Speakers Corner came into its own between 1914 and 1918 as anti-conscriptionists, communists and socialists denounced the war, which they viewed as a trade war for markets that would only benefit British and American capitalists. During the stormy conscription referendum debates of 1916 and 1917, the Domain was crowded with thousands of people every Sunday. One of the largest crowds was when the premier of Queensland addressed an anti-conscription rally of an estimated 100 000 people.

There were also speakers who were virulently pro-conscription and anti-German, and many local Germans were either interned or assaulted. Even prominent Sydneysiders were not protected by their positions or wealth.

'Swifts' was an extraordinary mansion in Darling Point, its design based on Government House, with sandstone masonry, façades, castellations and a tower, a long arcade and porte-cochére. It had an enormous staff of cooks, housemaids, butlers, footmen, gardeners, coachmen and grooms. Originally built for one brewer, Robert Tooth, it had been purchased in 1900 by another brewer, the German emigrant Edmund Resch. Born in Bavaria in 1847, Resch had migrated to Australia in 1863 hoping to make his fortune on the goldfields, but over the next decades, in league with his brothers Emil and Richard, he earned a fortune making beer.

During World War I, when anti-German sentiment was rife, Edmund contributed generously to the war effort, but on 4 March 1916 the *Mirror of Australia* published a vicious editorial pointing out that 'The Resch family live at Swifts, Darling Point, a house which has a commanding view over Sydney Harbour, and could, if so desired, be easily used for purposes inimical to this country. No German should be permitted to occupy such a residence.'

Edmund managed to avoid any action against him until November 1917, when he was arrested for an 'indiscretion' (as a joke flying a German flag atop of 'Swifts') and interned for four months until, due to poor health, he was sent home. He remained under house arrest with a guard to ensure he did not leave or receive German visitors.

The Domain was also a place where women could speak out about the evils of alcohol. There was a strong temperance campaign to limit the hours that hotels could trade. At the time they opened at six o'clock in the morning and closed at 11 p.m. The temperance movement was driven primarily by women but was also backed by newspapers like the *Sydney Morning Herald* and the churches – except for the Catholic Church, which made sense given most of the publicans were Roman Catholic. The movement had grown for decades and its visible successes were the many coffee palaces and temperance hotels. The publicans fought back, but one event during the war gave victory to the temperance movement and dramatically changed Sydney society.

On St Valentine's Day 1916, 5000 Australian soldiers at a training camp in Casula went on strike, protesting against the bleak conditions and an increase in drill hours. Not content with a vocal protest, they hurried on to Liverpool, where hundreds more troops joined them, the protest forgotten as they drank two hotels dry. After a drunken melee at the railway station, which caused the death of one man and the wounding of six others, the soldiers hijacked a train and headed to the city, where the thousands of intoxicated soldiers, like a plague of voracious khaki-coloured locusts, descended, damaging shops, restaurants, hotels and, out of drunken self-righteousness, the German Club. They assaulted any man or woman who got in their way. The debauchery continued for three days. The reaction of the appalled Army chiefs was swift, and five days later over 1000 soldiers were discharged from the AIF for drunkenness, misconduct and being absent without leave. Another 116 were ordered to be court-martialled.

The *Sydney Morning Herald*'s reaction to the drunken mayhem was typical of the public's horror: it shamed Australia and confirmed that 'no amount of clever dodging or denial can mask the demands of people for early closing'. A referendum was held on the issue of hotel closing hours on 10 June 1916. The rioting soldiers had created a wave of public sympathy for the cause of the temperance movement, and the referendum gained an overwhelming majority of votes for six o'clock closing.

It may have been a moral victory, but it was to also have disastrous consequences for Sydney, just as Prohibition would have in America. Since the rum-soaked days of the early settlement, Australians have been great drinkers. Six o'clock closing wasn't going to change this. The era of sly grog and razor gangs had arrived.

A DAY IN CONCORD

THE LAWN IS IMMACULATE. On one side it gently rises to the top of an incline, where an imposing two-storey Italianate mansion, complete with a four-storey tower hovering above the entrance, dominates the grounds. On the other side the lawn slopes down to mangroves and, partly hidden behind clumps of trees, the waters of the wide, sluggish Parramatta River slap languidly against the banks of sandstone rocks. Screeching parrots whirl overhead, their gaudy feathers flickering in the hot autumnal sunlight.

We have started a tour of the once-great estate of 'Yaralla', and have just passed two wooden houses built in the 1850s now used as rest homes for soldiers suffering from post-traumatic stress. The middle-aged guide is telling our small group that we are standing on one of the last and, at 10 hectares, largest nineteenth-century estates remaining in Sydney, which once belonged to the wealthiest woman in Australia. I hadn't heard of Yaralla until a couple of months ago.

I first learned of Dame Eadith Walker when I was having lunch at the Old Fitzroy Hotel in Woolloomooloo. Built in 1860, the pub is three storeys high with a red brick façade and metre-wide stripes of white concrete demarcating each floor, as if bandages are keeping the building together. There is nothing imposing or grandiose about it, unlike Dame Eadith's mansion. The Old Fitzroy seems ancient and decrepit, yet there is something eccentric about it, as if it had been designed by the author of Victorian fairytales with a sense of humour. Inside it is just as eccentric, with plastic chandeliers, a ceiling the colour of congealed blood, scruffy chairs, a fireplace, and the whole bar cluttered with a delirious and incongruous mix of objects.

Karoline Chardon had been a barmaid at the pub for nearly a year. Twenty-one, vivacious and studying part time, she was well liked by the clientele, many of whom, like me, had been coming to the Old Fitzroy for over a decade. It has always been a working-class hotel, as were all the many pubs and sly grog places that were a feature of nineteenth-century Woolloomooloo.

Knowing I was researching this book, Karoline told me how, in her final year of high school, she had designed and made a Victorian bustle dress to play the 25-year-old Eadith Walker at the Concord Fair – Eadith had been 25 when she inherited her father's estate in 1886. Karoline showed me her project – the patterns, samples of fabric – plus a photograph of her wearing the gorgeous many-layered frock on stone stairs in the grounds of Yaralla. She told me what she knew about Eadith's remarkable life and her enormous estate where the teenage Karoline had walked her dog and played hide and seek among its trees and artificial grottos. But Karoline's connection with Eadith was even closer. Her father, the Reverend Chardon, is the senior minister in the small Holy Trinity Church just outside the estate, which was Eadith's gift to the community. It was consecrated in late 1913 and was where her funeral service was held.

I had visited grand mansions like Vaucluse House, Elizabeth Bay House and Bronte House in the east, but Yaralla is in Concord, on the western side of the city. Its history of family wealth, on a scale seldom seen in our society, is unknown to most Sydneysiders.

The grounds Yaralla stands on were once populated by the Wangal clan, part of their country that they called 'Wanne', which began at about where Birchgrove is now and followed the course of the river to Parramatta. Because this is shale country, it was unsuitable for rock carvings, and so there is little evidence of the Wangal now, except for a few midden sites. As for the people of the First Fleet, they barely knew the Wangal before the clan was ravaged by the smallpox epidemic of April 1789, so our knowledge of them is meagre at best.

What we do know is that in late 1797 Governor John Hunter granted a former convict about 20 hectares fronting the Parramatta River mangroves, several kilometres outside Sydney. Isaac Nichols, born in 1770 in Wiltshire, England and sentenced to seven years transportation for stealing in 1790, proved to be a model prisoner. At six feet (1.8 metres) tall, he was an arresting figure in the colony, diligent and sober, so much so that he was appointed chief overseer of the convict gangs labouring around the fringes of Sydney Town. When he was granted the land at Concord, he waived his salary as overseer in exchange for two convicts as workers and, after years of toil, established a farm that proved so successful that Nichols eventually owned several pubs and built a shipyard, as well as running the post office in town that so impressed the young Obed West.

The first house he constructed on his Concord property was a small stone cottage. A vicious gale and hailstones reduced it to rubble. The second house he built caught fire when sparks from the chimney landed on the wooden shingles of the roof. Sailors on a boat anchored on the river went to help, rescuing furniture and valuables, while the desperate Nichols clambered up onto the roof to throw water on the flames, only to lose his footing and fall to the ground. Miraculously he was uninjured, and the roof was only partially burned.

He had fallen in love and married Mary Warren in 1796 but, as the years went on, her behaviour became erratic and one night in October 1804 visitors described her as exhibiting 'extravagant conduct'. Then she disappeared. Some grass cutters working on Goat Island discovered her body; she had thrown herself into the river, which had carried her downstream towards the Heads. Coroners were reluctant to give a verdict of suicide because the victim couldn't be buried in consecrated ground, so in this case the verdict was 'accidental death by insanity'.

Nichols wasted no time in finding a new bride and four months later he married Rosanna Johnson, who was to bear him three sons. Not long after the marriage a group of Aboriginal people, having raided the government stock farm in Seven Hills the previous night, attacked Nichols' farm, plundering it, and 'dispers[ing his cattle] ... in all directions'. Fearing for his life, Nichols fled into the bush. As the *Sydney Gazette* reported of the raid, 'These people still continue troublesome wherever they find access.'

In a few years his farm was a major supplier of fruit, vegetables and meat, including that of emus. The birds were so valuable that when one was stolen he placed an advertisement in the *Gazette* warning people not to buy it but to return it to him.

He took on more responsibilities in 1809 by becoming superintendent of public works and, to stop the practice of people illicitly obtaining mail from incoming ships, was made the first colonial postmaster the same year. His duty was to board incoming ships and collect the mail and parcels. Sydney's only post office was in his home in George Street. For those who wanted their mail, he charged one shilling for a letter, two shillings and sixpence for a small parcel, while any parcel over nine kilograms was five shillings. He sold books and lent others for a fee. His house held many social functions, including the annual highlight, the Bachelors' Ball. By the time of his death in November 1819 this well-liked and esteemed emancipist owned 283 hectares of Concord and large hunks of land in Lane Cove and Hunters Hill.

The Concord property was now called 'Woodbine', and Isaac's wife and sons continued to supply Sydney with vegetables and meat until they sold the property to a Scottish immigrant, Thomas Walker, who kept their cottage, Woodbine, which, somewhat altered, still stands in the shade of a clump of old trees.

Thomas Walker had arrived in Sydney by himself in 1822 at just 18 years old. He was employed in his uncle's business, a company of general merchants. A hard worker, he soon took over the firm and in the late 1830s travelled to Melbourne, where he speculated in land, which made his fortune. Back in Sydney he made even more money, but the 1840s depression that saw friends ruined and banks collapsing made him an ultra-cautious director and president of the Bank of New South Wales from 1869 until his death in 1886. He opposed needless expenditure and shrewdly maintained the bank's shabby building and furniture. This extravagant display of frugality won the confidence of customers who, it was said, 'abhorred the display and gilt of modern fashions'.

He had enough money to buy 500 acres (200 hectares) of the land Nichols had owned, including the promontories Rocky Point and Nichols Point. He commissioned the colony's most celebrated architect, Edmund Blacket, to build 'a cottage', and paid close attention to the plans, annotating them with his ideas: 'Sash windows instead of French windows' and 'What sort of window for hall?' He named it Yaralla, a Wangal word reputed to mean 'my home', honouring its original owners.

Now he was financially well off and the building of the mansion was in train, albeit slowly, it was time to get a wife. In 1860, at the age of 58, he married Jean Hart, 28 years his junior. The following year a daughter, Eadith, was born. In 1862 the family travelled to Scotland and Europe and, back in Sydney, lived in town, spending their weekends at Woodbine, watching the mansion slowly rise, its sandstone foundations laboriously cut from a quarry dug out of the mangrove shoreline. Jane's health was always precarious and in 1870, the year the family finally moved into Yaralla mansion, she died of consumption. Photographs and paintings of Walker in later years show a reticent Victorian man with bushy sideburns and distant eyes that seemed to hide the deep grief of his young wife's death beneath lush eyebrows.

He was now nearing 70 and, unable to care for Eadith by himself, asked his unmarried sister, Joanna, to look after her. Joanna realised that the eight year old would be lonely on the vast estate and convinced her brother to adopt six-year-old Annie Masefield, the daughter of her friend George Masefield. Annie and Eadith became inseparable, their education provided by private tutors on the estate. They were regulars at theatres, concerts and art galleries, took singing and dancing lessons every Saturday in town, learned European languages, played tennis, practised archery, and went sailing and travelling overseas together. The plainer of the two, Eadith, like her father, held the world at one remove with a commanding façade of Victorian reserve and a strong sense of the social responsibility that came with her wealth. Her adopted sister was high spirited and adventurous, rowing by herself on the Parramatta River and riding astride rather than side-saddle. Intelligent and curious, Annie was fascinated by nature and, years later, having developed an interest in photography, published several influential books of photographs on Australian wildflowers and how to identify them.

Thomas's life revolved around his many businesses and his immense conchological (shell) collection, which he was to donate to the Australian Museum. Displaying great personal courage, in 1885 he spoke out against Australia sending an army to avenge the death of General Gordon in Khartoum. In a noisy and heated debate at the Theatre Royal, one member of the audience yelled out, 'We must avenge the death of the brave General Gordon.' Thomas, one of the few cool heads in the packed auditorium, answered, 'Gordon is dead, so must you spill more blood?' But of course jingoism triumphed, and in March of that year nearly two-thirds of Sydney's population of 300 000 lined the streets to cheer 758 men who, accompanied by suitably martial music, marched proudly to Circular Quay where they boarded two steamers to join the British forces in the Sudan. The soldiers returned to Sydney a few months later without having engaged in more than a brief skirmish in which three men were slightly wounded. For Thomas the folly proved that once again prudence and common sense were overruled by a mob's irrational passion.

Now in his early eighties, he was aware that his time was running out. He'd go for long walks with his silent daughter through the estate and along the river, warning her of the dangers of being an heiress: many a mercenary man would want to marry her for her money alone. It was advice she would take to heart.

He died with a reputation as a skinflint. It was only after his death that a hidden self was revealed. He had secretly given much to charities and employed an agent to privately nominate people in distress or poverty and provide them with money anonymously. In his will he set aside £100 000 for the building and continuing financial support of a convalescent hospital he wanted built on 13 hectares in the corner of the estate called Rocky Point. The rest he left in trust to Eadith. Her father, desperate for the Walker line to continue, hadn't bequeathed Yaralla to her but 'to a child of her marriage'. Eadith was now the wealthiest woman in Sydney, if not Australia.

Nowadays as the visitor approaches the Thomas Walker Convalescent Hospital it doesn't seem to be the imposing structure that features in photographs and paintings for the simple reason that today one approaches it from the road. The hospital was built facing the Parramatta River, because in the late nineteenth century this waterway was the most convenient and calm route to Concord, especially for physically fragile patients.

One of the most eminent architects in Sydney, John Sulman, knew that the approach from the river had to provide a sense of the theatrical, even awe. He was so keen to get the commission that he shafted another architect who had won a competition to design the hospital. What he didn't know was that this project would forever bind him to the Walker family.

He had practised as an architect in England but after his wife Sarah contracted TB, he sold up everything and in 1885 the two of them immigrated to Australia, where he would live out his life designing churches, office buildings and schools, and pushing the innovative concept of town planning. His buildings were distinctive, yet conservative. Modern art for him was 'awful rubbish'. Tall, thin, with a trim beard, he was a smooth performer in social circles, meticulous, a great networker, with the tunnel vision and towering ego common to his profession. *Architecture* magazine of May 1919 described him as:

> ... a typical Englishman – polished, aggressive, debonair always:
> forceful and decisive in action and speech. He knows exactly
> what he wants to achieve and goes straight for it, and it is a
> stubborn obstruction that turns aside the great wind of purpose.

The public did not see that beneath the patrician exterior was a man who was prey to severe physical and mental breakdowns and at times had to stop working for up to a year to slowly recover. The day he showed the Walker family his plans for the convalescent hospital and signed on for the project, his wife Sarah died.

Sulman undertook extensive research in England and Europe, studying similar hospitals, the size of wards and the average length of a patient's stay. What Australia offered was sunlight. Every ray of sunshine was valuable. As he said, 'Modern investigations have proved direct sunlight can be efficient in destroying germs of disease.' The recuperative powers of fresh air were also crucial. He configured the wards in such a way that they caught the sea breezes that travelled up the river from the coast.

Architecturally, the building should have been a mess. Designed in what can only be called the Australian mongrel style that was beloved of Victorian Sydney, it borrowed influences from everywhere. Although its general appearance is in the Queen Anne style, it has eclectic elements such as an Italianate tower, Gothic Revival finials, Georgian shuttered windows, Renaissance balustrades, Doric and Ionic columns and Greek-inspired caryatids (supporting columns in the shape of a woman). The stonework of the façade is embellished with floral motifs, cartouches, swags, lion heads and friezes of plump cherubs. Despite this heterogenous mixture, it all magically hangs together.

The interior verges on the palatial. Eight buildings make up the complex. On either side of the main buildings are two wings with cloisters. The two-storey main building has a three-storey tower over the entrance and a sumptuous vestibule with intricate brickwork and marble columns. There are two enclosed courtyards, a concert hall, and a gorgeously decorated recreation hall. Even the walls are special: they are among the first examples in Australia of 'cavity walls' created as insulation against Sydney's summers. Stained-glass lunettes depicting the virtues of justice, temperance, prudence, hope, faith and charity are positioned alongside a frieze inscribed in gold: *This hospital for convalescents was founded by the late Thomas Walker of Yaralla in the hope that many sufferers would be restored to health within.*

It went £50 000 over budget, which Eadith willingly coughed up. But it was worth it. Sydney had seen nothing like this striking building. It opened in 1893, despite the severe depression. Patients boarded a boat from Circular Quay and on arrival either walked or were carried through a rotund water gate onto dry land where, past the small but elaborately carved gatekeeper's lodge, the luxurious hospital awaited them. Those arriving were greeted by heraldic lions, and those departing were farewelled by carved dolphins on a sandstone panel.

A few years later the hospital was treating 1000 patients annually. One of the most grateful was the writer Henry Lawson, who spent time there in 1902 recovering from a drunken cliff fall. His ode to Thomas Walker, titled 'The Unknown Patient', opens with:

> The moonlight breathes on Walker House and softens scrub
>   and hill;
> The native trees are strangely stirred, the pines are very still;
> The nurse's lantern flits and flits, and pain and sorrow cease …

Although the feelings were heartfelt, the lines prove that Lawson was a better fiction writer than poet. Sulman's building functioned as a convalescent hospital until 1978 when it became the Rivendell Adolescent Unit for emotionally disturbed adolescents, including those who were refugees from war-torn countries.

During the construction of the hospital, Eadith's aunt Joanna knew she was dying. What was clear to her was that Eadith wouldn't marry; there had been no beaux in her life, and she had taken to heart her father's advice that any man who wanted to marry her was probably a gold digger. Realising this, Joanna turned her attention to Annie. The adopted daughter, as she relates in her youthful diaries, had many a suitor, but the dying Joanna, wanting to push Annie to marry, acted as matchmaker, pairing up Annie with the widower Sulman as often as possible. Annie may have been 15 years younger, but Joanna thought that her artistic aspirations would be encouraged by the talented architect. In the same year the hospital opened, Sulman married Annie in an extravagant wedding at Yaralla. His two daughters, Florence and Edith, were bridesmaids and Eadith was maid of honour. With this marriage Sulman's career became inextricably bound up with the Walkers. He designed the grand Yaralla Chambers in the city and several buildings on the estate, including the sumptuous stables. He also extended the second floor of the main house originally designed by Edmund Blacket.

Now that Annie had left the estate, Eadith was alone. She commandeered the first floor of the mansion and, as if a queen bee, installed nine maids in rooms surrounding her huge bedroom with its balcony overlooking the grounds. A few years later, her twin cousins, Egmont and George Walker, came to live at Yaralla, each having his own room. There was also a bedroom for the staff who worked in the substantial library downstairs. The ground floor had drawing rooms, dining rooms, smoking rooms, a billiard room, 'Indian' rooms, a massive kitchen and an interior courtyard.

This was a world unimaginable to other Sydneysiders, except for a privileged few. Yaralla had an enormous staff of 35: cooks, maids, grooms, engineers, butlers, farmers and gardeners. There were two wharves, extensive orchards, rose arbours, rare rock orchids, and ten hectares of garden, 'boasting grounds more akin to the Botanic Gardens'. It was a self-contained village with a power station, dairy, bakery, slaughterhouse, fire station, piggery, fowl house, lodges for the staff, and golf course, squash and tennis courts. It even had its own post office.

The rich and famous came to visit. The guest books kept from

1897 to 1937 contain the names of Sydney high society, artists like Melba, English royalty, even the celebrated aviator Ross Smith, who, in a piece of theatre, landed his plane on the front lawn. The parties were legendary, as were the charity fundraisers. For the children's carnivals no expense was spared for the decorations, costumes, specially composed music, razzle dazzles, pony rides, puppet shows, toy railways and papier-mâché caves. For the adults there were croquet tournaments, rowing regattas and pleasure cruises along the Parramatta River. Women's rowing races were extravagant affairs, with the boathouse 'gaily decked with flags', expensive prizes to be won, and an enormous marquee with food and drinks for the guests. The race was from the Convalescent Hospital to the Concord jetty. Spectators boarded a steamer to watch. As the *Sydney Morning Herald* reported of the time Eadith's team won, 'The ladies rowed with vigour and enthusiasm which surprised their friends, and the graceful effect of their work was much admired.'

The grounds held fancy dress parties and many theatrical spectacles, including elaborately staged tableaux like the witches' scene from *Macbeth* and half a dozen scenes from *Sleeping Beauty*. Eadith, with her 'refined, lilting voice, never raised in anger or annoyance', always appeared immaculately dressed, conscious of her lofty position and wealth. At one fundraising ball she wore an empire gown of ivory Roman satin with diamonds and pearls sewn into the fabric, a string of plump pearls (she was extremely fond of such necklaces), an exquisite diamond tiara and, as a gossip columnist gasped in her article about the occasion, 'an electric light was in her powdered hair and produced a dazzling effect'.

Weddings at Yaralla were elaborate affairs, with arches of blossoms picked from the many flowerbeds and brilliantly decorated candlelit marquees with wooden dancefloors. For the expensive wedding of the poet 'Banjo' Paterson's daughter, a special carpet was laid outside for her walk down the aisle. A honeymoon at Yaralla was a sign that one had climbed to the highest echelon of Sydney society.

For the camera Eadith always adopted a reserved, even grim expression, determined not to give away any private thoughts, but there is one candid photograph of her seated in the gardens, wearing a heavy Edwardian dress, her face partly shaded by a huge hat. She is watching two men sitting on a rug and firing at an unseen target with miniature rifles. What is unusual is that she seems genuinely amused and gazes fondly at one of the men, a burly figure with a florid moustache. This was her mechanic and chauffeur, Charles Burnside, who seems to have meant much to her. He appears in many of her photograph albums, and his signature occurs more often in her guest register than any other (over a hundred times, according to Patricia Skehan in her book *The Walkers of Yaralla*). He drove her on sightseeing outings and to social events, frequently pictured wearing his jaunty peaked cap, holding her hand as she alighted from the latest model car. When not at Yaralla he stayed at the Union Club in the city, 'a base for gentlemen who had no permanent residence' in Sydney. Whether he was her lover or not, it seems that his unpretentiousness and male gallantry appealed to Eadith. But after a decade as her companion he suddenly disappears from history, rumoured to have returned to England.

Now Yaralla is silent, except for the birds and the voice of the guide. I look up at the mansion and the building glows in the sun. With its columns and four-storey towers, it has the unmistakable appearance of a Tuscan villa. Karoline and I follow the guide down to the water's edge, where there was once a jetty for guests to disembark. Across the river are rows of apartment blocks, quickly and recently erected, with all the charm of hideous Gold Coast towers. Perhaps little has changed.

Articles about Yaralla written in the social pages decades before often remarked on the juxtaposition of the beautiful estate with the nondescript apartments and cheap houses across the river. A writer for the prestigious *Australian Home Beautiful* in 1929 thought Yaralla maintained a 'dignified seclusion from the restless tide of suburban buildings ... Twisted tangles of fern dangle from the rocky enclaves on the lower shoreline, where thick mangroves screen the sight of high-rise development.'

The original path of sandstone blocks down to the water still exists, but on either side huge clumps of bamboo block out the mansion. The guide tells us this was deliberate; it was a piece of theatre so that those who arrived did not see the house until they emerged from the bamboo thickets. The guide is wrong. All the photographs in Skehan's two books on the Walker family and Yaralla show no bamboo at all. In fact, once one disembarked the mansion was clearly visible and Eadith would have been standing at the top of the rise or in the shade of the patio to greet the guests, her staff ready to serve those arriving who on occasion were serenaded by a band on a separate boat that accompanied them as they came up the river.

Our group walks up the hill to the side of the mansion and we're confronted by a grass plain of a hundred metres or more in length. The empty space is a telling example of how time mocks humans' futile attempts to create permanent monuments. For me, there is a sense of elegiac melancholy; I know what had been there from the photographs of Yaralla's past. The tennis courts have vanished, the swimming pool has been filled in, the hothouse is long gone, as is the orchard, the Turkish bath, and the conservatory with its decorative fountain. The grotto is fenced off, the power station demolished, as is the cottage Eadith had shipped over from Norway with its intricate wooden structure, brilliantly crafted and reassembled without using a nail.

Her lifestyle was the epitome of Edwardian glamour and upper-class wealth. She travelled the world, shooting Bengal tigers in India (in one photograph she poses with a dead tiger, a gun slung over her shoulder, next to Lord Kitchener, who clutches his own rifle), winning a grouse-shooting competition in Scotland, taking part in boat races (she was an excellent rower) and visiting Pompeii. The photograph of her at Pompeii is typical of practically every one I've seen: she's wearing a heavy Edwardian frock and a huge florid hat, unsmiling and watchful, with an aura of absolute rectitude and emotional distance.

World War I brought a sense of purpose into Eadith's life, and she flourished, throwing herself into charity work, especially for the Red Cross. She established a tent city on her estate for up to 30 soldiers suffering from TB (it only closed in 1920). Even her Leura home in the Blue Mountains became a retreat for wounded and shell-shocked servicemen.

After the war Yaralla became the site of more parties and celebrations, returning to its Edwardian role as the cynosure of Sydney high society. Eadith was fascinated by movies. She bought and showed copies of silent comedies featuring Charlie Chaplin, cartoons like Felix the Cat and shorts that featured the loves of her life – dogs.

It was entirely in keeping with her sensibility that she allowed part of a film to be shot on her estate. Made in 1918, *Cupid Camouflaged* now exists only as a series of stills. The story is simple fare; it could have been written on a couple of beer coasters. There is an attempt at matchmaking, mistaken identity, a cad pretending to be a lord, an elopement and true love victorious. The cast were amateurs, mostly from Sydney society. Reviews were scathing, with *The Mirror* finding the film, 'a poor advertisement for the acting talent of the nobility of Sydney'. Despite this, *Cupid Camouflage* ended up making a considerable profit of £45 000 for the Red Cross.

What intrigues are the stills from the production, especially those taken at Yaralla. The characters seem stuck in an Edwardian time warp. The women wear gorgeous Edwardian gowns, many carrying exotic feather fans, while the men wear tuxedos and white bow ties. The 'Open Air Dancing' scene, where nine young women dance on the lawn, is reminiscent of the Isadora Duncan school of extravagant improvised dancing. It's as if the war never happened, and the halcyon world of luxury and upper-class supremacy has returned. The reality of flappers, hot jazz, sly grog and dance halls does not feature.

In 1920 the Prince of Wales (later Edward VIII) stayed for a week at Yaralla on a private holiday after his official visit to Sydney. As Patricia Skehan, the historian of Yaralla, mentions, Eadith had a squash court especially built for him, but he never played on it because it had a concrete floor. The royal visit gradually turned into a nightmare, though you would never think it reading the prince's published diary:

> We've been to a small party at the house of a very rich old
> woman (Miss Walker). It's a very luxurious house complete
> with squash court, swimming bath etc. We went up about
> teatime and had a game [of tennis] before dinner after which
> we danced, and it developed into God's own rag.

Lord Louis Mountbatten, whose task it was to accompany the scatterbrained royal, wrote a detailed and perhaps more realistic entry about the night in his own diary:

> The entire party was spread out throughout the house,
> crawling under beds, squeezing through windows and
> generally doing quite the maddest things imaginable ...
> Colonel Grigg ... seized the mattress, blankets and sheets

and threw them over the scrapers … after that, everybody
started getting out sponges and throwing them at each other
… pandemonium spread all over the house … Tablecloths,
towels, sheets and sponges were dipped in water and thrown
about. Eventually, one of the Walker twins took a bucket of
water and tried to throw it at the Admiral, (who was dressed
as a Chinaman), but only succeeded in completely drenching
the unfortunate Miss Walker's very valuable oriental carpet.
Her nerve gave way completely and with tears in her eyes, she
implored everyone to spare her carpet.

A society matron saw the occasion even more clearly:

The Prince got very tight that night. He got halfway up the
stairs with some wine and poured it down on the heads of
everybody down below … The thought that at twenty-six the
prince was old enough to behave himself, but he didn't really.

If Mountbatten believed he could control his wayward charge,
he realised he couldn't when one night the Prince of Wales slid
down a banister and accidentally smashed an expensive vase.
Eadith, now at breaking point, had had enough of these pranks
and demanded the royal pay for it.

There is also a sense that the exasperating royal visit caused
her to reconsider her life. She approved a major subdivision of her
estate in 'the land sale of the century'. Gradually the world outside
began to encroach on the grounds of Yaralla as it shrank in size.
Nullawarra Avenue was built in front of the entrance gates. There
was a second subdivision a couple of years later (both sales now
account for a major portion of Concord West). Turning 60, she
decided to escape from Yaralla with its endless responsibilities.
She purchased shares in the Astor, constructed in 1923, Australia's

tallest and most elegant residential block at the time, and settled in there on the all-woman tenth floor. Situated in Macquarie Street, the Astor, wrote one architect:

> ... looked like an up-to-date piece of concrete and glass New York or Chicago dropped into late Victorian sandstone Sydney; a tall, sophisticated 'skyscraper' of the type associated with American modernist architecture ... making it one of the most enduring and identifiable residential buildings in Sydney.

She struck up a deep friendship with furniture-maker and antique merchant Captain Francis de Groot, an Irish-born former soldier who had served with the 15th Hussars on the Western Front in the Great War. One of his proudest possessions, which he constantly boasted about, was a ceremonial sword he had been awarded for bravery. The Bolshevik Revolution had made him into an ardent anti-socialist and his right-wing views were shared by Eadith, although she probably didn't know he had joined a secret paramilitary organisation, the New Guard. Most of the New Guard's members had served in the war and were willing, even to the point of staging a *coup d'etat*, to protect Australia from any threat of communism.

After a year's stay at the Astor, the restless Eadith returned to Yaralla, where she encouraged one of Australia's great photographers, Harold Cazneaux, to photograph it over several years, mainly for Warwick Fairfax's magazine *The Home*, which featured architecture, domestic interiors and the world of high society. One of the most evocative photographs is of the mansion and tower, partly hidden by dense trees and shrubs – the estate as a glamorous sheltered outpost of wealth and privilege. As the magazine put it: 'Amid an ever-growing restless tide of suburban building, Yaralla still maintains the dignified seclusion of other days.'

You can tell that Eadith began to trust Cazneaux. He took many pictures of her with her beloved dogs, and these revealed a different Eadith. Whenever she was photographed with the animals there was an expression of tenderness and affection on her face. It's as if she only lost her wariness and reserve with the adored dogs. The dogs' importance is evident in the collection of headstones now in the squash court the prince never played on. Lined up on the floor are memorials to 'Digger', 'Cobber', 'Wog', and others, collected from the graves where the dogs were buried with the same care and reverence given to humans.

After selling her place in the Astor, Eadith bought into the Savoy apartments, a 1919 building designed by Claud Hamilton in the American art deco style. In its narrow Darlinghurst street, it stands out as something special, as I can attest when, most evenings, my wife Mandy and I walk our dogs past it. A couple of doors down from the Savoy is St John's, the Anglican Church Eadith attended, its spire designed by Blacket, who, years before, had been Yaralla's first architect. Her Darlinghurst apartment was a bolthole, one she could retire to when the running of Yaralla became too much. It was a haven where she preferred to meet friends and relatives without undue ceremony.

She continued to travel overseas (accompanied by a valet and a maid) and entertain the rich and famous at Yaralla. When the Duke and Duchess of York stayed in 1927, Eadith commissioned a unique set of crockery featuring her insignia, and de Groot designed special furniture for the dining room. She became celebrated for her philanthropy and in 1928 was made a dame. Her car collection grew; the stables now transformed into an enormous garage, and her chauffeur had a choice of a Daimler, Rolls-Royce or Cadillac to drive, though Eadith forbade him using the main avenue when driving her out of Yaralla. The ungrateful local residents had objected to the shady brush box trees that originally lined the street and replaced them with scrawny *Butia capitata* palms that Eadith thought ugly and gave no shade at all.

From then on, her health deteriorated. Those who met her remarked how ancient she looked, even her clothes were from another era. She became a recluse and her estate, an island, was gradually hemmed in by commonplace suburbia, whose residents rarely saw Miss Walker, except perhaps for a glimpse of her in the back of one of her chauffeur-driven cars on Sunday mornings, making the short journey to the local Holy Trinity Church.

Unable to walk very far, she used a motorised wheelchair to inspect her property. The motor was silent and, as one gardener said, shivering at the memory, 'You couldn't hear her coming.' Once they saw her, the men would, as they had for decades, respectfully doff their hats. She had difficulty getting upstairs, so a special chair, like an inclinator, was installed for her. Long before she died, Eadith had become a shadowy presence on the estate.

In October 1937, with her dog Cobber at her bedside, she died. Her death marked the end of the Walker family, which had been a unique part of Sydney's history since the 1860s. Her name, and that of her father, still exists in the Thomas Walker Convalescent Hospital and the Dame Eadith Walker Hospital, significant monuments few other Sydney families could match. She seems more an elegant upper-class woman out of Proust, rather than one of the stoic, weary women populating Lawson's social realist stories. But as in Proust, time is the enemy. Time quickly forgot her father and, just as quickly, Sydney would forget her.

ON THE BEACH

IF ANYTHING SUMMED UP SYDNEY'S LOVE OF ITS BEACHES, it was during the early days of the pandemic in 2020. People defied government warnings about maintaining social distancing and flocked to Bondi Beach. The *Daily Telegraph* ran the headline, 'Eager Beachgoers Bury Their Heads in the Sand' on its front page. A Melbourne radio host was outraged by the scenes: 'It will do those self-righteous, smug and self-important Sydneysiders some good to be knocked off their high perch.' There were photographs of many thousands of people on the beaches at Bondi and Manly flouting the pandemic restrictions. Eventually police on horseback had to be brought in to disperse the crowds. For the rest of the nation the photographs only proved that hedonistic Sydney played by its own rules.

The beaches have become integral to Sydney's idea of itself. The sand and bracing Pacific surf sum up Sydney for visitors. For Seymour Hicks, an English actor-manager who toured in 1925 and wrote the travel book *Hullo Australians*, it was the classlessness of the beaches that appealed: 'Everybody from butcher boy and housemaid upwards or downwards can enjoy themselves during six months of the year. The sea is for the people ... not for the favoured few.' What amazed him was how many people there were, 'Thousands of people stand in a solid mass in water up to their knees ... You see all sorts and sizes of male and female in their bathing suits as the police will allow them ... You get a bit of a shock. It's all so naked you feel as if you were in a butcher's shop.'

Around this time in the mid-1920s an estimated 60 000 people were visiting Bondi Beach each summer weekend. Footage from a six-minute silent documentary filmed on Bondi Beach in 1925 shows just how quickly the culture of the beach had ingrained itself in the life of Sydneysiders. *Sydney's Sunny Beaches* shows huge crowds frolicking on the beach, with cartwheeling girls, men forming human pyramids, picnicking families, young women and men flirting or covertly ogling each other, excited children wading into the shallow waters holding on to their mothers' hands, and the more adventurous men swimming out to sea. The beach and the swimming costumes convey an air of easygoing informality where the beach belongs to everyone, no matter what station of life you were from, and, most of all, there is a pervasive sense of communal happiness, as if the sand and the sea are the sacred site of an Austral paradise. The documentary finishes with an engrossed crowd watching a lifesaving drill; heroic, muscular lifesavers holding on to their safety rope, heading out into the waves to save a man and carrying him back to shore, where they use a stroking technique on his body to bring him back to life.

Every experienced swimmer and lifesaver knew that the sea could be treacherous, even deadly. As Colin Wills wrote in *Australian Passport*, recalling Manly Beach in this period:

There were cross currents and undertows, and sometimes a wave that looked promising enough was really a 'dumper' – one that curled over forwards from the top and became a furious spinning coil of water, from which the unwise swimmer would emerge breathless, battered and bruised, with a bleeding nose ... or with even a broken limb, or at times, with a broken neck.

Aboriginal people knew the beaches well. They called Bondi 'Boondi', a name that can be translated as 'water breaking over rocks', 'noisy water' or 'falling water' or our simple monosyllable: 'surf'. It was a popular spot for the local clans to hunt wildfowl along the reedy lagoons that once extended from Bondi Beach to Rose Bay. It's said that near the northern headland of Ben Buckler was a 'kooradgee ceremonial ground'. On North Bondi golf links are rock carvings of sharks, whales and a creature like a thin man with an iguana's tail. It's not known if Aboriginal people surfed, but people at the turn of the twentieth century would find skulls and weapons on Bondi Beach.

Further south the name Coogee is said to be a local Aboriginal word *koojah*, which means 'smelly place'; another translation of a similar word means 'the smell of the seaweed drying'. Further south still, Cronulla is derived from the word *kurranulla*, meaning 'place of the pink seashells'. Maroubra apparently means 'place of thunder', while Manly has the simplest derivation of them all.

It was named by Captain Arthur Phillip for the men he met there – those of the Kay-ye-my clan of the Guringai people – writing that 'their confidence and manly behaviour made me give the name of Manly Cove to this place'. On another visit Phillip encountered members of the clan and, after a misunderstanding, he was speared in the shoulder. In a remarkable gesture, despite hovering on the verge of death, the governor ordered that there be no retaliation.

By the late 1870s so many people were flocking to Bondi Beach, then private property, that in 1882 it became a public beach, and the first tramway to the beach commenced in 1884. By the end of the century a tramway guide described the area's charms for visitors:

At the southern end of the bay a picturesque rocky nook, where one may sit in the shade, while the whole stretch of the bay affords unlimited opportunities for paddling, fully availed of, by juveniles, particularly on a holiday. A very large swimming bath. The Bay is a great place for sharks during the season, and some exciting sport in the way of shark fishing can be witnessed almost any night during the hot months.

Drinking and carousing were common, and on one occasion a large crowd of drunken hooligans rioted after a quarrel over a woman. Police who tried to restore order were badly beaten. By this stage Bondi was becoming a byword for violence, and 'to give him the Bondi' meant to kick a man to death.

Over at Manly Beach, Mr Leahy, the zealous inspector of nuisances, was having a torrid time of it as bathing in the nude became very popular with boys and men (women were regarded as 'loose' if they even took off their shoes and stockings and lifted their skirts to paddle in public). An entry in the inspector's diary, dated 23 December 1888, provides a typical note: 'At North Harbour taking the names of those bathing in a nude state from 10.30 till two o'clock.'

But it wasn't just nude bathing that was against the law. Bathing in daylight – clothed or unclothed – was outlawed. When the Fig Tree baths were opened at Woolloomooloo in 1833 men could swim naked enclosed by a fence. It wasn't long before there were male and female baths, with a high fence modestly hiding the women from the men.

The man who helped open the beaches was William Gocher, a newspaper editor in Manly, who announced in his local paper that he would publicly bathe at midday on 8 September 1902. In front of many onlookers Gocher ostentatiously bathed in the sea, but on leaving the water the police were not to be seen. The following Sunday the police were again absent. His third appearance drew an even larger crowd. It was later said he entered the surf wearing a frock coat and top hat, but in reality he went in wearing his usual neck-to-knee. On his way out of the water he put on a shabby mackintosh. This time the police, who were under pressure from politicians and outraged locals, were waiting for him. The Manly police sergeant emerged from behind a tree and greeted him with, 'Hope you enjoyed your swim, Mr Gocher.' By then it was obvious that even the police couldn't stop people swimming in daylight hours and the battle for Manly Beach was over. 'Crowds flocked to the novelty of all-day bathing.' In 1903 Manly Council rescinded the by-law prohibiting bathing after 7 a.m., but a new law was enacted that everyone over the age of eight had to wear a neck-to-knee costume and mixed bathing was still not permitted.

It's said that the forerunners of modern Bondi surfers were the boys and handful of men who swam in the lagoons behind the beach from the early 1870s, but it was not until the late 1880s that a few 'cranks' and 'exhibitionists' started bathing naked in the sea. These law-breakers were often chased by the police up and down the sand dunes. As one shocked witness wrote to a newspaper:

> It's a shame that the prettiest beaches round Sydney should be rendered unavailable to women and children by this wanton desecration; that every pretty little spot should be monopolised by swimmers to the violence of modesty in the young of both sexes.

Emboldened by Gocher's example, in 1903 Frank McElhone, a bank clerk, and his friend, the Reverend Robert McKeown, rector of St Mary's church, Waverley, defied the law. The police prosecuted the two men, but the trial only gained more publicity for the resolution of the issue. In 1906 a local committee supporting McElhone and the rector was formed, resulting in the establishment of the Bondi Surf Bathers' Lifesaving Club, the first organisation of its kind in the world. In late December the same year, the first public demonstration of the newly designed lifesaving reel was given at Bondi Beach and, a fortnight later, the lifesavers, using the new equipment, rescued two boys, Rupert Swallow and a Charlie Smith of North Sydney, who, thanks to this new piece of equipment, would live to become one of Australia's most famous airmen, Sir Charles Kingsford Smith.

Sydneysiders gloried in their beaches. In a 1925 article, the *Sydney Mail* was effusive:

> The beaches give you the impression that all Sydney girls are
> well shaped. Slim, graceful, lithe, slender and virile ... To
> watch them coming in, shooting the breakers, eyes sparkling,
> teeth flashing, their heads tied up in a handkerchief or covered
> with a bright-coloured waterproof cap, is a sight for the gods.

It wasn't long before photographs of these Sydney models became sought after and commercialised. In *Our Girls: Aussie Pin-ups of the 40s and 50s*, author Madeleine Hamilton spends some time on Adelie Hurley, daughter of famous photographer Frank Hurley. She was photographed for *Pix* and *The Sun* as the typical Australian beach girl. As Adelie remarked, she and the other girls were photographed 'always at the beach or looking through a shark net or looking through a palm tree with a towel wrapped around your head like a turban'.

Women pushed the boundaries of what constituted modesty on the beaches. In May 1943, *Truth* published a photograph of skimpily attired Beryl Lawes being banished from a Sydney beach by a disapproving inspector. One woman wrote to Beryl congratulating her 'for standing up for your rights against those old wowsers and old fogies who try to condemn your beautiful Australian womanhood ... if you would be sweet enough to send me a snap of yourself to stand on my dressing table, I would be highly delighted'.

The men, too, were admired. The lifesavers who protected the beachgoing public were praised as physical exemplars of the male body, virile specimens of stamina and muscular perfection.

Lifesavers were at the forefront of promoting Australia to tourists. A poster commemorating the opening of the Sydney Harbour Bridge in 1932 portrayed the lifesaver as the perfect model of Australian manhood. They were lifesavers with muscles as strong as the steel girders of the bridge and just as perfectly constructed.

The lifesavers not only rescued swimmers in difficulty, but helped people recover from bluebottle stings and cuts from oyster shells or sharp rocks. Then there were the shark attacks. Sydney's worst year for sharks was 1929. Colin Stewart was attacked while waist-deep among a crowd of swimmers at Bondi and died the next day. A young man was mauled at Maroubra, another died at White Bay and a girl was badly maimed at Collaroy.

It's quite remarkable to think how quickly swimming and surfing caught the popular imagination. During World War I the federal government was annoyed at the small numbers of men signing up and in 1917 put out posters of a surfer with the words: *It is nice in the surf, but what about the men in the trenches? Go and help.*

In 1906 the first plucky woman ventured into the sea at Bondi during daylight hours. Nobody seems to have known who she was, but she headed down to the shoreline one Sunday wearing her neck-to-knee swimming costume. A large crowd had gathered and she had to walk into the surf between a double line of gawping spectators.

Many Sydneysiders were still not won over by this new public spectacle, including Mayor Watkins of Waverley who, after an inspection of the beaches, told the *Daily Telegraph* in 1907:

> What we saw at Bondi was disgusting. Some of these surf bathers are nothing but exhibitionists, putting on V trunks and exposing themselves, twisted into all shapes on the sand. They are in worse manner than if they were nude. Their garments after contact with the water show up the figure too prominently. Women are often worse than the men, putting on light, gauzy material that clings when wet too much to be decent. But they won't continue doing it at Bondi Beach, not so long as I am Mayor Watkins.

The mayors of Waverley, Randwick and Manly, acting together, directed that all bathers, men and women, had to wear skirts from hips to knees. There was a tremendous outcry.

An Irishman wrote a letter to the *Sydney Morning Herald*:

> This edict is another Injustice to Ireland. As a self-respecting Irishman my feelings are outraged that I must wear skirts when I go into the surf. What will I be – a Highlander in kilts, or a serio-comic-Aphrodite in the foam? Neither is to my taste.

Over a thousand Bondi men marched to the city singing 'John Brown's Body' behind a dead seagull on a pole. They dressed in their sisters' petticoats, 'flounced, laced, and embroidered'. They wore frothy ballet frills around their bellies and made red flannels and damask tablecloths into sarongs. Others marched in their mothers' kitchen curtains.

The public ridicule was too much for the mayors and they

never enforced their skirt edict. But over the years the matter of what men and women wore on Sydney beaches became a regular and much publicised test of the changing mores of the nation.

The paintings of Ethel Carrick Fox give a good idea of how people, especially women, dressed for the beach just before World War I. In *Manly Beach – Summer is Here* (1913) the many women are dressed in Edwardian finery, the men in suits, and there's a distant cluster of men in their swimming costumes. The central figure on the crowded beach is a woman sitting on a deck chair, her large umbrella shading her from the sun, while we see the backs of many holidaymakers gazing out at the azure waters. In another Fox painting from the same year, *Promenade at Manly*, women of fashion in heavy Edwardian dresses amble in the shade of the trees along the beach, showing off their attire. In *On the Sands* a couple of men hover near the water, handfuls of women and children in their best clothes sit on the sand gossiping, the rolling waves tantalisingly close. In *Balmoral Beach*, women in their fashionable dresses and hats walk their children alongside the rim of the incoming tide and stare at the enticing water as if it's beckoning them to go in.

Before the Great War there were some daring young women who were willing to be photographed in bathing suits. Colin Caird, 'a gentleman of leisure', liked to take waitresses from restaurants in Pitt Street to Collaroy for picnics. He bought them swimsuits and photographed them in their beachwear. In one evocative photograph, five of them are pictured wearing swimsuits that cover their whole bodies from neck to knee, the costumes cut to make sure that their feminine figures were hidden. Once they finished swimming and posing for the lifelong bachelor, they dressed in old shirts and loose football shorts that came halfway to their knees and were happy to be photographed as boys as they played around the sand and rocks.

These old-fashioned bathing suits gradually gave way to the daring new woollen costumes favoured by the famous Australian swimmer and aquatic film star Annette Kellerman, who noted the difference in swimwear in her 1918 book *How to Swim*:

> There are two kinds of bathing suits; those that are adapted for use in the water, and those that are unfit for any use except on dry land. If you are going to swim, wear a bathing suit. But if you are merely going to play on the beach, and pose for camera friends, you may safely wear the dry land variety.

After the Great War women took to the water wearing the 'Canadian swimwear' Kellerman recommended as an example of the spirited independence of the flapper.

In 1936 a man was fined a shilling for having rolled his one-piece costume down to his waist. It was an example of how rigorously the modest bathing costumes of both men and women were enforced by beach inspectors. After knee-length bathers went, they were replaced by two-piece suits (pants and a singlet-like top) and for women, a one-piece suit with a modesty skirt.

But it was after World War II that beaches, especially Bondi, became a site for sunbakers and swimmers, especially women, to flaunt the new skimpy bathers. Aub Laidlaw, the chief inspector of Bondi Beach for three decades, became infamous (or legendary, it all depended on which newspaper you read) for his conservative interpretations of what constituted indecent swimwear.

In 1946, 17-year-old Pat Riley, described by one tabloid as 'a platinum blonde with shapely hips', was ordered from the beach by Laidlaw when he determined that the fine net on the sides of her trunks was transparent. A crowd of 2000 shouted to her, 'Come on, Pat, give us a look.' After changing into a black moss crepe suit, she climbed on the bonnet of a car, counted to three and threw her blue net briefs into the crowd, 'which fought for the swimsuit and in the process tore it to pieces'.

The first girl to wear a bikini on Bondi Beach created a sensation. One witness recalled, 'She came out of the dressing sheds and the men on the beach went mad. It was a near riot. She was surrounded. When she tried to run all the men ran after her.' Laidlaw arrived on the scene and, with the help of a local, managed to escort her into a shop where her two rescuers turned hoses on the crowd to stop them breaking down the door.

Laidlaw was a one-man army against immodesty. He ordered men off the beach if they wore V-shaped bathers, especially if they were made of cotton ('We won't stand for anything like that,' he warned). By the early 1960s he was still ordering women off the beach if he considered a bikini 'unsuitable' and the offender refused to 'resume normal dress'. One woman defiantly wore a gold bikini and when warned by Laidlaw she called him a fool. Laidlaw wasn't deterred, 'Despite the trend overseas, I don't think bikinis will ever be allowed on Bondi … We have seen women on the beach with little more on than two hankies.'

Ridicule ended his reign and by the late 1970s not only were bikinis ubiquitous, but women were going topless. In 1979 an outraged Father James O'Reilly of St Patrick's church channelled his inner Laidlaw, declaring: 'Bondi Beach is now a mecca for the sick in mind – the sex perverts and deviants who come in increasing numbers, many armed with binoculars …' His words failed to arouse the authorities and little notice was taken of his jeremiad. Soon Sydney had four nude beaches.

The beaches were for the parade of bodies, the health of swimmers, the joy of physical exercise and the tonic effects of tanning. By 1937 more than 6 million Sydneysiders were going to the beaches each year. The 1930s saw beach culture and the Australian body – a tanned, muscular archetype shaped by sand, surf and sun – become an essential part of the Australian identity. The more physically fit entertained beach crowds with 'beach acrobatics' or 'beachobatics'. Gymnastic feats were popular, such as one shown in a photograph of a woman bending over in an L shape while a man does a handstand on her buttocks. And then there were the parades of sun-worshippers wearing the latest beach swim wear.

If anything caught the spirit of the beaches and the sun-worshipping Sydneysiders it was what has been called 'one of Australia's most recognised photographs', Max Dupain's *Sunbaker* (1937), a close-up of a man lying face-down in the sand, photographed at ground level so we only see the top of his head and his two muscular arms; a monumental form of the bronzed male body framed against a summer sky.

If Dupain's photograph has become an iconic image of our beach culture, then so has Charles Meere's painting *Australian Beach Pattern* (1940). This work, which encapsulated the 1930s trend to mythologise the Australian way of life as symbolised by the beach, is one of the most popular paintings in the Art Gallery of New South Wales and has appeared on many book covers. It has also inspired many artists, and was chosen as one of the images for the Opening Ceremony program at the 2000 Olympics.

The painting depicts an action-packed family day at a Sydney beach. It's both strange and familiar – even eerie to some – and over the years has been the focus of many a fervid interpretation. It's a tableau of beachgoers whose athletic perfection is of such monumental proportions that it almost verges on the satirical. Meere set out to present a crowded, complex composition that seems suspended in time. The tanned men, women and children are gods and goddesses in bathers.

One of the ironies is that Meere was not an outdoors type. According to one of his students, Flora Robertshaw, 'Charles never went to the beach. We made up most of the figures, occasionally using one of Charles' employees for the hands and feet.' Early reactions criticised it as inhuman, lifeless and lacking in lyrical feeling. Later critics accused it of glorifying racial purity, suggesting the painting celebrated the Aryan ideals of Nazi Germany or had a 'sun-soaked eugenic argument'. Others advanced the theory that it was inspired by rampant nationalism. Linda Slutzkin argued that the work is connected with the war, and that the figures are 'Spartans in Speedos'. Another suggests it shows our naïvety at what was happening in Europe and our unpreparedness for battle.

In the late 1980s Anne Zahalka, whose career is defined by an obsession with the painting, made a photographic parody of it, *The Bathers*. Instead of heroic poses, the characters are rather awkward, their bodies all too real and unheroic. She made the sexes more evenly balanced, and the woman holding the beach ball has been made more central. And, as a dramatic contrast, there are more non-Anglo people populating the foreground. The original painting was of Anglo Australians, which was a reflection of Meere's time, but Zahalka is trying to realise the demographic changes of Sydney society and beachgoers of her era.

Meere's painting is not political like Zahalka's many photographic variations of it. It has to be remembered that it was painted by an Englishman who, having fought in the horrifying battles of the Great War, came to Australia and saw in our beaches, our hedonism and enjoyment of life, a luscious alternative to the bleakness of postwar Europe.

*

If an Englishman created one of the most fascinating images of our beach culture, it was three Polynesian men who would transform

Australian swimming and inaugurate the surfing craze. At the age of seven, Alick Wickham from New Georgia in the Solomon Islands arrived in Sydney in the 1890s on his father's schooner. As a schoolboy Wickham worked as a houseboy, and in his free time he swam in the sea baths at Bronte Beach (Australia's oldest ocean pool). A local swimming coach, observing the impressively fast Wickham, would shout, 'Look at that kid crawling!' From this time Wickham became known as the man who brought the stroke now known as freestyle or 'the Australian crawl' to the world, although this style of swimming was widespread in many parts of the Pacific. In 1899 a Polynesian, Tommy Tanna, came to Sydney to work as a gardener and taught the locals to body surf.

Near Christmas in 1914 the NSW Amateur Swimming Association invited several newspaper reporters to Freshwater Beach on the north shore, to witness an exhibition of surfboard riding by Duke Paoa Kahanamoku from Hawaii. A large excited crowd turned out to meet the world champion sprint swimmer, named after his father, who had been given that name when the Duke of Edinburgh visited Hawaii and it was noticed that the son 'had something of a regal air'.

The young Duke had learned board-riding as a youngster on Waikiki Beach, Honolulu. For his Sydney demonstration of the art he had carved his board with his own hands from a slab of sugar pine purchased from a local lumber yard in Freshwater. A few people had been surfing in Australia, but the Duke brought board-riding to a whole new level.

He entered the water and, lying flat on the board, paddled out about 365 metres where he waited for a suitable breaker. When it came, he swung his board around and came in with it. He rose slightly, knelt on the board, and then stood up for almost 100 metres. The conditions were against good surfing due to the dumping waves that followed closely on top of each other. But, as one report put it, 'it must be admitted it was wonderfully clever'.

The crowd had seen nothing like it, He seemed to be floating on the waves, effortlessly controlling his long wooden board that weighed a hefty 45 kilograms, whereas the boards he used back in Hawaii weighed less than 12 kilograms. Another enthusiastic witness called it 'a magnificent display, which won the cordial applause of the onlookers'.

This first public demonstration proved so popular that he returned in January 1915 to give lessons. He invited 15-year-old Isabel Letham to have a go. She was soon able to stand up on a board, and later in the day sat on his shoulders as they tandem surfed. A few years later, unable to join a surf club because she was a woman, Letham would drive to the more obscure beaches of Bilgola and Bungan with her friend Isma Armor and they would spend weekends surfing and camping together.

The Duke, as he was called, became a major figure in the revival of a centuries-old Polynesian custom that became a global craze. Among sports writers his demonstration on 23 December 1914 is widely regarded as the most significant day in the development of surfing in Australia. His importance is still celebrated: there's a Duke Kahanamoku Park on the northern headland of Freshwater Beach, and a bronze statue of him stands gazing out at the pulsating Pacific in front of the Harbord Diggers Club.

Surfing became a way of life for many along Sydney's beaches. Surfers lived a life more Polynesian than puritan. As one surfer explained to journalist Hugh Atkinson in the early 1960s: 'I dunno, it's hard to describe. When you're driving hard and fast down the wall, with the soup curling behind yer, or doing this backside turn on a big one about to tube, it's just this feeling. Yer know, it leaves yer feeling stoked.'

THE GOLDEN TWENTIES

TWO ENGLISHMEN CAME TO SYDNEY IN THE EARLY 1920S.
The first, the author DH Lawrence, arrived in 1923 and stayed
two and a half days in Sydney before heading down the south
coast to Thirroul for an extended stay. He thought Sydney was
'all London without being London ... all, as it were, made in
five minutes, a substitute for the real thing'. In Martin Place,
he longed for Westminster; in Sussex Street 'he almost wept for
Covent Garden'. As far as one character in his Australian novel
Kangaroo is concerned, the country had no genuine culture, 'it
had no real magic'. As usual, Lawrence's views of the countries
he visited were seen through his morose or elated states of mind.

Seymour Hicks, a West End actor, writer and producer, toured
Australia with his hits *The Man in Dress Clothes* and *Broadway
Jones*. He saw Sydney as 'the playground of the Commonwealth'
and marvelled at the differences between the country's two
major cities, writing in one of his several travel books, *Chestnut
Reroasted* (1924), that 'Melbourne people entertain you in their
homes, Sydney people entertain you in their restaurants.' Sydney
was a 'fun city ... with a slight dash of Paris about it. Streets
branching off everywhere, so unlike the mathematical block
system of Melbourne.' To Hicks, Sydney was a pleasure-loving
town, a 'Venice seen from the Lido in the dusk may rival but not
equal its beauty'.

Hicks was probably closer to capturing the spirit of Sydney in the 1920s than the dyspeptic Lawrence, who was even appalled at the high cost of a taxi ride. What both didn't see in their fleeting visits was the city's transformation from a genteel, culturally backward Edwardian city into one with an exuberant embrace of modernism. Part of this was the lifestyle of bohemianism for a small but visible minority that challenged the numb conformity and conservatism of the suburban dream.

Nowhere was this more evident than in Kings Cross, where artists and writers like Dulcie Deamer (who daringly attended artists' balls in a leopard-skin toga) and the poet Christopher Brennan (who eventually drank himself to death) could be found. According to Tony Moore in *Dancing with Empty Pockets: Australia's Bohemians*, 'bohemia is in part created in the act of its telling, or more particularly, remembering'. To the bohemians, making art was less important than one's life as art.

But to the three McDonagh sisters, living in a part of town, not known for its bohemianism, making art was vitally important. The sisters, Isabel, Phyllis and Paulette, were the eldest of seven children of John McDonagh and wife Anne, a nurse. Their father was a gregarious and lively doctor known across Sydney for his seemingly incongruent interests. He was a superb athlete, a trick roller skater, an owner of most of the skating rinks in Sydney, including The Imperial next to Hyde Park ('closed to the rowdy elements'). He collected exquisite antique furniture and mixed in such disparate social circles that he astonished many. He adored boxing and was honorary doctor for boxing matches held down at the Stadium in Rushcutters Bay, patching up bloodied boxers, and can be seen in 1908 footage of the African American Jack Johnson and Tommy Burns world title fight, wearing a top hat in the ring as he attended to the bruised and battered Canadian between bouts. He was also honorary doctor for the J.C. Williamson's theatre empire, caring for famous local and overseas singers and actors like Sarah Bernhardt, entertaining them at his home and joining in their impromptu singalongs and skits.

His three eldest daughters were born within three years of each other and became extraordinarily close. Isabel, Phyllis and Paulette were fascinated by the showbusiness people that their father invited home and, from an early age, were drawn to theatre and exhibiting their skills at roller skating rinks. They grew up in a world of artists and Sydney's social elite. Later, when the family shifted to the huge, stately Drummoyne House, built in the 1850s, they entertained themselves, mimicking the actors they had seen, creating their own shows and designing even more outrageous fancy dress costumes.

Then their world collapsed. In 1920 their 61-year-old father died in strange circumstances when they found him dead on their doorstep after another doctor had administered an accidental cocaine overdose. Two years later their mother died. The siblings continued to live at Drummoyne House. Despite their father dying almost broke, the three attractive sisters were considered wealthy 'society girls'. They held two- or three-day parties at Drummoyne. One friend said years decades later, 'they were more Bohemian than anything around now'.

Films became an obsession. The three of them had no time for what they called 'hayseed' movies with their 'Dad 'n Dave idiot stupidity'. They preferred European pictures, especially the German films of Fritz Lang and Hollywood movies which they thought had an emotional rhythm that Australian films lacked.

The trio started their own film company with the idea said, Paulette of writing 'stories that we felt were entertainment ... that's all.' They quickly sorted out their roles; gorgeous Isabel, under the name, Marie Lorraine, would be the star, Paulette would direct and write the initial scripts, and Phyllis would be production manager. They thrashed out scenarios and refined them in long, intense meetings

The McDonaghs were alluring, persuasive and charming, the epitome of the modern woman of the twenties and, using their father's social network, they called in favours, whether it be for expensive props or filming locations like the swish Ambassador's nightclub. Drummoyne House was an obvious set with its huge number of rooms and antique furniture. Their small budgets were financed by relatives and friends. As one writer said of them, 'the sisters had a sense of themselves ... they just wanted to do it and they did it.'

Their first film was *Those Who Love* (1926) and its theme was one that preoccupied them – the social collision between the upper middle class and working class, in this instance, Barry, the son of moneyed Sir James, falling in love with Lola, a dancer. All sorts of melodramatic events ensue until years later Barry is living in an attic, having rejected wealth and position and taken to drink. He ends up in hospital where Lola, working as a nurse, recognises him. She visits Sir James, asks him for money for a specialist and the family is united. The film was a success (it bumped off Chaplin's *Gold Rush* as Sydney's most popular film). Typically, the high-spirited sisters spent much of the profits on lavish parties at Drummoyne House.

The next film was *The Far Paradise*. The story is, again, an entertaining and delirious melodrama with similar elements as their first film. James Carson is involved in crime and is investigated by the Attorney-General, Howard Lawton. Carson's daughter Cherry falls in love with Lawton's son Peter. Of course, his father forbids the relationship. A year later Peter finds Cherry selling flowers in a mountain tourist resort, trying to support her now-alcoholic father, who conveniently dies of a heart attack so Cherry can marry Peter.

But the film is more than its story. It is visually striking, the acting subtle, and the *mise en scene* (under Phyllis's careful supervision) is superb, with huge Venetian mirrors obsessively reflecting the inner most thoughts of the characters. Paulette's direction had gained confidence and the German Expressionistic lighting is unique in Australian pictures at that time. What the startled crew and actors had to get used to were the times the film shut down for the three sisters to loudly thrash out their ideas until they were resolved. Paulette was now experienced enough to drill the actors, and tone down the overacting of stage actors. Isabel's acting was exceptional in capturing the heroine's complicated emotional journey while Paulette lingered over her sister's beauty with the intimacy of a lover's gaze

Their second film was even more popular than their first and the impressed *Sydney Morning Herald* reviewer said it showed 'decision in every detail', while *Smith's Weekly* observed that the film was 'something of the art that conceals art.' As Graham Shirley in *Australian Cinema* (1989) says, '... it is one of the best-directed of all Australian features prior to the coming of sound'. The quality of the picture was obvious, even to those reviewers who had once dismissed the sisters as dilettantes. The magazine *Everyone* noted that 'With very little else but pluck and determination they went ahead, and the results of their enterprise have been more than amply justified ... These young ladies have certain very definite ideas with regard to motion pictures and have the courage of their convictions.'

Their next film, *The Cheaters*, is about an embezzler, Bill who works with his daughter Paula robbing wealthy people. Bill also seeks revenge on a businessman, John Travers. In a familiar McDonagh twist Paula falls in love with Travers' son Lee and begins to have doubts about her life of crime. Eventually Paula reforms and marries Lee. Filmed on the cusp of silent movies being replaced by sound, *The Cheaters* was shot as a silent in 1929 but had trouble securing a release. The McDonaghs decided to adapt it into a partial talkie and filmed some additional scenes in Melbourne in 1930 using an improvised sound-on-disc system.

The McDonaghs had made no pretence about tackling social issues, but went on to make Australia's first anti-war film in 1933, *Two Minutes Silence*, now lost, was set some years after World War I has ended. Four people gather in a London drawing room and, as the clock strikes eleven, they think back to their horrific experiences of the war, which include death, rape and suicide.

The sisters had always been preoccupied by the fate of Australian soldiers in the war and had attended and held many a benefit for ex-soldiers. But for an audience in the Great Depression, especially women, this was grim stuff and it flopped. They wanted comedy and romance, in other words, movies more like the sisters first three.

The McDonaghs were criticised by some ardent male nationalists for not making 'authentic' Australian films, regarding their movies as frivolous, fluffy and too feminine. But women audiences loved their sophisticated Hollywood style ethos and the complicated, intelligent and beautiful heroines that Isabel played. Unlike more serious fare, the handsome male leads, the fancy dress parties, the worlds of the criminal and upper classes, the chic dresses, wonderful Sydney locations, moody nightclubs, lush hotel rooms, the rich visual style, and the optimistic endings seem, even at this distance, to sum up the buoyant and vibrant twenties and a special feminine sensibility to be found in a city like Sydney.

*

A woman's flaunting of her sexuality was also a consequence of the emergence of the 'city girl'. For her the city became a theatre. To avoid anonymity in the faceless, fast-paced crowd, she became a public performer, emulating Hollywood actresses, those dreamy, gorgeous flappers with their cloche hats, short skirts, pouting sensuality and ribald backchat.

Two of Sydney's popular artists' haunts were both founded by women. Red-headed Betsy Mathias started Betsy's – or, more formally, Café La Boheme – out of her own meagre savings in a rickety tenement in Wilmot Street, a laneway between George and Pitt streets. She was an idealist, anarchist, communist, member of the notorious International Workers of the World (IWW) and a soapbox orator in the Domain. The café was said to be an 'extraordinary resort of lost souls' and, as a *Smith's Weekly* journalist wrote in 1925:

> Every Bohemian in Sydney has visited at least once that tiny café redolent of garlic and spilt wine, swallowed the spaghetti and joined lustily in the chorus ... 'Oh, Heidelberg!' which is, of course, the 'Red Flag' in disguise.

Her kindness towards poets, communists and broke writers soon financially ruined her and she had to close Betsy's. A few years later when she was interviewed, the reporter noted how frail and little she was and how she was 'a strange example of energy outrunning purpose, of fervour robbed of a natural outlet – the unsatisfied and eternal anti'.

The other meeting place for bohemians, artists and intellectuals was the Pakies Club, started by Mrs Augusta 'Pakie' Macdougall, wife of theatre director Duncan Macdougall. It opened in 1929, decorated by the hip modernist painter Roy de Maistre, and operated from rooms on the second floor of 219 Elizabeth Street (opposite the War Memorial in Hyde Park) until 1966.

Countless writers and artists came to talk, gossip and lecture, including Mary Gilmore, Miles Franklin and Xavier Herbert. It held conferences, like the Writers' League National Conference in 1935, where one afternoon was spent discussing the novels of the American writer John Dos Passos, whose work was banned in Australia, and after dinner there was a reading of Katharine Susannah Prichard's new one-act play.

Fancy dress was popular, and in 1929 there was a Mexican-themed party. Rugs were borrowed from the home of the Mexican consulate, a Mexican ballet was performed, and the guests wore outsized sombreros. 'It seemed a little slice of the famous *outlaw* country had been transported to Sydney,' said one gossip columnist. The costumes were colourful. One woman came as a moon goddess. Never one to miss a chance at fancy dress, the American architect Marion Mahony Griffin came as 'Ahpuch', the Lord of Death, with a headdress of long golden spikes four feet (1.2 metres) across. Her husband, Walter Burley Griffin – like his wife, the architect and designer of Canberra and the exclusive north shore Sydney north shore suburb of Castlecrag – wore a robe of 'highly coloured Oriental embroidery and a large headdress … somewhat Egyptian in design – he was "Itzamma" – The Father of All', and no doubt Griffin, who had a high opinion of himself, played the role with great conviction.

THE DREAM WEAVERS

FOR FOUR DECADES FROM THE 1920S, Jim Bendrodt and Azzalin Romano were Sydney's dream weavers, offering Sydney Hollywood glamour, New York sophistication, European elegance and, most importantly, a romantic heart.

By the 1950s, Jim Bendrodt's fame had been fading. But when he sat for his portrait in 1957, he was back in the game. The year before he had opened the Caprice, a luxurious floating restaurant in Rose Bay. It quickly became a magnet for wealthy Sydneysiders and international celebrities. He was a Gatsby figure, mercurial, charming, elusive, with an exotic Canadian drawl, a jewelled cigarette case always at the ready; an exquisite dancer, a showman, a former lightweight boxing campion, a reckless gambler, a man famous for his glamorous and exciting restaurants, dance palaces and ice-skating rinks. He had imported American jazz bands to Australia and, as a 2013 *Sydney Morning Herald* article put it, 'Jim Bendroit brought class to the Harbour City in the Age of Swing.'

The painter was Judy Cassab. She had been born in Vienna to Hungarian Jewish parents. During World War II she had evaded the Nazis by posing as a Catholic maid. After the war Cassab and her husband, Jancsi Kaempfner, learned that their immediate families had died in concentration camps. The couple moved to Sydney with their two sons in 1951, settling in Woollahra. Cassab established herself as a celebrated portrait painter, depicting her subjects in her familiar ersatz expressionist style.

Through her society connections she had heard of Jimmy Bendrodt, and painted him for the Archibald Prize. He was 62, and for his portrait wore an imported grey silk suit, red carnation in the buttonhole, a white silk handkerchief peeped out of his jacket pocket, his hands, as usual, perfectly manicured. A quick impression is that he looks an elegant, slightly world-weary figure, much like an older Fred Astaire, a comparison that would have thrilled him. But Cassab also saw something else – the unflinching and distant stare of a man who had seen much. As one friend noted, 'He looked like a man who had lived, but one you didn't mess with.' Indeed, back in Canada he had been a professional boxer and lumberjack. In his years in Sydney he had dealt with threats from gangsters and angry drunks, and was not afraid to use a gun. Yet his face did not have a single scar from his violent run-ins, even during the era of the razor gangs.

He had been born in British Columbia and, after a rough and tumble youth, the 'dark, lithe and muscular' 19 year old made his way to Sydney as a stoker, arriving in 1910 with just £5. The only skills he had were dancing and rollerskating, and as luck would have it, he ran into Sydney identity Dr John McDonagh, whose interests included boxing and, as a lucrative sideline, he owned several rinks. Bendrodt's trick skating proved popular, but as McDonagh soon realised, the young Canadian had a strong entrepreneurial spirit and he made him manager of his classy rink, the Imperial, in Hyde Park. The Canadian soon bought out McDonagh and reopened it in 1914 as the Imperial Salon De Luxe, where he introduced the latest dance fads to Sydney and patrons could dance to the Imperial Orchestra.

Bendrodt fuelled the dance craze by opening the Palais Royal Dance Hall in 1923 at the Showgrounds in Moore Park. It was large enough for 5500 people, with 3000 able to fit onto the enormous dancefloor. The music was supplied by Billy Romaine leading one of Australia's first jazz bands.

Bendrodt lived in a luxury apartment in Kellett Street, Kings Cross. On the afternoon and evening of 8 August 1929, two rival gangs – one aligned with brothel madam Tilly Devine, the other with sly grogger Kate Leigh – faced each other in Kellett Street, taunting each other, throwing bottles, and yelling obscenities for hours. An exasperated Bendrodt poked his head out of his first-storey window and told them to stop. The gangsters threw bottles and stones, forcing him to retreat. Not easily intimidated, and known for 'bouncing' drunks, he grabbed his revolver, leaned out the window again and fired a warning shot into the air. The shot galvanised the 40 thugs into action, and a vicious, bloody brawl broke out with the gangs using revolvers, bottles, stones, fists and razors to settle their scores.

By 1931 the Depression had hit Bendrodt hard. He was fast running out of cash, and only had enough money to either pay his staff or meet his operating costs. He suggested to his employees that they gamble all their last wages, amounting to £1200, on his horse, Firecracker, even though it was an unknown quantity. When they agreed, he sent a number of his staff to place bets with as many bookmakers as possible. They got good odds and the horse won by a length. The employees were paid and the business survived.

*

Another dream weaver like Bendrodt, Azzalin Romano had arrived in Sydney in 1923 to run the plush Ambassador's Café in Pitt Street. An elegant Italian with slicked-back hair and a pencil moustache, he had been head waiter in the finest hotels and restaurants in Europe. He also spoke French, German, Spanish and

English. Known quite simply as Romano, he brought a European sophistication to Sydney.

The city had seen nothing like the Ambassador's; it was like entering a movie set. The foyer's oriental carpets led to a marble staircase with bronze balustrades, the steps lined with bronze statuettes. Once on the landing, doormen opened the doors into the main dining area and ballroom, where long rows of damask-covered tables could seat 700. The panelled ceiling and walls were covered in specially painted friezes. The polished dancefloor was made of rare Western Australian timber that was slip-free and noiseless, and the music was played by imported American and British jazz bands.

By 1931 the Ambassador's was broke and had to close. Romano opened his eponymous restaurant in York Street, then in 1938 he shifted it a short distance to a large basement in Martin Place. The ambiance was even more striking, with 138 wall mirrors reflecting the glamorous customers, an impressive bust of Napoleon patrons had to pass by as they entered, a staff of 80, an orchestra, and a menu of 370 dishes. The most popular dish was steak diane, said to have been invented by Romano's *maître d'hotel* Tony Clerici at his London restaurant Tony's Grill in 1938 and named in honour of Lady Diana Cooper, the famous society hostess.

Dressed in white tie and tails, Romano greeted customers with the suave manners of an aristocrat. While diners ate and drank, a violinist moved among the tables, playing Hungarian music. It became a rendezvous for the wealthy, the smart set, international film stars like Vivien Leigh and Maurice Chevalier, and important visitors from interstate. It was also a dreamland where the wide-eyed suburbanite, having saved for a special occasion, could spend an evening they would remember for years.

*

Bendrodt opened the Trocadero in 1936 on the western side of George Street, south of Bathurst Street. He had overseen the construction, which cost a huge £150000 but ended up a brilliant example of modernism executed in the art deco style with seating for 2000. The entrance was a floodlit tower of the best Hawkesbury sandstone, the vestibule had marble floors and walls of polished granite. The three sides of the auditorium and dancefloor were covered in scarlet carpet with a pattern of fleurs-de-lis in cream, gold and black. The walls held bas-relief murals depicting famous international dancers, the bandstand was shell-shaped with coloured lights that presented constantly changing scenes.

Dressing up and going dancing became Sydney's favourite pastime. Couples who couldn't afford to go to Romano's or Bendrodt's own upmarket restaurant, Prince's, flocked to the Trocadero, as did royalty, governors, military men, actors and the elite of Sydney society. The Troc held dances, charity functions, debutante balls, receptions, gala parties, radio broadcasts and pageants. On Friday and Saturday nights it was 'dance central'. The debonair trombonist Frank Coughlan was the band leader for most of the Troc's 35 years, with the best jazz and swing musicians in the country. In the early years you could get thrown out for calling it a 'dance hall'; the proper name was *palais de dance*. It represented the Hollywood glamour of Astaire and Rogers, the enchantment of movie-style romance and, during the Great Depression, hope and optimism.

Bendrodt was busy. In the summer of 1937, he transformed the Palais Royal into the extravagant Ice Palais. Even with that a success, he was envious of Romano's restaurant and in 1937 he bet all his money on his filly, Gay Romance, whose win helped him finance Prince's restaurant, also in Martin Place. As he told the press when it opened in 1938, 'It will not be a nightclub or cabaret. It will be a restaurant specialising in the serving of food in superlative surroundings.'

It was just as sumptuous as Romano's, with its own air-conditioning plant creating what was said to be its own weather, a huge bakery, a head chef (Jules Weinberg) imported from Paris, a French head waiter (Monsieur Pierre), a staff of 80 composed of 22 nationalities, and 'fine French cuisine', all contributing to Prince's 'soft lights and sweet music' vibe.

The acoustics were perfect, patrons were able to dance in the early evening and at supper time to two bands, one of them the world famous Weintraub's Syncopators, its six musicians able to play 47 instruments and specialising in Viennese waltzes, French chansons, swing music and Chicago jazz. They had been one of the most sought-after bands in Berlin, even appearing in Sternberg's great film *The Blue Angel* in 1930. During a world tour they landed in Australia in 1937 and wanted to stay. In the beginning they had to fight the chauvinistic and anti-Semitic Australian musicians' union and, eventually, were able to become permanent residents and perform.

The two restaurants became favourites of the social pages and tabloid gossip columns and featured in posh magazines like *The Home*. The two venues were the epitome of chic and sophistication. During World War II they became destinations for American officers and their Australian dates. Bendrodt and Romano were criticised for their lavish entertainment but, as they both argued, the restaurants played a part in helping American morale.

Both the men had a love of horseracing and owned several winners. But their personalities were very different. Romano was married with two children, Bendrodt was married, but had no children. He and his wife, Peggy (his former dancing partner), campaigned for animal rights. Romano was a firm but gentle man, unlike his rival who was a hard taskmaster but one who rewarded initiative, an opportunist more than ready to bend the law, paying off police enforcing liquor laws. Underneath the charming demeanour, 'Jimmy' was a tough nut. He had to be, dealing with razor gangs, weeping drunken women, staff on the take, alcoholic musicians, corrupt police, obnoxious customers and standover merchants.

The men were masters at tapping into what the public wanted and possessed Hemingway's ideal of grace under pressure when disaster beckoned. They were entrepreneurs who kept the machinery of their operations functioning without the customers being aware of the effort and money it took. They created adult fairylands, baubles of illusions. They knew the aphrodisiac power of music, the romance of candles and neon lights, exotic murals, the Hollywood fantasy of tuxedos and gorgeous gowns, the flash of cameras from newspaper and magazine photographers, the reporters looking for tittle-tattle for their gossip columns and the allure of famous names. They knew that cities need a safety valve; so their dance palaces, restaurants and nightclubs promised pleasure and romance, love and sex.

Their nemesis would be rock and roll. The quickstep, the foxtrot, the waltz and the tango became passé. Romano sold his restaurant only to see it became a discotheque with vulgar go-go dancing. The Trocadero closed its doors in 1971 and was demolished to make way for an ugly cinema complex.

Both men are forgotten now, except perhaps in the memories of old men and women who once dined and danced in Sydney's dreamlands.

THE 1930s

THE 1929 WALL STREET STOCK MARKET CRASH and the resulting
Great Depression hit Sydney suddenly and hard. Factories closed
and the unemployment rate rose to just over 30 per cent in
1932. People not only lost their jobs but their homes. Makeshift
camps and shanty towns sprang up across Sydney in suburbs like
La Perouse, Rockdale and Long Bay; Clontarf was the only major
camp on the North Shore. Hundreds of homeless men dossed
down in the Domain, as the Botanic Gardens was locked at
night. On Sundays they had to mingle with the crowds listening
to soapbox orators shouting over hecklers and lecturing about sex,
God or a socialist world government. In the inner city, Surry Hills
and Darlinghurst were crime-ridden dens of prostitution, drugs,
sly grog and vicious gang battles. Eventually vast government
spending on public works, including the Harbour Bridge (begun
in 1923), the city underground rail system and power stations
created employment that was to support many through harsh
times.

Hotels and boarding houses flourished, as did the reign of
dreaded landladies and landlords. Sydney's pubs and boarding
houses were concentrated in the city. In 1933 over half of Sydney's
632 hotels and 6278 boarding houses were in the city municipality,
which included Alexandria, Darlington, Erskineville, Glebe,
Newtown, Paddington, Redfern and Waterloo. The heaviest

concentrations were around Circular Quay, the wharf and warehouse areas on the western side of George Street, and around Haymarket.

Peter Harrison, whose mother ran several rooming houses in Kings Cross in the 1920s and 1930s, recalled that:

> They were seedy and noisome smelly places. There was always
> a fair sprinkling of new Australians in them. Mostly they
> were blokes from an unsettled domestic kind of background
> … tradesmen working in and around the city, painters on
> the Sydney Harbour Bridge, wharfies, blokes on the wharfs
> … I used to shudder at the whole thing. I thought the whole
> operation was just too sordid.

Catherine Edmonds' novel *Caddie, a Sydney Barmaid*, a fictionalised autobiography, provides a vivid portrait of a woman surviving misfortunes and the Depression. Born in 1900 to an alcoholic and abusive father, Edmonds lost her mother in childbirth and her brother at Gallipoli. She escaped her family and poverty only to marry the wrong men and, needing to work, had to temporarily place her two children in a church-run home. She moved from dive to dive, her experiences not unlike Sumner Locke Elliott's description of flat life in his novel *Water Under the Bridge*:

> The stairs smelled of stale fat; the dusty smell of cheap rooming
> houses. There was the conviction of grey clothes soaking in
> basins … Dirty skylight, electric bulb lit under pink-fringed
> shade, room so stuffy windows probably not opened for years
> … smells of stale talcum, wallpaper once gold-flecked faded to
> brown measles, stalagmites of frozen grease drippings around a
> gas ring …

One time when she was living in a cockroach-infested flat in Darlinghurst Edmonds realised that most of the other women in the block had to earn money as prostitutes.

For most of the Depression she was a barmaid. Her description of the 'six o'clock swill' is grimly fascinating as the men drink as much beer as possible between 5 and 6 p.m. in packs of fellow boozers, vomiting where they stand, crowding the bar and shouting out for more schooners as the barmaid cries 'Last drinks!'

There was a stigma attached to the job, with the barmaid often the only female in the main bar. She was morally suspect and Caddie, as she was called (one lover named her after a Cadillac), had to deal with a publican who ordered her to shorten her dress because 'she was an artwork and he liked his artwork on display'. Then there were the sleazy customers who made crude sexual comments and openly asked her for sex. Even a teacher at her children's school offered to pay her to be his mistress.

All through this she was determined to remain morally respectable, but during the Depression tips were few and money was scarce, so she pretended to be out of work to collect the dole while running tabs for the pub's SP bookmaker. Later she ran the pub's SP books herself when the bookmaker moved on to legal bookmaking at the racecourses. Eventually she earned enough money to support her children and move to the country.

Caddie was made into a film in 1976 with Helen Morse as a very attractive and ethereal Caddie, a contrast to the author, who was described as plump, round-faced, with 'narrow grey blue eyes and wavy brown hair'. It's a romantically tinged movie, unlike the book, but does retain the real Caddie's lack of self-pity and is a moving example of the quintessential Aussie battler.

Edmonds could hardly wait to escape the daily grind of her job and life in dismal houses and flats, but for others, like Eileen Kramer, a young dancer who would go on to join the famous

Bodenwieser modern dance company, the inner city was magical. Eileen lived in Phillip Street at a time when it was undergoing change. There were new office buildings, some three storeys high, a couple of cafés, and once elegant houses now operating as boarding houses. She lived in a small white cottage, 'a lodging house at a respectable establishment, which meant there was no bringing a girlfriend home for the night'. There were four rooms for regular tenants and three for casuals. A 20-year-old Rosaleen Norton, who years later would achieve infamy as the Witch of Kings Cross, rented a ground-floor room (Eileen always remembered her upper-class voice). Every morning the residents would wake up to the roar of an old lion at Taronga Park Zoo on the other side of the harbour.

For the author Shirley Hazzard, the fashionable conjunction of Market and Castlereagh streets was raffish and rural at the same time:

> There were windows brilliant with coloured gloves and handbags and silk shoes and shopping arcades lit like rainbows. The women passing along Pitt Street or Castlereagh had cooler faces and wore hats of violets or rosebuds, with little veils. Kegs of ale were nonetheless drawn on drays right past the best shops by pairs or teams of Clydesdales: chestnut necks straining in collars of sweated leather ... manure underfoot, and a bruised smell of dropped cabbage trodden by blinkered ponies harnessed to vegetable carts. Along the curb, barrows of Jaffas and Navels, or Tasmanian apples.

Donald Horne, author of the seminal cultural critique *The Lucky Country: Australia in the Sixties*, was a young boy in the 1930s and was awed by the city's opulent cinemas with their 'copies in marble of famous statues, copies in oil of famous paintings, copies in glass of famous chandeliers, copies in bronze of famous suits of armour, copies in wood of famous styles of furniture, copies in stone of famous orders of architecture'. He remembered the lush red curtains, hundreds of metres of thick carpet, the kaleidoscopic lighting effects, a full orchestra and, mightiest of all, the Wurlitzer organ, which rose onto the stage on a hydraulic lift. For him and his circle of relatives shopping at upmarket stores such as David Jones, Mark Foy's, Farmers and Anthony Hordern's was 'one of the significant ceremonies of Sydney'.

In Brian James' novel *The Advancement of Spencer Button*, the protagonist finds travelling from the beaches of Manly to working-class Redfern 'depressing'. The shops were small and drab with stale food and rotting fruit, the meat in butchers' shops was covered with flies, and dozens of nasty-looking pubs sold alcoholics their early morning slops. To Spencer the area was unbearably hot, noisy and dusty:

> There was the grind and rattle of trams in Castlereagh Street and Redfern Street, the ceaseless clopping of horses' hoofs and jarring accents of lorry wheels ... the very air smelt stale of horses and was filled with flecks of dried manure whenever a breeze stirred along those drab streets. The ground was fouled everywhere with manure and pieces of paper, cardboard boxes, scraps of vegetables, banana skins ... Loutish youths, tough, vocal, conceited and pugnacious, known to the vulgar as 'sparrow-starvers', plied to and fro with yard brooms ... collecting manure and other refuse.

But this Sydney was at odds with what was happening elsewhere. The architectural critic Robin Boyd called the 1930s the 'flat building era'. The blocks of flats of the 1920s and 1930s were walk-up structures, usually of two or three storeys, with between four and 12 self-contained flats in each block. What all these flats had in common was their relative closeness to the city centre and the harbour. In parts of Kirribilli, Neutral Bay, Elizabeth Bay and Manly almost everyone lived in flats or boarding houses. Except in Vaucluse, two-thirds of eastern suburbs residents were tenants. Beyond the city centre the only suburb that had as many flats was Manly. Flats comprised about 40 per cent of all dwellings built between 1933 and 1941; in comparison, Melbourne had less than half of Sydney's numbers.

Flats were most highly visible in Kings Cross, which had the highest population density in Australia. In 1933 some 6000 flats represented a third of the total number of residences, 90 per cent of them tenanted. For one journalist, Kings Cross and Darlinghurst were 'the home of the flat dweller'.

As far as many people were concerned the Cross, as it was nicknamed, was rife with immoral lifestyles, despite a 1933 census showing 70 per cent of residents were married couples with only 2 per cent divorced. Still, it was a world away from the North Shore, which the comic author Lennie Lower, who lived in Woolloomooloo and the Cross, described, citing a representative suburb, Chatswood, as:

> ... one of those places that are a stone's throw from some other place and is mainly given over to the earnestly genteel. Here, respectability stalks abroad adorned with starched linen and surrounded by mortgages. The clatter of lawn mowers can be heard for many miles on any sunny Saturday. Sunday evenings, the stillness of death descends on the place.

As far as the middle class in the staid North Shore suburbs were concerned, Kings Cross was an island of sin. The reality was different: it was a site of modernism, art deco buildings and beauty.

Every night around midnight on the other side of town, a flaneur for God carrying a pocket full of yellow waterproof chalk in his overcoat, walked the city's streets and wrote one word, *Eternity*, in perfect copperplate on Sydney's pavements some 50 times a night. Few saw him at work, but he was known throughout Sydney as Mr Eternity.

Born Arthur Stace in Redfern in 1885, he grew up in poverty and was made a ward of the state by the age of 12. His two sisters were prostitutes and his two brothers died homeless alcoholics. He was a drunkard himself and in 1916, at the age of 26, signed up to fight in France, where he served as a drummer boy and stretcher bearer.

A 'birdlike little man with wispy white hair', he returned home to live a life of thieving, scrounging and drinking. In 1930 he wandered into St Barnabas Church on Broadway and, as he put it, 'I went in to get a cup of tea and a rock cake but I met the Rock of Ages.' He gave up drinking then and there, and two years later found his calling when he heard a Baptist minister give a sermon at the Burton Street Tabernacle in Darlinghurst, which made him want to 'shout eternity through the streets of Sydney'. Stace later recalled that he 'felt a call from the Lord to write eternity'. He had a piece of chalk in his pocket and 'I bent right down there and wrote it.' The word eternity took on a mystical significance for Stace and he thought it was his God-given duty to write it throughout Sydney.

He took to walking the streets and ended up writing the word some half a million times on pavements from Kings Cross to Parramatta. His mission attracted the wrath of Sydney City Council officers, who tried to arrest him for 'defacing pavements' on 24 occasions, but shied away from booking him when he said he had permission 'from a higher source'. He once calculated that when he was 'running hot' it cost him 'six bob a day in chalk'. His one word would last up to six months, and one in Surry Hills, he was pleased to note, lasted a year.

Stace's grand obsession continued for 35 years, and the word eternity stamped itself on Sydney's subconscious. In 1977, ten years after his death, a plaque was unveiled near the waterfall in Sydney's Town Hall Square with *Eternity* rendered in Stace's distinctive copperplate. The pop artist Martin Sharp celebrated Stace and created artworks prominently featuring the word eternity. A filmed opera, *The Eternity Man*, was made in 2008. On New Year's Eve 1999 the word was emblazoned across the Sydney Harbour Bridge and beamed to the world, welcoming the new millennium.

THE COATHANGER

THE AMERICAN GENERAL DOUGLAS MACARTHUR ARRIVED IN SYDNEY on 19 March 1942, the tenth anniversary of the opening of the Sydney Harbour Bridge. He had escaped the Japanese invasion of the Philippines and come to Australia in his role as Supreme Commander of the Allied Forces in the South-West Pacific. His idea was to use Australia as a base to regroup and start planning the defeat of the Japanese. A month before, the Japanese had made their first bombing raid on Darwin, and at the end of May 1942 Japanese midget submarines entered Sydney Harbour.

MacArthur was afraid that the Japanese would invade Australia from the north. His plan was that, if the defensive situation deteriorated dramatically, he would stop the Japanese from an easy harbour crossing from the North Shore by blowing up the Sydney Harbour Bridge. He envisioned it being brought down by spectacular explosions, with demolition charges placed at the northern approach and towards the southern end of the bridge deck.

Army engineer Brian Nicholson was ordered to plan its destruction. He spent a day crawling around the bridge, over the arch, picking spots in which to place the charges. He estimated that six men could plant explosive charges at eight points along the giant arch in less than a day. Charges would be wired to an electronic detonator near Millers Point. The firing of the eight charges would cut free a large section of the arch on the southern half of the bridge. With this section removed, the remaining sections would collapse into the harbour. Nicholson calculated that the bridge, which weighed 52 800 tonnes (in steelwork) – its arch spanning 503 metres and rising 134 metres above sea level – would clog the harbour with debris. So, he next set about experimenting with underwater explosives that could clear the shipping lane.

Of course, the Japanese never invaded Australia and the plan was never put into effect, but if it had, MacArthur had no idea just what a shattering blow it would have been to Australians and, most immediately, Sydneysiders. It would have been a symbol of imminent defeat – the obliteration not only of an engineering marvel that put Sydney on the world stage, but also of a beacon of modernism, optimism and pride.

The bridge had a long gestation. Just two years after the arrival of the First Fleet, William Dawes included a bridge across the harbour in his plan for the settlement, and in 1815 the civil architect, Francis Greenway, wrote to Governor Macquarie proposing a bridge. Even after he had been pushed out of his post by Governor Brisbane, the idea still haunted Greenway's imagination, and in April 1825 he wrote to *The Australian* about his visionary plan:

> Thus in the event of the bridge being thrown from Dawes' battery to the North Shore, a town would be built on that Shore; and would have formed with these buildings, a grand whole, that would indeed have surprised any one on entering the harbour; and had given the idea of strength and magnificence that would have reflected credit and glory on the colony, and the mother country ...

The bridge may have been a pipe dream in the early days of the settlement, but as the population on the North Shore grew, it gradually became obvious that a tunnel or bridge needed to connect the north and south shores. Watermen and later ferries were carrying an increasing number of customers to and from the North Shore and, if the area were to be properly developed, something had to be done. A bridge seemed to come a step closer during the 1880s when Sir Henry Parkes, as MP for the North Shore constituency of St Leonards, campaigned with the slogan: *Now who shall stand on either hand and build the bridge with me?*

In 1900 a competition to design a bridge across Sydney Harbour was announced. One of the great believers in the idea of a bridge, rather than a tunnel as advocated by some, was John Bradfield. Born in Brisbane, he was a brilliant engineering and chemistry scholar at Sydney University. He joined the New South Wales Department of Public Works as a temporary draftsman, becoming permanent in 1895. In 1912 he proposed a suspension bridge to connect Sydney and North Sydney; a little later he designed a cantilever bridge that would stretch across the water from Dawes Point to Milsons Point. By 1922 he was suggesting the government build an arched bridge.

Bradfield had been an eager bodysurfer in his youth, loved the outdoors, and was a keen gardener. For most of his working life he commuted to the city from the family home in the North Shore suburb of Gordon, taking a train to Milsons Point, then a ferry to Circular Quay, a journey that no doubt reminded him every morning and evening of the need for a bridge.

Behind Bradfield's bushy moustache, immaculate conservative suits and balding dome was a man keenly aware of public relations, and he did countless interviews and wrote hundreds of articles about his vision for Sydney: a city-wide underground rail line, electrification of the suburban railways and construction of an additional loop and spur lines to the eastern, western and northern suburbs. His vision was an attempt to write history in 'ineffaceable characters of steel and stone'. The bridge was the lynchpin of the whole scheme, with lanes for vehicles as well as footpaths, rail and tram tracks. The four granite pylons, two at either end, would not be 'meaningless masses of masonry' but would be, he said, something elegant and artistic, 'the showpiece of Sydney'.

In 1923 construction of the bridge started. Most Sydney-siders saw it as a sign of progress and necessary in order to connect the two halves of the city, but it was not without controversy. Some critics queried the colossal expense. There were also concerns about the social cost of the obliteration of old Sydney – the impacts on the North Shore communities of Milsons Point and Kirribilli, and the densely packed working-class area of the Rocks. Over 500 homes were destroyed to create the bridge's northerly approaches. The resumptions continued for several years, affecting both owners and tenants.

Among these many victims were waterside workers, shop-keepers, business owners, real estate agents, tobacconists, butchers, and women running residential and boarding houses. Those without leases were regarded as 'merely tenants' and given scant consideration. Even those not affected by the resumptions and demolitions saw just how devastating the project was to areas like the Rocks. After the bubonic plague of 1900 caused the obliteration of many lanes, streets and houses in the Rocks, these new resumptions were 'a further coffin nail in the once vibrant, living neighbourhood'. Old mansions from the 1840s and 1850s were demolished. As the *Daily Telegraph* reported, 'whole streets were torn up like a battlefield. The Rocks and thoroughfares had a special place in the history of Sydney. It was the cradle of our early settlement.'

Most affected were Cumberland Street – 'mangled beyond recognition' – and Princes Street, which disappeared altogether. So too went the southern side of Argyle Street and the western side of York Street. This sense of a social catastrophe is beautifully memorialised in the photographs of Harold Cazneaux, Herbert Gallop and Henri Mallard, which show old Sydney making way for the new. As the population was forced to move out, the old terraces and treeless thoroughfares seemed resigned to their fate, the streets empty except for a handful of urchins, or a lone cat or dog bereft of owners. Old people especially felt betrayed, witnessing houses being demolished around them as they waited to find new accommodation far away from the homes they had lived in their whole lives. As one old widow wrote in a letter to an indifferent government, articulating the fears of many, 'Fate seems to have singled me out for disaster.' Even Bradfield had to recognise the social impact and in 1928 noted the 'many touches of pathos where owners of properties, grown grey in occupation, heard they must find residences elsewhere. These interviews were the most trying phase of the construction of the bridge.'

A year later a new controversy gained traction in the press over who really designed the bridge, inspired by articles in the *Sydney Morning Herald* by Ralph Freeman, a consulting engineer who conveyed the impression, bolstered by the newspaper, that he was the designer. Freeman and Bradfield could barely stand to be in each other's presence, and photographs of them together reveal uneasy smiles and distant looks. Freeman's attacks had a distinctly personal air. In 1933, the year after the bridge opened, the Director of Public Works stated unequivocally that Bradfield was the designer of the bridge and that 'no other person by any stretch of the imagination can claim that distinction'. Even so, the controversy was to continue for decades with modern historians suggesting that it was designed by the British firm Dorman Long and based on that company's own Tyne Bridge in Newcastle upon Tyne.

Besides the basic design of the bridge, Bradfield demanded four pylons, which, as critics said, were unnecessary and not load-bearing. But Bradfield wanted the public to have confidence that the bridge would not collapse and would find the pylons aesthetically pleasing. Concrete was suggested, but he wouldn't back down from his determination that they had to be made from granite, which he thought 'would humanise the landscape in simplicity, strength and sincerity'. It was strong, durable and attractive, but also expensive, costing an extra $130 million in today's money.

After an extensive search it was discovered that the best granite came from Moruya, 300 kilometres south of Sydney. It appears grey from a distance but up close shows specks of white against dark grey that sparkle in the sun. It was quarried and shipped by sea to Sydney. Granite workers and their families built 'Granitetown' next to the quarry, which even had a school. The site employed up to 250 workers with special stone masons imported from Scotland and Italy. The Italians were mostly single, but the Scots brought their families with them, celebrating their toils on their days off with Highland dances. One 18-year-old Australian apprentice was enthralled by the 'fast and furious' dancing and the 'rippling cadenzas' of the music. 'I have never seen people so fired with enthusiasm on a dancefloor as the Scottish people are.' It was on the rosewood floor of the new quarry hall, he said, that he was 'introduced to social life'.

The finished pylons, built in an art deco style, give a warmth and beauty to the steel arch. For the poet Dorothy Hewett, they were 'as paws crouched on the harbour/ like a huge, dark cat'. To the artist Jessie Traill, the bridge was the epitome of modernism and the power of industrialisation. By 1927 her etchings of its construction had become immensely popular, and the *Daily*

Telegraph acknowledged her unique bond with the structure: 'Miss Traill is an artist after the engineer's own heart, with a special gift for embracing steel and stone with poetry.'

But to her the workshops at Milsons Point, which she was allowed to visit in 1929, truly revealed the magnitude of the undertaking:

> Next to looking at the construction itself ... the wonderful thing is to see the huge workshops at Milsons Point ... One machine cuts through solid steel as if it were matchwood, another planes the sides of sheets to the utmost nicety of hairsbreadth measurements, the shavings of steel coming off hot and smoking in great curls, blue and purple in colour. Another machine bores holes for bolts, and another cuts out great holes, planing them round to a minute exactitude. There are furnaces where the iron is heated and anvils on which it is bent – red hot bolts are thrown from one operator to another, in fact it all seems like a mysterious forge of Vulcan with crowds of pigmies continuously doing his bidding.

The population in the workshop was mostly made up of Scottish, Irish and English workers. During the busiest period of construction in July 1930, the workshops ran 24 hours a day in three shifts with a workforce of about 800 men. The workshops were demolished in 1932 and the site became home to Luna Park and a swimming pool, two places of fun totally at odds with the hardships and enervating heat of the labour-intensive workshops.

Like Traill, many artists – and most Sydneysiders – were enthralled by the bridge and closely followed its seemingly languid construction, unable to look away as the work dominated the business centre of Sydney and the waterway. A photographer like the Reverend Frank Cash, the Rector of Christ Church,

Lavender Bay on the lower North Shore, saw the gigantic project as reflective of the 'hand of God'. He photographed each step of the construction, plus the demolition of the buildings being torn down to make way for it, even as his congregation declined due to so many losing their homes. His dwindling but devoted congregation sat through many a lantern slide presentation of what he was witnessing from his vantage point over the bay. He also had privileged access to the bridge construction site. Cash created an extraordinary legacy of over 10 000 photographs, many published in 1930 as the book *Parables of the Sydney Harbour Bridge*. It contained 534 pages of images and text chronicling every aspect of the bridge's construction.

Henri Mallard's photographs were reminiscent of Lewis Hine's extraordinary images of the construction of the Empire State Building. Mallard climbed hundreds of metres in the air, clinging precariously to cables and standing on small steel plates to document the workers in heroic poses; he wanted to give dignity to the workmen who he believed were often forgotten. The pictorialist photographer Harold Cazneaux relished the curves of the bridge and juxtaposed its mighty scale against the decrepit and vanishing old Sydney. Similarly, Robert Curtis in his photograph *Down Alfred Street, Milsons Point* contrasted the monolithic presence of the bridge with the surviving buildings in Alfred Street, which almost tremble next to this massive symbol of technological supremacy.

For painters, the bridge represented a new era, the twentieth century's rejection of the dun-coloured realism of much Australian painting and a bold reimagining of how to view cities as centres of modernism. Two women artists were especially attracted to this mighty structure, Grace Cossington Smith and Dorrit Black. Smith savoured the curves of the bridge and how it reflected the undulating nature of Sydney itself, and how its two feminine arches were designed to meet and meld into one giant arch, all this she rendered in striking fauvist-like planes of colour. Black's *The Bridge, 1930* has been called 'the finest of all Australian cubist paintings' by the art critic Daniel Thomas. She was strongly influenced by the modernist and cubist art movements she had been exposed to on a visit to Europe. *The Bridge, 1930* is a portrait of industrial dynamism, with an almost spiritual aura reflected in its colours of pale greens, blues, greys and 'shimmering peacock'. The bridge, yet to meet in the middle, is like two mechanical animals leaping towards one another. It's a monument to modern engineering, with the five-mast clipper anchored beneath it a memory of another, older Sydney. A year after painting this masterpiece, Black founded the Modern Art Centre in Margaret Street, the first gallery to devote itself to modernism, and one of the first galleries in Australia to be established by a woman. Soon it would inspire a generation of Australian modernist painters, including Roland Wakelin and Grace Crowley.

Like most people, Black waited and watched in awe as the arches slowly inched their way across the sky, a crane on either apex. Public anticipation grew as the arches incrementally moved closer to consummation. Finally, the gap was reduced over a period of ten days until the extremities of the two arches finally connected on a central bearing pin near midnight on 19 August 1930, 'as perfectly as truth itself', a glorious example of precision engineering. After five years relieved Sydneysiders could see that the bridge was becoming a reality. Once the arches were joined, work then began on hanging the deck, which was erected from the centre outwards.

The construction came at a cost. There were 16 deaths. Some workers were crushed by cranes or granite blocks or drowned. In October 1930 Roy Kelly slipped off the bridge in wet weather and fell 52 metres into the water below.

I am often working near the edge of the bridge, and on many occasions, I have thought to myself, 'Now, if you ever fall Roy, you had better make sure that you hit the water feet first or headfirst.' So when I slipped and fell today, I concentrated on saving my life. That is all I thought about. It was the only thing in my mind; the desire to live. I knew that I was very near death. I hit the water. I went under. There was a roar of water in my ears. My lungs felt as if they would burst. Then I came to the surface. I was alive, marvellously alive.

Ferry passengers and other bridge workers who witnessed the fall saw his 'body hurtling downward with terrifying speed', and when his body hit the water 'a fountain of spray' rose some six metres.

When it was completed, the bridge had a width of 159 feet (48.5 metres) to allow for six lanes of road traffic, four railway lines and two footways. Initially the two eastern railway tracks were used for trams. Yet from a distance the bridge doesn't look ponderous at all; it seems as if it is floating above the water, the girders and arch a delicate metal filigree.

It was set to be officially opened on 19 March 1932. The official commemorative 'Bridge Scroll' includes a central panel outlining the history of New South Wales from Cook in 1770 to 1932, as well as a short history of the Sydney Harbour Bridge. Flanked on either side are signatures of the governors, government officials, politicians, bridge contractors and organising committees. The top shows a coloured panoramic view of the bridge from the Heads and in the clear sky is a biplane. To the left above the New South Wales coat of arms are ghostly images of 13 Aboriginal people. The tone of the scroll is exultant:

Since the days of Captain Cook Sydney has progressed phenomenally and, as the preceding century has passed into

a limbo of the forgotten, modern devices and science have
brought this great City on a line of parity with the greatest
cities of the world, and in this year, 1932, it is our proud boast
that we now possess the greatest bridge in the world.

If the bridge was an advertisement for modernism, the supremacy
of technology and Sydney's arrival on the world stage, the opening
also became the fulcrum of seething political forces that were in
danger of tearing the city, even the country, apart.

Around 750 000 people came to witness Premier Jack Lang
cut the ribbon to open the bridge. A special pair of gold scissors
was on hand to do the job. Lang had been a great supporter of the
bridge and said of Bradfield, 'He wanted to be the Napoleon III
of Sydney. He wanted to pull down everything in the way of his
grandiose schemes. He was always thinking of the future.'

The Depression had polarised politics. Lang's Labor Party
first won government in 1925 and had held the reins of power
for seven years, but Lang was barely able to suppress the growing
struggle between communists and fascists. He assumed that on
such an important day as the long-awaited opening of the bridge,
none of these political conflicts would matter. But in the crowd,
sitting on a horse borrowed the day before from a teenage girl on
the North Shore, and wearing his old army uniform, was Eadith
Walker's old friend, furniture maker Francis de Groot.

An ex-cavalry officer, he was attracted to the right-wing
politics of the paramilitary organisation the New Guard, a
diluted version of Mussolini's Black Shirts. The New Guard had
been formed by Colonel Eric Campbell and other officers who
strongly opposed Lang's socialist Labor government. A virulent
anti-communist, Campbell had been fined £2 for calling Lang 'a
nasty tyrant, a scoundrel, a buffoon and a hated old man of the
sea'. De Groot and the New Guard were angry that the NSW

governor, Sir Philip Game, the representative of the king, had not been invited to open the bridge. De Groot's plan was to upstage Lang.

Eadith was seated in a special section of the VIP stand roped off from the crowd of 300 000. A fiercely patriotic woman described as 'a Britisher to the Backbone' with anti-left-wing views, she had nevertheless during the lead-up to the celebrations invited the left-wing Premier Jack Lang and his family to stay at her Yaralla estate. A socialist and critic of Britain, Lang seems an unusual guest. But for Eadith, as for so many proud Australians, the bridge represented an achievement that transcended anyone's political affiliations.

Now she watched as the premier, clutching the large gold scissors, prepared to cut the ribbon and formally open the bridge. Then the familiar figure of her 44-year-old friend de Groot, riding a horse more suitable to the glue factory than the Light Horsemen, jogged towards the premier.

What Eadith thought of what happened next is impossible to guess. She had tried to avoid controversy all her life and now she was caught between two men of diametrically opposed political beliefs, one staying under her own roof, the other a friend who designed the very furniture the premier had been sitting on in her home.

When the premier approached to cut the ribbon, de Groot urged his horse forward, and with a downward motion of his sword tried to cut the ribbon, but it was not taut enough, so he tried again with an upward motion of his sword and successfully sliced the ribbon, shouting to the bemused crowd, 'I declare this bridge open in the name of the decent citizens of New South Wales.'

Amid chaotic scenes de Groot was arrested. The two halves of the ribbon were quickly reattached, and a fuming Lang cut the ribbon. De Groot was sent to a Darlinghurst mental facility to be assessed but was soon released, his gesture regarded as comical more than political, though the image of him on his horse with sword held high eclipsed any memory of the premier cutting the ribbon. After the dismissal of the Lang government by Sir Philip Game in May 1932, the New Guard faded into obscurity.

During the first 24 hours it was open, over a million people crossed the bridge in trains, trams, vehicles and on foot. On the same day, Sydney newspapers were full of advertisements for land on the North Shore. The car ferries immediately went out of business. The impact of the bridge was profound. It shifted commercial activity up the new highway to Crows Nest and devastated those businesses that had survived along lower Alfred Street. It emptied the harbour of much of the hectic ferry trade and made most boatyards redundant. It turned North Sydney from a transport hub where ferries, trams and trains met at the waterfront, into a corridor to be passed through on the way to somewhere else as the suburbs rapidly expanded northwards.

But the bridge also kick-started Sydney's push to modernise. Even now it is still considered a feat of world-class engineering, one that signalled Australia's maturity as a nation. As historian Peter Spearritt puts it:

> During the thirties the bridge became a symbol for the city,
> linking its two halves. It was a prosperous symbol, planned
> in better times. In the middle of the Depression, it was a sign
> that a return to suburban prosperity was possible.

Of course, on the night of the bridge's opening there were fireworks, a tradition that has flourished over the last few decades on the last night of the year, when the fireworks on the bridge try to outdo the spectacular brilliance of the previous year with a display seen all over the world.

Five months after the 'Eternity' sign lit up the bridge on the last night of 1999, the iconic status of the bridge made it an obvious location for a public act of support for reconciliation. About 250 000 people, Indigenous and non-Indigenous, starting at the northern end and walking south towards Darling Harbour, made their way across the bridge in a continuous stream that lasted nearly six hours. People marched carrying banners, flowers, pushing prams and wheelchairs, and wearing badges and stickers. Despite the chill wind there was an exhilarating sense of optimism. The Australian and Aboriginal flags flew side by side at the top of the bridge's arch. When a skywriter wrote the word 'Sorry' in the sky above the harbour, the marchers cheered. It was the largest political demonstration ever held in Australia.

The bridge has become part of Sydney's psyche, and when people think of Sydney, the image that comes immediately to mind is the Sydney Harbour Bridge.

THE WAR COMES TO SYDNEY

ONE OF THE FIRST SIGNS OF THE APPROACHING WORLD WAR
was the refugees. Nazi persecution forced 8000 Jewish refugees to
Australia before the war, with 5000 of them settling in Sydney.
Many of them gravitated to Kings Cross, a locale frequently
described as 'cosmopolitan' by the rest of the Anglo-centric
country. People of diverse races and ethnic groups, especially
Italians, Greeks and Jews, had settled into Kings Cross and East
Sydney. The Jews were attracted to the Cross for several reasons: it
was a short distance from the docks, they were used to apartment
living, the rents were cheap and, like many migrants, they sought
out their own kind, finding solace among those with the same
language and culture. Many of the new arrivals were sponsored
by the Jewish Welfare Organisation, which had an office in the
Cross.

Despite the fact that Jews were being persecuted in Europe,
Australians were generally not welcoming. In 1938 Thomas
White, Minister for Trade and Customs, was appalled by the
prospect of large-scale Jewish immigration, saying, 'As we have no
real racial problem, we are not desirous of importing one.' Around
the same time the Immigration Department analysed the 'quality'
of Jews, and came to the conclusion that Berlin Jews were good,
the Viennese had bad characters, Budapest Jews were even worse,
Polish Jews were thieves and Romanian Jews were gangsters.

They stood out in their appearance for a start: 'They wore long overcoats, heavy material and padded shoulders. Their hats were different and they always carried a briefcase with them and the men had money purses.' The women, on the other hand, were thought to be shorter than Australians and plumper, with some female residents of Kings Cross finding the Jewish women had 'a kind of excessive femininity about them'. The refugees, according to one government report, were 'arrogant and they treated locals as inferior beings, the Russian Jews were said to be particularly haughty and glib'.

In a panic once war broke out in September 1939, the government interned German Jews, despite them being anti-Nazi, as well as Italians and any Japanese they could find.

They also interned Australians such as Percy 'Inky' Stephensen, and the Englishwoman Adela Pankhurst, of the famous suffragette family.

Stephensen was raised on a farm in Queensland where he learned to ride and shoot. He attended Oxford as a Rhodes scholar, and established a publishing house in England where he promoted the novels of his friend DH Lawrence, and edited the first uncensored edition of *Lady Chatterley's Lover*. Back in Australia, in 1932 he started the Endeavour Press in Sydney with Norman Lindsay, publishing such writers as Banjo Paterson and Miles Franklin, before going out on his own and publishing Eleanor Dark, Henry Handel Richardson and Xavier Herbert's *Capricornia*.

In 1936 he wrote his most famous work, *The Foundations of Culture in Australia*, which laid the groundwork for the Jindyworobak poetry movement of the 1930s and 1940s. This was a strongly nationalistic, anti-British literary movement of white writers who believed that the only way to create a unique Australian culture was through the assimilation of Aboriginal subjects, language and Dreamtime stories. He also fell in love with his adopted city and later wrote what was considered a definitive *History and Description of Sydney Harbour.*

Always strongly political, Stephensen was a communist until he became disillusioned by the Moscow show trials of 1936 to 1938, which convinced him that communism was not the answer. With a suddenness that amazed his friends, he swung from the far left to the far right. He saw America as a malign influence on Australia, with its comics promoting 'demonology, witchcraft and voodooism [that had] a raving mad view of the world'. He was virulently anti-Semitic, pro-fascist, a defender of Japan, pro-monarchist and anti-communist.

One curious and unusual aspect of his politics was his unpopular pro-Aboriginal stance. As far as he was concerned, they were the original Caucasians and therefore Aryan people, which meant white Australians had to be in solidarity with them. He helped finance the newspaper *Abo Call*, which was written and edited by Aboriginal activist Jack Patten. In 1938 he helped organise the Day of Mourning and Protest to mark the sesquicentenary of the founding of Australia, a protest that may have been overlooked in the euphoria of celebrations at the time, but which has now taken on a huge symbolic significance.

Stephensen co-founded the magazine *The Publicist*, which propagated his extreme views, but not content with this he founded the Australia First Movement two months before the Japanese bombing of Pearl Harbor. Like Pankhurst, 'Inky' as he was known, advocated peace with Japan. Military intelligence originally failed to have his party banned for its pro-Japanese views but concocted a supposed plot that resulted in Stephensen's arrest in March 1942. He and 15 other members of his Australia First Movement were arrested on trumped up charges of suspicion of collaboration with the Japanese and of planning sabotage and assassinations.

He was held without trial and vicariously shifted around the many internment camps across the country for the rest of the war. The official war historian Paul Hasluck wrote that the detentions were the 'grossest infringement of individual liberty made during the war'. Stephensen went on to ghostwrite 70 books for Frank Clune, many of them about Sydney's past.

Stephensen's anti-American and pro-Japanese views could not have been more at odds with the general public, which had reason to fear the Japanese as the chance of an enemy attack on Sydney, or even an invasion, became a real possibility. Wealthy Sydney parents sent their children to boarding schools in the Blue Mountains or Southern Highlands. Those children remaining practised for air raids. Suburbs darkened with blackouts at night.

Anne Walsh, 87, remembered how, as a seven year old at that time, 'All I knew was something terrible was happening out there, because everyone seemed so tense and worried.' Her father, a warden, donned a helmet every night to check their Darlinghurst street was blacked out. There were food scarcities. Children were issued with a kit containing a piece of wood to 'place between your teeth when the bombs fell so we didn't break our teeth'. For Maev O'Meara, then a student at the Convent of the Sacred Heart Rose Bay (later Kincoppal), her vivid memory was of large dark panels and heavy drapes placed across the boarding school windows at night. There was also the sudden and startling presence of soldiers, sailors and airmen on the streets, wearing khaki uniforms with slouch hats, naval uniforms, and the dark blue outfits of the RAAF. Shop windows were taped up in readiness for an air raid and the banks in Martin Place were fortified with sandbags.

After the Japanese carried out an aerial reconnaissance of Sydney Harbour, three midget Japanese submarines entered through the Heads on the night of 31 May 1942 with the aim of laying waste to American and Australian warships. In the event only one vessel was sunk – the requisitioned harbour ferry *Kuttabul* – killing 21.

Soon it seemed as if the whole world had come to Sydney: Americans, British, French, Dutch, sailors, soldiers and airmen. Kings Cross was the favourite destination for American troops for their five- to ten-day furloughs. At the height of the war it seemed to locals that there were six Americans to every Australian soldier.

The Trocadero became a haven for American servicemen, and famous musicians like Artie Shaw and his American Navy Band played there. Fights often broke out between the Americans and jealous Australian men, and as soon as they did, the Troc orchestra would strike up 'Stars and Stripes Forever' until the cops arrived. Taxis and tables in restaurants were scarce unless the woman had an American escort. It was no wonder Australian men were jealous. Most of the fights between them and the 'Septic Tanks' were over women.

But for many women it was wonderful. Nancy Keesing, in a poem about a tired mother with children, 'Reverie of a Mum', has her remember a romantic night with an American serviceman in the Domain, the air full of the scent of frangipani, whispers and giggling; and how one soldier climbed up the light pole and removed the bulb, so the urgent lovemaking could continue unseen.

The phenomenon of American servicemen fraternising with Australian women attracted novelists such as Dymphna Cusack and Florence James, who co-wrote *Come in Spinner*. Their novel offers a vivid picture of the impact of American forces on the city as it traces the fortunes of a group of young women who work in a beauty salon. One woman's younger sister succumbs to toiling in a brothel and there is a scene where the mistress of an American soldier dies as the result of an abortion, dramatising the fear of Americans morally contaminating Australians. But the novel doesn't whitewash Australian men, who complained bitterly about the success of the Americans with their women. The character Guinea expresses the common thought that Australian men who whinged about the success of the Yanks with their women were hypocrites: 'You'd think they were a lot of monks themselves.'

Taxi sharing was mandatory, and it was a rare luxury to ride alone. Everyone had amusing stories about exasperating fellow passengers, riding with men who made passes at anyone in a skirt, drunks, mad old ladies, vulgar soldiers. Cars with muffled headlights and filtered streetlamps overhead gave out weak eerie light. For Sydneysiders it was the colourlessness of everything that loomed large – brown lights, khaki, yellowish newspapers, books printed on cheap paper that turned brown. The dreariness of brown was everywhere. The beautiful neon lights were off, and the clock tower of the General Post Office was taken down and stored away. The windows of the upmarket stores were unlit and had wire where there had been plate glass. The double-decker buses were drab with camouflage, and camouflaged army vehicles were everywhere.

In one of his autobiographical novels, *Fairyland*, about his time during the war, Sumner Locke Elliott writes of how 'the prossies were out in force ... the queers were lolling in doorways, their desperate eyes flicking like snakes' tongues'. He conjures up a scene in a pub of the time:

> Geraldine, sipping her shandy, felt that after all the war was not
> exclusively drab, only that up to now she'd been excluded from
> this congenial side of it, the what-the-hell evening celebration
> of the monstrous event that touched them all one way or
> another, the Yanks, and the WACs, Aussies and AWASs, all
> getting a bit tiddly, the smoky back ladies-only-with-escorts
> room, the noise, the chatter and coarse laughter, the open

kissing, the going to and from the 'loo' because of the many
beers having to be consumed before six o'clock closing, the
calling out to the barmaids to 'stack 'em up, love, give us two
more rounds ...

The activity at Garden Island, where the huge graving dock was
being constructed, was a spectacular event in the city where most
other building work had come to a halt. A labour force of 3500
men reclaimed 12 hectares from the harbour to join the island to
the mainland. 'All day and throughout the night in the blaze of
myriad lights which contrasted strikingly with the blacked-out
city, thousands and thousands laboured in the scene of almost
bewildering activity.'

For five years the whole world seemed to pour into Sydney.
Through the Heads came Americans, British, French – soldiers,
sailors and airmen of many nations, but once the war had ended,
they left, as did the excitement and melodrama of love affairs,
wild times, and the imminent threat of death on the battlefield.

THE 1950s

IN 1950 THE AMERICAN NOVELIST JAMES A MICHENER visited Sydney. He had just won the Pulitzer Prize for his collection of stories about World War II, *Tales of the South Pacific* (soon to become the hit musical *South Pacific*). As his plane landed, darkness fell and he was thrilled by the sight of the 'explosion of one million lights of Sydney ... On hillsides, down many bays, is the brilliance of Australia's metropolis, home of nearly two million people. Few approaches to the nations of the world can be so spectacular, so portentous.'

He thought that Sydney was like London, only prettier. The Harbour Bridge was a national symbol like the Statue of Liberty or the Eiffel Tower. But housing, rent, food, eating out, hotel accommodation and transport were much more expensive than other Australian cities.

His glib take on Sydney was deceptive. The city was stagnating, few new blocks of flats were built compared to the manic 1920s and 1930s. Neon lighting banned during the war was not as brilliant as before. Few new restaurants opened. The City of Sydney promised that new venues 'would help restore the pre-war nightlife of Kings Cross. The neon lights of Kings Cross are rapidly being turned on again.' When 3000 American sailors from Admiral Halsey's 'Goodwill Fleet' arrived in 1954, they had all heard of the famous Cross, but those who had experienced it during the war remarked that it was much quieter now.

Rationing was slowly coming to an end, as was the housing crisis. After the war desperate families squatted in derelict houses and empty apartments. In March 1946 ten squatters took possession of the vacant mansion 'Maramanah' in Potts Point. Most of them were returned servicemen who were homeless. As a spokesman for them put it, 'We have done everything to find a home, but it is hopeless ... it is disgraceful that the council should tear down a beautiful old building like this when thousands are homeless in Sydney alone. We can sleep here. We cannot sleep in the parks.'

This action captured the imagination of Sydneysiders, who were all too aware of the housing shortage. Though there were others who thought it was a communist plot and pointed to the fact that the Communist Party held meetings and weekly dances at Maramanah. Even so, the authorities realised that the squatters had the public on their side and did nothing to evict them.

Two photographers captured these torpid, fraught years. In 1946 Max Dupain was taking photographs of queues after the war, 'queues for buses, vegetables, fruit, when I just happened to come across this butcher shop in Pitt Street'. He photographed five women, dressed in black and wearing black hats as if going to a funeral. In reality they were waiting in line to buy what little meat was available. They were grim, anxious, resigned. As Dupain said, 'Not looking too happy about the world.'

Not much had changed in the slums when David Moore, another brilliant photographer, shot *Redfern Interior, 1949*. It's a devastating image of poverty and hopelessness. In a small dingy bedroom, a pensive and haggard grandmother is beset by anxiety and obvious money worries, her gaunt daughter is in bed with a newborn, and a grubby child sits on the floor gazing up at its granny as if seeking an answer to all of this.

Finally in 1954 Greenway opened at Milsons Point. It was the largest public housing complex in Australia. It says something about the times that materials and labour were in such short supply after the war that its construction took six years. Despite its spectacular views of the harbour, the windows were small so as to reduce the cost. It housed 309 one- and two-bedroom flats and consisted of four structures, the two taller 11-storey buildings had steel frames and the smaller two were concrete framed. It soared 40 metres, just under the height restrictions of 45 metres.

It was designed in the modern functionalist style that rejected unnecessary decoration and had obvious similarities to the postwar apartment blocks in New York's Bedford-Stuyvesant area. The ugliness of Greenway, named after Macquarie's architect Francis Greenway, seemed an affront to the man who had designed Sydney's elegant Georgian buildings. But the first tenants were delighted.

When Mrs VWH Briggs moved into her flat, she declared to the *Sunday Herald*, 'If I won the lottery seven times over I wouldn't leave here. This will do me!' What excited the occupants were the modern appliances – electric stoves instead of gas, stainless steel sinks, and built-in cupboards. The Greenway consumed so much electricity that the local council had to install a special substation beneath the complex to provide power to the many washers, stoves, lights, dryers and lifts.

Sydney gradually left behind the austerity of the postwar years. Six o'clock closing was repealed in 1954, and in 1957 Sydney's first shopping mall opened in suburban Ryde. Height restrictions were lifted in the same year and skyscrapers began to rise up from the CBD. Even so, Sydney remained stubbornly conservative. Most shops closed on Saturday afternoon and on Sundays theatres and pubs were closed and sporting events banned, giving Sydney the appearance of a ghost town one day of the week.

One of the biggest changes to Sydney's demographics was the arrival of increasing numbers of migrants and refugees from Europe. For older white Australians this was disturbing. One character in Hugh Atkinson's novel *Low Company* complains, 'Bloody Australia's becoming a nation of Nuts and Balts.' Still, change was unavoidable, and Atkinson describes how:

> A trickle from the Baltic countries ... had swelled later to proportions of a flood and greatly altered the Sydney scene. Cafés which, from the earliest days, have served steak, eggs and tea, delivered by a slattern in slippers and her thumb on the plate, now advertised raviolis, pizzas, goulash and squid. Soft-eyed Italians waited on the tables, and delicatessens crammed their windows with spectacular patés and cheeses. A suddenly sophisticated citizenry dawdled over small cups in arty espresso bars and on the streets the young went about in crepe-soled suede shoes and oily, duck tailed haircuts.

One book about migrants that became immensely popular was *They're a Weird Mob*, published in 1957. Written by John O'Grady using the pseudonym of Giovanni 'Nino' Culotta, the novel is a satire about an Italian journalist who arrives in Sydney to write articles about Australians and their way of life. Nino takes a job as a labourer. Because he has learned 'proper' English he is puzzled by the Australian vernacular spoken by the working class. The world Nino inhabits is the strongly male one of the period, but he does get to know a Kay, whom he spots in a Manly café. And in a rom-com meet-cute, he helps to teach her not to eat spaghetti with a spoon. They eventually marry. Although it's a comic novel, its clear message is that immigrants should realise their good fortune to live in a lucky country and should endeavour to assimilate as soon as possible. Read now, the novel reveals a socially insular, masculine culture, cocksure of its superiority, with its cavalier ethnic slurs (dagoes and wogs), and puritan morality.

The enforcers of the morality of the time, the police, were convinced that 'male sex perversion' had increased in alarming numbers since the end of the war. In 1952 the chief of the Vice Squad, Inspector SC Crothers, stated in court that men who 'contaminated youths' were becoming a serious menace and that perversion offences were very prevalent 'among certain foreign elements'.

The police didn't have a spotless record regarding homosexuality. A decade before there had been a sensational case. Clarence McNulty, editor-in-chief of the *Daily Telegraph*, had been arrested in a public toilet by a Constable Carney on a charge of wilful and obscene exposure. Instead of pleading guilty and avoiding public shame, McNulty protested that he was innocent.

The court case revealed that Carney and his partner Grigg, working as a two-man team visiting public toilets, had arrested 200 men on the same charge in one year. The men, whether guilty or not, had paid off the two blackmailing cops to avoid going to court. The case against McNulty was dismissed.

For the police and the government, homosexuals, and men who dressed as women, were corrupters of youth, and they took every opportunity to arrest the 'perverts'. Drag was not new in Sydney. After World War I there were men who liked to dress as women who paraded around College Street, risking arrest because it was illegal to dress as a woman under the *Offensive Behaviour Act*. To avoid the law, gays gave private performances in flats. There was a curious caveat to wearing drag: if a real woman were present at a drag party, then the men weren't doing anything illegal. But even this law did not stop the police from raiding the parties.

It seemed to the police that it was impossible to stem the tide of vice. One only had to look to the United States, where pornography and striptease clubs were prospering, to realise that Australia would soon follow suit. Their fear was realised by the gangster Abe Saffron who, at the end of the 1950s, launched the first legal strip club in Kings Cross. The Staccato was an immediate hit and stayed open due to bribes paid to politicians and high-ranking police. It was just the beginning for Saffron, who opened several more clubs and would become known as 'Mr Sin'.

THE PUSH

IF ANYTHING DEMARCATED THE INTELLECTUAL TRADITIONS of
Melbourne and Sydney, it was the Push. According to the historian
Manning Clark, from the late nineteenth century Melbourne
radicals gravitated towards Karl Marx while Sydney's radicals
tended towards Friedrich Nietzsche. One embraced collectivism
and the all-powerful state, the other was suspicious of the state
and championed individual liberty.

Although these differences remained a somewhat esoteric
affair, a loose confederation of men and women in Sydney ended
up embodying the stark intellectual and cultural division between
the two cities.

The Push was a name derived from the larrikin gangs of inner
Sydney during the late nineteenth century – the Plunkett Street
Push, the Straw Hat Push, the Glebe Push and the Waterloo Push.
The difference was that the members of the Push of the 1940s and
1950s were middle class and their philosophy had originated from
one person, John Anderson. Anderson was to dominate Sydney's
intellectual life for over three decades from 1927 to 1958 when
he was Challis Professor of Philosophy at Sydney University.
According to many, he was the most important philosopher who
had taught in Australia, let alone Sydney.

Born in Scotland, he arrived in Sydney in 1927. After a
torrid flirtation with communism, he developed his own unique

philosophy. His libertarian ideas emphasised joy, playfulness and beauty to be enjoyed by the intellectual and artistic elite. He hated the 'servile state' and rejected the very idea of society itself. Christian concepts of good and evil were only meant for slaves. In *Corrupting the Youth: A history of philosophy in Australia*, James Franklin sums up Anderson's belief that:

> ... the world was going downhill fast. It was the age of socialism, religion, communism, rationalism ... in Australia the Labor and Liberal parties were both committed to destroying freedom and independence. The churches, the universities and media were servile to the ruling interests.

He was such a charismatic presence at university, and his ideas so attractive, that even a confident student like Donald Horne, soon to be an author and newspaper editor, was in awe of him. When he saw him walk by, 'My skin might stiffen and my hair prickle at the roots ... I was gripped by the need to know him.'

Anderson's philosophy was the crux of debates in the Libertarian Society, which published the *Sydney Libertarian Broadsheet*. It proved to be extraordinarily influential and gave rise to the Push. This was a loose and ever-evolving group of men and women who were atheists, enemies of the repressive institutions, especially the political state, and who ridiculed the notion of social engineering the perfect human as hopelessly naïve. Social and political engagement was useless. They exalted anti-authoritarianism, extolled sexual liberation and freedom from the constrictions of society, especially those of the 1950s, with its conservative and suffocating morality, wowserism, suburban drabness and cultural philistinism. To one member, 'The Push was an island of excitement in a sea of dullness.'

The group argued and debated in the Lincoln Coffee Lounge,

and in their favourite watering holes – the Royal George in Sussex Street, the Newcastle on the corner of Essex and George streets, the Tudor in Phillip Street, and the Assembly on the corner of Phillip and Hunter. In the 1960s the Newcastle was unusual for allowing women to drink in the public bar, rather than exiling them to the Ladies Lounge. When Barry Humphries first stepped into the gregarious, loud and opinionated Royal George crowd, 'I stood in that packed throng of artists' models, academics, alkies, radio actors, gays and ratbags, drinking large quantities of cold beer, and I felt as though my True Personality was coming into focus.'

These hotels were a focus of the Sydney Push during the 1950s and 1960s. Ironically Anderson would have nothing to do with its bibulous pub culture. But what an extraordinary collection of individual talents they were: Robert Hughes, who would become a significant author and art critic (a mural of his adorned a wall of the Newcastle for a time); Germaine Greer; the poet and gambler Harry Hooton; the philosopher George Molnar (not to be confused with the *Sydney Morning Herald* cartoonist of the same name); film director Michael Thornhill (*The FJ Holden*) and his writer friend Frank Moorhouse; Richard Neville and Richard Walsh, who went on to publish the controversial and sometimes banned magazine, *Oz*; Margaret Fink, film producer (*My Brilliant Career* and *For Love Alone*) and lover of Hooton and Humphries; Clive James, author and critic; and the acerbic wit and poet Lex Banning.

Banning had been born with cerebral palsy, which left him with involuntary movements and uncoordinated arms and face. He 'grimaced and spat as he spoke … Frequently he was taken to be drunk.' Despite these handicaps he graduated with honours from Sydney University in 1948 and gravitated towards the Push. He had to lift and drink the beer using his elbow, resting on the table as a fulcrum. Once he was drinking conversation flowed and the group soon learned to understand him.

His poetry ranged from the formal to the lightly colloquial; it has a darkness, a deep love of women, and an especial love of Sydney.

Geoffrey Lehmann, a fellow poet who drank with Banning, remembered first meeting him: 'The impression I had of Lex as a personality ... is that somehow, he symbolised for me the Sydney line in poetry ... it seems to be a rather hedonistic type of line. You enjoy life; you have intense experiences. You find the same sort of thing in Slessor.' In 1965 a sick Banning returned home to die in his mother's house at the age of 44.

A major preoccupation of the Push was sex. Clive James was enchanted by it: 'Endorsing the critique of sexual guilt as a repressive social mechanism, the Libertarians freely helped themselves to each other's lovers.' Later feminists thought the Push sexist and some female members of the group retrospectively thought that this sexual liberation was of dubious benefit to them.

One woman who was transformed by this sexual freedom and anarchist philosophy was Germaine Greer. She came up to Sydney from her home town of Melbourne where she had been having a miserable time mixing with the socialists. One member of the Push said to her, 'You're a Sydney person, Germaine. You're simply in the wrong place. Come to Sydney.' Greer recalled that one of the things that impressed her were the rigorous arguments. 'I was already an anarchist; I just didn't know why I was an anarchist.'

It was said that one of the reasons she stayed was her infatuation with Roelof Smilde, a professional gambler and a leader of the Push. His intellectual and personal journey was a strange one. A Dutch migrant, he became school captain at the prestigious North Sydney Boys High School and won a place at Sydney

University. The siren call of the Push made him drop out of university, and he spent his time drinking, debating, gambling, playing bridge and poker, and promoting libertarian philosophy.

In *Sex and Anarchy*, her history of the Push, Anne Coombs sees a thread of its ideas and philosophy in Greer's most famous work:

> The Libertarian legacy shines through *The Female Eunuch* – revolutionary, but not Utopian, smashing icons but not erecting new ones, self-reliant without being self-blaming, attacking the conventional family while not opposing motherhood or sexuality or men.

Doctrinaire Melbourne feminists never forgave her. As Greer wrote, 'I had that ad hoc training that used to be meted out to me in the beer-stained purlieus of the Royal George.'

The church hated the Push's free sexuality and their fight against all censorship. The state saw them as a threat. Intrigued and not a little alarmed, an ASIO report summed them up as 'anarchists who wouldn't hesitate to drop a bomb on the Sydney Harbour Bridge or derail a train'. Others saw them as a drunken gang of verbose middle-class poseurs. Barry Humphries later wrote scathingly of the group as:

> … a fraternity of middle-class desperates, journalists, drop-out academics, gamblers, poets *manqué*, school teachers and art students, who each night after their working hours exchanged their irksome respectability for a little liberating profanity, drunkenness and sex.

But as Mervyn Bendle wrote recently, 'The Push provided vital ideological and psychological foundations for the resolute individualism that came to characterise the culture of Sydney.' It was such a refreshing change from the collectivism, the idealisation of the state and Marxist social engineering of the grim ideologues down south. It was no wonder that, by comparison with the Push, Melbourne began to acquire the nickname of 'Bleak City'.

FLAT LIFE

SUMNER LOCKE ELLIOTT LEFT SYDNEY IN 1948 to live in the United States, where he worked as an actor and television writer. In the early 1960s he turned to strongly autobiographical novels, writing about Sydney between the 1920s and the 1940s saying, 'I still see the Sydney of 1937 in my mind's eye ... a Sydney locked like a fly in amber.' What he missed the most were 'the trams in George Street'. When he briefly returned to Sydney in the 1970s, he was appalled to see that they had been replaced by buses polluting the air with petrol and diesel fumes. The destruction of the tram lines was more than a case of civic vandalism, it was a brutal act of urbanicide.

Sydney's tram network was once one of the largest in the world, undertaking 405 million passenger journeys at its peak in 1945. But material shortages and a lack of funding during World War II caused the system to deteriorate alarmingly. The government realised that upgrading the infrastructure, plus buying new trams, would be financially prohibitive. It sought overseas advice, and in 1952 a British expert recommended that Sydney cancel 250 new trams and replace the entire system with buses: 'London has resolved its traffic problem by replacing trams with buses and Sydney should do the same.'

Representatives of the government went to the United States, and as one American expert put it, 'All large American cities that were beating traffic tangles were getting rid of trams.' The future was the car and expressways. Trams were shabby, an embarrassing and sentimental anachronism in an age of speed. Like America, it was predicted that Australia would see a rise in private car ownership and the car represented modernity and progress. Sydney was hilly and had narrow streets, unlike Melbourne, which was perfect for trams with its grid of wide flat streets.

In the late 1950s Sydney tore up its tram network. Nearly a thousand trams were driven to the workshops in the eastern suburbs and stripped of everything that could be sold, then sprayed with sump oil and set alight. The last trams, scrawled with graffiti and filled with enthusiasts, made their final journeys in 1961. When the trams were removed, mass transport plummeted, private car usage soared, and belching, groaning buses dominated the streets.

Another sign of what Labor premier Joe Cahill called 'a striking symbol of Sydney's growth and maturity' was the elevated roadway across Circular Quay, a brutalist disfiguring of the historic gateway to Sydney. The Cahill Expressway was controversial from the beginning, with critics lambasting it as a 'tragic blunder'. Others saw it as an example of a revitalised Sydney as skyscrapers began to fill the skyline. It was an era of concrete and glass, the new buildings visible symbols of modernity and new technologies.

The Cahill Expressway, built to alleviate city traffic congestion, continues to be a scar on Sydney's urban landscape, oppressing everyone and everything below it. Architectural critic Elizabeth Farrelly described it as 'doggedly symmetrical, profoundly deadpan, severing the city from the water on a permanent basis'.

One of Jeffrey Smart's most well-known paintings is *Cahill Expressway* (1962). The image is a stylised view of the approach to the northern end of the expressway's tunnel. The only human, a plump middle-aged man, stands to one side, as if embodying the anomie one experiences when overwhelmed by a huge impersonal construction. Cahill died in 1959, one year after the opening of his eponymous expressway. No doubt he would be nonplussed to learn just how much it's reviled today.

The skyscraper that began the transformation of the city's skyline was the AMP building on the corners of Alfred, Phillip and Young streets. When it was opened in 1962 by Prime Minister Menzies, it was the tallest building in Australia. Many more followed, and in the mid-1960s the journalist and historian Gavin Souter marvelled at this new Sydney:

> Just as the inner-city once seemed unlikely ever to change,
> now it seems unlikely ever to stand still again. The other day I
> counted 16 cranes on the skyline ... It is too early yet for a final
> verdict on the new city, but already I prefer it to the old. That's
> not to say that I would wish to see the city lose all its sandstone
> piles. I like the GPO, the clock tower at Central Station, the
> Customs House at Circular Quay, St James' Church and mostly
> other buildings designed by Francis Greenway, but otherwise
> are perfectly willing to surrender everything built before 1930.

A counterweight to International Modernism, which gloried in glass and concrete high-rises, was the Sydney School, also known as the 'Nuts and Berries style'. This loose collection of like-minded architects was drawn to rustic materials, clinker bricks, and raked roof lines. It was a style that was heavily influenced by traditional Japanese architecture and Frank Lloyd Wright. The architects favoured organic and natural structures, often built on steep slopes. Their projects were largely homes on the North Shore and in the eastern suburbs, as well as ski lodges in the alpine hamlets of Thredbo and Perisher. The Sydney School residences were labelled 'nuts and berries' because in contrast to most of the modern houses being built, they exposed rustic materials like brick, timber and stone. It tried to bring a human scale to the juggernaut of towering architecture, represented by the high-priest of modernism, Harry Seidler.

The NSW Housing Commission built high-rise blocks in the inner city. They were dreary, unimaginative, their apartments cramped and noisy, the end station for the working class, the mentally ill and pensioners. The tenants struggled to live a good life in these high-rise chicken coops, which puzzled some experts because the wealthy enjoyed living in the sky in their privately developed apartment towers. On a fleeting visit to Sydney in 1973, the American anthropologist Margaret Mead was baffled by these two opposing views and remarked, 'Only the poor seem to suffer from high-rise neuroses.'

Flat building in the 1960s and early 1970s surpassed even the phenomenal growth rate of the 1920s and 1930s. In 1970, for the first time in Sydney's history, more flats were built than houses. Very few of the blocks of flats were built in the city in comparison with the suburbs. Demand was higher in the suburbs and, as developers quickly learned, land cost much less. Developers revelled in the readily available finance and lax local government building regulations. It was a sure way to make a quick buck.

The result was blocks of flats out of character with the rest of their suburban streets. They resembled barracks and were often cramped, with views that looked on to another block next door or had no views at all. The developers didn't care about shoddy workmanship or architectural aesthetics. As Ruth Thompson notes in her *Sydney's Flats: A social and political history*, anyone could set themselves up as a builder. There were no licensing requirements and little or no enforcement of building standards by local councils. The legacy of the 1960s unit-building boom is seen throughout suburban Sydney: 'Rows of uninspired and uninspiring three- and four-storey blocks sprung up along the main transport corridor and rail lines to dominate the streetscapes of suburbs like Ryde, Lane Cove, Rockdale, Botany and Kogarah.'

But what was it like to live in these buildings? What went on inside them that was different from life in suburban homes? A Sydney television series set in an apartment block showed a voyeuristic Australia one version. In early 1972 the first episode of *Number 96* was broadcast. The soap opera explored the lives and relationships of the residents of a four-storey block of flats at 96 Lindsay Street, Paddington (in reality, the façade was 83 Moncur Street, Woollahra). The building had eight apartments, a ground-floor delicatessen and a chemist shop (later to become a wine bar).

It screened weeknights at 8.30 and soon became the most popular show on Australian television. Its adult storylines were controversial for the time, with much nudity (the first time full-frontal nudity was on Australian television screens, with some actors contractually obliged to strip), a world-first gay character on television, an interracial romance and other taboo subjects, including a transgender character (Carlotta from *Les Girls*), marijuana use, teenage drug addiction, rape, illegal abortions, a black mass, a panty snatcher dubbed the knicker snipper and the pantyhose murderer. It made stars out of many of the large cast, such as the blonde sex siren, Abigail.

The show attracted many complaints, especially in its early years. The Australian Broadcasting Control Board sent their censor, a highly religious man, up from Melbourne every week to ensure each episode complied with the Control Board guidelines. Sometimes offending scenes would be cut from an episode after its Sydney airing, and Sydney found itself in the curious position of being able to watch scenes that would be censored for the rest of the country.

The soapie finished in 1977 when ratings declined, but it had proved itself one of the most daring and groundbreaking Australian TV series of the 1970s. At its peak it was a cultural and social phenomenon. As McKenzie Wark writes in his book *Celebrities, Culture and Cyberspace*:

> Once, when I was a kid, I was walking down a suburban street at night, when I noticed a rhythmic flickering of light from inside the houses. Though screened from view by the drawn curtains, the lights from a row of separate houses were all pulsing in time. And then I heard the music and I knew everyone was watching the same show ... *Number 96*.

THE ASKIN ERA OF THE 1960s

DAVID HICKIE WRITES IN HIS BOOK *The Prince and the Premier* that 1965 'was the turning point in the development of organised crime in Australia, and especially New South Wales'. The reason for this was the election of Robert 'Bob' Askin as Liberal premier in 1965. During the war Askin had been the SP bookie for his battalion as well as a loan shark, and had run two-up games. It was in the army that he acquired the nickname 'Slippery Sam'.

Askin was to be premier for a decade. Short and plump, he was fanatically tidy, a genial boss who presented himself to the electorate as an ordinary bloke with common tastes, a superb raconteur, and fond of a punt. When an inquisitive reporter once asked where he got all his money from, he explained he was a very successful punter.

His affability hid a loner, and few who worked closely with him thought they really knew him. His wife certainly didn't know of his extramarital affairs. One staffer accidentally poked his head into Askin's office one night and gasped on seeing him dancing nude with a naked woman.

He hated journalists and became infamous all over Australia when, in 1966, he was in a car with Prime Minister Harold Holt and President Lyndon Johnson. A mob demonstrating against the Vietnam War was blocking the vehicle and a furious Askin was reported to have ordered the driver to 'run over the bastards'.

What was also little known during his lifetime was his friendship with the gangster Abraham 'Abe' Saffron, a man who had made his early money selling sly grog. Saffron was born to Russian Jewish parents in Sydney in 1919. His father ran a drapery store, a vocation that didn't appeal to young Abe, whose criminal tendencies started early when, at the age of eight, he sold black-market cigarettes. At 19 he was fined £5 for allowing premises to be used for gambling. Two years later he was sentenced to six months hard labour for receiving stolen goods. The magistrate gave him a suspended sentence, hinting that it would be a good idea if Saffron joined the army to fight for his country.

He enlisted in the Citizen Military Forces but never served overseas. It took him two years to reach the rank of corporal and even then he was considered so useless that the army discharged him. He quickly saw that there were fortunes to be made in sly grog, especially in nightclubs, where patrons would pay a premium for a drink. He was only 23 when he took over the running of the swanky Roosevelt nightclub in Kings Cross. A few months later he bought the Gladstone Hotel in William Street, just a ten-minute walk from his nightclub. By buying up hotels he cornered the market, selling the illegal booze out of the nightclub and also to sly groggeries.

Only 5 feet 6 inches (167.6 centimetres) tall, he had a swarthy complexion and grey reptilian eyes, a formidable priapic drive, and if crossed would get one of his standover men to beat or even kill the offender. He had a shrewd grasp of the weaknesses of others, and believed that every woman and man had a moral flaw that he could exploit, whether it be sex or money. For his budding empire to survive and flourish he bribed the police and important officials and blackmailed politicians after secretly having photographs taken of their illicit sexual exploits.

Saffron found the greedy Askin easy to corrupt. Soon the premier was on Saffron's payroll and was given tips on fixed horseraces as 'a courtesy to Premier Askin'. Saffron also ran illegal casinos, and to keep them from being raided he paid the premier and the corrupt police commissioner, Norm 'The Mushroom' Allan, $5000 to $10 000 per week each.

Sydney bookmakers nicknamed Askin 'crime', because even though he was to say to the media, 'crime doesn't pay', he was crime's best friend, presiding over an explosion of organised crime in New South Wales. He allowed illegal casinos to thrive. Askin and later Police Commissioner Fred Hanson were given bribes from illegal casinos from 1967 until they retired. Perce Galea, head of an illegal gambling empire, paid the premier $100 000 in bribes a year. One of Galea's illegal casinos, dubbed 'The Double Bay Bridge Club', would spend $10 000 on wages, $1000 on rent and $5000 on bribes a week. It had an annual profit of $2 million. Not content with these large bribes, Askin also had a side hustle in selling knighthoods.

Askin and Saffron regularly had dinner together at the legendary Bourbon and Beefsteak Bar and Restaurant in the Cross owned by former CIA operative Bernie Houghton, a secretive man with a penchant for youths barely out of their teens. The restaurant was home to gangsters and corrupt cops. It had come into existence during the arrival of American servicemen on R&R (Rest and Recreation) leave during the Vietnam War.

The first Americans on R&R arrived in 1967. At its peak, a planeload of GIs landed every day for six days of rest and recreation. By the time of the last flight in 1972, 280 000 American servicemen had descended upon Sydney, spending close to $80 million (about $760 million today). Some of the servicemen arrived with drug habits picked up in Vietnam, especially the insidious heroin. Most, however, were spending their R&R picking up willing girls and paying for sex. Prostitutes hadn't been seen in Kings Cross in such numbers since World War II.

The colossal earnings from the drug trade resulted in gang violence and police corruption.

It was also an era when people didn't seem to care about the city's history or architecture that reminded them of the past. A hatred of Victorian-era buildings was common. Many people, including architects like Harry Seidler, wanted the Queen Victoria Building demolished. Newspapers ran headlines like 'Tear Down This City Horror' and advocated that a car park be put in its place.

If that wasn't bad enough, Askin, who had no interest in history or culture, allowed developers free rein to demolish buildings on sites they were keen to develop. It was a prime example of a feral hyper-capitalism, until it met opposition from the NSW Builders' Labourers' Federation (BLF). Led by outstanding union leaders, including the charismatic Jack Mundey, the union chose to take on a role of social responsibility, as Mundey outlined in the *Sydney Morning Herald*:

> Yes, we want to build. However, we prefer to build urgently required hospitals, schools, other public utilities, high-quality flats, units and houses, provided they are designed with adequate concern for the environment, than to build ugly unimaginative architecturally-bankrupt blocks of concrete and glass offices ... More and more, we are going to determine which buildings we will build ... The environmental interests of three million people are at stake and cannot be left to developers and building employers whose main concern is making profit.

The BLF was as good as its word. In June 1971 a residents' group of women from middle-class Hunters Hill wanted to save Kelly's Bush on the harbour foreshore, where AV Jennings intended to build luxury houses. The BLF placed a green ban on unions having anything to do with the project. Jennings said it would use non-union labour. In response the union threatened to stop work on another AV Jennings construction project, saying: 'If you attempt to build on Kelly's Bush, even if there is the loss of one tree, this half-completed building will remain so forever as a monument to Kelly's Bush.'

If developers thought this was a one-off, they were mistaken. Resident action groups began to mobilise to save their areas from mindless destruction. A crucial part of the green ban movement was the emphasis on preserving working-class residential areas, and the Rocks was a perfect example. The site of the first European settlement in 1788 and home to a wealth of historic buildings, it was also home to the underclass and low-income workers – sailors, maritime workers, pensioners, street cleaners, factory workers and transients. The BLF placed a ban on its destruction from 1971 until 1975, saving some of the oldest buildings in Australia and protecting the picturesque foreshore parks. After much protest, plans were drawn up that eliminated high-rise buildings. The bans had been a complete success, as can be seen in the Rocks today, which attracts millions of visitors a year.

The next confrontation would be with Sid Londish, a Woolloomooloo boy who, by hard work, ruthlessness and huge ambition, achieved wealth and prestige. In the early 1970s he had a grand vision for his old suburb that involved bulldozing the old buildings and creating high-rises of 20 to 30 storeys with rooftop gardens, the whole suburb crisscrossed by two monorails. This would be the culmination of his achievements as an entrepreneur. And he had contacts at the highest level on side. With the help of

Premier Askin, he was able to acquire a loan of $20 million from the Moscow Narodny Bank – quite a feat during the Cold War, given the Soviet Union was communist.

But Sid hadn't counted on the opposition of the locals, nor the power of the builders' labourers – in February 1973 the BLF placed a green ban on the entire suburb. Sid was irate. But the ban was not lifted until early 1975, when two-thirds of the area was obtained by the Housing Commission to create medium-density apartment blocks and houses for low-income earners, with trees lining the once bare streets and parks. Londish's failure rankled with him and way into his nineties he would, as I can personally attest, buttonhole strangers in shops and on the street, telling them, 'I used to own Woolloomooloo.'

Around this time another fight was underway up on the ridge overlooking Woolloomooloo. This was the battle for Victoria Street, Kings Cross, where developer Frank Theeman was determined to demolish the street's rows of dilapidated Victorian terraces and erect high-rises. The conflict would not only culminate in the limitation of development along the ridge and the preservation of many gracious old terraces, but also lead to one of Sydney's most enduring mysteries: the disappearance of activist, heiress (to the Foy fortune), and newspaper proprietor Juanita Nielsen.

It was not just residents opposing the development on Victoria Street – many of them had been offered money to move out or had been made offers they couldn't refuse – but a motley collection of students, intellectuals, feminists, communists, anarchists and working-class people who took over the buildings as squatters.

To Theeman's fury, the BLF placed a green ban on Victoria Street. He contacted his 'good friend' Police Commissioner Fred Hanson – later revealed to be one of a long line of corrupt police – to get rid of the squatters. For two days in January 1974 police stood by while about 30 eager pupils of a karate school set out to demolish the terraces and frighten the squatters into leaving. Dozens of squatters were arrested.

Meanwhile divisions in the BLF had opened up and the NSW branch was taken over by corrupt leaders from Victoria who prioritised lifting the ban. This was where Juanita Nielsen played a significant role, not just in campaigning against the development in her newspaper *NOW*, but in her relationship with John Glebe, Secretary of the Water and Sewerage Employees' Union. Glebe banned the connection of water services to the development, and once again Theeman was stymied.

In July 1975 Juanita Nielsen went to a meeting at the Carousel Club in the Cross, and was never seen again. An inquest officially declared her dead in 1983, but failed to determine the place and manner of her death. Nonetheless, there was evidence of police corruption and links between her disappearance, property developers and Kings Cross.

Askin retired as premier in June 1975, leaving behind a toxic public culture where you could become a major player in the city by whatever means necessary, whether through drugs, gambling or brutish building development. All that mattered was that you became a wealthy Sydney identity. As a parting gift Perce Galea gave Askin $100 000.

Alfred McCoy, author of *Drug Traffic*, summed it up: '[with] the Liberal-Country parties in power, the state endured a period of political and police corruption unparalleled in its modern history'.

RED LIGHTS

SEX WORKER ANNE MCGARRY WAS IN HER EARLY SIXTIES WHEN she had to fight for her life in the Love Machine brothel in Kings Cross. In the early hours of 3 May 2013, she was leaning on a car outside the Love Machine during her shift when Michael Kay, a man half her age, approached her. He had bleached blond hair and was mumbling. Although McGarry thought him 'very strange', she asked if he wanted to go upstairs with her and he said yes, explaining that he had been rejected by all the other brothels and had been 'ripped off' by a girl in one of them. He wanted sex 'involving a chain'. McGarry said she didn't do 'bizarre sex' and, after confirming he had money to pay her, she took her client into Room One, which was fitted out with a bed, spa, towels, scented candles, a large television, a table with condoms and an ashtray.

When he gave her $285, she told him he could stay for an hour if he gave her another $100. She ordered him a bottle of beer and rang downstairs for a staffer to collect the money, as was the custom (a percentage of it would be paid as a wage to her at the end of the night).

Kay stood in the middle of the room 'umming and ahing' until, frustrated, McGarry told him to take off his clothes, otherwise 'you're wasting your time'. Eventually Kay undressed and lay on the bed. McGarry tried to make him erect and put a condom on him. Kay started to talk about himself, saying 'he hated his father and had just had a fight with him'. Then he explained that he hadn't had sex before. The exasperated prostitute said, 'Yes, you have. I'm not silly. I've worked. You've had sex before.'

The client rolled on top of her and was starting to have sex with her when he grabbed McGarry by the throat. She flung him off and told him to get dressed and leave. He jumped up and dressed while she put on her clothes. He was standing by the spa and, as she was about to leave, he suddenly grabbed her from behind, jabbing his right hand into her throat and she fell to the floor. He began kicking her in the head, then choking her. McGarry thought she was going to die and fought her client for what she said was seven or eight minutes. 'I would have been dead if God hadn't given me strength,' she later told the court.

She managed to reach out and open the door. Kay grabbed her by the back of her hair. She thrashed around, biting and scratching. The two rolled down the stairs as he punched and kicked her, and both landed against the fire door. McGarry pushed it open and yelled out to the bartender to call the police. Her phone, secreted between her breasts, fell out. Kay took it, jumped up and shouted, 'I've set the place on fire.' And he had. The fire brigade was called and it took some time to put the fire out. Hundreds of bystanders in Darlinghurst Road watched the smoke billowing out of the windows. The owner of the Love Machine described McGarry as 'an icon of the Cross', who had worked in the area since the 1970s. Other owners and sex workers called her a 'legend'.

During Kay's trial the court learned about the inner workings of the Love Machine. Kay had been McGarry's first customer of the night. Depending on the night of the week, she might have to wait hours for a client, sometimes up to eight hours. She had worked 'on and off' at the Love Machine and had three prices on offer, $165, $220, and for $330 the client could stay for an hour. On the night she was assaulted, four much younger prostitutes were working at the brothel. She described them as 'Candy, she's Asian, Nicole, she's a tall blonde girl, Champagne, and Tessa, black hair, a Māori girl.' McGarry occupied Room One on the first floor because 'I was one of the older ladies'. Each woman had a room, and they shared a communal toilet on level one, as well as dryers and a washing machine to clean the towels used by clients. There were strippers on the ground floor, with a continual show. McGarry summed up her encounter with Kay: 'It was the biggest mistake of my life. I'm very lucky to be here. I have gone through a lot of drama and shock and stress.'

It's a cliché that Adelaide is known for its churches, Melbourne for its boulevards and sober suburbs, and Sydney for sex and sin. Its reputation started when the first women convicts stepped ashore in 1788.

The Rocks had always been a centre for brothels, prostitutes working out of hotels and street walkers catering to sailors and wharfies. The most infamous street was 'Suez Canal' (supposedly a pun on 'sewers') that still runs from George Street to Harrington Street and was regarded as one of the most unsavoury places in Sydney. It was haunted by prostitutes and larrikins, and featured sly grog shops and an opium den.

Another side of town also became notorious. By the 1850s Woolloomooloo was becoming a byword for lawlessness and sexual immorality. Part of this reputation was based on the number of brothels in the area. In 1859 a Woolloomooloo police constable said that 50 houses were inhabited exclusively by prostitutes, not one of whom was over the age of 20.

In the city itself prostitutes haunted the theatres, and after a show at the Theatre Royal male theatre patrons could visit nearby brothels. In the 1870s a man could walk out of the Theatre Royal, head to the intersection of King and Castlereagh streets, stroll on up King Street and stop at one of the most famous bordellos,

Café Blind, with its huge frosted plate glass windows. There he'd tap against the side door with his cane, not caring about being spotted by passing policemen – they'd been paid to turn a blind eye to what went on inside – and would be welcomed in by the proprietor, an Austrian with a black beard and a diamond ring.

The woman behind the counter was Madame Blind, who effected pencilled eyebrows, blackened eyelashes, hair dyed a grim yellow and deep red lipstick, liberally applied. The bar and parlour had enormous mirrors, crimson hangings, marble-topped tables, sofas and easy chairs. The customers ranged from drunken young men to well-known politicians. The barmaids were mainly teenage girls wearing thick make-up and one of the madam's cast-off dresses. There was a small saloon bar at the rear, and upstairs was a billiard room with two other saloons. In one of these was a piano player who, on busy nights, especially after the theatres closed, would be surrounded by drunken men singing along and teenage girls cajoling their clients into buying the most expensive French champagne.

In 1891 the inspector general of police told the government that there were 403 known 'fallen women' in Sydney. Brothels and hotels gave the area around Elizabeth and Liverpool streets an 'evil' reputation. By 1903 there were an estimated 2000 prostitutes in Sydney. The Sydney Rescue Society counted 560 prostitutes from Bathurst Street to Circular Quay. In the same district there were 25 houses of ill fame and prostitutes worked out of about 100 hotels.

Newspapers wrote articles about white girls who sold themselves for opium. It was reckoned that 25 opium dens were known to exist and that there were a further 25 shops and offices where opium was smoked. For example, in 1909 Ada Price, aged 19, was living in a 'Chinese den' in Alexandria. She said she had no other place to go. She had been sent to the Industrial School in

Parramatta in 1904 and after three years was discharged. She did some occasional work before a friend brought her to the den. Two Chinese men lived there. For a year four young girls lived and worked at the den. While the two Chinese men were at work, the young girls sold themselves to the Chinese customers.

By the 1920s the slums of Surry Hills and Darlinghurst had become Sydney's new red-light district. In the heart of Surry Hills was Frog Hollow. This gully was crowded with ramshackle dwellings literally piled on top of each other where gambling, drug dealing and prostitution flourished (it's now a delightfully peaceful public park with only a plaque noting its past infamy).

By 1929 there were over 600 prostitutes in the city itself, with many under the age of 16. Tabloid newspapers often featured sensational stories about underage girls working in brothels. During World War II, American servicemen were stationed in areas like Kings Cross and Woolloomooloo (the red-light areas of Woolloomooloo were reserved for black servicemen) and prostitution was rife. In March 1943, 25-year-old Joy Phillips was sentenced to three years in prison for allowing Joan Duffy, 16, to work in her Surry Hills brothel. Duffy, a country girl from Cowra, was visited by as many as 20 soldiers and sailors a night. She was told by Joy that if she 'entertained' soldiers and sailors for seven and a half minutes, the charge would be £3, while an hour's 'entertainment' would cost them £10.

In the late 1960s and into the 1970s, Aboriginal and Islander prostitutes worked out of pubs in Haymarket, servicing the market workers. The racket only stopped when the markets shifted to Flemington. Those prostitutes who catered to merchant seamen or foreign sailors were called 'ship molls' and operated in certain hotels in the city and nearby Pyrmont. Occasionally these women were invited on board the ships for 'parties' or 'orgies'.

In the 1960s and 1970s Darlinghurst Road, Kings Cross, or the Golden Mile as it was commonly called, was the epicentre of Sydney's sex trade. The Forbes Street steps, off William Street, were famous for transgender hookers.

The tradition of brothels in East Sydney, Darlinghurst and Surry Hills was directly descended from notorious madam Tilly Devine's Palmer Street trade of the 1920s and 1930s, and the little brothels of the lanes continued into the 1960s. If sex workers didn't work in a brothel in this period, most of them had pimps. As one prostitute of the era put it, 'Most of these hoons only had one lady, but there were the few clever ones who managed to have two – one at one end of Kings Cross and another at the other end – and spent the whole night running backwards and forwards between them.' During these decades some prostitutes turned over between 80 and 100 clients per week and at least half of these men saw them on a regular weekly to monthly basis. Married men represented half to three-quarters of their clientele; two-thirds were equally mixed working-class and middle-class men. Call girls on the North Shore and in the more exclusive areas of the east like Double Bay, were more likely to have middle-class clients, while men visiting brothels in western and southern Sydney were predominately working class.

In the early 1980s, 71 brothels (massage parlours or bordellos) existed in Sydney. There began a general decline in commercial sex with the increase of casual sex in society. For instance, in 1983 there were 22 brothels throughout East Sydney and Darlinghurst. Three years later only four remained, but there were several houses in discreet streets and lanes that catered to clients. One or two women usually occupied one of the little terrace houses at a time. They stood in an open doorway to attract attention from male passers-by. The open door and red light indicated it was a brothel. When the girls were busy the front door was closed.

In the terraces the furniture and décor were simple but, as one prostitute said, 'Men like the homey atmosphere of our houses.'

Those women with records of soliciting, consorting and other prostitution offences were very likely to be women who worked prior to the laws changing in 1979, when few sex workers escaped arrest. One prostitute, Sharleen, said of that time, 'We used to get arrested every night, and once I got arrested seven times in one night. In all, I've probably been arrested about 2000 times, at least.' The occupation the women engaged in may have been grubby and dangerous at times, but one of the worst aspects was dealing with the police. The women had a lingering mistrust of the cops who physically assaulted them, blackmailed them for money, demanded free sex and, if that was not forthcoming, planted drugs on them.

As one sex worker said, 'During the late seventies, early eighties, the police were more interested in money; the "freebies" they could get anyway. There's a lot of cops' wives whom I've helped put fur coats on their backs, and a lot of cops' kids whom I've helped to educate right up until the laws changed in 1979, and all of a sudden I had surplus money.'

Another danger was addiction. In the 1920s and 1930s many of the women working for brothel madam Tilly Devine were addicted to cocaine – encouraged by Devine, who would pay them with the drug rather than cash. By the mid-1980s heroin was the drug on the street and almost a third of women working in inner-city brothels and on the streets were regular drug users. Around this time many Asian women (from the Philippines, Thailand, Malaysia, Cambodia and China) began to work illegally in Sydney's massage parlours and bordellos. A new feature in Kings Cross was street boys and girls selling themselves for drugs. A notorious male brothel, Costello's in Kellett Street, sold underage boys to paedophiles.

Violence was common. Between December 1984 and December 1985, 46 prostitutes on William Street were victims of some outrage, including being burned on the breasts with cigarettes; one woman was dragged along the footpath by her nipples, another was lassoed and dragged for half a block behind a speeding car.

By the 1990s the main areas for prostitution in Sydney were Kings Cross and William Street. Kings Cross had the advantage of proximity to private hotels or rooms that could be rented for the occasion. Most of the clients were tourists, country visitors, young men from the outer suburbs having a night out in the Cross, and sailors from the Woolloomooloo naval base.

Although William Street was only a short walk from the Cross, it may as well have been a different world. Here the women worked in clusters for safety and no more than 100 metres from their houses. Each house had a hired 'sitter' whose job was to organise rooms as the women arrived with clients and to try and stop aggressive men from assaulting the girls. Most of the prostitutes were addicts and many had stories of bashings, robberies and rape. They copped verbal abuse and ridicule from passers-by that they either ignored or responded to with their own abuse or sharp repartee.

The aim of the women on the street was to catch the eye of cruising motorists, rather than to invite conversation as in the Cross. Here on the street dresses were scantier and more revealing, with tiny skirts, leotards and fishnet stockings, with eye-catching colours that immediately dazzled the male motorists. Unlike the Cross, the cruising men were more likely to be married, preferring the anonymity of gloomy streets to the bright lights of the Cross.

Once the driver was attracted to a woman, he pulled up at the kerb and beckoned her. She approached the car from the passenger side and spoke to the man through the open window, being careful not to place her head inside the car – there was a possibility of being seized by the hair and dragged in. Then the bargaining began.

The William Street women lived in a world of danger and potential violence, unlike those who worked in one of the most famous brothels in Australia, A Touch of Class, which opened in Riley Street, Surry Hills, in 1972 and grew to fill three Victorian terraces. Described as the 'most controversial piece of real estate in Sydney', among the 'Touches' clients were some of the country's best-known figures from business, entertainment and sport, as well as generations of sailors from visiting warships. To protect its clients, their visits would appear on credit card statements as 'Staff Call'.

There is no doubt that A Touch of Class had some friends in high places so it could continue its brazen business – street prostitution may have been decriminalised in 1979, but brothels were not legalised in New South Wales until the *Disorderly Houses Amendment Act* of 1995.

A Touch of Class closed in late 2007 and was to transform itself into Misty's, with the new manager hiring psychics to get rid of any lingering bad karma. At its peak it proved just as successful as its predecessor. The madam, Suzelle Antic, bragged to the *Sydney Morning Herald* that 'We could get 200 jobs a night through the place, I'd say it was the busiest brothel in the city.' But the gentrification of Surry Hills meant fewer clients and it closed in late 2016 when the madam moved her girls to Newtown.

Around the time Antic shifted her activities out of Surry Hills, Darlinghurst remained a haven for prostitution as it had for a hundred years. Appalled residents of the Seidler-designed Horizon building, which towered over the area, casting its long shadow over the terraces below, complained to the police about what they were witnessing. Prostitutes had spread into the area because of a turf war with the transgender prostitutes who operated along William Street, where police allowed them to work. For Darlinghurst locals it was becoming increasingly depressing to see prostitutes performing sex acts in the open in the small parks, and in cars during the middle of the day. As one resident said, 'On a Sunday I can walk out my front door and see a girl giving a guy oral sex in broad daylight. We've had guys strip naked in the park. We've seen prostitutes have their children with them while they're doing drugs.' Another complained of yelling and screaming late at night and acts of violence outside their homes.

The law as it stands in Sydney allows prostitution as long as the women are not working within 100 metres of a home, school or church. Most prostitutes targeted by the police were not charged but told to move away from residential areas and back onto William Street, where there were nightly fights and screaming matches between the transgender sex workers and other prostitutes.

When I first shifted into Kings Cross 30 years ago there were many sex workers openly accosting any male, especially on Darlinghurst Road, watched by their hawk-eyed pimps, and a dozen or so brothels. Now, except for an occasional prostitute touting vainly for customers, sex workers and brothels have vanished into the suburbs.

UNDERCURRENTS

AFTER I'D WORKED WITH THE PRODUCER JAN CHAPMAN on three telemovies, in 1987 she asked me if I'd create a TV series, perhaps set in Bondi. I had rarely been to Bondi, even after eight years of living in Sydney.

Never having really explored the area before, I walked down the grassy knoll to the white sand, passing the Spanish Mission–style Bondi Pavilion. The bay with its cliffs on either side seemed like an amphitheatre devoted to the flesh. The bluish-green sea was flat, the lackadaisical waves struggling onto the sand. Children paddled or pretended to be surfers on their styrofoam boards; adults swam into the gentle waves and cruised back to shore with them. Men and women candidly showed off their physiques. The sunbaking bodies turned slowly in the sand, toasting both front and back. It reminded me of chickens in a rotisserie as they browned. In the shimmering heat it seemed as if these people were supplicants to a pagan god.

Returning up the hill, passing flocks of aggressive noisy seagulls dive-bombing families for their chips, I saw shabby art deco apartment blocks from the 1930s, and the main street filled with men, women and children (their noses covered in white zinc) in bathers and beach towels, buying fast food and ice creams. The scene had an unapologetic crassness and tattiness. My eyes were attracted to a four-storey 1940s building on Campbell Parade, its cream exterior dull and grubby. I knew then that was where I would base my story of three adult sisters whose lives have spiralled so far out of control that their father, in a gesture not unlike Lear, gives them that weary little Bondi hotel to run. This became the series *The Last Resort*.

The characters who lived in my Isis Hotel were surfers, criminals, an unemployed widow making money doing telephone sex, the teenage daughter of one sister, and a Japanese surfer, a character who came into being after a local surfer told me that Bondi was becoming too famous and Japanese surfers were starting to surf there, and the trouble was that they didn't know the proper surfing etiquette. So the Australians learned the Japanese word for shark and yelled it out when they wanted to scare the interlopers back onto the shore.

The 30-part series wasn't a success (though it was big in Malaysia), but I learned to like Bondi, with its mixture of working-class residents, backpackers, and Jews who had flocked there after World War II to escape an anti-Semitic Europe in ruins, and found they could afford Bondi's cheap houses and flats. Two books published around the same time as the TV series, *Life's a Beach* and *Life's a Beach II: The adventure continues*, both by the photographer Rennie Ellis, gave a vivid portrait of just how sensual Sydney beaches were, how paganistic, tanned and shameless, with bodies sexy, bloated or misshapen, all accepted. One looks at the photographs now and can only marvel at how little attention the sun worshippers paid to the threat of skin cancer.

The television show that made Bondi Beach internationally famous premiered in 2006, and continues today. *Bondi Rescue* is a reality series that is broadcast in over 100 countries. Unlike *The Last Resort*, whose exteriors were filmed in winter because it was cheaper and less crowded, accidentally undermining the sunny image of Bondi by showing bleak skies and few swimmers in the surf, this series is shot during the summer, with a central episode reflecting incidents that occur on Christmas Day. It shows the daily lives and routines of the professional lifeguards who patrol Bondi Beach. Between November and February the lifeguards perform around 5000 rescues. They also have to deal with lost children, shark scares, bluebottle stings, injuries, sexual deviants, drunkenness and thieves.

The show's theme song may be 'In the Summertime' and promises good times, but Sydney's beaches have another side, with tribal loyalties, ethnic hatreds, territorial disputes, and even religious visions.

*

A darker picture of the surfing culture and the girls who were part of it was published in 1979. Written by Kathy Lette and Gabrielle Carey, *Puberty Blues* is an autobiographical novel about two 13-year-old girls, Debbie and her best friend, Sue, from Sutherland Shire. For the girls, 'The beach was the centre of our world. Rain, snow, hail, a two-hour wait at the bus stop, or being grounded, nothing could keep us from the surf. Us little surfie chicks.' It was a small world with nuanced differences. North Cronulla was the same as South Cronulla except the waves were bigger, the boys were older, the shops were closer, the hair was longer, and the status was higher.

Over the course of one summer the two girls desperately try to ingratiate themselves into the 'Greenhills gang', a close-knit coterie of males into endless surfing, casual sex, drugs and heavy alcohol use.

The novel introduced older Australians to phrases like: 'pash off', 'rack off' and 'surfie molls' and panel vans called 'shaggin' wagons' with stickers that read *If it's rockin' don't bother knockin'*.

This brutish world is tribal and male-dominated; the girls spend their time sunbaking and watching the boys surf. The surf culture was irredeemably sexist, with nonstop bongs and underage sex. Rape, abortion and miscarriage were part of it, but not spoken about. In the novel gang rape is unremarkable, mindless violence is amusing. Hard drug use, largely heroin, was common and a killer. Of the 19 original members of the 'Greenhills gang' the book was based on, nine developed heroin habits and at least two died from it while in their teens. Finally, fed up with this ugly male culture, Debbie and Sue abandon the blokes to surf on their own.

The book was made into a film in 1981, directed by Bruce Beresford, who was intrigued by a world he knew nothing about, as he had grown up in Toongabbie in the outer-western suburbs. The surf culture of southern Sydney was a mystery to him. For censorship reasons the age of the two girls was raised to 16. The novel is generally darker than the film, and Kathy Lette complained that:

> ... the film sanitised the plot by omitting central references to miscarriage and abortion. The movie depicts a culture in which gang rape is incidental, mindless violence is amusing and hard drug use is fatal, but it was unable to address the consequences of the brutal sexual economy in which the girls must exist.

All this may well be true, but Lette's film version would never have been as successful as the movie turned out to be, so much so that a television series aired in 2012 and a second series was made in 2014. Although Lette would have criticised these for the same reasons as she did the film, both series were still unsettling for what they did show. The *Sydney Morning Herald* reviewer wrote that, 'like the book, the series is racy, confronting, often quite brutal, heartbreaking and coruscatingly entertaining. It sparkles even as it disturbingly illuminates a culture of adolescence that seems not so much dated as distressingly contemporary.'

The worst aspects of surfie culture reached a malign apogee in the 1990s, with the Bra Boys, a gang based in the beachside suburb of Maroubra. It gained its notoriety through violence and alleged links to organised crime. The gang was held together by surfing as well as strong ties to the suburb. 'Bra' was a reference to Maroubra, and street slang for brother. This group of semi-literate men had tattoos saying 'My Brother's Keeper', 'Bra Boys' and the suburb's postcode, '2035'. An extremely territorial mob, it took control of the reef break off the coast of Kurnell known as Cape Solander, renaming it 'Ours' and keeping outsiders from using it. The gang was probably unaware that it had been named after Swedish botanist Daniel Solander, a colleague of Joseph Banks. A plaque commemorating him is secured to the cliff face to mark the spot where the *Endeavour*'s crew first landed.

In 2002 about 160 gang members were involved in a violent brawl with police during a Christmas party that injured 30 cops. Three years later one of its leaders, Jai Abberton, was acquitted of murder. He and his brother, Koby, would spend time in jail for other crimes. In 2007 a full-length documentary about the gang received international attention. *Bra Boys* was written and directed by a couple of members of the group and narrated by Russell Crowe. It was amateurish and self-serving and could not avoid a tone of swaggering menace.

One aspect of surfing culture that would result in violence was its chauvinism. Surfers guarded their territory with zealous bigotry. In *Puberty Blues* the list of adversaries was large. There were 'bad surfboard riders on their "L" plates ... the Italian family groups and the "uncool" kids from Bankstown' who swarmed to South Cronulla creating a 'Dickheadland'. But the most dreaded 'enemies to keep an eye open for' were 'the Bankies, from the greasy western suburbs'.

The Bra Boys liked to brag that westies, and Muslim men from the western suburbs who harassed girls, were kept from their beaches. 'The beach should be for Aussie kids,' said Koby Abberton. 'If these fellas come out to Maroubra and start something, they know it's going to be on, so they stay away.'

In the summer of 2005 leading up to Christmas there had been tension between the Cronulla locals and Lebanese youths from the western suburbs. There were accusations young Lebanese men were harassing local women, calling them 'Aussie sluts'. In the early afternoon of Sunday, 4 December 2005, three lifesavers approached four young Lebanese men on Cronulla Beach and a series of verbal assaults escalated. One Lebanese man attempted to defuse the situation but one of his friends threw a punch that spiralled into a fight. A lifesaver was badly hurt after falling and striking his head.

The Sydney tabloids and radio shock jocks leapt on the events, with the most influential, Alan Jones, thundering on 2GB, 'What kind of grubs? Well, I'll tell you what kind of grubs this lot were. This lot were Middle Eastern grubs.'

The newspapers and talkback radio inflamed the situation to such an extent that by midday on Sunday, 11 December, around 5000 people had arrived at the beach and begun attacking anyone they thought was Lebanese. The violence spread to other suburbs, including attacks on ambulances and police officers.

There was a hysterical media reaction and the whole idea of multiculturalism was up for debate. This became an Australia-wide moral panic totally out of proportion with the actual events, and a minor series of incidents compared with racial conflicts in other parts of the world. But it was the natural consequence of the territorial nature of Sydney beach culture. Some local surf clubs later issued statements rejecting racism and violence. Others argued that the gathering was justified as a protest against 'ethnic gangs', with alcohol blamed for the rioting and violence and the agitation of far-right groups. In a surprising gesture, the Bra Boys, who had proudly boasted that 'the beach should be for Aussie kids', made an apology to leaders of the Islamic community.

There is an even grimmer flipside to the picturesque image we have of the beaches. Murders and hate crimes have also been associated with particular spots. In January 1965 two 15-year-old girls, Marianne Schmidt and Christine Sharrock, were brutally killed on Wanda Beach near Cronulla. It had been a popular picnic spot for the Schmidt family, but on this occasion the two girls had wandered off by themselves. Their partially buried bodies were discovered the next day. The case has never been solved.

During the 1980s vicious homophobic gangs from the western suburbs would go to known gay beats in Manly and Bondi in order to rob, assault and even kill gay men. Since the 1960s, the North Head area at Manly was known as 'the shy man's beat' or the 'last stop on Sydney's gay sex tour'. Men would sunbathe and wait to connect with other men. Gangs referred to this gay beat as 'an ATM', stopping to rob the defenceless men to get money for their heavy drinking on a Friday night. They'd king hit a target, take his money, his jacket, his jewellery, anything of value, and did not have to worry about police coming after them. The injured men were often too scared to report assaults because the police treated them as if they were the perpetrators, not the victims. Several men were killed by gangs who threw their victims off a cliff. One such victim was an American, Scott Johnson. In 1988 his clothes were discovered folded up at the top of a 50-metre cliff, his naked body at the bottom. Police ruled it a suicide and it was not until 2022, after bungled police investigations, an inquest, and a long campaign by his family, that a man was convicted of the murder.

Bondi's reputation was worse. In two separate attacks in 1989, gangs threw television reader Ross Warren, 25, and barman John Russell, 31, to their deaths. The homophobic police showed little interest in investigating their deaths, ruling them probable suicides as they had several others, and it was not until 2005 that the coroner found that they had been murdered. The area became known as the Bondi Badlands.

*

But Sydney's beaches have had another side as sites of religious fervour. In 1924 the Star Amphitheatre opened at Balmoral Beach. It was constructed by the Order of the Star in the East, founded by the president of the Theosophical Society, Annie Besant. The amphitheatre was intended as a platform for lectures by the mystic Krishnamurti.

An urban legend persists that it was built in order to watch Christ's second coming, when he would walk through Sydney Heads. The crumbling amphitheatre was demolished in 1951.

In January 2003 one of Sydney's most popular beaches, Coogee, a favourite party zone for backpackers, became a site of religious veneration. One day, a man was looking out his front window when he suddenly noticed an apparition of the Virgin Mary at the end of a wooden safety fence. He called his friends to have a look. By the next day, word had spread, and several hundred people flocked to the park. Soon the crowds swelled to several thousand a day, especially in the late afternoon when the apparition materialised. As the *Sydney Morning Herald* reported:

> Some wept, others sang, most prayed. Scores more hiked
> up the cliff path to touch and kiss the post which had been
> transformed into something like a shrine. Pictures of the Virgin,

rosary beads and flowers were piled up around the whitewashed fence. Most agreed they could discern the shape of a veiled figure.

The rational explanation was that the vision was an unlikely combination of the fence's design and colour, late afternoon shadow, and a small rise that changed the angle at the end of the railing. Even so, the Catholic Church didn't know how to react, with the Sydney Archdiocese issuing an anodyne message: 'If people are experiencing a sense of peace by being there, then it is a good thing.' Ten days after the Virgin Mary arrived vandals destroyed the fence where she had appeared, disappointing thousands of believers. The fence was quickly rebuilt but with a slight alteration to the original design. Although the Virgin Mary hasn't returned, a tiny garden has been planted to mark the spot and people still come to pray.

REMAKING SYDNEY'S SKYLINE:
HARRY SEIDLER

ARCHITECT HARRY SEIDLER WOULD COME TO SYDNEY via a tortuous route. Born in Vienna in 1923, the son of a successful Jewish clothing manufacturer, he fled to England in 1938 after Nazi Germany occupied Austria. After a brief period studying building construction, he was arrested by the British authorities as an enemy alien and interned on the Isle of Man. He was only 16, and one of the youngest internees. Furious, confused and hurt, he took the imprisonment as a personal slight. He eventually wrote a secret 130 000-word diary about his experiences there and in Canada, where he was interned until October 1941.

The experience was to scar him for life. As his biographer Helen O'Neill writes, 'The transcript of the diary makes harrowing reading. It ricochets with trauma, confusion, controlled depression, and the searing pain of pure injustice.' It was to affect Seidler profoundly, and while it made him less empathetic towards others (he could be obnoxious and insulting to everyone), it also seems to have given him the rebellious energy he needed to overcome all opposition to his vision.

After his release from internment, he studied architecture and became a Canadian citizen at the end of the war. In America he studied under German Bauhaus teachers, including Walter Gropius. By this time was he an enthusiastic and committed modernist, fascinated by the Parisian architect Le Corbusier. His parents had migrated to Sydney in 1946, and his mother wrote to him, commissioning him to design a home for her and his father, Max. Intrigued, and also wanting to see his parents, Seidler arrived in Sydney in the middle of 1948 with the aim of designing a house for his mother and then returning to America and 'civilisation'.

Rose had chosen a site in Wahroonga on the upper North Shore, at that time remote bushland. Her friends were appalled, telling her she was crazy. There was only an unmade road, no neighbours, and market gardens. For her son this was *terra nullius*. Anything was possible. His design for the Rose Seidler House overturned virtually every convention of suburban architecture in Australia. The geometry and layout would be closely based on his hero Le Corbusier's famous 'Villa Savoye'.

Rather than facing the street, the house sat in the middle of the bushland. Six external doors gave access to an outdoor area, while each room, with the exception of the bathrooms, had a view onto the bush. Floor-to-ceiling glass gave panoramic vistas of the outside. On sunny days the interior would be incandescent with light. The typical suburban houses of the time were a series of boxy rooms with a dark hall down the middle, designed as if afraid of sunlight. They featured overstuffed armchairs and kitsch wallpaper. Seidler's furniture was made from lightweight materials with thin legs, lounges with minimal stuffing. The house was divided into two distinct zones: the living areas and the sleeping areas. Some of the walls were flexible dividers. There were sliding doors, and a huge sandstone fireplace. Its roof was flat and Seidler, always fancying himself an artist, painted a flamboyant and colourful piece of abstract art on the wall facing the sun deck. He called the house 'a machine for living'. To many Australians its stark, cube-like form seemed like something out of a science-fiction movie.

Seidler may have loved his mother but that didn't mean he allowed her to interfere with his design and its uncluttered paean to modern living. He got rid of his parents' heavy Viennese furniture and replaced it with items he had brought with him from New York. Even Rose's precious cutlery was tossed aside and replaced with simple functional utensils, her son admonishing her as if she were merely a client and not his mother, 'I will not eat with this decadent cutlery because I bought you flat stainless steel, the newest from America and that fits into this house.' Everything had to be perfect and complement Seidler's vision. But Rose always backed him, even to the extent of sewing the curtains and bedspreads for the new house according to her son's design and preferred colours.

On 17 December 1960, a hundred invited guests came to inspect the new house. Over the next few years design magazines, newspaper reporters and women's magazines came to gawp at this extraordinary home. Even years later uninvited visitors would troop through the garden, staring at the house and taking photographs, while Rose tried to shoo them away. But whether the house was liked or not, it exuded an aura of optimism, a sense of a future filled with adventure, sunlight and modern glamour. For a country like Australia that had embraced cosy suburbs, the Rose Seidler house was a revolution. Even now admirers flock to inspect the house on Sundays.

From the first time he flew into Sydney and looked down on the hundreds of thousands of bland suburban roofs and the squat city centre, Seidler had an ambiguous attitude towards his parents' adopted country. He despised the mediocrity of its government officials, the lack of artistic vision, and the ignorance of what was happening in progressive architectural circles overseas. But there was one redeeming feature for him – Sydney was an architectural wasteland that he could stamp with his self-proclaimed genius.

One of his first major commissions would become a signature building for those who disliked his architecture: Blues Point Tower. After designing some more houses and a few minor buildings, he was offered a blank canvas for what he considered a visionary project. The waterfront streets around Berrys Bay, Blues Point and McMahons Point on the lower North Shore were filled with slums that embodied the worst of the Depression years. Many locals regarded the buildings with disdain, and couldn't wait for them to be demolished. So, here was a large patch of land on which Seidler could create his ideal village. Only this time, he would reach for the sky. Once cleared, the waterfront would have uninterrupted harbour views and the area would be a model metropolis unto itself.

Seidler took his cue from Le Corbusier's radical 'Plan Voisin', his provocative idea for rebuilding a large part of the centre of Paris. The Swiss–French architect proposed to bulldoze a large area north of the Seine and replace the narrow streets, monuments and houses with giant 60-storey cruciform towers placed within an orthogonal street grid and park-like green space. His audacious and arrogant scheme was met with scorn from French politicians and the public. But Seidler had Sydney politicians and the press on his side. He envisaged a squadron of functionalist housing blocks of varying heights and orientations that would be a perfectly planned community.

Models were exhibited, and it was only then, on seeing the structures in three dimensions, that critics emerged. The plan seemed a hideous conglomeration of tall buildings, a crowded urban nightmare where it seemed people did not matter. At ground level the towering structures created a Stygian world where sunlight could not penetrate. It was as if human beings were reduced to ants.

This plan ran counter to another architectural movement in the United States as set out in one of the most sustained and influential critiques of modernism, *The Death and Life of Great American Cities* (1961). Written by a New Yorker, Jane Jacobs, it argued that the best urban places were those that grew organically, were layered and had a sustaining community of all classes, a vibrant mix of the well-off, the middle class and the poor, the old and the young.

This movement meant nothing to a stern modernist like Seidler. As far as he was concerned, people had to adapt to buildings, not the other way around. Modernist architecture extolled the ideal of an immaculate structural vision untroubled by context or anything as messy as life and human desires. Like Le Corbusier, Seidler disliked hedonism and had an almost messianic belief in the purity of his vision.

The only thing that stopped this monstrous development was lack of money and political will. Only one structure was built – the Blues Point Tower, for a time the tallest residential building in Australia; the solitary manifestation of Seidler's brave new world on a gorgeous peninsula. It cannot be ignored and remains an eyesore, a bleak exclamation mark of modernism on the harbour.

Yet Seidler's career flourished the more he lambasted the parochialism of local architects, the backwardness of governments, the cosy conformity of artists. Combative and needlessly rude, he found energy in these fights, whether against councils, bureaucrats or government ministers. Everyone was a fool, except him. With his bespoke suits, colourful bow ties, and the cocky strut of a short arse, he imposed himself on Sydney.

In 1964 he shifted into the top floor of his newly designed apartment building Ithaca Gardens in Elizabeth Bay. He and his wife, Penelope, lived there for three years. The building looks into the 1930s apartment block next door. As I know from visiting friends who lived there, the front entrance is brutally plain, its bricks now stained a dirty greyish-green. The nondescript façade facing the street is only matched by the uninviting interiors. The minimalist rooms are poky, and the ceilings so low I found myself stooping.

Seidler's low ceilings were based on his shortness and his desire to cram as many levels into a building as possible, uncaring of those taller than him. As one anonymous employee remembered, he used to say to the builders and workmen, 'When the building inspector comes on the site, you all kneel down, so he gets the impression the ceiling is higher. Don't stand up when the building inspector is there. Hunch, hunch.'

He was all for tearing down the old sandstone buildings, including the Queen Victoria Building, believing it a monstrosity. Yet he had a soft spot for Georgian architecture – especially Greenway's buildings – writing that the only time Australian architecture had been truly Australian 'was in the early days when settlers took the Georgian architecture and modified it to suit the local climate, since then it has slipped back into copying suburban England'. As such he attacked the decision to name the severely functionalist Housing Commission apartment block in North Sydney after Greenway as an 'insult'.

He, in turn, knew how to insult. Anyone who disagreed with him was a 'cretin'. One lawyer who dealt with him several times called him 'a complete fanatic ... A martinet.' Like Greenway, he took to print to defend his vision, writing self-published books he gave to all and sundry. If not writing, he was garrulously selling his new religion to anyone who would listen. One reporter described the verbal barrage as 'like a high-pressure American salesman'. He never entirely lost his ambiguous attitude towards the country he eventually became a citizen of, believing Australia to be 'a disadvantaged outpost of the Western world, tied to Western culture, and steeped in the prejudices of the nineteenth century'.

Also like Greenway he was humourless, and if anyone made jokes he'd stare at them uncomprehendingly. In any event his intense focus left little time for levity, as his assistants quickly learned. One recalled, 'People didn't approach him because they were afraid of getting their heads bitten off.' He lived in a world of high art (he played recordings of Bach endlessly as he created), modern sculpture and painting, and expensive epicurean tastes. As Penelope once said of the couple, 'We truly are the beautiful, privileged people.'

The Blues Point Tower was Australia's tallest residential building until the 1970s, but it attracted increasing criticism, and was often described as 'Australia's ugliest building', although some architects admired it. Seidler privately bridled at these criticisms but finally broke in 1982 when cartoonist Patrick Cook lampooned it as the 'Harry Seidler Retirement Park' in the *National Times*. His cartoon depicted a barren landscape on which had been erected ten structures resembling refrigerators. Each featured a slot at the front through which the sole occupant was being given a sandwich while a dunny man collected their shit at the rear. Seidler fumed that the cartoon defamed him by suggesting, among other things, that he 'lacked aesthetic sensibilities'. Only a man whose prickly pride overwhelmed his common sense would take a cartoonist to court.

The case was a sensation. In the witness box Cook described Blues Point Tower as 'hideous and a real offence against the harbour'. His cartoon pointed out that, in his opinion, 'the Seidler buildings were ugly and induced claustrophobia'.

Seidler's lawyer, his brother-in-law Clive Evatt, thought that, given his cocky client's articulate defence of his buildings in the media, he would be more than capable of holding his own under questioning. But as Evatt later ruefully recalled, Seidler turned out to be 'the world's worst witness. He rambled on, wasn't able to concentrate on the questions.' As Seidler meandered in the witness box, his stunned barrister reflected that had he known how badly his client would perform on the stand, he would never have recommended going ahead with the case. Seidler was out of his depth. He was used to pontificating without interruption, but having his expertise questioned in a courtroom, he wilted. The Supreme Court jury found in favour of Cook, judging that his cartoon was fair comment.

Seidler was publicly ridiculed. He never forgot the media assault, and it reinforced his contempt for the 'cretins' in the mass media, and he developed an even more contemptuous attitude towards those who did not agree with him. This was not helped in 1988 when the *Bulletin* magazine included him in a feature headed 'The Hundred Most Appalling People in Australia'.

Architects in other parts of Australia didn't want to work in Sydney because they thought Seidler 'owned the place'. In a way he did. Even though his 'relationship with Sydney continued to be fretful', according to one of his biographers, his buildings were strewn across the landscape, from houses built on prominent ridges, solitary in their modernist glory, to skyscrapers dotting the city. He was to design 180 houses and buildings here and overseas, but for Sydneysiders three stand out, unmissable due to design, height and location.

His most celebrated, and perhaps most important to Sydney's growing confidence as a world city, was Australia Square. It was conceived shortly after height restrictions were lifted. Thirty buildings around George and Pitt streets in central Sydney were demolished in 1961 to make way for the circular tower. It was 170 metres high, had a revolving restaurant on the forty-seventh floor, an observation deck on the floor above, a public plaza, a retail complex and a car park.

Completed in 1967, its construction employed the latest technological advances, including the structural system developed by Pier Luigi Nervi, one of the world's leading engineers. It was the world's tallest lightweight concrete building at the time, and was Australia's first modern skyscraper. For nine years it would be Sydney's tallest building. From the time of its completion it was described as one of the most beautiful buildings in the country, and remains, as one architect put it, 'iconic to Australian architecture'. One admiring architecture critic said it 'gave Sydney a sense of growing up, a sense of confidence. It was our first glittering version of a skyscraper.'

His next major project wasn't far from Australia Square – on the corner of Martin Place and Pitt Street. This was another sky-scraper (228 metres and 67 storeys), and its construction entailed the demolition of some of Sydney' s most cherished buildings: the beautiful nineteenth-century Hotel Australia, the Theatre Royal and, perhaps most missed of all, the historic Rowe Street precinct, a small but glamorous laneway. This obliteration of Sydney's past caused much controversy at the time, with headlines like 'Destruction of one of Sydney's most stunning buildings' and editorials condemning the obliteration of the Hotel Australia. The articles and opinion pieces didn't faze Seidler, the history meant nothing to him. All he cared about was his vision, and that meant dragging soporific Sydney into the twentieth century.

The MLC Centre, as it was known (it is now simply '25 Martin Place'), is a stark white modernist column, an octagon with eight massive columns in the corners that taper towards the top. It is one of the world's tallest reinforced concrete buildings. Again there was praise, but there was also criticism and ridicule, much of it focused on the strange mushroom-like roundhouse next to the main tower. As one NSW Treasurer observed caustically, 'It lends weight to the theory it was built by authoritarian surveillance state aliens to spy on unsuspecting pedestrians of Martin Place.'

Despite increasing criticisms of his work, architectural honours here and overseas multiplied. Books, not all of them self-published, praised his work and, in a nice riposte to those who had once imprisoned him, his diaries of his internment were published to acclaim and gave him every right to criticise Australia's recent mistreatment of refugees.

One of his last designs was the Horizon, a 43-storey block of 256 apartments in Darlinghurst. It's hard to avoid as I sit on my balcony writing these words. It's to my right, an enormous white tower erupting imperiously out of the squat terraces that seem to cower beneath it. It was built on the site of the former ABC radio studios on Forbes Street, between William and Liverpool streets. Frustrated by the City of Sydney's height restrictions, he had pleaded in the press that 'the views of our incomparable magnificent harbour are denied by local councils disallowing free-stranding residential buildings which people want'. By that he meant, what rich people want. Not long afterwards, a lawyer found a loophole to circumvent the council's intransigence. Because the land was owned by the federal government, Seidler didn't have to worry about the council's height restrictions.

The building towers over its neighbours. Its scalloped balconies are designed to give sweeping views of the harbour, the bridge, the Opera House, and the distant Blue Mountains – vistas only the wealthy owners can appreciate. Having paid so much for these views, the owners could demand that the less salubrious areas around them be cleansed of prostitutes, drug dealers and other riff-raff. Despite its cheerleaders, the Horizon stands as a glaring example of a modern architect's callous disregard for *hoi polloi*.

There is no doubt that Seidler's insistence on modernist architecture was necessary for Sydney to engage with the rest of the world's urban design, though it could be said that his Rose Seidler house probably had the greatest and most lasting impact on our sense of the possibilities of suburban houses. But compared to Seidler's skyscrapers, Greenway's buildings seem to be built to a human scale that tries not to crush the human spirit.

As the writer and architectural critic Jonathan Meades put it: 'The actuality of architectural practice [is] a morass of compromise, horse trading, maniacal hubris, brinkmanship, unjustified optimism, tantrums, slobbering sycophancy and frequent humiliation.' Both Greenway's and Seidler's careers could be summed up by these words. Yet without these two men, we wouldn't have the Sydney we do.

THE PACKERS

THE PACKERS' RISE AND FALL was to have a different arc from their long-term rivals, the Fairfaxes. The media dynasty began in 1902 when Robert Clyde Packer arrived in Sydney from Hobart aged 22. He spent some time writing for regional newspapers, never proving himself more than a mediocre journalist, before returning to Sydney to work on the *Sunday Times* in 1908. By 1913 the hardworking Packer was editor and had increased the paper's circulation. He rose to the position of sub-editor of *The Sun* and later editor of the *Sydney Sun* in an era of increasingly bitter rivalry among the many morning and afternoon newspapers.

In 1918 he joined three others to start *Smith's Weekly,* which he designed and managed. It was a very Sydney paper, with its irreverence, copious illustrations and ribald sensationalism, just the right popular mix for postwar optimism. His third share in the business made him wealthy and he launched the *Daily Guardian* in 1923. It was soon successful, appealing to readers with news as entertainment, whether it be politics or crime, served up with a voyeuristic interest in sex and scandals (frequently the same thing). This was to be a template for modern newspapers. Packer was driven by a compulsive need to make as much money as possible, and that meant taking a cynical attitude to his readers, whom a contemporary magazine said had 'a mental age of fifteen'. Titillation reigned and Packer found he could capitalise on this by organising the first Miss Australia contest in 1926, a move that pumped up the paper's circulation to an astonishing 275 000 copies. He was to sell his newspaper and in so doing became a wealthy man and managing editor of Associated Newspapers.

This gave him time to spend sailing, kangaroo shooting and dabbling in the quasi-fascistic movement the New Guard. His hobbies did little to help him relax, however, and the pressure of work, and a sailing accident, proved fatal. In 1934 he died returning from England, where he had gone to seek medical help for his ailing body.

His son Frank was devastated. All the Packer men, down to the present day, forgave their fathers for their anger, ruthlessness and harsh treatment of them, justifying the behaviour as necessary, even an aid to toughen them up.

Also like these Packer men, Frank was a wayward youth and a poor student, finding solace as a youngster in sport. He was a physically strong lad, aggressive and confrontational. At the age of 17 Frank found himself carrying out menial duties in the basement of the *Daily Guardian*, as his father insisted he learn every aspect of the newspaper business. Three years later he shifted over to *Smith's Weekly*, and his father quickly promoted him to advertising director, a decision that rankled with the reporters who thought the son a reckless gambler and playboy.

But in 1933 Frank helped initiate the publishing venture that would be a cash cow for the family for decades. The *Australian Women's Weekly* appeared in June that year and proved successful beyond his wildest dreams, achieving a circulation three times what he had hoped for. Its topical in-depth features, modern fiction, stylish fashion pages and social gossip made its rivals seem tame and behind the times.

In all things Frank had an unquenchable energy, whether for the newspaper business, boxing, sailing or the pursuit of women.

He pursued one woman in particular, Gretel Bullmore, who, despite his desperate infatuation, proved unattainable. Striking, intelligent, sports loving, a constant feature in society pages, she ignored or laughed off his entreaties until after years of persistent wooing the exhausted Gretel gave in. They were to have two sons, Clyde and Kerry.

Three years after starting the *Australian Women's Weekly*, he acquired the failing *Daily Telegraph*. Part of Frank's success can be put down to his ability to pick the best people. For the *Telegraph* this meant giving the job of editor to Sydney Deamer, who pushed a modern agenda that promoted progressive ideas. Frank, conservative in his values, didn't care as long as the paper made money, but he was obsessed by the Fairfax papers.

The success of the *Sydney Morning Herald* always rankled, so he ordered his reporters to attack the Fairfaxes at every opportunity. But of more immediate concern in the cut-throat world of Sydney newspapers was Ezra Norton, owner of the salacious *Truth*, a man of notorious temper and half-crazed social behaviour. Frank's launch of the *Sunday Telegraph* in 1939 seriously cut into *Truth*'s readership. Norton reacted by ordering his reporters to satirise and belittle his rival. In retaliation, Frank, never one to let something like that pass, published unflattering photographs of Norton in his paper.

In the members' enclosure at Randwick Racecourse on Derby Day 1939, Packer jeered Norton and deliberately provoked him, despite Norton's two burly bodyguards. Packer was taller than his enemy at 185 centimetres, thickset and dangerous in any physical altercation (he had won the NSW amateur heavyweight boxing championship in 1929). Finally, Norton snapped and threw the first punch. The brawl was ferocious and brief as both were quickly separated by their friends. What Frank was not to know was that 75 years later his grandson would also brawl in public, creating, as he and Norton had done, headlines and public ridicule.

Much to Norton's chagrin he had to apologise to the Australian Jockey Club, but he didn't forget this slight. Envious of Packer's success, and conscious of his own paper's declining fortunes, he continued to needle Frank. During World War II, he seethed at Packer's commission in the Australian Imperial Force. For a couple of years *Truth* ran photographs of 'Captain Frank Packer' enjoying himself at the races with the cutting caption: 'Captain Packer will be leaving for the front shortly'. But Packer did, eventually, serving in New Guinea.

The war changed him. He no longer tried to stay at one remove from the political stance of his papers and forced them to support the Liberal Party. At the same time, in what seemed crazed behaviour to those close to him, he threw himself into a frenzy of work, starting and buying magazines, launching newspapers, becoming involved with book publishing, printing, television, films, tourist resorts – he even bought a piggery. Although his Channel Nine television stations were successful, he felt more at home with print. He terrorised his staff with sudden threats, contrary orders and nonsensical sackings, and overwhelmed them with constant memos regarding petty cash, whether it be for models' brassieres, camera bulbs, even string. He may have had the ability to choose the right talent (never giving them the credit they deserved), but when that talent was no longer of use he disposed of people without remorse. Like his father, he could turn on the charm when he wanted, but this was a rare gift he seldom bestowed.

As he grew older, he became obsessed with winning the America's Cup yacht race and made two attempts with his boats *Gretel* and *Gretel II*, but failed both times. He was knighted in 1959 and his wife Gretel died a year later, having long forgiven him for his blatant womanising. Four years later he married a twice-wed divorcee, Florence Adeline Vincent. His sons were now working for his Consolidated Press, starting out at the bottom, just as his father had forced him to do, except that Frank was a greater bully, terrorising his sons and treating them as if they were strangers he had to bend to his will rather than his own flesh and blood.

He had hoped that Kerry, 'the dumb ox' as he called him, might be able to compensate for his stupidity with his physically imposing body. And so in 1960, when Frank was attempting to take over the Anglican Press, a small publisher run by the truculent, Walter Mitty–like writer Francis James, he enlisted his son to do some dirty work for him. Frank was angry that James refused to sell the press, so he sent an all-too-eager Kerry and some of his beefy friends to pressure James into selling. A boisterous Kerry, pleased that his father had given him the task, led his gang of hoons, broke down doors, smashed windows and forced their way into the building, vandalising the premises as they did so. A frightened James barricaded himself in his office and phoned Rupert Murdoch, owner of News Limited and Packer's most powerful media rival at the time. Without a moment's hesitation Murdoch quickly gathered together a team who threw an embarrassed Kerry and his friends out onto the street, leaving them with bloody noses and black eyes. The Murdoch press gleefully reported this incident in graphic detail, delighting in telling the public that the son of Australia's biggest media tycoon had been caught brawling in the street and had come off second best.

As he grew older, Frank Packer increasingly saw himself as a kingmaker in politics, proud of using his newspapers as a political bludgeon. As one obsequious long-time editor said, 'you learnt how to sniff the breeze'. In 1970 Packer – his political nous blunted by friendships with the powerful and his unbridled egotism – ordered

his media empire to attack Prime Minister John Gorton, and help
the inept and devious Billy McMahon to undermine him. Frank
succeeded in his campaign in 1971, only to realise too late that
McMahon was a disaster, becoming one of Australia's worst prime
ministers during his short time at the top.

An occasional rival in the hothouse of Sydney newspaper wars,
Rupert Murdoch once observed that Frank Packer 'is the biggest
crook in Australian newspapers, but equally he is the cleverest'.
What Murdoch didn't know was that despite an impressive
circulation, the *Daily Telegraph*'s losses were subsidised by the
goldmine of the *Australian Women's Weekly*. It had infuriated
Packer for years that the *Sydney Morning Herald*'s money-spinner
was its lucrative classified advertising. He had never ceased
viewing the Fairfaxes as pretentious, art-loving snobs. In June
1972, a harassed Frank allowed his sons to convince him to sell
the *Telegraph* to Murdoch, whose best feature was that he was not
a Fairfax. For weeks afterwards he'd burst into tears whenever the
sale was mentioned.

But this didn't soften his attitude towards his sons. In 1972,
after many disagreements with his father, Clyde resigned and
Frank disinherited him. Increasingly weakened by a poor heart
and glaucoma, Frank ranted and raved about the new Labor
government and fretted that the son to take over his empire was
one he and Gretel regarded as 'the family idiot'.

When Frank died in 1974, at first Kerry was at a loss. He
adored his father and excused every cruelty that had been meted
out to him as punishments he deserved. To the surprise of all
who knew him as a child and teenager, Kerry went on to become
one of Australia's most powerful media proprietors. This would
have also stunned his parents, who seldom saw him when he
was a child, and, when they did, despaired of him, calling him
'Dummy' and 'Boofhead' to his face.

Kerry's early life had been full of setbacks. When he was eight, he was stricken with polio and confined to an iron lung for eight months. At school the written word was an unsolvable jumble of letters due to undiagnosed dyslexia. As he was to recall years later, 'I was hopelessly behind everyone else and a bit of a laughingstock … and kids are pretty unkind to kids.' His memories of his childhood were of his unhappiness and loneliness. He survived by throwing himself into sport, working hard at it, trying to prove himself to other boys. His experiences at school hardened him. He saw the world as a hostile place and life as a relentless Darwinian struggle for survival. His view of humanity was a bleak one: he expected to dislike people when he met them, and expected to be disliked in turn.

At the age of 37 he took over the running of the business and gradually emerged from his father's shadow. He started out cautiously but then the realisation hit him that his bluster and aggression could make grown men cower. He intimidated people. Physically this was easy, he was nearly two metres tall and his weight hovered around 130 kilograms. Although he found it difficult to read any memo longer than a page, he had a sharp wit, a remarkable intelligence and didn't suffer fools, whether they were bankers, journalists or government ministers. His office became a terrifying chamber for his employees. Even the images on the walls were confronting – pictures of bull elephants, lions, and his favourite painting, a pack of dogs tearing a terrified sheep apart. He gloried in humiliating his staff, dressing them down in front of each other as he stood at his desk, arms akimbo, shouting, 'You're fucking stupid. Now tell me you're stupid and tell me why you're stupid.' One nervous head of programming nearly fainted when Kerry pulled a .44 Magnum out of his desk, pointed it at him and snarled, 'If we don't see an improvement in ratings, son, this is how you'll end up.' He clicked the trigger and smiled.

He had been bullied by his father, but he had become an even more malicious bully, gloating over his power and not ashamed to use it.

Like his father he could be charming when he wanted to be, but most times the effort was too great, and his default positions were rudeness, aggression and vindictiveness. He never let his dreams get in the way of reality. The world was a grim place and, like all pessimists, he was never surprised by dastardly human behaviour. Unlike the Fairfaxes, he had the common touch; at home with locker room talk, desperate to be one of the boys, scorning high culture and intellectuals, devouring fast food and action movies (often at the same time). An insomniac, he watched hours of television and had an understanding of what the average viewer wanted. His first love was television and he seldom showed interest in the printed word. With a sort of joyful strut, he paraded his uncouth manners, especially to the English, whose caricatured ideas of vulgar, uncultured Australian businessmen always in pursuit of the dollar were personified by Kerry. Shocked American executives had never met anyone so rude.

In the 1970s he wanted the television rights for Australian Test cricket, and when he wasn't given them, he signed up 50 of the world's best cricketers for World Series Cricket and staged his own matches. The first of these were dismal failures, but he toughed it out. His actions outraged the cricket establishment in Australia and England, which gave him enormous pleasure. The British press savaged him, called his cricket matches a 'circus', but he won. He revolutionised cricket and the televising of it, paid the cricketers what they truly deserved and, they in return, would always have the highest respect for him.

Throughout his career, Kerry, like his father, was haunted by the Fairfaxes. He wanted to crush the family by owning their newspapers. He was angry when he couldn't, and the frustration gnawed at him. He dreamed of revenging himself on them and rubbing those posh noses into the dirt. In the early 1970s it was his anger at losing the Australian rights to *Cosmopolitan* magazine to his rival Fairfax that led him to create, with journalist and editor Ita Buttrose, a women's magazine that would become an instant success. It may have been modelled on the American magazine, but it had its own distinct voice, and one that matched the optimism of the new Labor government. *Cleo*, launched in November 1972, was for women aged between 20 and 40 who were looking for something more than the recipes, knitting tips and royal news that the *Australian Women's Weekly* focused on. It had controversial feminist content, male centrefolds, and detailed sexual advice. As Buttrose said: '*Cleo* gets women, and it also strikes the perfect balance, offers a bright, light-hearted tone and aesthetic without shying away from the more serious issues that are important to their readers.' Kerry was not only pleased that his magazine outsold the Fairfax *Cosmopolitan*, but also that he had launched a popular women's magazine just as his father had.

Years before Packer had married Roslyn Weedon and had two children, Gretel and James. Like his father, he was a womaniser, having one long affair with a model, Carol Lopes, who committed suicide after Kerry dropped her. There was a long-term mistress, Julie Trethowan, manager of his fitness club (she was well provided for in his will). He knew that money bought him women's affection, as he had always been fully aware that he was no Adonis. Phillip Adams, broadcaster and author, remembers talking to Kerry in his study one evening, where he had a glass cabinet full of elephant guns, an elephant's foot filled with fire irons, and a pair of elephant tusks on the wall. Packer was in a morose mood. He had just seen the movie *The Elephant Man* and told Adams, 'That's how I feel,' convinced that he was as monstrously ugly as the title character.

The Fairfax empire continued to taunt him and in 1991 after Young Warwick's attempted privatisation of the company collapsed, Packer again attempted to acquire it. The bid failed, which he blamed on his legal advisor Malcolm Turnbull, later to become prime minister. In June 2009 Turnbull related how an angry Packer confronted him:

> He told me he'd kill me, yeah. I didn't think he was completely serious, but I didn't think he was entirely joking either. Look, he could be pretty scary. He did threaten to kill me and I said to him: 'Well, you'd better make sure that your assassin gets me first because, if he misses, you better know I won't miss you.' He could be a complete pig, you know. He could charm the birds out of the trees, but he could be a brute.

What Turnbull didn't grasp was just how desperately Packer wanted Fairfax. For him, it would be the natural culmination of his career, his ultimate victory over a rival who had tormented the Packers for decades. This setback would rankle until the day he died.

In 1994 Kerry tried for the licence of Sydney's first casino but failed. It was another devastating defeat and he took it personally, believing that the establishment did not consider him upstanding enough to own one. His revenge four years later would be to acquire the Crown casino in Melbourne. He knew casinos intimately – after all, he was one of the world's biggest gamblers, losing $19 million in one night at the Ritz in 1987.

He liked to pay for female escorts during his gambling forays. In *Friends and Enemies: A memoir*, Barbara Amiel, the present wife of Conrad Black, describes how Packer once paid her to be his date. He played cards with a stake of £500 000 a game, and she afterwards received a cheque for £100 000 from his winnings.

He gave her another £100 000 a night later from backgammon profits. She seemed open to a fling, but he was jolted from his sexual pursuit when he went to her flat and, for a man acutely aware of his dyslexia, was intimidated by her extensive collection of books. Packer, she said, had a 'primitive ugliness that can be very sexually attractive, particularly when presented in an immaculate suit'. She appreciated his thuggery, 'as if at any moment he would abandon all civilised convention, tear his food with his hands and physically maim anyone in his way'.

On the racetrack he would terrorise bookmakers by placing such huge wagers that they would bankrupt the bookie if his horse won. Many bookmakers gave up their licences rather than deal with him. He despised politicians and only supported those who could do something for him. In 1984 the Costigan Royal Commission suspected him, on little evidence, of fraud, tax evasion, drug trafficking, distribution of pornography and even murder. This was a horrendous time for Packer and although no charges were ever laid (in truth he was a tax avoider par excellence), he never forgot the smears and was convinced the public wouldn't either.

Kerry cared little for other people. Despite being one of the richest people in Australia, he possessed no sense of civic duty like the Fairfax family. He worshipped money and believed his greatest strength came from a belief that it was him against the world. He had none of the Fairfaxes' interest in the arts (this would be the realm of his wife and daughter). His passion was polo. He established teams and lavish polo complexes in Australia, England and Argentina. In 1990 he suffered a heart attack while playing polo. His heart stopped beating for eight minutes but he was revived and, as he was to say to many people later, with a sense of triumph, 'I've been to the other side, and let me tell you, son, there's fucking nothing there.'

But he continued to smoke (though he never drank, unlike his father who extolled the virtues of martinis), didn't exercise and had several bypass operations, as well as dealing with a chronic kidney infection. By 2005 he knew he was dying. He was becoming thinner, his face larger in relation to his body, as if it was morphing into an Easter Island statue. It's interesting that he didn't take leave of employees and friends but flew to Buenos Aires, Argentina, a very sick man, to say goodbye to his favourite polo players. In December of that year he died.

His media empire passed to his son, James, who, like his father and grandfather before him, had been bullied by his father since he was a boy. James was 38, about the same age Kerry had been when he took charge of the company after his own father's death. James was a diffident, shy boy who seemed to buckle under the demands of his father and the Packer name. When he was boarding at the prestigious Cranbrook school, his fellow boarders would often hear him crying himself to sleep. His father thought him a sook, and knowing that, like all the Packer men, James was without academic nous, tried to instil a liking for sports in him. This included setting up a cricket net in the backyard and having a bowling machine bowl cricket balls at his teenage son at 150 kilometres an hour, a pace even the best batsmen in the world would flinch at.

James was not interested in the arts, newspapers or television, and a year after his father died, he began to offload Channel Nine and the Consolidated Press magazine and newspaper group to fund his move into international gaming and tourism. If he did have one thing in common with his father, it was a love of casinos. Although not especially interested in gambling himself, he liked being in casinos, mixing with high rollers and feeling cocooned from the world outside. He jumped from relationships to marriages and divorce with a disconcerting eagerness, as if desperate for affection but not knowing how to relate to women.

His business interests over the years would also follow this pattern; a plunge into a new business, and then a highly public withdrawal. He would have intense friendships and then, without explanation, would drop those friends. Even before his father died, he seemed at a spiritual loss and, after developing a friendship with the actor Tom Cruise, began attending the Church of Scientology. He said it was 'helpful' but did not elaborate in what way. After leaving the church he distanced himself from it. However, his involvement with Cruise gave him a taste of the movie-making business and he stumped up $100 million in 2013 to form a production company, RatPac, with his business partner Brett Ratner.

He was also thinking about his father's legacy and how he could both honour it and outdo it. In 2012 he made a pitch to the New South Wa had lobbied his political les government to open Sydney's second casino, something his father had failed to do. He promised it would bring in millions of tax revenue. His aim was to build what he called 'an iconic Sydney building' that would be a tribute to his father. Kerry Packer's own casino design had been described as a 'shopping centre', low, wide and square, more in keeping with his 'pragmatic earthbound sensibility'. But James aimed higher – literally. He would build a tall, imposing building, so spectacular that it would dwarf the rival casino, the Star, and dominate the Sydney skyline. Eventually the Crown casino rose 271 metres, costing around $2.2 billion. This gambling mecca was also a six-star hotel, with exclusive restaurants and apartments that had unparalleled views of Sydney. As it ascended into the sky at an astonishing rate, an excited James handpicked an apartment worth $60 million for when he returned to Sydney to live.

In 2014 his wealth was assessed at $7.19 billion, making him the third-richest person in Australia. He had a superyacht, a luxury cruise ship, a private jet, a 12-seater helicopter and a stunning selection of cars, most of which he didn't drive. But things began to spiral out of control. In the same year he was involved in a brawl on a Bondi footpath with his best friend David Gyngell, the head of Channel Nine. Apparently, Gyngell had made remarks about James's girlfriends and he had retaliated. The photographs were graphic and humiliating: two middle-aged men wrestling in the gutter. It was a disconcerting echo of his grandfather's public brawl with Ezra Norton.

His film company had successes and failures, but James grew tired of the hard work it entailed. Instead of being a glamorous lark, he found it tedious and publicly unrewarding. He sold his shares in 2017, a year after he became entranced by Israel and its prime minister, Benjamin Netanyahu. There was talk that James might convert to Judaism, but he was too mentally fragile for this huge spiritual step. He threw himself into a relationship with the singer Mariah Carey. Although he loved her, he broke it off, paying her a multi-million-dollar settlement.

Around the same time this was going on, 19 of his employees in China were arrested for organising junkets for wealthy Chinese high rollers to visit his overseas casinos, circumventing China's strict capital controls. Of the 19 staff arrested, 16 spent nine to ten months in jail as an example to other foreigners illegally recruiting gamblers on Chinese soil.

As the pressure began to get to him, his behaviour became alarmingly erratic. One time he dropped to his knees and kissed the feet of former prime minister of Israel, Shimon Peres, at other times he would suddenly burst into tears.

More woe would follow in his hometown. For three days in October 2020 Packer appeared before an independent inquiry into Crown's suitability to hold a casino licence in New South Wales. He spoke via a videolink from his 108-metre superyacht in the Pacific and appeared a sad figure, glassy-eyed and puffy-faced, halting and devoid of energy. He accepted Crown had operated an unlicensed business in China. The head of the inquiry questioned him about Crown's links with organised crime, to which Packer only gave vague answers. The inquiry accused Packer of setting in train a strategy of bringing rich Chinese gamblers to Australia during his time as chairman. He had no answer to this, and as the *Australian Financial Review* put it, he 'brutally [threw] old mates under the bus'. When shown emails – which he accepted were 'shameful', 'disgraceful' and 'threatening' – that he had written to a financier who pulled out of a deal, he said he was mentally ill and didn't know what he was doing: 'I am being treated for my bipolar disease ... I was sick at the time.' The inquiry questioned why he hadn't told shareholders he was unwell. In his more morose moments Packer thought of himself as Icarus, who had flown too close to the sun and plummeted to earth.

In February 2021, the inquiry found that Crown was unfit to hold a casino licence, due in part to Packer's threats to the financier, as well as its 'continued commercial relationships with junket operators who had links to Triads and other organised crime groups'. Worse was to come as other inquiries looked into the affairs of Crown's casinos in Melbourne and Perth and also found them fostering a cultu re of corruption and money laundering, and provided examples of the casinos' predatory behaviour in enticing gambling addicts into their casinos, reducing them to poverty and suicidal thoughts.

His humiliation was complete. Although still wealthy, James Packer had become an abject, wretched figure, a flabby hulk (the stomach stapling operation to stop his compulsive eating hadn't worked) who said he would never return to live in Sydney; the one who had tarnished the Packer name. He would sail across the oceans on his superyacht in a medicated fog, dealing with the ghosts of his disappointed father and grandfather, drifting into an unknown future.

The curious thing is that Sydney and the rest of Australia never really took the Fairfaxes to their hearts. They were respected, even envied for their wealth and power, but they hid themselves from *hoi polloi*. The Packers were different. There was no mystery to them, they seemed to have a quintessentially Australian larrikin aura that the old money Fairfaxes didn't.

The Packer who has left the strongest legacy as far as the Australian public is concerned, is Kerry. A sacred monster, a hulking, loud-mouthed bully who, in his reincarnation in several popular television series, became an admirable but flawed man who did much to enrich popular culture and stood up to the snobby establishment, the government and faceless bureaucrats

In three straight years there were three television series devoted to him. The 2011 miniseries *Paper Giants: The Birth of Cleo* told the story of the creation of the magazine, and the sometimes turbulent relationship between its creators, Ita Buttrose and Kerry Packer. A year later came *Howzat! Kerry Packer's War*, a miniseries about World Series Cricket. Although not a hagiography, there is no doubt that Packer is the hero, an Aussie bloke fighting the snobby cricket establishment in England and Australia. *Power Games: The Packer–Murdoch War* centres on the rivalry between the two families going back to the infamous brawl when Frank Packer was trying to take over the Anglican Press.

In 2019 Tommy Murphy wrote the play *Packer and Sons*, which was performed at Belvoir Street Theatre. It had a mixed reception, with reviewers noting two things: when the Kerry character was off stage, the play lagged, and James seemed too nebulous a character, just as he is in real life.

It's easy to imagine the Fairfax family fitting into Melbourne's wealthy circles, but not the Packers, especially not Kerry. They were too vulgar, too foul-mouthed, too contemptuous of tradition and old-world values – in other words, too Sydney. All that's left now of both these Sydney media dynasties is some telemovies, a few stories, and James Packer's beautiful casino tower, an exquisite elongated silvery object, imperious in the sunlight, leaving its haughty shadow on those below.

HYDE PARK SOUTH

HYDE PARK IS DIVIDED INTO TWO SECTIONS, separated by busy Park Street, which delineates two very different experiences, the arboreal central pathway the only constant in each. While the northern section celebrates nature and pagan pursuits, the southern section is dominated by the remembrance of war.

Even the buildings that fringe the southern section of Hyde Park are different from the gigantic buildings on the eastern side of northern Hyde Park. The two most prominent are sandstone Victorian testaments to learning and culture, the Australian Museum (constructed between 1846 and 1857) and Sydney Grammar School (originally Sydney College, opened in 1835). Their grandeur and earnest tributes to classical Greek and Roman architecture are apparent, and they stand out in an even more monumental fashion in paintings of Hyde Park in the nineteenth century as there are no trees, shrubs or other buildings of such magnitude to hide them.

At the far south, on what is now Liverpool Street, was the Lyons Terrace, built in 1841. There's an evocative painting of Lyons Terrace done in 1849 that gives some sense of the beauty of the three-storey terraces and their isolation. These were terraces only the wealthy could afford, sited behind brick pillars and iron railings near the corner of College Street. The view across the unmade Liverpool Street shows Hyde Park fringed by a tottering wooden fence, the park itself a desolate and barren ground.

On the Elizabeth Street side of the park is a structure seldom noticed now, much of it hidden by fig trees. The Obelisk, irreverently known for years as 'George Thornton's scent bottle', was erected in 1857, facing Bathurst Street. It's an air outlet for the underground sewer that, in a comical gesture, was disguised as a full-size replica of Cleopatra's Needle, the famous Egyptian antiquity now in London.

To look from the far south-west corner of the park across Elizabeth and Liverpool streets is to see a remarkable building, its exterior a blend of white-glazed brick from Glasgow and yellow-glazed architectural terracotta mouldings and decorative panels from Yorkshire. The top of the building features mansard roofs on the corners. Along the Elizabeth Street façade ceramic tiles still advertise silks, linens, hosiery, laces, shoes, gloves, corsets, costumes and flowers.

This was one of Australia's foremost shopping landmarks. Its closure in 1980 ended a spectacular era of retailing. Mark Foy's department store was established by Francis Foy and his brother Mark. Francis, a prominent Catholic, is remembered as flamboyant, kind, generous, impetuous, and with a remarkable memory for transactions. Born in 1856, he worked for his father in a Melbourne drapery shop before shifting to Sydney with his brother Mark. At the time the future site was occupied by a cluster of rundown shops owned by Chinese and Hindu merchants. Francis patiently acquired them all, one by one. The store was modelled on Bon Marche in Paris, the world's first true department store.

Named after their father, Mark Foy's opened in 1908 and quickly became the most stylish emporium in Sydney. Inside were oak and cedar fittings and a grand stairway. There were large uninterrupted floor areas, chandeliers and marble finishes, and a rooftop ballroom. It claimed a number of firsts for Sydney, including the first escalator to carry customers from floor to floor, the first restaurant in a drapery store, the first motorised delivery service, and a circulating library. It was not only the fashion centre of the city, but also became a meeting place, especially for women.

In 1913 a prescient Francis predicted that a world war would happen, so he bought up all the imported stock he could find in Australia. As well as this, he opened an office in Japan to acquire glassware, textiles and other Asian goods. In his spare time, he gambled recklessly and bred horses. In November 1918, as was his habit, he attended the Melbourne Cup (although he was ill) and, prescient as usual, bet a bookmaker three to one that he would not return to Sydney alive. Foy won the bet when he died on the train to Sydney.

The board continued to run the profitable emporium and when the underground Museum station was opened in 1926, a tiled umbilical cord was created between Hyde Park and the building in the form of a subway between the underground station and Foy's. Just inside the station were posters advertising Foy's and a ceramic tile still proclaims *Mark Foy's Subway to Museum Station*. What the board hadn't predicted was that when Wynyard and Town Hall stations opened in 1932 the commercial heart of Sydney would begin its slow crawl northwards, leaving the once great emporium to steadily decline.

In a startling makeover, the building re-opened as the Downing Centre in 1991 and the floors that once thronged with shoppers now swarm with lawyers, judges, magistrates, victims, criminals, juries, witnesses and reporters, the vast areas accommodating local criminal courts, district criminal courts, civil claims courts, court services and sheriffs' offices. The former ballroom and fifth floor were converted into seven courtrooms, with offices and public areas. In the morning one can stand on the south-west edge of Hyde Park and watch the grim defendants, escorted by their lawyers and on occasion hounded by shouting journalists, quickly mounting the stairs in Liverpool Street and hurrying inside.

It's impossible, however, to avoid the military nature of much of the southern end of Hyde Park. In the south-east corner is the Emden Gun. This war trophy is a four-inch gun wrenched from the German cruiser *Emden*, which was sunk off the Cocos Islands by HMAS *Sydney* in 1914, Australia's first Australian naval victory. What's slightly unsettling is that it points down Oxford Street as if warning pedestrians, drivers and revellers at the Gay Mardi Gras parade to behave.

On the western side of the park, facing Elizabeth Street, is perhaps one of the most disturbing pieces of statuary in all of Sydney. It consists of four five-metre hyper-realistic upright bullets and three fallen shells. Titled *Yininmadyemi* ('Thou Didst Let Fall'), the sculpture is by Aboriginal artist Tony Albert, and is a tribute to the Aboriginal and Torres Strait Islander men and women who have served in the nation's military. The sculpture represents those who survived and those who were sacrificed. Although well intended, the realistic bullets (in shape and design, if not in size) seem overly aggressive and brutal. It's an unintentionally callous, even alarming monument, not conducive to contemplation but a reminder of how weapons kill in war.

The largest structure in the park is its most beautiful: the Anzac Memorial, a collaboration between two remarkable artists, the architect Charles Bruce Dellit and the sculptor Rayner Hoff. The Sydney-born Dellit, an imposing figure who wore a 'fearsome sombrero', was described as 'a human dynamo' with a work ethic that exhausted his assistants. Despite his conservative architectural education, he introduced Australia to art deco, a style he refashioned in his own way, influenced by American skyscrapers. Once embarked on the huge project, he engaged sculptor Hoff to create the statues and bas-reliefs for the monument. He and Dellit had similar tastes, both admirers of Norman Lindsay, American architecture and drawn to stylistic modernism in art. Like Dellit, Hoff was physically imposing, with an extraordinary devotion to his vision, one that was to be sorely tested by the conservative views of the establishment.

The project began in 1927 and it occupied Hoff almost full-time for three years, with his assistants and students from the art school in the old Darlinghurst Gaol working long hours alongside him. He and Dellit collaborated closely. The architect had planned that the four standing figures would represent the traditional allegories of the 'Four Seasons' and the 'Arts of Peace and War'. But Hoff demurred and replaced them with depictions of stylised figures representing the four Australian services: the Army, the Air Force, the Navy and the Army Medical Corps. The men and women are in modern military uniforms and the reliefs portray soldiers in battle and working behind the lines. The reliefs synthesise both the classical and art deco reduction of superfluous detail. The result was 20 enormous single figures for the exterior.

The marble reliefs of the interior represent 'The March of the Dead', and in the centre of the interior is Hoff's bronze sculpture *Sacrifice*, which depicts a limp young man lying naked on a shield and sword, supported by his mother, his sister, and his wife, who is nursing a child. It can be viewed from two levels, from above and from the side. It's the only sculpture in an Australian war memorial showing a completely naked male and caused quite a kerfuffle when it was unveiled. Hoff tried to explain to his critics that the sculpture was to distil the 'essence of war sacrifice. A great burden of pain, horror and annihilation was laid on the youthful manhood of this nation. The quiet, continuous influence of women throughout the war ... [who] received no honour, praise or decoration.' He went on to point out that although many women were not directly involved in the war, they lost their sons, husbands, friends and lovers, all the time enduring their sacrifices without a murmur, in other words, 'sacrificing themselves'.

The Catholic Church was vociferous in its outrage, especially disapproving of the naked human body. For Hoff the male and female bodies were beautiful, sex was beautiful – everything natural was. He was also vilified by his own artistic brethren, the Master Builders Association, and the local chapter of the Royal Australian Institute of Architects over the 'immorality' of the stylistic figures and the symbolism of the groups' 'Crucifixion of Civilisation' and 'Victory after Sacrifice'. Other criticisms were that Hoff and Dellit did not depict the glory of war, rather its tragedy and horror. For both men the heroism of the dead shines more brilliantly when the viewer recognises the ghastly circumstances in which it was enacted. 'That,' said Dellit, 'is why the statuary is so gaunt and uncompromising.'

For the official historian of World War I, CEW Bean, the structure was disappointing. He had lent Hoff his own photographs from the war and bemoaned the result:

> I do not think the conventional modern style should be
> adopted in any figures on a memorial. The style at present in
> vogue demands the portrayal of figures with triangular facets,
> stiff angles, and dumpy swollen limbs, which give them the
> appearance of totems ... I'm afraid that they may someday be
> laughed at.

Despite the carping, the memorial is an exquisite collaboration between an architect and a sculptor and has come to be seen as such. It lacks pomposity and melodrama, and invites contemplation and awe at the sacrifices that the war wrought. The large tranquil pool of reflection leading up to the entrance is precisely that. Visitors become part of the building as they walk towards it and are reflected in the water.

In November 1934 Prince Henry, Duke of Gloucester, opened the Anzac Memorial before a crowd of 100 000 people. The ceremony was preceded by 20 000 ex-servicemen and women marching from the Domain, all singing wartime tunes as they approached Hyde Park. But the building was unfinished. Because of the Depression there was no money to complete Dellit's design – a large water cascade on the southern side of the memorial was missing, as was a new entrance and walkway. These were finally opened in 2018.

The huge crowd attending the opening in 1934 had only been matched in 1879 when 60 000 people attended the unveiling of the huge statue of Captain Cook to mark the centenary of his death. That monument dominates the highest point in the park, the corner near Park and College street. The larger-than-life bronze figure shows the great British explorer, cartographer and navigator holding out a telescope in his left hand, his right hand extended upwards. Created by the English artist Thomas Woolner, it was described by the British *Art Journal* at the time as 'unquestionably a work designed with force and spirit that raise it to the character of the sensational'.

Four inscriptions surround the base of the statue. On the front face: *Captain Cook, this statue was erected by public subscription, assisted by a grant from the New South Wales government, 1879.* On the western side: *Born at Marton in Yorkshire 1728.* On the eastern side: *Killed at Owhyhee 1779.* And on the southern side: *Discovered this Territory 1770.*

Over a hundred years later that inscription on the southern side has caused much heated debate. As the prominent Indigenous journalist Stan Grant says, the idea that Cook discovered this land was 'a damaging myth'. In 2017 a vandal sprayed the statue with graffiti reading *Change the Date* and *No pride in genocide*. The first was a reference to the controversy over celebrating Australia Day on 26 January, when Governor Phillip raised the British flag at Sydney Cove (a majority of contemporary Sydneysiders believe that Cook was part of the First Fleet). There is no doubt that the First Fleet was, in its way, an invasion that was to have terrifying and long-lasting consequences for the First Australians.

What would amaze the thirsty people of Sydney who came to collect water from Busby's Bore in the early nineteenth century is the ubiquitous presence of water in Hyde Park north and south. Huge volumes of water are visible everywhere, from the cascade bouncing down the southern entrance of the Anzac Memorial, the vast Pool of Reflection, the water-filled sculpture dedicated to Busby in Hyde Park north, and the Archibald Fountain's lavish choreographed display of water.

THE HEDONIST DECADE

THE BEAUTY AND MAGIC NEVER FADE. Every time I walk from Circular Quay down the footpath towards the Opera House is like the first time. I momentarily stop and inwardly gasp at the sight. There before me, as if rising from the harbour itself, are the curvaceous and brilliantly white shells of the Opera House.

The building and its surrounds sit on Bennelong Point (Dubbagullee), once home to Governor Phillip's Aboriginal friend Bennelong, then Fort Macquarie with its castellations, then a ramshackle tram depot. From this eyesore rose one of the most innovative architectural achievements of its time.

Begun in 1959, it was finally opened in 1973. Designed by the Danish architect Jørn Utzon, the construction had been dogged by controversy, especially its escalating costs and frequent delays. In the beginning an optimistic Utzon suggested it would only take two years to build. Its prolonged gestation was a mixture of tragedy and triumph, involving much personal turmoil, conflicts, divorces, disappointment, political bungling, petty-minded officials, stormy walkouts and sullen silences. The building changed lives, and an ABC reporter and her crew died when their helicopter crashed while they were filming it.

After enervating arguments with philistine government bureaucrats, Utzon resigned. The Opera House was completed by an Australian architectural team led by Peter Hall. Hall, a workaholic, found himself with plans that were chaotic and unfinished. His achievement has always been undervalued. In later years he ended up bankrupt and homeless, his immense effort forgotten, dying an alcoholic at 64. For the rest of his life an indignant Utzon stubbornly refused all overtures to return to Sydney to see his magnificent creation. As the architect Philip Cox said, 'All involved were losers – except the people of Australia, who gained the Sydney Opera House.'

English diarist and snob James Lees-Milne visited Australia in 1980 and marvelled, 'The Opera House is astonishing … Architecturally it is a revelation of dare-devilry and outrage. And it succeeds.' Some Australians thought the structure resembled a beached whale; others, nine nuns playing football; or a bunch of nails clipped from an albino dog. It was a precious fluke, a rare instance of Australia reaching for the stars – or, as former prime minister Paul Keating said, 'It's more art than architecture.'

I had come to Sydney from Melbourne at an exhilarating time. By the late 1970s the strict financial markets were relaxing, global trade was increasing, as was merchant banking. Most of the trade in mining stocks originated in Sydney, with the result that Melbourne was losing its reputation as the nation's business centre. The globalisation of markets encouraged a shift to Sydney because it had an international airport and faced the Pacific with its American and Asian markets. As one Melbourne banker put it, 'It's more New York and we're more Boston.'

Sydney had also become the headquarters of Australian media companies: John Fairfax's empire and Kerry Packer's Consolidated Press had deep roots in the city, and Murdoch's rapidly expanding News Limited had its head office in Sydney.

Melbourne still regarded itself as the arts capital of Australia, but the more exciting theatre and film was happening in what Melburnians called 'Tinsel Town'. They sneered that Sydney was materialistic and facile, whereas their city was a breeding ground for the serious and non-commercial arts. The left-wing Australian Performing Group (APG) in bohemian Carlton, a defiantly heterosexual theatre, dismissed Sydney theatre as being run by the 'gay mafia'. What I was to discover was that, unlike the factional theatre scene in the southern capital, in Sydney there was no rivalry between companies, even though they each had singular sensibilities and politics.

A playwright who escaped the suffocating ideological bonds of the APG and its Marxist apparatchiks was David Williamson, who came to Sydney in the early 1980s. He would write a highly successful play satirising the cultural divide between the two cities, *Emerald City*.

Like most of his works this was highly autobiographical. The central character in *Emerald City* is Colin, a Melbourne screenwriter with principles still intact (a rare creature indeed), who moves to Sydney 'along the yellow brick road' in search of its vitality, while constantly comparing the cities: 'It never rains in buckets like it does in Sydney.' His wife is a publishing executive and, according to Colin, her friends are 'chardonnay socialists'. Of course, she protests at the move to Sydney because of its commercialism and materialism. Colin's struggle is between art and commercialism, between being broke and having money, between artistic integrity and the nightmare of selling out. Then there is the allure of owning a house with a harbour view. As the actress Ruth Cracknell, who played a film producer in the original production, said in an interview, 'In *Emerald City*, Sydney's playing the same role as New York or London ... it's a battle between ethics and material gain.' Or as her character Elaine puts it, 'Don't blame the city, the demons are in us.'

In reality Sydney theatre was invigorated by an extraordinary range of talent that made Melbourne theatre seem stagnant and naval gazing. Jim Sharman, who had directed musicals like *Jesus Christ Superstar* and *Rocky Horror* in London, had earlier made *Hair* a success back home and was now in a productive artistic relationship with Patrick White, directing plays like *A Cheery Soul*. Sharman and Rex Cramphorn set up the daring Paris Theatre Company in 1978 as an alternative to the major theatre, the Old Tote. The Paris was underfunded and went broke quickly, but its brief presence weakened the importance of a moribund Old Tote, which folded. From the ashes emerged the Sydney Theatre Company, run by Richard Wherrett. His early decision to look to American plays and musicals for inspiration rather than English ones shocked the more conservative audiences. Unlike Melbourne, which underutilised its set and costume designers, Sydney embraced them, giving its productions a special sheen that enhanced the theatre experience. There was also a wonderful flowering of acting talent that would endure on our stages and screens for years, such as John Bell, Judy Davis, John Gaden, Robyn Nevin and Colin Friels.

In the late 1970s the most compelling Australian films originated from Sydney directors: Phillip Noyce's *Newsfront*, Peter Weir's *Picnic at Hanging Rock*, Gillian Armstrong's *My Brilliant Career* and Bruce Beresford's *Breaker Morant*. I remember sitting in a Melbourne cinema before I came to live in Sydney and experiencing one of the most marvellous and original Australian films I had ever seen, Weir's *The Last Wave*.

The story centres on David Burton, a white solicitor in Sydney whose seemingly normal life is disrupted after he takes on a murder case and discovers that he shares a strange mystical connection with a small group of local Aboriginal people accused of the crime. Sydney becomes inundated with heavy and never-ending rainstorms, sometimes resulting in disturbing black sludge falling from the sky. Only the Aboriginal people seem to know the cosmological significance of this freakish weather.

The film climaxes with Burton escaping through a sewer tunnel and emerging onto a beach not unlike Bondi, where he gazes up in horrified awe as a huge apocalyptic wave rises into the sky, threatening to engulf him and Sydney.

The film's ambition was something I had never seen before in Australian movies and, as I was to experience in my first years living there, the story could only have come out of Sydney. Sometimes the summer rainstorms seem as apocalyptic as those in Weir's movie.

The visiting Englishman James Lees-Milne remarked in his diaries, 'Sydneyans try to be like New Yorkers ... the tempo is rushed, the temper frayed.' What he didn't pick up as a visitor was the effervescent excitement in the air, the sense that Sydney was changing in profound ways.

One of the first times I was aware of a particular Sydney style of restaurant and food was at the Blue Water Grill at the northern end of Bondi Beach. It seemed open to the elements with a spectacular vista of the beach and the Pacific. The dress code was casual, unlike stuffy Melbourne's formality, and the young chef, Neil Perry, created a quintessential Sydney fusion of Asian and Australian influences: chargrilled ocean fresh seafood, chilli sauces, coconut sambal, fragrant green curry, delicious white wine and views of the iconic beach, with its strutting lifesavers, handsome surfers and sunbaking hedonists. It seemed so Sydney, so dazzling. After the restaurant closed Perry opened Rockpool in the late 1980s, a formal dining room in the Rocks with a pricey menu that offered more extravagant variations of the Asian-spiced seafood at the Blue Water Grill. The lavish interior set a pattern for the next decade, when investors would spend millions on the fit-out of a new restaurant.

But it was the Bayswater Brasserie in Kings Cross that was to epitomise the 1980s. The design was French brasserie, including the black and white tiled floor and paper covered tables. It was the place to be, a hugely popular spot, cheerful, light-hearted and buzzing with businesspeople, lawyers, journalists, publishers, film producers, directors, writers and actors. It was said that probably every film that got made in the 1980s and early 1990s had its beginnings over lunch or dinner there. Like Perry's Blue Water Grill, the atmosphere was informal and during the summer evenings the windows along the street were open and the scent of the jasmine creepers outside mingled with the humidity to create a heady fragrance. The food was adventurous and not expensive, a compelling blend of Mediterranean dishes with Asian and Middle Eastern influences. This Sydney style of food at the Bayswater Brasserie and Perry's restaurants eventually found a name – Modern Australian.

Fashion also developed a unique Sydney style through the efforts of Jenny Kee and Linda Jackson. In 1973 Kee and Jackson opened Flamingo Park, a boutique in the stylish Strand Arcade. At the entrance a sign invited you to 'Step into Paradise' – and indeed, it was. It was quite a shock for someone like me who had been used to Melbourne women dressed in funeral black to walk into the boutique and be visually assailed by such electric colours. The shop lived up to Kee's aim 'to create an experience like no other'. It had taken off immediately and became a mecca for overseas celebrities like David Bowie, George Harrison and Lauren Bacall. Even Princess Di wore one of Kee's jumpers with its deliberately twee koala motif.

Kee was born in Bondi, with Chinese ancestry on her father's side and Anglo-Italian on her mother's. Jackson had been brought up on Melbourne's beaches. The two were very different. Kee's clothes were a bright riot of colour, and she favoured fiery red lipstick and glasses with vividly coloured frames. She was gregarious and outgoing compared to the quieter Jackson, who had a disarming shyness mixed with steely determination and the disconcerting stare of someone sizing you up. Their first fashion show had been held in a Chinese restaurant and completely changed how fashion shows were done in Australia. Their collaboration reached its apotheosis in 1983 with a startling parade in Jackson's studio, a showroom in William Street.

Their muse was the Australian landscape, flowers and fauna and, in Jackson's case, the flashes of colour in opal stones. There was nothing demure about their colours, which took inspiration from the bright light of Sydney. Sometimes it took a brave woman to wear Jackson's dresses and not be overshadowed by their flamboyance. The pair's clothes achieved the level of art and, as Sydney's cultural impresario Leo Schofield said, 'They are the wizards of Oz fashion.'

Colour helped explain the immense popularity of the artist Ken Done. Art critics may have scorned his work, but he, perhaps more than any other artist, defined a Sydney look in the 1980s, one that appealed to locals, tourists and overseas visitors, especially the Japanese. His detractors have been many. The artist Brett Whiteley sneered that 'I would rather take methadone than Ken Done', and the *Sydney Morning Herald*'s art reviewer John McDonald dubbed him, 'The DJ of Sydney's perpetual dance party.' One critic, Scott Bevan, more open to the artist's work, remarked, 'If you had to put a face to Sydney, it could be that of Ken Done ... it is through Done's eyes that so many people have seen Sydney. The art of Ken Done has helped millions around the globe put a face to Sydney.'

Done was born in 1940 in Belmore, a suburb of Sydney well beyond the siren call of the harbour. He always remembered the regular ferry trip from Circular Quay as a boy to visit his grandparents across the harbour at Fairy Bower during World War II. He relished watching the 'foam boiling under the Manly ferry' and the vessel threading its way through an anti-submarine gate near the harbour entrance. As a teenager he went to live on the North Shore close to the harbour in Cremorne and Balmoral.

The harbour became his playground, its water, sand and light a catalyst for his paintings. His boyish enthusiasm shines through in ebullient, explosive colours as if he's thrown his palette at the canvas. His Sydney is a constant party. There's no wallowing in introspection. Life is optimistic and intoxicating. Sydney seems on a permanent holiday in an eternal summer, even his night-time scenes of moonlight shining off the water have a joyous luminosity.

His subjects are simple, and all based around the harbour and the beaches, the Opera House, the bridge, sunbakers on the sand, sailors, children paddling in the water. He's painted the harbour from every conceivable angle, in every colour: aquamarine blue, bright yellows, red, intense greens, calm whites. But yellow is probably the colour Done uses most, indeed his cadmium yellow is almost a visual signature. 'Some people will say I took the beige out of Australia,' he boasted.

The paintings became so popular that he opened up the lucrative Done Art and Design shop in the Rocks. By the end of the 1980s there were 15 Ken Done stores across Australia. His 'product' (his word) was seemingly in every house in the nation – doona covers, swimming costumes, T-shirts, towels, sunglasses, cufflinks, coasters, place mats. He even became like a trademark himself with his florid moustache and uniform of striped sailor's top.

His designs were everywhere, and copycats flagrantly plagiarised them. In the 1980s, as the artist said, 'If anything had a lot of bright colours on it they would say, "That's a Ken Done".'

If any one person epitomised the excesses of Sydney in the 1980s and its darker consequences, it was Geoffrey Edelsten. He had trained as a doctor, started a record company that released some of his songs, and became known for his unconventional medical clinics and glamorous lifestyle. He had worked as a doctor in the early 1970s, spent three years in Los Angeles, and on returning to Sydney started to operate innovative 24-hour medical centres fitted with chandeliers, grand pianos and mink-covered examination tables. The clinics attracted much media attention, which he craved. He dressed in white suits that matched his pasty face, owned mansions, helicopters and a fleet of Rolls-Royces and Lamborghinis with licence plates such as *Macho*, *Spunky* and *Sexy*. In 1984 he married his first wife, Leanne Nesbitt, a blonde model 20 years younger than him. Part of his flamboyant image was that he was said to have a pink helicopter. Even though it was actually blue and white, pink seemed to suit his public persona.

A year after he was married, he became the first private owner of a major Australian football team, South Melbourne. The team had been a basket case for years and it was hoped that by shifting it north it would prosper. Melbourne football writers could hardly believe that this doctor with his gimmicky medical clinics, who outrageously flaunted his wealth in typical Sydney fashion, would be the team's saviour. It was renamed the Sydney Swans, and Edelsten gloried in even more media attention.

Then, towards the end of the decade, his life and career began to unravel. In 1988 he was removed from the New South Wales medical register for using unqualified staff for laser surgery. Convinced he was above the law, Edelsten approached the psychopathic hitman, Christopher Flannery, to assault a former patient. In 1990 he was jailed for one year for perverting the course of justice and soliciting an assault. He divorced, gave up the Sydney Swans, and fled Sydney for a suburban life in Melbourne, where he started up a new series of clinics. In 2015, still craving media attention, he was a contestant in the reality TV show *Celebrity Apprentice Australia.*

*

In the 1980s Oxford Street became the locus of gay social life. By the beginning of the decade it was home to a string of bars, clubs, saunas, sex shops and cafés known as Sydney's gay 'Golden Mile'. This emergence of a gay heartland was an extraordinary social change, as male homosexuality remained illegal in New South Wales until 1984.

Of course, what couldn't be ignored was the annual Gay and Lesbian Mardi Gras. It had its beginnings on the night of 24 June 1978 when more than 500 people gathered on Oxford Street in a 'festival' calling for an end to discrimination against homosexuals, an end to police harassment and the repeal of anti-homosexual laws. The crowd grew to nearly 2000 as gays poured out of the bars and clubs to join the celebration. Although the organisers had obtained permission, the police rescinded it without warning. As the parade was dispersing in Kings Cross, the police viciously broke it up and arrested 53 people. Although most charges were eventually dropped, the *Sydney Morning Herald* published the names of those arrested, leading to many people being outed to their shocked and occasionally disgusted family, friends and workmates.

By the late 1980s the Sydney Mardi Gras was one of the largest such festivals in the world. It attracted hundreds of thousands of people from around Australia and overseas. Some stood on wonky shop awnings or stolen milk crates to get a view of the extravagant floats, the muscular semi-naked men covered in oil and glitter, the drag queens and lesbians all making their joyful way along Oxford Street and down to Moore Park. Despite conservatives and churches railing against it, the Sydney Gay and Lesbian Mardi Gras became one of Australia's biggest tourist drawcards.

Sydney's exuberant gay scene was a favourite subject of the photographer William Yang. He was born to Chinese parents in Mareeba in far north Queensland and came down to Sydney in the 1970s. His unique images document gay life, its loves, drugs and wild parties. As AIDS ravaged the gay scene, he was on the front line, revealing the tragic suffering behind the glamour and glitter of nightclubs and drag shows. One of his most moving series follows the decline of a friend dying of the terrible disease as he becomes incapacitated and slips into a final coma.

But Yang was more than a photographer of gay social life, he was a photographic Pepys, documenting the world around him – the pleasures of the beach and its iconic lifesavers, the social world that revolved around the writer Patrick White, weddings, actors, theatre directors, social events, artists, writers, Jenny Kee and Linda Jackson of course, and the movers and shakers of the city. He documented the decade with lucidity, humour and sometimes with the necessary cold-hearted gaze of the artist.

His 1984 book *Sydney Diary* is the perfect time capsule of the 1980s, recording the emergence of the gay community and party scenes, the city's prominent identities and the exuberance of the era when Sydney perfected hedonism.

THIS SMALL BLOCK
OF DARLINGHURST

IT'S JUST AFTER FIVE ON AN AUTUMN AFTERNOON. As usual my wife Mandy and I are having a late weekend lunch at Una's in Victoria Street, Darlinghurst. It's been here for over 50 years. The interior is cosy with kitschy wooden chairs and reproductions of snow-capped mountains. The restaurant specialises in German, Austrian and Hungarian food. The schnitzels are enormous, and I defy anyone to finish the giant pork knuckles.

We sit at one of four outside tables, our dog Basil, a chihuahua cross, sits on my lap as we wait for our meals. Mandy bought him as a puppy over a decade ago from a local drug dealer on the streets of Kings Cross. He was a tiny, dismal thing, a skeleton cloaked in thin fur with huge ears he had yet to grow into. Now he's plump and happy, except when visiting the vet a few doors down from where we sit.

Una's has a diverse collection of patrons. There is the grey-bearded widower who arrives a little after us for his dinner, which he demolishes quickly and leaves. There's the glum former dentist whose stellar career was ruined by cocaine, the large middle-aged Anglo men with their petite Chinese or Filipina wives, the ones who live by themselves and have an aura of loneliness as they eat. There are birthday parties, as there is this evening – a girl dressed as a princess in a frilly pink frock is celebrating her fifth birthday. There is the smartly dressed woman who is quiet and demure inside the restaurant but outside is loud and foul-mouthed. Divorced fathers caring for their children of a weekend are frequent customers, as are bleary-eyed unshaven men hoping the comfort food will rid them of their hangovers. There are gay couples, and people of Austrian and German background who come for food that reminds them of home. If the Swans are playing an afternoon game then families wearing red and white, will drift into the restaurant from the Sydney Cricket Ground to celebrate or commiserate. Unlike other restaurants, this is one where the man has chosen where to eat and a reluctant wife or girlfriend tags behind him, concerned at how rich the meals are and the huge number of calories involved. As usual, always at the same time, three tiny Filipina nurses, still wearing their uniforms, seemingly inseparable and chatting excitedly all at once, hurry past our table heading home. Two dogs tied up outside the grocer shop next door whine and bark, one annoyed, the other upset, at their owners disappearing inside without them.

Una's is near the corner of Surrey Street, and 50 metres further down Victoria Street is Liverpool Street. This small block between Surrey and Liverpool streets is a vivid microcosm of the suburb of Darlinghurst. Two Italian restaurants face one another across Victoria Street, two Thai restaurants also face each other, and two Japanese, one on each side of the street.

Directly across from us at Una's is Rough Edges. A colourful mural depicting St John's church and its environs stretches across its wide frontage. Staffed by volunteers, it's opened six nights a week for two hours each evening. Free drinks and food are given to the homeless, the needy, the mentally disturbed. This evening it's closed because it's Saturday.

While we wait for our food, Barry, the gaunt ice addict, restlessly walks back and forth across the road, oblivious to the traffic of cars, police paddy wagons, incessant fire engines (Basil howls in unison with their sirens), motorbikes and delivery bicycles. As always, Barry is ranting about the evils of parents drinking alcohol in front of their children. In the deepest throes of an ice binge he will create a miniature garden of twigs around the base of the towering plane tree outside the restaurant, lambasting delivery riders who come to pick up takeaways and accidentally crush the precious garden with the wheels of their bikes. Today he is shouting to the world, 'I wish my mother hadn't committed suicide ten years ago on her birthday'. He seldom eats during these benders and Andy, the German waiter, will come outside and hand him food in a container. Barry promises he will eat it, but I have never seen him do so. He has more important things to do, like gardening or warning the world of the ills of drink and drugs.

A hundred metres behind us is William Street, dividing Kings Cross from Darlinghurst (named after the martinet, Governor Ralph Darling). The two suburbs couldn't be more different. Kings Cross is vanishing as the affluent Potts Point seeps slowly towards William Street. Real estate agents have come to regard the name Kings Cross as a liability. To them, it's Potts Point South.

Sydney's lock-out laws were introduced in 2014 to combat alcohol-fuelled violence in the area. In addition to a number of restrictions (such as not serving shots after midnight), legislation was introduced requiring 1.30 a.m. venue lockouts and 3 a.m. last drinks. Assaults decreased, but many businesses closed due to lack of trade, and gradually the Cross lost its mojo. It was no longer party central. Swish restaurants and cafés, antique shops and hipster bars have become common. One of the biggest projects in the last 50 years is about to begin. The block between the El Alamein Fountain and Roslyn Street will be demolished and iconic sites such as the Bourbon and Beefsteak and the Empire

Hotel (once the home of Les Girls and then the Carousel Club, where Juanita Nielsen was last seen) will be no more. In their place will be an 18-storey block of apartments with a café, restaurant and shops on the ground floor. The plan will transform Darlinghurst Road and the social fabric of what remains of Kings Cross.

For the middle class and upper middle class of Potts Point, pressing matters are finding senior yoga classes, the best manicurists, exclusive cheese shops, the most prestigious perfumier and ways to rid Macleay Street of beggars and the unsightly homeless.

Just over William Street to the south is the Tropicana Caffe that opened in 1980. It specialises in focaccias, pasta and coffee. The chairs are simple and the tables functional. It was once home to Tropfest, the international short film contest that became so successful it had to shift to the Domain. You still see customers sitting by themselves, lingering for hours over their coffees as they write screenplays on their laptops. Across from Tropicana, on the eastern side of Victoria Street, is a line of empty shops that were once thriving restaurants, cafés and pizza bars. The Covid pandemic made them unprofitable, and they stand as abject witnesses to those cruel two years, most of them now with For Lease signs plastered on their windows.

Mandy and I can walk to Una's, which is just a few minutes from our apartment opposite the sandstone fire station, built in 1912. Because of Darlinghurst's high density, it is one of the busiest suburbs in Australia. There's an evocative 1930 photograph of it in the City of Sydney archives: the fire station stands proudly alone, its rounded front like a puffed-out chest. Now the building is hemmed in by two busy streets either side of it. A needle disposal unit is bolted to the outside wall.

On our way we usually take a short cut from Darlinghurst Road to Victoria Street through the walkway of Hammond Care, a social housing project for the destitute and disabled. The site, owned by the church, was once a petrol station, then a car wash. On warm days, silent old men sit in their wheelchairs, faces upturned to bask in the sun, as if they are warming their blood. Sometimes stoned teenagers sit on the narrow sloping strip of lawn under the jacaranda tree, giggling and staring at their phones.

A cyclone fence is the boundary between the care home and St John's Anglican Church, whose spire can be seen towering over this part of Darlinghurst. Opened in 1858, the sandstone church complete with tower, spire, transepts and chancel, is one of the few unaltered Edmund Blacket buildings in Sydney and a glorious example of Gothic Revival.

Mandy and I were married there in 2003. At the time I had a vague recollection that it had been briefly famous. And it had. In 1987 its rector, Reverend John McKnight, was in Washington to support Israeli technician Mordechai Vanunu, who was on trial in Jerusalem for treason and espionage after divulging his country's nuclear secrets. Eighteen months earlier, Vanunu had been a backpacker living in a Kings Cross hostel, earning money as a dishwasher and later a taxi driver. One night Vanunu, a Moroccan Jew, walked into the church and accepted an invitation to join its Bible study group. He developed an intense interest in Christianity and McKnight baptised the former yeshiva student in his Darlinghurst church.

While in Sydney Vanunu told a journalist about a nuclear facility in Israel's Negev Desert where he had worked. It was a secret that Israel, an ally of the United States, didn't want the world to know. After the truth was exposed, Vanunu, a stubborn and at times naïve man, flew to London, where he was seduced by a woman working undercover for the Israeli secret police. She lured him to Rome, where he was kidnapped, drugged and flown to Israel. He was given a deliberately harsh sentence for betraying state secrets in a closed trial. Defiantly Christian, and refusing to speak Hebrew, he spent the next 18 years in prison, 12 of them in solitary confinement.

St John's church once had a school next door, and two of its graduates would become important players in Australia's early film industry. The actress Louise Lovely was born Nellie Louise Carbasse in 1895. Her Swiss mother had come to Australia in 1891 as a member of Sarah Bernhardt's theatre company. She decided to stay in Sydney, and married an Italian. From a young age Lovely wanted to act, and after starring in Australian films, moved to America, becoming the first Australian actress to have a successful career in Hollywood. In 1924 she returned to Sydney, where she and her husband wrote and directed *Jewelled Nights*. It was a success but never recouped its costs. The disillusioned actress retired from the movie business, remarried and moved to Hobart in 1946, where her new husband became manager of a theatre. She ran its lolly shop until her death in 1980.

Raymond Longford's father was a warder at Darlinghurst Gaol not far from his son's school. Longford became a film director, writer, producer and actor during the silent era. Perhaps his most famous movie was an adaptation of CJ Dennis's 1915 verse narrative *The Sentimental Bloke*.

If Mandy and I don't take this short cut through Hammond Care, we continue along Darlinghurst Road, past the church and its large rectory, and the gorgeous art deco apartment building the Savoy, where Eadith Walker had resided for a period. Then we come to the Darlo Bar on the corner. It was the pub where Mandy held a wake for her father after he died at the hospice a block further south. Half a dozen well-known comedians used to drink in a corner of the pub that overlooked the footpath, but one by one cancer killed them until no one would sit there for fear of an early death.

If we turn right, it's only a short walk to Margaret Fink's heritage house. An original member of the Sydney Push, she remained friends with others of the group, including Germaine Greer. The stylish and vivacious Fink held so many dinner parties and soirees with painters, writers, actors, directors and producers that her home became the Australian equivalent of a French salon. Her last produced film was *Candy*, about the doomed love affair between two junkies in Kings Cross, with Heath Ledger playing the lead.

If we were to continue in a straight line, we'd pass the Jewish Museum. Originally it was the Maccabean Hall, commemorating the Jewish men and women who served in World War I, and was opened by the great Australian Jewish general Sir John Monash in 1923. It has a surprisingly bland exterior given what is inside. In 1992 Holocaust survivors opened the museum to commemorate and pass on their experiences of the Holocaust so they will never be forgotten.

Across the street from the museum is Green Park, stretching down to St Vincent's huge hospital complex. The first thing that strikes you is a giant pink triangle made of enamelled steel. The artwork, just across the road from the Jewish Museum, commemorates the homosexual men and women who were victims of the Nazis and of Soviet labour camps. On the western side of Green Park is the former Darlinghurst Gaol with its imposing sandstone walls. In 1841 the prisoners from the jail in the Rocks were marched up streets lined with curious spectators to be its first inmates.

The park was named after an Alderman Green, although some think it's named after the hangman Alexander Green. Alexander arrived in Sydney as a convict in 1824 and became the town's assistant hangman in 1828. By the time he moved to Darlinghurst Gaol in July 1841 he was Sydney's permanent hangman. Described as simple-minded, very ugly, with pockmarked skin and stumps for teeth, he had a livid scar down one side of his face courtesy of an axe attack by a prisoner. He was given a whitewashed hut in what is now Green Park, but was forced to move inside the jail when larrikins burned his house down in 1842. After a career that saw him hang 490 people, the despised executioner fell into insanity and was committed to the Tarban Creek Asylum in 1856, where he remained until he died 23 years later.

If you look closely, you can see the Victor Chang Memorial on the corner of Burton and Victoria streets, which commemorates the surgeon who performed Australia's first successful heart transplant in 1984 at St Vincent's Hospital. He was murdered in a bungled extortion attempt in 1991. I have an emotional connection to him because one of the last lives he saved was my Uncle Bob, who had written a successful play *No Names, No Pack Drill*, based on my mother's relationship with an American who went AWOL during World War II. The play was set in an apartment block just the other side of William Street in Kings Cross.

During the 1970s and early 1980s, teenage boys used to line the eastern wall of the former jail waiting to be picked up by men cruising past in their cars. We knew one such prostitute who ended up being 'cared for' by a much older gay man. He was from Newcastle originally and had escaped his abusive childhood to work the Wall. By his late twenties, his mind was permanently scattered, he was virtually illiterate and, when in the grip of paranoia and fear, would put black paper over all his windows so no sunlight could get in and there he would live in darkness for months.

More often, unless walking Basil, we don't go as far as Green Park, and instead we turn left at the Darlo Bar and head down Liverpool Street towards Victoria Street. As we stroll, the thing that impresses are the large number of five- and six-storey apartment blocks built between the 1920s and 1940s. Seventy-seven per cent of people in Darlinghurst live in flats or apartments, another 21 per cent in semi-detached or terrace houses. In fact, just 0.5 per cent live in freestanding houses, compared to the national average of 73 per cent.

Basil and Coco, our deceased chihuahua, used to demand to stop at the entrance to grotty Hayden Lane so they could sniff the rubbish bins and urine stains left by other dogs. Not so long ago the narrow, grim laneway underwent a remarkable transformation, the rubbish bins replaced by luxuriant shrubs and tropical plants.

Sebastian Vasquez had lived in the lane for two decades and one day when he was tending to his 'guerrilla' garden, which he had established to try and make the laneway more attractive, a passer-by told him how a young woman's body had been found in the lane back in 1997.

Rebecca Bernauer was adopted, but she didn't get on with her parents. The troubled teenager ran away from home and headed to Kings Cross. A heroin user since she was 15, she had started to attend Narcotics Anonymous the year she died. Known as 'Charlie', she worked as a prostitute near the corner of Forbes and William streets. The 18 year old was found on 9 June 1997, stuffed behind an abandoned refrigerator. Initially police believed she had died from a heroin overdose, but the autopsy revealed she had been raped and strangled. She was killed just days before she was due to give evidence against a former policeman in a drug case. In 2000 police conducted DNA testing of clients and workers at a brothel near the laneway where Rebecca's body was found. After several years they found a match with a cleaner at the brothel. They arrested him in a boarding house near the murder scene.

Vasquez now has a plant growing in a rusted pot that marks the spot where Rebecca's body was found. The plant is a bromeliad, which brings a touch of the tropics to the lane. It's a variety prized for its thick foliage that grows in a natural rosette. The wide leaves grow around a central cup that catches water to sustain itself. The bromeliad is a moving memorial for a victim who was another instance of how this area can destroy the vulnerable.

A further 20 metres along the street, we come to the corner with Victoria Street, and diagonally opposite stands the Federation-style Green Park Hotel. For 127 years the pub was a fixture in Darlinghurst, an extremely popular place for nurses, doctors and staff of St Vincent's, gays and straights. But in 2020 it was bought by the hospital as a mental health clinic and suicide prevention centre. It stands empty, its conversion paused because of the pandemic.

We turn left into Victoria Street and squeeze past a long queue of customers waiting to get into the Messina gelato bar. It's so fashionable that people come from Potts Point and as far away as the inner suburbs to buy the ice cream. The eager swarm is well dressed and affluent, their children squirming with impatience. A little further on, past an upmarket florist, is Gino's an Italian restaurant and bar. Occasionally in summer Mandy and I sit at an outside table watching the passing parade and are amazed at just how different the people are from those across the road at Una's. These people are young and hip and strut with confidence. There are many gay couples in their late twenties and early thirties with close-cropped hair, trimmed beards and taut gym-fashioned bodies, some of them holding hands. They're an indication of a unique Sydney demographic: the suburb has a higher percentage of male residents than the national average, which is nearly 50 per cent. In Darlinghurst 58 per cent of residents are male and 42 per cent female. At Una's many of the gay men who come to eat are older, their bodies succumbing to middle-aged spread.

After we sit down at Una's, without being asked Andy hands me a glass of white wine and Mandy a lemon, lime and bitters.

This evening as we wait for our meal, a woman we know stops at our table, Robyn Greaves, who helps run the Kings Cross Community Centre. She's wearing a white mask and has just visited a mutual friend in St Vincent's, Peter Young, who has been diagnosed with terminal lung cancer. Peter was a voluble and staunch opponent of the City of Sydney's planned destruction of the Ilmar Berzins–designed Fitzroy Gardens. Peter, along with many others, defeated the project that was going to rid the Gardens of its opulent greenery of trees, ferns and flowers and popular use as a peaceful oasis, and replace it with pathways and banal lawns.

'You know,' Robyn says, 'Peter's always been a gloomy sort of bloke. Well, now he seems really sprightly at getting the bad news that he'll die soon.'

With a cheerful goodbye she heads off as Andy places a chicken schnitzel in front of Mandy and for me, a plate of *Kassler* (boiled pork). Basil is now at my feet waiting for scraps.

Loud giggles and shouts come from across the street. A hens' party of about ten young women has emerged from Gino's after downing cocktails. They stop outside Rough Edges and take selfies of each other before heading to another bar. They're wearing miniskirts, fishnet stockings and tottering high heels and are already tipsy. Their mother looks bemused, knowing she will have to be sober enough to get her daughter and her friends home safely. Once there used to be stag nights in the Cross but now there are only a couple of strip joints, so the boys go elsewhere.

We're halfway through our meals when a father, mother and ten-year-old daughter, wearing red and white scarfs, trudge into Una's.

'Did they win or lose?' I ask.

The father shakes his head, still trying to process what he's seen. 'Lost. I thought we had a real chance this year.'

'Maybe next year,' pipes up the daughter.

We finish and say goodbye to Andy. 'You coming tomorrow?' he asks. We say we are. We head home, taking the short cut through the Hammond Care walkway. We stop at the liquor shop, a few doors from our apartment, to buy a bottle of wine. Brett, the owner, is Greek. His family comes from Kythera, and generally there's a book about the island on his counter. He has no sons, but six daughters, which means he's going to be out of pocket when they all marry. When we enter, he's berating a customer.

'What do you mean, Vegan wine? What the fuck is that?' The chastised young man hurries outside. 'Now,' he says to us with a grin, 'what's new?'

A GLOBAL CITY

THERE WERE ABOUT 40 000 OF US TAKING PART in one of the largest marches ever held in Sydney. The crowd was made up of men, women and children, Indigenous and non-Indigenous. Busloads of Aboriginal and Torres Strait Island people had arrived from interstate and rural and remote communities to join the protest. People carried Aboriginal flags; hundreds wore T-shirts emblazoned with the flag. Placards lamented the British invasion of 1788. The marchers were protesting the colonisation of Australia that had caused injustice and suffering and the dispossession of the Aboriginal people. It was Australia Day, 26 January 1988. The mood of the marchers was surprisingly cheerful as we made our way to Hyde Park.

Not far away, in brilliant sunshine, two million people lined the foreshores of the harbour, the sky swarmed with raucous helicopters and 10 000 boats packed the water as a fleet of replica tall ships came through the Heads, re-enacting the events of 200 years ago. The *Australian Women's Weekly* summed up the euphoria:

> Well! What a party ... the eyes of the world were on us. January
> 26, 1988, was a day to remember! The focus may have been on
> Sydney Harbour with the royal visitors, majestic tall ships First
> Fleet and dazzling fireworks, but the celebrations were Australia's.

During the sesquicentenary 50 years before, a hundred Aboriginal men and women gathered at a hall in Sydney for 'A Day of Mourning'. Only four non-Aboriginal people were allowed to attend: two policemen, a journalist from *Man* magazine, and the right-wing, pro-Aboriginal author Percy 'Inky' Stephensen. The first speaker, Jack Patten, got straight to the point:

'On this day the white people are rejoicing, but we, as Aborigines, have no reason to rejoice on Australia's 150th birthday. Our purpose in meeting today is to bring home to the white people of Australia the frightful conditions in which the native Aborigines of this continent live.'

Other speakers recounted the horrors of dispossession and their desire for citizen rights, pointing out that the land had belonged to their forefathers and refusing to be pushed into the background of Australian society. Doug Nicholls expressed the meeting's frustration that the Australian public did not realise 'what our people have suffered for 150 years'.

Those protesters 50 years earlier would have been amazed at the size of the crowd marching to Hyde Park. The huge attendance was a visible sign of how many Aboriginal people had come to live in Sydney since the 1950s, reversing the trend of the early nineteenth century that saw their dispersal to La Perouse and rural areas. It was estimated there were 35 000 Aboriginal people living in Redfern and Waterloo in the 1960s, and the numbers kept increasing.

By the 1990s there was not only a highly politicised Indigenous population making its presence felt in Sydney, but the beginnings of a cultural movement that was as significant as the Harlem Renaissance was to America. Painters, actors, designers, filmmakers and dance companies like the internationally acclaimed Bangarra were all in one way or another addressing what Bangarra's manifesto described as, 'the burden of intergenerational trauma and crucially, the extraordinary power of art as a messenger for social change and healing'. By the middle of the nineteenth century the numbers of Aboriginal people in Sydney were so tiny, the settlers believed the population was dying out. But as the millennium approached, Indigenous people were living in Sydney in large numbers, reclaiming their culture and refashioning it in one of the most extraordinary social and cultural transformations the city has experienced.

But there were some disagreeable features to Sydney in the 1990s that were hard to ignore. By the 1990s hard drugs had made Kings Cross an epicentre of degradation, wretchedness and cruelty. A decade before, it had seemed the heroin epidemic couldn't get worse. The son of NSW Premier Barrie Unsworth died of a drug overdose in 1977, and in 1984 it was revealed that the daughter of Prime Minister Bob Hawke and her husband were heroin addicts. A legend of rugby league, Jack Gibson, would wander through the Cross talking to anyone who could tell him just how his son ended up an addict, dying of an overdose. Drugs had crossed all barriers of background, education and class.

If addicts found it difficult to score in the Cross or Darlinghurst, then they would take a train to Cabramatta in the western suburbs, where dealers offered cheap and reliable supplies of heroin. Cabramatta had been a centre for immigrants and refugees from Asia, particularly Vietnam, China, Laos, Cambodia and Thailand, since the 1970s, and Asian gangs ran the drug trade. One politician who tried to stop them was John Newman. He had arrived from Austria with his parents as Johann Grauenig (he later anglicised his name). His family settled in Cabramatta, and he attended local schools.

Newman had served as a member of the NSW Legislative Council from 1986 and was dismayed at how the suburb he grew up in was being terrorised by gangs. He waged a campaign to combat Asian organised crime and the political corruption, drug dealing, home invasions and prostitution that had turned his beloved Cabramatta into a hellhole. His car was vandalised, and he received numerous death threats. On the evening of 5 September 1994, he had just parked his car in his driveway when a hitman shot him twice, killing him instantly. It was Australia's first political assassination. Phuong Ngo, a political opponent who had run against Newman in 1991, was convicted of the murder in 2001.

What was becoming obvious was that the drug trade couldn't flourish without the help of corrupt police. In 1995 the Wood Royal Commission into the NSW Police Force spent 451 days hearing from 902 witnesses, and in the process revealed to the nation the extent of corruption, in Kings Cross especially, including bribery, money laundering, drug dealing, fabricating evidence and protection of paedophiles. Police Commissioner Tony Lauer resigned, his position untenable given the level of corruption. Many policemen joined him in resigning; others were arrested and 12 committed suicide.

Police corruption had always been a problem in Sydney. Premier Askin had presided over a corrupt regime in the late 1960s and early 1970s, but there were two men who, despite initially hating each other, would combine in the state parliament of the 1990s and 2000s to achieve a level of political corruption not seen, as one prosecutor put it, since the Rum Rebellion.

In 1988 Ian Macdonald, a member of the Labor Party's socialist left faction, was elected to the NSW Legislative Council. For people who, like me, knew him from university days back in Melbourne, it was a surprise. As a student leader he was regarded as a narcissist and a chancer who endlessly networked in order to reach the top rungs of student politics. He pretended an intimate knowledge of Marxist theory, but his mind was a junkyard of slogans, clichés and received opinions. He joined the Victorian Labor Party but his naked ambition and unwillingness to wait years for a parliamentary seat was anathema to many so, in a sensible move, he shifted to Sydney, where his cunning and ambition were admired. He was to head several ministries, but his Machiavellian political dealings meant he was in and out of favour with the revolving door of Labor premiers. A loudmouth and opponent of the right-wing faction of his own party, he loathed above all Eddie Obeid, the Labor party's 'power broker'.

Obeid arrived in Sydney from Lebanon as a six year old. Officially he had worked as a taxi driver and property developer, and had inherited property in Lebanon from his father, but no one knew exactly where his wealth came from when he was elected to the Legislative Council in 1991. After he made his maiden speech he never made one again. He was a shadowy figure who worked the back rooms, bestowing and receiving favours from other politicians and developers. He had a gift for manipulating factional numbers and votes. He was one of the richest members of parliament with nine children, a mansion, 'Passy', in posh Hunters Hill, properties in Lebanon, Port Macquarie, Terrigal, Concord and others tied up in a complex web of companies. Despite his wealth he always seemed to be on the prowl for more financial opportunities.

One of his great abilities was to recognise the character flaws of others. Even though Macdonald made it obvious that he despised people like Obeid, Eddie ignored the left-winger's abuse and set about gathering information about him. Macdonald had expensive tastes in food and wine, had recently remarried to a younger woman and had a considerable overdraft for his farm. Macdonald's enemies spoke about his duplicitous nature and his misuse of public funds.

An intrigued Eddie invited Macdonald to a dinner at a

Chinese restaurant where they ate the best foods and drank the most expensive wines. The rabid socialist made it clear that he didn't like what Eddie stood for politically. The meal didn't seem to help resolve their political and personal differences. When it came time to pay, Eddie paid half the bill in cash. He saw Macdonald pocket the cash and pay the whole bill with his Labor Party credit card.

Eddie now knew Macdonald's weakness – money. He began to flatter him, asking after his wife, his daughter, and listened sympathetically to his financial problems. Macdonald, who always thought he was the smartest guy in the room, fell for Eddie's oleaginous charm. The man who was constantly spouting Marxist rhetoric was now in thrall to a man who believed in nothing but money.

Macdonald began to be seen as a liability to the Labor Party over his perceived misuse of public funds and was being pushed to retire. It was then that Eddie saw his chance. During his final days in parliament Macdonald was Minister for Mineral and Forest Resources and Eddie knew that even with his considerable superannuation the avaricious socialist would need more money if he were to live in the style to which he had grown accustomed. Obeid's plan, backed up by his greedy and dim-witted son Moses, was one that would benefit all three. Macdonald's fate was sealed.

Macdonald came up with what he thought was a cunning plan to enrich himself, Eddie, and Eddie's son Moses. In 2008 he rigged a tender process for a coal exploration licence. The licence was granted over the Obeid family farm in the Bylong Valley near Mudgee. The result was a $30 million windfall for the Obeids.

At the same time, insatiable Eddie was being hounded by the tax department who were chasing almost $9 million in tax and penalties, and investigators were sniffing around another of

Eddie's dubious deals involving lucrative concessions on café leases secretly owned by his family at Circular Quay.

The coal licence bonanza couldn't be kept a secret, and following investigations by the state's anti-corruption body, Obeid and Macdonald were put on trial. Eddie, cocky as ever, told the media he would never spend an hour in jail. Macdonald, now completely bald, looked like an aged foetus as he walked to court through the media scrum with a permanent toothy grin that seemed disconcertingly maniacal.

In 2017 Macdonald was found guilty of two counts of wilful misconduct in public office and was   ed for ten years with a minimum of seven. After serving two years he was released on a technicality and, full of bombast, railed against the media, saying it had 'victimised' him. Soon he was to face another court ordeal, this time with Eddie and his boofhead son Moses. Following a complex year-long trial, the judge was satisfied beyond reasonable doubt that the three men had conspired to ensure the Obeids benefited from Macdonald's granting of the coal licence. In late 2021, more than a decade after the coal licence was issued, the trio were sentenced.

Eddie Obeid was given seven years with a minimum sentence of three years and ten months, Ian Macdonald nine years and six months with a minimum of five years and three months and Moses Obeid five years with a minimum of three. In a desperate attempt to stay out of jail both Eddie and Macdonald played the health card, tendering a string of letters from medical professionals arguing why they shouldn't be imprisoned. These included letters from GPs, a neurologist, an ophthalmic surgeon, a gastroenterologist, details of an appointment with a psychologist and brain surgeon, and doctors worried they might be susceptible to Covid in prison. Macdonald also pleaded that he suffered from incontinence and might need surgery. But it was no good. All three men ended up in jail.

Eddie's Order of Australia Medal was cancelled. Both men were finally thrown out of the Labor Party. Macdonald's ignominious end wasn't surprising for those who knew him at university. Always out for himself, he had fallen in with an unprincipled Sydney identity who recognised a fellow grifter and, in perverting the political system, they got the comeuppance they deserved. Macdonald had come up the yellow brick road from Melbourne to the Emerald City to pursue fame and fortune, only to find himself in league with the Wicked Witch of the West.

A decision of Premier Bob Carr in 1997 was to have greater ramifications for the state than Obeid's and Macdonald's notorious behaviour. The Proust-loving, sports-hating Carr decided to allow poker machines into New South Wales hotels, saying with a shrug that it was 'a bargain with the devil'. The devil won. There are now 95 000 machines in New South Wales, which means the state has more poker machines per capita than anywhere else in the world outside gambling meccas such as Macau. Some of the highest losses occur in the poorest regions of western Sydney. The social costs of poker machines have been enormous, causing relationship breakdowns, mental problems, embezzlement and, of course, debilitating financial stress.

The economic boom continued from the 1980s as Sydney strengthened its position as the financial capital of Australia. John Carroll in his book *Land of the Golden Cities: Australia's exceptional prosperity and the culture that made it*, said of Sydney that it's 'Australia's only global city. It is pre-eminent in attracting international tourists and corporate headquarters. It's Australia's media capital.' It was also, because of the bridge, the harbour and the Opera House, the most immediately identifiable Australian capital city for film audiences across the world. In *Mad Max: Beyond Thunderdome* the tribe of children abandoned in the desert finally return to civilisation only to find a shattered

Harbour Bridge and a dust-covered city devastated by nuclear attack. Many a big-budget apocalyptic Hollywood movie shows Sydney being torn apart in spectacular fashion, such as *Independence Day, X-Men: Apocalypse,* the remake of *The Day the Earth Stood Still, World War Z* and *Pacific Rim: Uprising.* If that's not enough, Godzilla uses his giant tail to hurl his deadly enemy, Zilla, crashing into the Opera House.

Bubbling under Sydney's boom was a growing excitement. On 23 September 1993 it was announced that the city would host the Olympic Games in 2000. At that moment Sydney received more worldwide publicity than at any other time in its history. The deputy lord mayor, Lucy Turnbull, wife of the future prime minister and a maven of Sydney society, was worried about her city. She issued a warning that Sydney's 'gloating and boasting' had 'partially unglued the sticky stuff that bound us to our fellow Australians'.

She need not have worried. The Games were held from 15 September to 1 October 2000 in perfect weather and an atmosphere of friendliness, joy and high spirits that was palpable. The Games garnered universal acclaim, with the organisation, the volunteers, the sportsmanship, and Sydneysiders themselves being lauded in the international media. Author Bill Bryson in *The Times* called the Games, 'one of the most successful events on the world stage', adding that they 'couldn't be better'. Journalist James Mossop called the Games 'such a success that any city considering bidding for future Olympics must be wondering how it can reach the standards set by Sydney'.

NOW

I CAN HARDLY BELIEVE WHAT I SEE. I'm standing at the entrance
to Dick Street, Chippendale, where I first lived when I moved to
Sydney. It was always in shadow. Dingy buildings lined one side
of the street, on the other were garages and six forlorn terraces
clinging together as if for support, their façades dirty white or
grim ochre, their front steps a metre away from the cracked
narrow footpath. The short one-way street was too tight for one
car to easily pass another. There was not a tree or plant or blade
of grass in sight.

Now, four decades on, the street resembles a plant nursery.
Dark green foliage sprouts out of garden boxes on the footpath.
Because the street still exists in a penumbra, the plants and shrubs
are mainly indoor varieties, with large fleshy leaves. Not only
that, but halfway down a clump of palms and banana trees and
bamboo stretch towards the light and are beginning to overtake
one side of the street. The former garage's dark brown exterior is
now a riot of colours.

The six terraces are each painted different colours, including
trendy grey, white and yellow. Outside my former cockroach-
infested home is a garden box with a profusion of plants flourishing
in the dim light. The once sagging wooden balcony is now sturdy
and obviously able to bear the weight of people. The houses look

immaculate and cared for and, as I ruefully note, have something that was missing in my time there – a sense of pride.

I walk the length of the street, passing an art gallery with two Dalmatians roaming around inside it, and make my way back to the cross street, Balfour. The first thing I notice is the absence of the sickly sugary smell of the White Wings cake factory. The factories have long gone, their buildings refitted for business and culture, many of them obscured by trees. Across from the entrance to Dick Street is the White Rabbit Gallery, which contains one of the most significant collections of contemporary Chinese art in the world.

The White Rabbit is one of a dozen galleries in Chippendale and I've read that there are many cafés and upmarket restaurants to the south of Dick Street. When I was living here there were no such places, only the grubby malodorous pub, factories and clusters of grim terraces rented by people who didn't have enough money to live anywhere else. Now those people couldn't afford to live here.

I turn left and after a few paces stop. Where once stood the many buildings of the huge Carlton and United Brewery, there are now lawns and a narrow sculptural cascade whose descending water ripples along on a 20-metre journey. The transformation is astonishing. There is not one remanent of the brewery remaining. It may as well not have existed for 168 years (it closed in 2006).

What also amazes is the enormous park, a rare feature indeed for Chippendale. There are dogs playing on the lawns and strolling mothers with children enjoying the winter sunshine, and trees. This is Balfour Street Park, a pedestrian gateway to Central Park where two monolithic towers reach for the sky. This project was one of two massive developments that changed inner Sydney, the second being Barangaroo. Both came after the decade of lethargy that gripped Sydney after the excitement of the Olympics. During that time it seemed as if Sydney was drained of energy and vision. Construction was haphazard and tentative. These two projects revitalised the city.

One Central Park, on the north-eastern corner of this huge precinct, opened in 2013 and comprises two towers of residential apartments, an east and a west tower, in addition to a six-level retail shopping centre at the base of the towers. It's made up of four levels below ground and 34 above, a structure that comprises 623 apartments. What immediately strikes me are the vertical gardens attached to the towers, a living tapestry of plants, flowers and vines stretching 50 metres high, making it the world's tallest vertical garden. The towers would be sunlight stealers except for another unique feature, a cantilevered heliostat attached to the eastern tower. Suspended from the twenty-eighth floor, its purpose is to reflect daylight onto the gardens, the pedestrian corridors and atrium below. Its motorised mirrors are positioned 100 metres underneath the cantilever on the rooftop of the shorter western tower.

The whole complex of towers, parks and shops is like a self-contained world. As usual the public sculpture is prosaic when it is not kitschy, like the Tower of Love, a two-metre totem pole that's a visual sandwich of cute hippos, bears and pandas.

The population mix has also changed markedly. Chippendale was once a suburb for poor Anglos, Italians and Greeks. Now about 30 per cent of people living in Chippendale were born in China. Only 30 per cent speak English at home. In the late 1970s, fewer than one in four Sydneysiders was foreign-born; four decades later the figure is nearly 40 per cent. Two-thirds of today's Sydneysiders were either born overseas or have a parent who was born overseas. The demographic revolution is astonishing.

Out on Broadway, in what was once one of the filthiest thoroughfares in Sydney, I stand opposite Central Park and admire the beautiful tumbling gardens of the towers. But when I turn around, I face what its many critics – including the American architect, Frank Gehry – have called the ugliest building in Sydney. The University of Technology building, a 27-storey brutalist monstrosity, opened the year I came to Sydney in 1979. It has all the charm of a Soviet edifice meant to put the fear of God into you, hinting at the existence of torture chambers in the basement.

On the corner of Broadway and Harris Street, where the university bookshop used to be, is a minimalist space called Start Ups. Across Harris Street is the familiar Agincourt Hotel, another ugly building that only pokie addicts and alcoholics could love. Further on are Chinese takeaways, McDonald's and sushi bars. As it's lunchtime, they're packed with students and office workers spilling out onto the footpath.

I walk down the western side of Broadway and pass Central Station, which has been undergoing a major renovation for several years now. Commuters navigate their way around the detours and construction debris. The expensive makeover reminds me that an even greater transformation of the city is taking place out of sight, as a new subterranean world of tunnels is created. A rail crossing is being constructed under the harbour and will be part of a 31-kilometre metro network, connecting the railway line from Chatswood on the North Shore to Sydenham in the inner west, where I once lived directly beneath the flight path. The train trip under the harbour will take just three minutes between the new Barangaroo station and the new Victoria Cross station in North Sydney. New stations are also being built in Martin Place, Pitt Street and Waterloo, the immense projects plagued by cost blowouts.

As I turn the corner into George Street, a strange sight greets me. There are no longer bustling crowds ordering takeaways or students rushing to classes. Many of the shops are empty and clearly have been for some time. There are faded signs announcing closing down sales, including a few derelict bookshops, one offering 50 per cent off in its final sale. A light rail tram glides along the street, one of the reasons for this grim panorama. The project went over budget and took so long to complete that many cafés, restaurants and shops went broke. Two years of the pandemic finished off the remainder.

In one area of derelict shops is a doorway that is obviously the quarters of a homeless person. Amid the blankets and sleeping bag there is a shrine to Jesus and the Virgin Mary: a half-metre tall sculpture of Jesus on the cross surrounded by small reproductions of kitsch pictures of Mary and Jesus. Further on outside a nondescript church a sign reads: *How dark does the world need to get before we reach the light again?*

I pass a hotel on a corner that is covered in graffiti; old beer posters from the 1930s visible behind its dirty windows. The only people on the footpath are making for the benches to wait for a tram. Brown dead leaves blow across the tracks. This is a most depressing part of George Street, Sydney's desolation row.

One thing I'm grateful for is no longer having to flinch when the screech of steel on steel erupts over my head. The monorail is no more. Despite many protests this egregious structure was opened in 1988. The carriages travelled just above the heads of pedestrians along narrow streets that were not designed for such things. I travelled on one once and was amazed at how close the carriage came to the first floor of buildings, almost within touching distance. It was a voyeur's delight, peering into offices as workers went about their business oblivious to the passing stares, each window a picture of lonely office workers like something out of a Edward Hopper's painting. The folly never achieved the patronage it was supposed to and ceased operating in 2013.

Thankfully all sections of the overhead track and some of the stations have been dismantled

As I near Goulburn Street and the Town Hall, George Street springs to life again. Shoppers hurry in and out of stores, and workers rush through their lunch breaks. Unlike the wind in lower George Street, the air here is still and the sun warms the blood. I pause at Market Street and look north down George Street, which is now a mall with benches, trams and pedestrians. I know that as a Sydneysider I am supposed to be grateful for these improvements to George Street, but it seems tamed and sterile. I miss its unruliness, the car horns, the groaning buses, the crowds on the footpaths, the general cacophony and the wild jumble of shops, which have now been replaced by expensive stores and skyscrapers. Once Sydney's most exciting and colourful thoroughfare, George Street is now a timid shell of its former gregarious self.

Having passed several derelict bookshops on my journey so far, I cross York Street to visit one of the last that remains open. I enter Abbey's and find I am the only customer. The sight of all the books is comforting. One of the staff says to me, 'I haven't seen you in a while.' I realise with a shock that it's been two years since I ventured in here, deciding it was safer to order books online during the pandemic.

Soon I am heading down a side street and turn right into Kent, a banal street that has no distinguishing buildings. I hear a man on a megaphone, but the breeze whipping down the street carries his words away until I get closer and see about 30 protesters waving Ukrainian flags on the opposite footpath outside the Hungarian Embassy. Some hold up placards, saying 'Shame on Your Country', 'Support Ukraine', 'Shame on you Hungary' and 'Stop Putin now'. It's the third month of Russia's brutal invasion of Ukraine and the man with the megaphone is haranguing the office block before him, calling out 'Shame on you!' and mentioning the massacres committed by Russian troops in Bucha. On my side of the footpath half a dozen bored policemen keep one eye on the demonstrators and chat among themselves.

Further up Kent Street, I turn left at a sign pointing to Barangaroo. I leave the sunshine and descend two steep sets of stairs and find myself in deep shadows cast by three skyscrapers. There's an atmosphere of hustle and bustle as men and women in expensive and stylish clothes hurry urgently to their destinations. Sydney is the most intense place to live in the country, and moves at a faster, reckless pace. No doubt some of the people rushing around me have minds sparkling with illegal substances. Sydney loves cocaine and remains the nation's coke capital. It's synonymous with success and, as one expert in addiction pointed out, 'the average patient looks like someone you work with in the office day to day'. The typical user is said to be wealthy and working in finance or entertainment; the CBD and the affluent eastern suburbs are hotspots.

I walk down a long penumbrous laneway crowded with bars and cafés and out into the sun. Before me is the harbour. Sydney has put on a glorious winter's day and the sun sparkling on the dark blue water is incandescent. The foreshore has a long walkway lined with artfully arranged huge sandstone blocks. My memory of this area is completely at odds with how it looks now. Once most of this was a concrete apron, grubby with age, oil slicks and dirt, the hardy weeds growing through its cracks adding to its forlorn appearance.

Before the arrival of Europeans, this area was used by the Gadigal people for hunting and fishing. The evidence of their occupation is close by: shell middens and numerous rock engravings. It's named after Bennelong's second wife, the feisty Barangaroo. Looking out on the calm waters it's easy to imagine that she once fished out there in her *nawi*. In the Great Depression dock workers called the area the Hungry Mile. During those years hundreds of workers would line the mile-long stretch of wharves early in the morning and wait for work in what was a desperate game of the survival of the fittest, where the stronger men were chosen over the weaker, and union troublemakers were snubbed in favour of pliable workers. By the end of the 1930s wharves dominated the waterfront from Millers Point to Darling Harbour, but by the 1970s the vessels were becoming too big and once Port Botany was constructed in 1979, cargo ships were permanently redirected there and the docklands became a useless eyesore.

There's no sign of a working port today. The only movement on the water is a yacht and a small ferry chugging slowly to the Barangaroo wharf. On the foreshore office workers are bent over their phones, eating sandwiches, or sitting in the sun, eyes closed as if in blissful reverie.

Workmen have set up temporary fences so they can erect equipment for the upcoming Vivid festival, the first after a two-year hiatus. The theme this year is 'The Soul of the City' and coloured images will be projected onto the Opera House sails and the pylons of the Harbour Bridge. Indigenous artists will transform the Barangaroo foreshore with more than 90 artworks (several delightfully coloured wooden poles are being put in place as I watch). Ken Done will project his artworks onto Customs House in Circular Quay, dedicating the images to the city with his personal tagline, 'To Sydney with love'. Vivid is a modern version of the nineteenth century's *son et lumiere*. Sydney has always been fond of lightshows and fireworks and the festival is extremely popular and photogenic – catnip to Sydneysiders.

I continue my walk in bright sunshine, accompanied by the crunching footfalls of people jogging on the crushed sandstone. As they come towards me, I notice their flushed faces are damp with perspiration. I stop and look back. Towering over Barangaroo is the Crown casino. There are Sydneysiders who hate it. The architectural historian Philip Drew believes that it's like a giant finger given to Sydney: 'Everything about it is selfish and narcissistic: its excessive height, public exclusion, and monopolisation of harbour views for a wealthy few.' Some say it resembles a slowly twisted gherkin, but for me this curved tapering structure of 75 storeys is a beautiful reflection of Sydney's undulating topography and joins other great structures like the Harbour Bridge and Opera House in celebrating curves rather than straight lines and grids.

It was designed by an Englishman, Chris Wilkinson, another foreign architect who has defined Sydney's skyline. From the days of Macquarie when another Englishman, Francis Greenway, began building here, a virtual United Nations of architects have redefined Sydney's urban landscape. The Austrian-born Harry Seidler; the Danish Jørn Utzon; the American Griffins, the husband and wife team who designed the model suburb of Castlecrag; the Italian Renzo Piano, who created his marvellous building Aurora Place in Macquarie Street; and of course the American Frank Gehry, who designed the quirky Dr Chau Chak Wing building in Ultimo that resembles a soggy cardboard dollhouse left out in the rain.

Whatever happens to the Crown casino, which James has now sold, in the future the Packer family's media legacy may be forgotten but, ironically, it will be the sad sack James, the one who stamped the Packer name on the city with this glorious and commanding glass edifice, who will be remembered.

As I continue my walk, I pass several Muslim women in black hijabs and tourists from across the globe. A young Japanese woman stands on a sandstone block at the water's edge and poses for a picture. When it's taken she looks up at the cloudless sky.

Almost in a state of ecstasy she cries out, 'It's so blue! So pretty!' I want to join in and say *Yes, yes, it is.*

I find myself looking up to Millers Point and its ridge of Victorian terrace houses. A few years back they were the homes of maritime workers and their families, but now those houses belong to the affluent who have their prized water views. The removal of the working class and others who had family ties going back generations in Millers Point was not the only instance of the government selling public housing to greedy developers. The Sirius building near the Rocks may have been a brutalist grey structure that resembled a concrete honeycomb, but it had spectacular views of the harbour and was prized for its fine social housing apartments. The last occupant, a blind woman in her nineties, Myra Demetriou, was the face of the campaign to keep the Sirius for public housing. She lived on the tenth floor and every night a set of lights in her apartment flashed out a message across Sydney harbour and the Rocks, *SOS, Save Our Sirius.*

Millers Point, Sirius and Dawes Point are prime examples of the government's policy of resumption of social housing, expelling tenants and other low-income earners and siphoning them off to distant suburbs in acts of social cleansing.

I near Barangaroo Reserve, a 6-hectare park at the northern end of Barangaroo. It's a reconstructed, naturalistic headland based on the pre-1836 shoreline. After 1836, the original headland and foreshore was cut away to make space for wharves and stevedoring work as Sydney became a major international port. The Reserve claims to 'restore the relationship with other headlands' in and around the harbour.

Next to the walkway on my right are steep slopes covered in vegetation where some 75 000 native trees, plants and shrubs have been planted. A total of 84 species were chosen, 79 of them native to Sydney Harbour. The trees, shrubs and ferns grow in such profusion that it would be extremely difficult to try and walk through them. Instead there are several steep narrow sandstone steps that lead to the top.

The Reserve is a magnificent piece of landscape gardening and confirmation of the symbiotic relationship between Sydney's natural landscape and its architecture. The Barangaroo complex lives in harmony with its natural surroundings as if rising out of it, just as the bridge and the Opera House seem to be at one with the harbour. The houses that coat the peninsulas and inlets coexist with the waterways, as do the finger wharves. Those promontories and bays give Sydney its distinct suburban identities, Manly is as different from Watsons Bay as Elizabeth Bay is from Clontarf and Walsh Bay from Lane Cove.

Barangaroo is confirmation that Sydney is no longer a port city. Originally it was its role as a port town that gave Sydney its vitality, the excitement of the world constantly coming through the Heads. It created a city that has a vernacular air that no other Australian capital city has – one with a mischievous spirit, a larrikin energy, a sense of restlessness, as if it was hovering on the verge of chaos, a torrid place of possibilities where the wall between corruption and the law has always been porous.

The publisher and writer Michael Duffy canvassed people in Sydney as to their attitude to public scandals and found, 'There is little real outrage in Sydney when something smelly comes to the surface ... [Sydneysiders] don't consider themselves citizens, just an audience. And the rich and powerful are a show, from whom good behaviour cannot be expected.'

The attitude of the rest of Australia towards Sydney can be summed up in a vitriolic magazine article entitled 'Why the rest of Australia hates Sydney (and why Sydney couldn't care less)'. According to the Brisbane journalist Frank Robson, Sydney is seen as a smug, superficial city preoccupied with money and status. It's typified by the eastern suburbs with its fashion designers, models, hairdressers, celebrity real estate agents, chefs, and young tycoons who 'spend much of their lives performing for gossip writers … and spending an inordinate amount of time obsessing about real estate'. If that's not enough, Sydneysiders have short attention spans, no loyalty, 'and are always on to the next thing'.

There's many a cliché in these observations, but there's no doubt that Sydney doesn't care what the rest of Australia thinks of it. Yes, it celebrates the cult of the body, a sense of brazen corporality that can bemuse the visitor. It shows off in its fireworks, light shows and Mardi Gras, as if life were a dazzling Busby Berkeley production. For its critics it remains self-centred, as if no other capital city exists in Australia. Obsessed by the new and transient, it's considered to be facile and crass, with no sense of the past, only the present, but that's true only to an extent. Despite the worst intentions of developers, everywhere I go in Sydney, I am reminded of the past, the ghosts and echoes of past lives in the Rocks, the glories of the Victorian sandstone buildings that came out of the very earth itself, as if an act of self-creation, the terraces, the staircases that take one from one vista to a completely different one in only 50 steps. From the beginning of white settlement, the city has defied grids and straight lines and celebrated bends, curves and winding ways in its streets and architecture.

Polls say the top five challenges for Sydneysiders are the cost of living, the cost of housing, traffic and commute times, jobs, and the pace and stress of Sydney life. The author Peter Corris was right, 'Sydney is the perfect city – its beauty, atmosphere and culture providing a spectacular contrast to its underbelly of poverty, corruption and vulgarity.'

I turn my attention back to the water. It is a beguiling sight. Today the air and the light of the intense blue sky and how it plays with the water seems magical. It's like one great act of affirmation, an open heart that invites you to take Sydney personally. And I do.

NOTES

The basic sources were the digitised newspapers and magazines in Trove <trove.nla.gov.au>, the online *Dictionary of Sydney* <dictionaryofsydney.org> and the *Australian Dictionary of Biography* <adb.anu.edu.au>. Besides those books and articles I have mentioned in the main text, some of the important sources for various chapters are:

Prologue
D. Falconer, *Sydney*, NewSouth, Sydney, 2010.

Location, location, location
'Underground Sydney, Busby's Bore, an Eccentric Tunnel', *Daily Telegraph*, 21 January 1903.
W.V. Aird, 'The Water Supply, Sewerage and Drainage of Sydney', Metropolitan Water Sewerage and Drainage Board, Sydney, 1961.
J. Korff, 'Aboriginal sites, Tank Stream', <www.creativespirits.info/oznsw/sydney>.

The dispossession
Dawes' notebooks titled 'The Grammatical forms of the language of N.S. Wales in the neighbourhood of Sydney', are now held in the School of Oriental and African Studies, University of London.
D. Foley and P. Read, *What the Colonists Never Knew: A history of Aboriginal Sydney*, National Museum of Australia Press, Canberra, 2020.
A. Wood, 'Lieutenant William Dawes and Captain Watkin Tench', *Royal Australian Historical Society Journal*, Vol. X, Part 1, 1924.

Albion *and* Surviving
T. Flannery, *The Birth of Sydney*, Text, Melbourne, 1999.
M. Gillen, *The Founders of Australia: A biographical dictionary of the First Fleet*, Library of Australian History, Sydney, 1989.
G. Karskens, *The Colony: A history of early Sydney*, Allen and Unwin, Sydney, 2009.

P. Taylor, *Australia: The first twelve years*, Allen and Unwin, North Sydney, 1982.

T. Watling, *Letters from an Exile at Botany Bay, to his Aunt in Dumfries*, 1794.

The distance of your heart

Museum of Sydney website <sydneylivingmuseums.com.au/museum-of-sydney>.

J. Broadbent, *The Australian Colonial House: Architecture and society in New South Wales 1788–1842*, Hordern House, Sydney, 1997.

The new skyline: Francis Greenway

W.L. Havard, 'Francis Howard Greenway, Macquarie's Architect', *Royal Australian Historical Society Journal*, Vol XXII, Part III, 1936.

Mortdale, aka Valley of the Dead

An influence on the personal chapters was Georges Perec's *An Attempt at Exhausting a Place in Paris*. As reported in the *Sydney Morning Herald* on 5 September 2022 ('Village fans want a lid on heights') there were protests against the so called 'Mortdale Master Plan', which would mean an additional 969 dwellings and the lifting of height restrictions. The draft recommended building heights of 22 metres (six storeys) along the main roads while increasing some residential heights to 13 metres and extending low and medium density further into residential zones. Said a spokeswoman of the Save Mortdale Village group, 'Mortdale is a village, and we don't want it wrecked. We don't want another Hurstville concrete jungle...we want to keep it as it is.' The local shopkeepers were for it, believing that more people would 'bring life into the area'.

The cult of the body

D. Beck, *Rayner Hoff: The life of a sculptor*, NewSouth, Sydney, 2017.

Plotting Sydney's destruction

'Spanish "allies" had Sydney in their sights for invasion', *Weekend Australian*, 3–4 March 2018. An article on Christopher Maxworthy, maritime historian, who found the report in the Spanish archives in Madrid.

'Sacre bleu! French invasion plan for Sydney', ABC News, 10 December 2012.

P. Fregosi, 'Terre Napoleon: French colonial ambitions in Australia, 1793–1815', *Quadrant*, vol. 32, no. 6, June 1988, pp. 56–59.

Old Sydney Town

Old Sydney Town website <oldsydneytown.com>.

'Farewell to Old Sydney Town Forever', *Sydney Morning Herald*, 25 January 2003.

T. Dawson, *James Meehan – A most Excellent Surveyor*, Crossing Press, Sydney, 2004.

R.T. Dowd, 'James Meehan', Royal Australian Historical Society, Vol. 28, Part 2, 1942.

Howling at the moon

M. Conner, *Pig Bites Baby: Stories from Australia's First Newspaper*, Duffy and Snellgrove, Sydney, 2003.

J. Dunn, *Colonial Ladies: Lovely, Lively and Lamentably Loose: Crime Reports from the Sydney Herald relating to the Female Factory, Parramatta 1831–1835*, Ligare Pty Ltd, Sydney, 2010.

A new beginning
P. Butler, H. Dillon, *Macquarie: From Colony to Country*, Random House Australia, Milsons Point, 2010.
W. Dixon, 'Madame Rose de Freycincet's Visit to Sydney, November 18 to December 26, 1819', Royal Australian Historical Society (a translation).
M.H. Ellis, *Lachlan Macquarie: his life, adventures and times*, Angus and Robertson, Sydney, 1973.
A. Taylor, 'Clover Moore refers concerns about Macquarie statue to Indigenous panel', *Sydney Morning Herald*, 23 August 2017.
Distractions
Obed West as a source of reminiscences about early Sydney in 1882, came initially in his response to a series of articles in the *Sydney Morning Herald* under the title 'Old and New Sydney'. His contributions to the historiography of Sydney started with letters to the editor of the *Herald*, the first two of which were under pen names, 'A resident of the locality since 1810' and 'Patria'. The third letter, which acknowledged authorship of the earlier two, bore his own name, as did the next one. The newspaper then published further contributions from West as part of the 'Old and New Sydney' series with articles on George Street, Pitt Street, Sydney Harbour, Chapel Row, the old Sydney racecourse, Redfern and surrounding suburbs.

The shame of Clontarf
S. Harris, *The Prince and the Assassin*, Melbourne Books, Melbourne, 2017.
S. Lawson, *The Archibald Paradox: A Strange Case of Authorship*, Miegunyah Press, Carlton, 2006.

Pictures of Sydney
'Crowd Source', photos part of a collection of street photographer, Arthur K. Syer, State Library of New South Wales, an exhibition of 50 snapshots taken by Syer that ran from April to August 2015.

Ridding Sydney of the birthstain
R.L. Knight, *Illiberal Liberal: Robert Lowe in New South Wales, 1842–1850*, Melbourne University Press, 1966.
E. Napier, 'Robert Lowe and his Associations with Australia', *Royal Australian Historical Society Journal*, Vol. XVIII, Part 1, 1932.

Sydney creates itself
D. Baglin and Y. Austin *Historic Sandstone Sydney*, Rigby, Sydney, 1980.
P. Drew, 'The Trials of James Barnet', *Quadrant*, January–February 2022.
T. Flannery, 'In Praise of Sandstone', *The New York Review of Books*, 22 June 2017.
R. Irving, *Paradise, Purgatory, Hell Hole: The story of the Saunders sandstone quarries, Pyrmont*, Media Masters, Singapore, 2006.
G. Stuart, *Secrets in Stone*, Griffin Press, 1993.
S. Yates, 'Foundation Stone', *Daily Telegraph*, 'History', n.d.

How a dynasty ends: the Fairfaxes
'Revealed: Fairfax family treasures up for grabs', *Sydney Morning Herald*, 17–18 August 2019.

'From frock shop to media dynasty, raising eyebrows along the way [Lady Mary
Fairfax]', *Sydney Morning Herald*, 19 September 2017.

Hyde Park North
M. Palin, 'Subterranean Sydney: eerie underground world right beneath the CBD',
12 July 2017, <www.news.com.au>.

The world comes to Sydney
Information about the Shakespeare tavern comes from 'There's a Tavern in the Town
– a famous rendezvous for Sydney's man-about-town 90 years ago', *Sydney Sun*,
28 October 1954.

A young woman's world in the 1890s
N. Davis, 'A Fashionable Parade' [re Melbourne and Sydney Arcades] PhD thesis,
2022.
M. Mercedes, 'Pioneering tea king still haunts his beloved QVB', *Daily Telegraph*,
5 December, 2020.
R. Travers, *Australian Mandarin: the life and times of Quong Tart*, Rosenberg
Publishing, Sydney, 2004.

The plague
The 1908 Royal Commission for the Improvement of Sydney was a source. Some
of the more confronting reports about slums were in Archdeacon FB Boyce's
evidence, 'The Campaign for the Abolition of the Slums in Sydney'.

A day in Concord
J. Roberts, *The Astor*, Ruskin Rowe Press, Avalon Beach, 2003.
P. Skehan, *The Walkers of Yaralla*, P. Skehan Publishing, Concord, 2000.
P. Skehan, *Eadith: Concord's Royal Kin*, P. Skehan Publishing, Concord, 2003.

The golden twenties
M. Sayer, *Those Dashing McDonagh Sisters: Australia's first female filmmaking team*,
NewSouth, Sydney, 2022.

The dream weavers
J. Ford, *Meet me at the Trocadero*, Cowra, NSW, 1995.
'He bought class to the Harbour City [Jim Bendrodt]' *Sydney Morning Herald*,
20 January 2013.
G. Repin, 'Azzalin Orlando Romano, and Romano's Restaurant', *Pittwater Online
News*, 26 May – 1 June 2013.

The Coathanger
Former army engineer Brian Nicolson told the *Daily Mail* in April 1957 about his
order to prepare for the destruction of the bridge.
C. Mackaness, *Bridging Sydney*, Historic Houses Trust, The Mint, Macquarie Street,
2006.

The Push
M. Bendle, 'The Melbourne Crisis and the Sydney Push', *Quadrant*, November 2021.

Flat life
R. Thompson 'Sydney's Flats, a social and political history' PhD thesis, Macquarie University, 1986.
The Expressway opened on 24 March 1958. After a 20-minute speech by Cahill, and seconds before he was about to cut the ceremonial ribbon, three youths attempted to do it before him. A wild struggle followed with detectives grabbing the young men. Other youths joined in. Women screamed. It echoed the premature opening of the Harbour Bridge by Francis de Groot.

The Askin era of the 1960s
'Turn of the phrase made "green" a rallying cry that saved heritage [Jack Mundey, 1929–2020]', *Sydney Morning Herald*, 12 May 2020.
M. Duffy and N. Hordern, *Sydney Noir: The Golden Years*, NewSouth, Sydney, 2017.

Red lights
A. Davies, 'Sex and the city: take a walk on Sydney's steamy side', *Sydney Morning Herald*, 17 December 2014.
L. Harris, 'Sex in the city: Darlinghurst sees 460 per cent increase in prostitution charges', *Sunday Telegraph*, 8 November 2014.
R. Perkins, *Working Girls: Prostitutes, their life and social control*, Australian Institute of Criminology, Canberra, 1991.

Remaking Sydney's skyline: Harry Seidler
P. Drew, *Two Towers – Harry Seidler: Australian Square, MLC Centre*, Horowitz Grahame Books, Sydney, 1980.

The Packers
James Packer's public brawl with David Gyngell outside Packer's Bondi apartment was in 2014.
P. Adams, *Weekend Australian Magazine*, 20 October 2018.
B. Griffin-Foley, *The House of Packer: The making of a media empire*, Allen and Unwin, St Leonards, 1999.
T. Lane, *As the Twig is Bent; the Childhood Recollections of Sixteen Prominent Australians*, Dove Communications, Melbourne, 2005.
D. Kitney, *The Price of Fortune: The untold story of being James Packer, a biography*, Harper Collins, Sydney, 2018.

The hedonist decade
J. Lees-Milne, *Deep Romantic Chasm: Diaries 1979–1981*, John Murray, London, 2000.
H. Pitt, *The Dramatic Story of the Sydney Opera House and the People Who Made It*, Allen and Unwin, Sydney, 2018.
This chapter is also based on my social mixing with William Yang, Linda Jackson and Jim Sharman. I also met Edelsten, whose handshake was perfunctory and clammy.
Step Into Paradise, Powerhouse Museum, Sydney, 2019, exhibition of Jenny Kee and Linda Jackson's designs.

H. Grehan and E. Scheer, *William Yang: Stories of Love and Death*, NewSouth, Sydney, 2016.

W. Yang, *Starting Again, A Time in the Life of William Yang*, Heinemann, Melbourne, 1989.

This small block of Darlinghurst

M. Gorrey, 'Lane with ugly past transformed into an inner-city oasis', *Sydney Morning Herald*, 20 January 2022.

After this chapter was written Peter Young died at St Vincent's and his funeral was held at the Wayside Chapel, Kings Cross.

A global city

K. McClymont and L. Besser, *He Who Must be Obeid: The untold story*, Vintage Books, North Sydney, 2014.

While serving his prison sentence Ian Macdonald had to confront the NSW Supreme Court again in September 2022. He and his mate, former union boss, John Maitland, were facing a retrial on charges relating to a grant by Macdonald in December 2008 of a Hunter Valley exploration licence to Doyles Creek Mining, a company chaired by Maitland. The prosecutor said that Macdonald's illegal actions as the Mining minister cost the state up to $100 million by giving a coal exploration licence to a company linked to Maitland without a competitive tender.

Now

'The last to leave Sirius Building (Myra Demetriou 1926–2021)', *Sydney Morning Herald*, 10 November 2021.

J. Lemon, 'Sydney is Australia's cocaine capital', *Sun-Herald*, 18 September 2022.

F. Robson, 'Why the rest of Australia hates Sydney (and why Sydney couldn't care less)', *Sydney Morning Herald Good Weekend Magazine*, 2 February 2002.

ACKNOWLEDGMENTS

Craig Handley, Karoline Chardon and Ali Nasseri were my helpful guides. Philip Drew, architectural researcher and critic was incisive about architecture and Harry Seidler. Paul Ashton, Adjunct Professor of Public History at UTS, provided invaluable feedback. Many thanks to Ben Naparstek, who commissioned two Amazon Audible audio dramas, *The Goodbye Party* and *Beatrice Dark*, little realising I was drawing on much of what I had learned about Sydney during the researching of this book. Many thanks to Phillipa McGuinness who originally commissioned the book, Elspeth Menzies who saw it through, and of course Linda Funnell, whose editorial gifts have helped make my previous two books, *Kings Cross: a biography* and *Woolloomooloo: a biography*, better than I could have expected and, as for this one, her brilliant editing and cutting were razor-sharp, invaluable and very much appreciated. As they say, in the classics, all mistakes are mine. And, lastly, my wife, Mandy, who believed in it and had to live with it.